New Perspectives in History

DID SLAVERY PAY?

Readings in the Economics of Black Slavery in the United States

Edited by
HUGH G. J. AITKEN
Amherst College

Houghton Mifflin Company • Bosto
New York • Atlanta • Geneva, Illinois • Dallas • Palo Alto

Printed in the U.S.A.

Library of Congress Catalog Card Number: 79-130654

ISBN: 0-395-11237-0

Contents

Preface

This collection of readings has been designed for the use of students in courses on American economic history, though it may have a wider interest. In assembling the selections and writing the introductions I have been very conscious of how my ideas of what "works" in teaching today's students have been shaped by experiences in the seminar rooms of Amherst College. If I were to claim that these experiences have always been unalloyed pleasure, none of my colleagues at Amherst and none of the students I have taught there would believe me. Every teacher has his many defeats and his few carefully-remembered victories. He learns, perhaps, more from the former than from the latter. One lesson that my students have taught me is that knowledge cannot be passed like a commodity from producer (or more often, from retailer) to consumer. Knowledge is acquired only when students exercise their intelligence on problems that concern them. This is a cliché, of course; but what is a cliché when read or heard from others can be dearly-bought wisdom when experienced firsthand.

If, therefore, the tone of the editorial introductions in this book seems ocasionally more direct and personal than is usual, the explanation is simply that I have thought of myself as confronting students with ideas and problems for them to grapple with, rather than as presenting material for them to learn. One of my colleagues once remarked that the attitude of an Amherst student to his professor could be summed up in two pithy and inelegant phrases: "Is that so?" and "So what?" Inelegant or not, the questions express precisely the attitudes appropriate to all forms of intellectual inquiry, and I hope that readers of this book will be no less sceptical and demanding than my Amherst students have been. It is no part of a student's responsibility to make life easy for his teachers. The reverse, of course, is equally true.

While preparing this book I enjoyed the hospitality of the Eleutherian Mills Historical Library in Greenville, Delaware; for the temporary respite this afforded from the pressures of academic life I am most grateful. Among many friends and colleagues George

Rogers Taylor, Douglas F. Dowd, and Alfred H. Conrad were particularly helpful with suggestions and criticisms. Specific acknowledgements to the authors and publishers of the selections contained in this book are made at the appropriate points, but some more general mention should be made of the cooperation I received from all sources that I approached. If I have at any point by inadvertence misinterpreted or distorted the meaning of any of the authors on whose work I have commented, I give a blanket apology; these are the risks one runs when attempting to explain and interpret.

H. G. J. A.
Amherst, Massachusetts

Introduction

The central problems with which this collection of readings is concerned will be obvious to anyone who has read the title or glanced through the table of contents. A lengthy introduction by the editor would be a waste of time and paper. Did black slavery in the United States pay? Whom did it pay, how much, when, and how? What exactly do we mean by the question, anyway? How do we know these things? How sure are we? Why are we still arguing about it?

Because we *are* still arguing about it—and this is an interesting fact in itself. The first selection in this book refers to the argument as a "historical perennial." Historians have been worrying over it for a long time—in fact, ever since personal slavery was legally abolished. And before that, contemporaries worried over it. Is the matter settled now? Are all the relevant questions answered? Many people thought so in 1957, when Alfred Conrad and John Meyer presented their findings. In fact, some of their critics accused them of flogging a dead horse. But the horse was not dead, and the argument did not stop. I at first intended to conclude these selections with Stanley Engerman's review of the controversy, which he published in the winter of 1967. But then, less than a year later, Marvin Fischbaum and Julius Rubin found much to object to in Engerman's conclusions and assumptions, and it hardly seemed fair to you, the reader, to stop with Engerman and leave the impression that all the loose ends had been neatly tied together. Obviously they had not.

Why has this argument proved so hard to settle? Part of the reason is that the argument itself—the point in dispute—keeps changing. Sometimes the changes are subtle, and you must watch out for them as you read these selections. Are we talking about the plantation system of producing cotton, for example, or are we talking about slavery? They were related, clearly, but they were not the same thing. And sometimes the changes are quite marked. To argue that slavery did or did not retard the economic development of the South is obviously not the same thing as arguing over whether it was or was not profitable to slave owners. In other words, the dispute over the economics of slavery has had its own life history, and part of the purpose of this book is to illustrate some of the episodes in that history.

If you ask why the argument keeps changing, the first answer is that research and debate has produced some clarification. And when some issues previously obscure become clear, we move on to others and try to resolve them. This is the way rational inquiry is supposed to proceed. It is what makes learning cumulative and entitles us to talk about a stock of knowledge. In the natural sciences it usually does happen in this way. In the social sciences and humanities, not as often. In these fields of intellectual activity—perhaps because of the impossibility of controlled, repeatable experiments, perhaps because of the many variables involved and the difficulty of isolating their effects and perhaps because human communication is inescapably dependent upon the use of metaphors—it is unusual for any issue to be definitely settled. This does not mean, fortunately, that scholars continue to argue over the same old hackneyed topics indefinitely. Boredom itself sets limits to repetition and compels innovation. And fashions change in this area of human behavior as in others. But it does mean that if you hope for final answers in history or the social sciences, you will be disappointed.

Whether or not the prolonged argument over the economics of slavery has shown any of the characteristics of scientific advance, or contrariwise has been a matter of continuing confrontations between irreconcilable points of view, is a question which you should decide for yourself after reading these selections. For what it is worth, my judgment is in favor of advance. By this I mean simply that I think we understand the economics of black slavery in the United States better now than informed people did when, say, U.B. Phillips was writing his classic articles. The dialectic of the historians has not produced agreement, but it has raised conflict to a higher (more informed) level. Two processes have contributed to this: first, the hard, dirty work of digging up information where no information was previously thought to exist; and second, the refinement of logical analysis and the use of more powerful explanatory models. Each of these processes is represented in this collection of articles, although it is exceptional for the same investigator to be equally competent in both.

But it has taken a long time to reach even the level of partial understanding on which we complacently congratulate ourselves today. And the explanation for this lies in a problem more intractable than difficulties in securing data or complexities of logical analysis. The fact of the matter is that black slavery in the United

States was an immoral, inhumane business. It is very difficult to argue coolly and dispassionately about a matter of this kind. In fact, there is some question whether one ought to.

It is very easy today to pass these moral judgments against slavery. One does not have to be very brave to describe it as inhumane and immoral; in fact, it would take considerably more courage to say something in its favor. But it is extremely important that you, when you read the selections in this book, understand clearly that some of the authors represented here were respectable, moral men who nevertheless *did* believe that there was something to be said in favor of slavery and who presented reasons that were not nonsensical in support of their beliefs. They were racists, you say? If you wish to call them so, yes. But when you stick that label on them, you are giving me information about yourself and your attitudes—redundant information, incidentally—rather than giving me any information I did not already have about them. So call them racists if you will; but don't, just because you have used that word, stop thinking about the problem.

There have been other well-known controversies in the history of historical writing that have shown an amazing capacity to survive all attempts to end them. Turner's theory of the frontier is one; the so-called economic interpretation of the Constitution is another. English economic historians have argued for years over what happened to the standard of living of the working classes during the Industrial Revolution; and you can still get scholars to raise their voices a decibel or two by mentioning Protestantism and the rise of capitalism. It is characteristic of such enduring controversies that they have, or are thought to have, political and ideological implications. The evidence often seems to point in directions which scholars, for one reason or another, are reluctant to accept; or else it points less unambiguously in a favored direction than they would like it to. The result is tension and, to relieve tension, verbal violence.

The debate over the economics of slavery has proved to be a classic example of this type. It is no great exaggeration to say that the concern of American historians with the issue has been obsessive. Certainly they have found it difficult to leave the subject alone. Like a teenager with a boil on his face, they keep fingering it, even though (or because?) it hurts. There is, of course, a good deal of suppressed guilt involved, though it is seldom permitted to show clearly through the polished academic veneer.

This intermixing of emotion and reason has made the argument sometimes exciting. Those who attended the 1967 meetings of the Economic History Association, when a talented panel debated the issue, will need no reminder that emotions do not lie far below the surface, even on the most staid of occasions. At the same time it has complicated the task of rational analysis. It is necessary not to be too simple-minded about this point. If there ever was a time when the ideal mode of scientific inquiry was supposed to be a cold, unemotional surveying of objectively factual evidence, that time has surely passed by now. A man who doesn't care what he finds out is probably not going to find out very much; or else the type of analysis he is engaged in is so routine that it would be better done by a machine than by a human being. Emotional commitment to the issue is a necessary resource for creative inquiry, if only for the reason that motives less powerful than this are unlikely to sustain you through the drudgery of research and disappointment. Whether you are watching *planaria* finding their way through a maze (when the conventional wisdom says they shouldn't be able to) or finding evidence to suggest that plantation slavery was at least as profitable as any other investment available at the time (when the conventional wisdom says that it was really an economic burden carried by southern whites for the sake of racial peace), you have to believe that what you find out matters.

The selections in this book were written by people who thought that what they were doing mattered. That is one of the reasons why they were chosen, from among the myriad other pieces of prose that might have been selected. The particular objectives, the reasons why it seemed important, differed. Phillips, writing at the University of Wisconsin in 1904, thought it was important that southern history should be interpreted first by scholars who had inherited southern traditions; others could criticize and correct later. Conrad and Meyer, writing at Harvard in 1957 in the first exciting years of the econometric revolution, wanted to show what the new economic history could do when faced with an old problem. Yasukichi Yasuba, a young Japanese scholar—were his concerns likely to coincide with those of Ulrich B. Phillips?—wanted to clear up the definition of profitability as a matter of operational economic theory. And so on. In every case the scholar at his desk cared sufficiently about his self-selected task to do a job that was superior—not run-of-the-mill, not par for the course, but superior. And if he had not cared, he could not have done it.

But an author cannot be personally involved and neutral at the same time. If we want scholars to care about their subject, we cannot expect them to show the inhuman objectivity of a computer (which is, in any case, objective only in the sense that it follows someone else's program). And through this door enters ideology, and personal bias, and class interest, and ethnic point of view. This is the price we pay for permitting scholars to be human. It becomes amazingly difficult to filter out the ideological component, to make up our minds when a historian's statements are to be taken as rationalizations of a position in which he finds himself because of his personality, upbringing, and background—which is to say, because of *his* history—and when we may safely take them to be non-personal statements of what is probably the case. When we read a historian's work, do we get our payoff in personal currency, negotiable only within his private world, or in public money, usable for intellectual transactions far removed from the mint of origin? It is not, of course, a matter of deliberate intent to deceive, or to conceal evidence, or to distort the truth. It is a matter rather of the assumptions with which one begins, the things one takes for granted, the evidence one just does not see. It is necessary to have a point of view; but from a single point of view you can never see the whole landscape.

Did slavery pay? Of course it did. And of course it did not. It paid, in cash and in other ways, those who, because they controlled the distribution of power, were able to appropriate the surplus produced by slave labor. And it did not pay, because it nearly ruined the South and because it implanted in the core of American society a source of conflict, guilt, and hate that is still with us. Are these problems of today the legacy of slavery? Or are they the result of racism? Is slavery a necessary or sufficient condition for racism to develop? Or can the one develop and persist without the other? Can we discuss the costs of slavery to this country without discussing the costs of racism? Is this just playing with semantics? Or is it taking a quick look at the complexity of truth?

The debate over the economics of slavery has been long drawn-out because the issue itself is multidimensional and because it has been persistently bedevilled by emotion and ideology. This is one reason why it is worth our while to look back over the controversy and read a few of the more important contributions. Most of the writers represented in this book know how to handle the English language. They are thoroughly trained in their respective specialties. They honor the traditional canons of scholarship. They are not pamphleteers nor professional propagandists. Consequently it will not always be easy for you, the reader, to discern why they frequently differ so profoundly in their conclusions. You will, of course, be sensitive to the possibility that emotion or ideology has distorted a scholar's judgment. But possibly three other suggestions may be helpful also. First, look for the unexamined, unsupported, and sometimes even unstated assumptions; these, far more than the logical structure of the argument itself, determine what conclusions are reached. Second, scrutinize the way in which the problem is defined; apparent adversaries are often talking past, rather than contradicting, each other, because they are tackling different problems. And thirdly, watch for the problem that isn't. These are of two principal kinds: the problems that arise when you try to explain something that is not true in the first place; and the problems that arise if you insist that only one particular explanation of a true set of facts can be correct.

And with that I should stand aside and let the authors talk to you. But one final word is necessary. In American universities, colleges, and high schools today, black studies programs of many different types are being introduced, some well thought-out, others conceived in haste and urgency. In all of these programs a need exists for teaching materials, in particular for books relevant to the interests of instructors and students. This means relevant to the history of the black experience in America. There is a dearth of such material at the moment, although it will probably not last long, since the need is clear and there is a market to be served. If you ask me whether I think this book has a place in black studies programs, my answer must be that I do not think so, or perhaps only a marginal place. The readings in this book have much to tell us about slavery, and about the plantation economy, and the South, but they have little to tell us about the black man. To put it bluntly, they are highly relevant to the white experience in America, and in particular to a correct understanding of the ways in which white people have thought about the institution they developed to organize and use black labor. But they add little if anything to our understanding of what it has meant to be a black man in America.

This is not said in any spirit of apology, but in order that those who read this book may understand what it is they are reading and why it has seemed worthwhile to put it together. It is important, I believe, that white people know more than they do about slavery and its history. It is important that they free themselves from myths of their own creating. Slavery was the institution that first bound white and black men together in this country. For good or evil, we are all still bondsmen, bound together by what slavery did to us.

HAROLD D. WOODMAN
The Profitability of Slavery: A Historical Perennial

We begin with an article written by a professional historian of our own day which undertakes to survey the history of the debate over the economics of slavery, at least up to 1963. Note particularly the distinction Woodman draws between profitability in the accounting or economic sense (are these the same?), in which slavery is regarded as a business like any other, and profitability in the more general sense which involves consideration of the long-term economic, social, and political effects of the slave system on the South, and indeed upon the nation. Whether "profitability" is the right word to use when discussing these latter issues is a matter on which you should make up your mind. Clearly, if you want to talk about the long-run social consequences of slavery, you cannot remain within the narrow confines of accounting and economics; but it is only within these narrow limits that "profits" can be rigorously defined. As Woodman points out, however, though it is certainly necessary to make this distinction, it is hardly possible to stop there. An appraisal of the slave system in moral or political terms cannot be made without reference to the fact that some people were making money out of it (or perhaps failing to do so). Nor is it possible (though he seems less confident on this point) to discuss the effects of plantation slavery on Southern economic development without some reference to the earnings record of this major economic sector and its linkage effects on the rest of the regional economy. Thus the legitimacy of profits, or of profits gained in this way, and their size, are also issues at stake.

A major virtue of Woodman's article is the way in which it shows the persistence, through the entire history of the controversy, of a few dominant themes. For example, as early as 1859 it was being assumed as hardly worth arguing that the South was economically backward compared to the North, and it was being vigorously asserted that slavery was responsible for the differential. Leaving aside for the moment the asserted causal relationship between slavery and economic backwardness, you should ask yourself what made Southerners so sure that they *were* living in an economically retarded region.

The publication of the 1850 federal census provided much of the data on which comparisons were based, and statistics carried the same aura of precise authority then as they do today. But, as so often, the conclusion was implicit in the ways in which the data were interpreted. Specifically, there was involved a particular view of what constituted wealth and capital (Were slaves productive capital? Were they people? Or both? Or neither?) and a particular conception of economic progress which substantially identified it with the spread of manufacturing industry. We certainly have not completely escaped these definitional headaches today, but the point to note is the way in which a problem of explanation was generated. Granted that the North was developing economically more rapidly than the South it was surely reasonable to set up as one of the hypotheses to be examined an inverse relationship between economic diversification and slavery. But was the assumption correct? And why was this hypothesis the favorite? Perhaps it was the profitability of cotton production, and not slavery, that restricted the flow of capital into manufacturing. Perhaps, in New England, it was precisely the lack of a profitable agricultural staple like cotton that led entrepreneurs to risk their capital in manufacturing.

Unexamined assumptions and fuzzy theorizing are typical of the antebellum discussions. Slave labor, you read, was economically expensive because it tied up investment capital. It hindered the growth of local markets. It made impossible the development of a skilled labor force. It led to soil exhaustion and a neglect of agricultural improvement. Slaves (or did they mean black people?) could never learn to operate machinery. On the other hand, without slavery the negro would have remained an ignorant, slothful African savage. And so on. Many of these assertions, stated originally for polemical purposes while the slave system was still functioning, were to be picked up and stated—again as facts—by later historians and polemicists who were not personally familiar with the slave system but who accepted the stereotypes of the negro and of plantation slavery that they found in earlier writings. To the extent that the debate has moved to a more informed level, it has been largely through subjecting statements of this kind to critical scrutiny. Woodman identifies the men responsible for the most significant steps toward greater clarity, beginning with Phillips in the early 1900s and ending with Conrad and Meyer, Evans, and Genovese in the 1950s and 1960s. Most, but not all, of the authors to whom he refers are represented in the selections which follow, so you will be able to judge for yourself, in most cases, whether Woodman adequately summarizes their arguments and points of view.

ABOLITIONISTS and their proslavery antagonists in the ante
bellum period argued hotly over the profitability of slavery. Since
the Civil War, historians and economists have continued the argument, less acrimoniously but no less vehemently. In part, solution
of the problem of the profitability of slavery has been blocked by a
lack of agreement as to how the problem is to be defined. Either
implicitly or—as is more often the case—explicitly, contemporaries
and modern scholars alike have begun their discussion of the
profitability of slavery by posing the question: Profitable for whom?
For the slave? For the slaveowner? For the South as a section? For
the American economy as a whole? Answers to the general question, of course, depend upon how the question is posed. As a result,
conflicting conclusions often reflect differing definitions of the
problem as well as different solutions. What seem to be clashing
opinions often do not clash at all but pass each other in the obscurity
created by a lack of an agreed upon definition of the problem.

When a writer answers the question, "Profitable for whom?" by
limiting himself to the planter or slaveholder, he is dealing with the
question of profitability in terms of a business or industry. He is
concerned with such questions as: Did the planters make money?
Did *all* planters make money? Did planters make as much on their
investment in slaves as they would have made had they invested
elsewhere? Staple production with slave labor is regarded as a
business enterprise much as automobile manufacture is seen as a
business enterprise today. Profitability relates only to the success or
failure of slave production as a business and ignores the broader
questions of the effect of this type of enterprise on the economy as a
whole.

If, on the other hand, a writer answers the question, "Profitable
for whom?" by discussing the effect of slavery on the South, he is
treating slavery as an economic system rather than as a business
enterprise. The issue of profits earned by individual planters is
subordinated to the larger problems of economic growth, capital
accumulation, and the effect of slavery on the general population.

Debate over the years has ranged on both aspects of the topic,
with most writers emphasizing one or the other aspect and an
occasional writer dealing with both. Despite the many contributions
which have been made—and are still being made—historians and
economists have not been able to reach a consensus on this vexing
problem. The debate rages undiminished and, except for greater
subtlety of method and sophistication of presentation, often rests

today on substantially the same ground that it did a hundred years ago.

If we trace the development of this continuing controversy through the works of its most able participants, we can discern some reasons for the lack of substantial progress in solving the problem and suggest certain lines of approach which may lead to a more satisfactory solution.

Dispute on the profitability of slavery in the antebellum period was confined almost solely to the question of slavery as a system rather than a business. This is not surprising. Proslavery writers could hardly be expected to defend the peculiar institution on the ground that it made the planters rich. In the face of obvious Southern economic backwardness and poverty, such a position would be tantamount to an argument for abolition in the eyes of anyone other than the favored planters. On the other hand, the antislavery or abolitionist group would have a weak argument indeed if they confined it to the contention that slaveowners made a profit. The right to make a profit was uniformly accepted in the United States, and to point out that planters made a profit by using slave labor was no indictment of them. The nature of the situation, then, led prewar commentators to deal with slavery primarily as an economic and social system rather than as a form of business enterprise and to argue its merits on the basis of its effects on the well-being of the whole population.

This did not mean, however, that the contenders clashed directly. Specific arguments seldom met with specific rebuttal. Rather, the antislavery group picked out those aspects of the question they felt most damaging and most to be condemned; defenders answered by pointing to what they considered to be the beneficial features of the peculiar institution. The antagonists, of course, were directly involved. Their aim was most often not to convince their opponents by scholarly argument but to attack or defend slavery within the larger context of the sectional controversy.

The essence of the antislavery economic argument was that the slave system caused Southern economic backwardness. The words of Hinton Rowan Helper, the North Carolina white farmer, summarize this position and at the same time show the intense feeling which the argument generated in the ante bellum South:

> . . . the causes which have impeded the progress and prosperity of
> the South, which have dwindled our commerce, and other similar
> pursuits, into the most contemptible insignificance; sunk a large

majority of our people in galling poverty and ignorance, rendered a small minority conceited and tyrannical, and driven the rest away from their homes; entailed upon us a humiliating dependence on the Free States; disgraced us in the recesses of our own souls, and brought us under reproach in the eyes of all civilized and enlightened nations—may all be traced to one common source, and there find solution in the most hateful and horrible word, that was ever incorporated into the vocabulary of human economy—*Slavery!*[1]

The burden of Helper's argument was that even in the area of the South's touted superiority, agriculture, the North was far ahead. Using figures from the 1850 census, Helper argued that the value of agricultural products in the free states exceeded that of the slave states and that the value of real and personal property in the free states topped that of the slave states (when the value of slaves was excluded). Helper adduced figures for commercial and industrial development which told the same story. His contention that slavery was the cause of this economic inequality came from a process of elimination rather than from a direct analysis of the operation of the slave system. At the close of the eighteenth century the South stood in an equal or superior position to the North in all aspects of economic development. Since then the South had fallen further and further behind. Wherein lay the differences between North and South which could account for this? Slavery, obviously, was the culprit.[2]

The Kentucky editor, Cassius M. Clay, regularly condemned slavery in his newspaper, the Lexington *True American.* Slavery, he argued, was economically destructive. Because it degraded labor, whites refused to do physical work, thereby fostering idleness. Those who would work were faced by the competition of slave labor, and their wages never exceeded the subsistence level which was the pay accorded slaves. When whites did not work and slaves were kept ignorant, skill or excellence could not develop. In addition, slave labor was economically expensive for the South because capital was tied up or frozen in the form of labor:

The twelve hundred millions of capital invested in slaves is a dead loss to the South; the North getting the same number of laborers, doing double the work, for the interest on the money; and sometimes

[1]Hinton Rowan Helper, *The Impending Crisis of the South . . . (New York, 1859),* 25.
[2]*Ibid.,* 1-25, 33, 39, 66, 69, 72, 81, 283-86, esp.

by partnerships, or joint operations, or when men work on their own account, without any interest being expended for labor.[3]

Finally, slavery hindered the development of a home market for local industry and thereby retarded economic development:

> Lawyers, merchants, mechanics, laborers, who are your consumers; Robert Wickliffe's two hundred slaves? How many clients do you find, how many goods do you sell, how many hats, coats, saddles, and trunks, do you make for these two hundred slaves? Does Mr. Wickliffe lay out as much for himself and his two hundred slaves, as two hundred freemen do . . . ? Under the free system the towns would grow and furnish a home market to the farmers, which in turn would employ more labor; which would consume the manufactures of the towns; and we could then find our business continually increasing, so that our children might settle down among us and make industrious, honest citizens.[4]

Clay's arguments, written in the 1840's, attempted to *explain* the economic consequences of the slave system rather than to *describe* them as did Helper a decade later. Clay's three main points—slavery degrades labor and keeps it ignorant, thereby hindering the development of skills; slavery freezes capital in the form of labor, thereby making it unavailable for other enterprises; slavery limits the home market—were recurring themes in the economic attack on slavery. A pamphlet by Daniel Reaves Goodloe, written about the same time that Clay's articles appeared, raised the same arguments.[5] George Tucker, in a general economic treatise written a decade earlier, gave major stress to the problem of idleness which he felt was a result of the degradation of labor induced by slavery.[6]

The most detailed economic indictment of the slave system in the ante bellum period—published just after the outbreak of the war—

[3]Cassius Marcellus Clay, *Writings,* Horace Greeley, ed. (New York, 1848), 204-205, 224.

[4]*Ibid.,* 227, also 346-47.

[5][Daniel Reaves Goodloe], *Inquiry into the Causes Which Have Retarded the Accumulation of Wealth and Increase of Population in the Southern States: In Which the Question of Slavery Is Considered in a Politico-Economical Point of View* (Washington, 1846), *passim.* Goodloe added that the degradation of labor served to keep immigrants away from the South, thus depriving the section of the skills and capital which new arrivals brought to the North.

[6]George Tucker, *The Laws of Wages, Profits, and Rent, Investigated* (Philadelphia, 1837), 46-48. Tucker argued that as the number of slaves increased, the cost of raising them would be greater than the gain from their use, and emancipation would result. *Ibid.,* 49.

was made by a British economist. J. E. Cairnes stressed the detrimental effects of slavery as a form of labor and as a form of capital. The weaknesses of slave labor, he maintained, stemmed from three characteristics: "It is given reluctantly; it is unskillful; it is wanting in versatility." Soil exhaustion necessarily followed from the use of such labor. Scientific agriculture was impossible; slaves who worked reluctantly and in ignorance were incapable of learning and applying new farming techniques. Only the best lands, therefore, were used and, losing their fertility, were left desolate.[7]

Slave labor also hindered industrial and commercial development, Cairnes continued. Slaves were kept in ignorance and were thus unable to cope with machinery. If educated and brought to the cities as industrial workers, the danger of their combining to better their conditions or of their engaging in insurrection was increased. Commerce likewise was impossible. The dangers of mutiny on the high seas or of desertion in free ports would deter slaveowners from using their property in this work.

Cairnes agreed with Clay and Goodloe that slave capital was economically expensive because it involved a larger capital outlay than free labor. Available capital was tied up in slaves and therefore unavailable for manufacturing and commerce. As manufacturing and commerce were important sources for the accumulation of capital, the lack of these enterprises hindered accumulation in the South. This completed a vicious circle, accentuating the shortage of capital and making nonagricultural pursuits even more difficult to begin.[8]

Ante bellum defenders of slavery, for the most part, did not meet these economic criticisms head on. Except for those who charged that Helper manipulated his figures to produce the desired result,[9] upholders of slavery shifted the ground of controversy.

[7]J. E. Cairnes, *The Slave Power: Its Character, Career, and Probable Designs: Being an Attempt to Explain the Real Issues Involved in the American Contest* (2nd ed., London, 1863), 44, 54-56, 81.

[8]*Ibid.*, 70-72, 74-75.

[9]See Samuel M. Wolfe, *Helper's Impending Crisis Dissected* (Philadelphia, 1860); Elias Peissner, *The American Question in Its National Aspect, Being Also an Incidental Reply to Mr. H. R. Helper's "Compendium of the Impending Crisis of the South"* (New York, 1861). Obviously in response to Helper were two other works, Thomas Prentice Kettell, *Southern Wealth and Northern Profits . . .* (New York, 1860) and J. B. D. De Bow, *The Interest in Slavery of the Southern Non-Slaveholder* (Charleston, 1860). While Kettell presented figures which would dispute Helper, his main point was not to contend with Helper. De Bow was attempting to argue against Helper's contention that nonslaveholders were dupes of the planters. These two works will be discussed below.

Slavery was defended as an economic good because it transformed ignorant and inferior African savages into productive workers. "There is nothing but slavery which can destroy those habits of indolence and sloth, and eradicate the character of improvidence and carelessness, which mark the independent savage," wrote Thomas R. Dew.[10] Another defender, Albert Taylor Bledsoe, after his sketch of the horrors of life in Africa, concluded that "No fact is plainer than that the blacks have been elevated and improved by their servitude in this country. We cannot possibly conceive, indeed, how Divine Providence could have placed them in a better school of correction."[11] William J. Grayson versified the same argument:

> Instructed thus, and in the only school
> Barbarians ever know—a master's rule,
> The Negro learns each civilising art
> That softens and subdues the savage heart,
> Assumes the tone of those with whom he lives,
> Acquires the habit that refinement gives,
> And slowly learns, but surely, while a slave,
> The lessons that his country never gave.
>
> . . . .
>
> No better mode can human wits discern,
> No happier system wealth or virtue find,
> To tame and elevate the Negro mind.[12]

Thus slavery was not only an economic good but a social and humanitarian blessing as well.

Slavery, according to its defenders, was economically beneficial

---

[10]Thomas R. Dew, *Review of the Debate in the Virginia Legislature, 1831-32,* as reprinted in *The Pro-Slavery Argument . . .* (Charleston, 1852), 328. Chancellor William Harper echoed these sentiments but in a more general way. Slavery, he wrote, is the only road to civilization. "If any thing can be predicated as universally true of uncultivated man, it is that he will not labor beyond what is absolutely necessary to maintain his existence. . . . The coercion of slavery alone is adequate to form man to habits of labor. . . . Since the existence of man upon the earth, with no exception whatever, either of ancient or modern times, every society which has attained civilization, had advanced to it through this process." Harper, "Slavery in the Light of Social Ethics," in E. N. Elliott (ed.), *Cotton Is King, and Pro-Slavery Arguments* (Augusta, Ga., 1860), 551-52.

[11]Albert Taylor Bledsoe, "Liberty and Slavery; or, Slavery in the Light of Moral and Political Philosophy," *ibid.,* 413-16.

[12]William J. Grayson, *The Hireling and the Slave . . .* (Charleston, 1856), 34-35. See also [Stephen Colwell], *The South: A Letter from a Friend in the North, with Special Reference to the Effects of Disunion upon Slavery* (Philadelphia, 1856), 14.

in other ways. It was said to mitigate the class conflict which existed in every society.[13] "It is impossible to place labor and capital in harmonious or friendly relations, except by the means of slavery, which identifies their interests," George Fitzhugh wrote.[14] His *Cannibals All!* also stressed the well-being of the slave. Because capital and labor were united in the slave he was better cared for and suffered none of the privations visited upon the wage slave of the North for whom freedom was a condition of dubious value. Grayson employed his heroic couplets to make this point:

> If bound to daily labor while he lives,
> His is the daily bread that labor gives;
> Guarded from want, from beggary secure,
> He never feels what hireling crowds endure,
> Nor knows like them in hopeless want to crave,
> For wife and child, the comforts of the slave,
> Or the sad thought that, when about to die,
> He leaves them to the cold world's charity,
> And sees them slowly seek the poor-house door—
> The last, vile, hated refuge of the poor.[15]

Proslavery writers, virtually ignoring the view of slavery as economically debilitating to the South, argued instead that it strengthened the nation's economy.[16] They pointed to the products of

[13]"It is the order of nature and of God, that the being of superior faculties and knowledge, and therefore of superior power, should control and dispose of those who are inferior. It is as much in the order of nature, that men should enslave each other, as that other animals should prey upon each other." Harper, "Slavery in the Light of Social Ethics," 559-60.

[14]George Fitzhugh, *Cannibals All! or, Slaves Without Masters* (Richmond, 1857), 48. Governor James Henry Hammond of South Carolina, while admitting that economically speaking "slavery presents some difficulties" and that it was more expensive than free labor, nevertheless concluded that it was economically beneficial. There was no overpopulation in the South, he argued, no group of men so hungry that they would work for next to nothing. He concluded self-righteously, "We must, therefore, content ourselves with our dear labor, under the consoling reflection that what is lost to us, is gained to humanity; and that, inasmuch as our slave costs us more than your free man costs you, by so much is he better off." Hammond, "Slavery in the Light of Political Science," in Elliott (ed.), *Cotton Is King*, 646-47.

[15]Grayson, *The Hireling and the Slave*, 43-44.

[16]Southern backwardness could not be ignored. The tariff, rather than slavery, was frequently pointed to as the cause. See Thomas Dew, *Review of the Debate*, 486. J. D. B. De Bow, in *De Bow's Review*, regularly called for the introduction of manufacturing in the South and the establishment of direct trade to Europe to solve the section's economic problems.

slave labor, tracing their importance to the country as a whole. Upon slavery and slave labor, in fact, rested the economic well-being of the nation and the world. David Christy, writing that slavery was not "a self-sustaining system, independently remunerative," contended that "it attains its importance to the nation and to the world, by standing as an agency, intermediate, between the grain growing states and our foreign commerce." Taking the products of the North, slavery "metamorphoses them into cotton, that they may bear export." To the world it supplied cotton for manufacture into cloth and clothing, stimulating commerce and industry. For the United States it provided the largest cash exports (cotton and tobacco); it comprised a market for manufactured goods, supplied food and other groceries, and helped to pay for foreign imports.[17] Northern profits depended upon Southern wealth, argued Thomas Kettell in 1860; the North, therefore, should do everything in its power to keep the South, with its peculiar institution, in the Union.[18]

Whatever advantages did accrue to the South came, ironically, to those who did not own slaves, according to the editor J. D. B. De Bow. Not only did the nonslaveowning merchants benefit from slavery because they handled the goods produced by slave labor, but the white worker in the South also benefited. He had status by virtue of being a white man; he was not forced to work in unhealthy shops as was his white brother in the North; and most important of all, he had the opportunity of becoming a slaveholder and by so doing relieving himself and his wife of drudgery in the fields.[19]

Although ante bellum disputants thus came to opposite conclusions regarding the profitability of the slave system, not all of their arguments were mutually exclusive. This observation is most clearly illustrated by the manner in which Ulrich B. Phillips, re-examining the question in the twentieth century, was able to incorporate a large part of both ends of the argument into his economic analysis of the slave system. He accepted many of the conclusions of slavery's defenders while at the same time maintaining that the slave system was detrimental to the economic development of the South. He was able to unite the two points of view by clearly differentiating between the plantation system and slavery. At the same time he considered another factor in his discussion, that of slavery as a business enterprise.

[17]David Christy, *Cotton Is King* . . . (New York, 1856), 78-82, 163.
[18]Kettell, *Southern Wealth and Northern Profits, passim.*
[19]De Bow, *The Interest in Slavery of the Southern Non-Slaveholder.*

While slavery existed, for the most part, within the plantation system, the two, Phillips maintained, were not inseparable. Indeed, the plantation regime "was less dependent upon slavery than slavery was upon it." The plantation system was a means of organizing labor; slavery, on the other hand, was a means of capitalizing labor.

The plantation system had definite advantages both economic and social. By routinizing labor, dividing different tasks rationally, and instituting strict supervision, while at the same time caring for the health of the workers (slaves), the plantation made for efficient methods of production.[20] Such methods were required because of the crude labor used. In effectively organizing ignorant and savage labor into efficient production it was economically advantageous; and "in giving industrial education to the laboring population, in promoting certain moral virtues, and in spreading the amenities" it was socially advantageous. The plantation was "a school constantly training and controlling pupils who were in a backward state of civilization."[21]

But the ante bellum plantation system hampered the economic development of the South. Its weakness stemmed less from its role as an organizer of labor and more from its close tie-in with slavery as an economic system. If the plantation was a school, the slave system prevented the apt students from ever being graduated. Laborers whose abilities transcended crude field work were yet harnessed to it and could not establish themselves as independent farmers. Unskilled labor was what was required and planters found it economically wasteful to train many skilled laborers despite any ability they might exhibit.[22]

Slavery, then, was harmful to the South because it prevented full utilization of the potential skills and abilities in the labor force. But the detrimental effects of slavery went deeper than this, according to Phillips. The central economic disadvantage of slavery was that it required that the entire life's labor of the worker be capitalized. Under a free labor system, wages are paid as work is done, and income from the sale of products can be used to pay future wage bills as they arise. The planter, however, was forced to buy his

[20]Ulrich B. Phillips, "The Decadence of the Plantation System," American Academy of Political and Social Science, *Annals*, XXXV (January 1910), 37-38, and "The Origin and Growth of the Southern Black Belts," *American Historical Review*, XI (July 1906), 803-804.

[21]Phillips, "Decadence," 39; Ulrich B. Phillips, *American Negro Slavery* (New York, 1918), 291, 313-14, 342.

[22]*Ibid.*, 343; Phillips, "Decadence," 40.

labor; that is, his wage bill became a long-term capital investment. Thus the slave system absorbed available capital. "Individual profits, as fast as made, went into the purchase of labor, and not into modern implements or land improvements."[23]

Because capital tended to be absorbed by the slave system, its availability was at a premium and planters were forced to look to outside sources for credit: "Circulating capital was at once converted into fixed capital; while for their annual supplies of food, implements, and luxuries the planters continued to rely upon their credit with the local merchants, and the local merchants to rely upon their credit with northern merchants and bankers." The result was a continuous economic loss as capital was drained from the South.[24]

The capital shortage stunted Southern economic development by hindering diversification in the economy, thereby keeping the South dependent upon the North. While Ohio benefited New York by becoming a market and a supplier of food and raw materials, Alabama had no such reciprocal relationship with Virginia or South Carolina. On the contrary, the Southwest competed with the Southeast to the detriment of the older regions because it could produce cotton more cheaply on the better lands and because increased production and labor needs drove the prices of slaves up. Economic benefits accrued to the North where manufactured goods and services had to be purchased; the Southeast was prevented from opening mills because all available capital was absorbed in slaves.[25]

Phillips introduced another dimension to his discussion of the economics of slavery—the question of the profitability of slavery to the individual slaveholder.[26] Matching the continual public loss as

[23]Ulrich B. Phillips, "The Economic Cost of Slaveholding in the Cotton Belt," *Political Science Quarterly*, XX (June 1905), 271-72; Phillips, *American Negro Slavery*, 395-96.

[24]Phillips, "Economic Cost," 272; Phillips, *American Negro Slavery*, 397, 399.

[25]Phillips, "Decadence," 39; Phillips, *American Negro Slavery*, 396.

[26]This was not the first time this aspect of the problem was raised. Complaints by ante bellum planters that they made little money were common, and newspapers (especially during a crisis period) carried notices of sheriffs' sales of lands and slaves lost by planters. Slavery itself was seldom seen as the root cause of such difficulties. Low cotton prices, the closing of the slave trade, the tariff, the machinations of the middlemen, and other such factors were usually adduced as the reasons for poor return with slave labor. Antislavery disputants sometimes touched on the question also, but the emphasis was on the detrimental effects on the South in general. "Slavery *is* profitable to the few," Daniel Goodloe wrote to Frederick Law Olmsted, "because it is simply a privilege of robbing the many." Frederick Law Olmsted, *The Cotton Kingdom*, Arthur M. Schlesinger, ed. (New York, 1953), xxix.

capital left the South was the private loss in the form of interest payments on borrowed capital. Profits were absorbed by the need to capitalize labor, a situation which was greatly aggravated in the 1850's when prices of slaves skyrocketed. As a result, Phillips declared, by the end of the 1850's only those plantations on the best lands, under the most efficient supervision, could make a profit for their owners.[27]

For Phillips, then, the plantation system was often economically beneficial to the South.[28] Its weakness stemmed from the fact that it was inextricably bound to slavery. It was slavery as an economic system which hindered and warped Southern development and kept the South backward in the prewar period. And it was slavery which made staple production in the ante bellum period an unprofitable enterprise for all but the most favorably situated planters. Phillips concluded that slavery was "an obstacle to all progress." He had to explain the continued existence of a personally and socially un-profitable system on noneconomic grounds. Slavery, he wrote, was initially introduced as a means of labor control and at first had proved to be profitable. As the number of slaves continued to rise, slavery became essential as an instrument of race control. It became the means to police an inferior race, to keep the Negroes' "savage instincts from breaking forth, and to utilize them in civilized industry." For the moment private gain and social gain were united. But as time went on the question of race control became most important—and an end to be attained only "at the expense of private and public wealth and of progress."[29]

---

[27]Phillips,"Economic Cost," 271, 274; Phillips, *American Negro Slavery,* 391-92.

[28]Writing soon after the turn of the century, Phillips concluded that the continued backwardness of the South was due to the *absence* of the old plantation system. The problem of ignorant labor remained, Phillips argued, and its utilization in small-scale farming (through small landowning, tenantry, renting, or sharecropping) was inef-ficient. Restore the order, the discipline, the direction, and the large-scale methods which characterized the ante bellum plantation, and the South, relieved of the burden of slavery, would prosper. All of the advantages of the ante bellum situation would be present with none of the disadvantages associated with slavery. Ulrich B. Phillips, "The Economics of the Plantation," *South Atlantic Quarterly,* II (July 1903), 231-36; Phillips, "Decadence," 40-41; Ulrich B. Phillips, "Conservatism and Progress in the Cotton Belt," *South Atlantic Quarterly,* III (January 1904), 1-10; Ulrich B. Phillips, "Plantations with Slave Labor and Free," *American Historical Review,* XXX (July 1925), 738-53.

[29]Phillips, "Economic Cost," 259, 275. See also his "The Slave Labor Problem in the Charleston District," *Political Science Quarterly,* XXII (September 1907), 416-39, and "The Central Theme of Southern History," *American Historical Review,*

Phillips' work was immensely influential. In the 1920's and 1930's a series of state studies were published which tended to support his conclusions. Perhaps because they were local studies and not concerned with overall Southern development, these monographs gave major emphasis to slavery as a form of business enterprise rather than as an economic system. The question posed was simply whether the planters made money on their investment in slaves. Rosser Howard Taylor, basing his conclusions on the testimony of travelers and on extant plantation records, concluded that in North Carolina "slaveholding was not generally profitable."[30] Ralph B. Flanders, in his study of Georgia slavery, found that although some planters were able to amass a fortune, many others made but a marginal living. He found much evidence showing that ante bellum Georgia planters bemoaned the unprofitability of the peculiar institution.[31] Slavery in Mississippi was investigated by Charles S. Sydnor. He found that free labor was much cheaper than slave and would have been more profitable for the planter to use. A thirty-slave plantation required a $40,000 investment, while if free labor had been used only $10,000 would have been needed. The greater the capital investment, he concluded, the greater the interest costs which had to be charged against profits. Furthermore, the large investment in labor the slaveowner was forced to make "added nothing to the productivity of the soil or to the betterment of the farm equipment," and it was doubtful whether the increased efficiency gained by slavery justified the "enlarged investment of capital." After calculating the costs of production on a typical fifty-slave Mississippi plantation, Sydnor concluded that profits were low. Only by spending the interest and other hidden charges (interest on capital invested in slaves, depreciation of slave

---

XXXIV (October 1928), 30-43. In a more expansive mood, Phillips found the slave system socially useful for its benefits in building Southern character: " . . . In the large it was less a business than a life; it made fewer fortunes than it made men." *American Negro Slavery,* 401.

[30]Rosser Howard Taylor, *Slaveholding in North Carolina, an Economic View* (Chapel Hill, 1926), 94-98.

[31]Ralph Betts Flanders, *Plantation Slavery in Georgia* (Chapel Hill, 1933), 221-30. As Phillips had done earlier, Flanders found the continued existence of a largely unprofitable business to be explained by noneconomic factors. The planters, he wrote, confused the plantation system, slavery, and the race question. "This confusion made it difficult for anti-slavery critics to understand the tenacity with which slave-owners clung to a social and economic system they despised, and which seemed to them unprofitable." *Ibid.,* 231.

property, land, and equipment) and by not calculating their own wages as supervisors of the business could planters seem to make a profit. A similar situation prevailed in Alabama, according to the historian of the cotton kingdom in that state, Charles S. Davis. Even with cotton selling at eight cents per pound, production by slave labor "was a fair business and nothing more." While some planters did make a great deal of money, "for the great majority the planting profession meant only a living."[32]

Further support for Phillips' views came from an influential article by Charles W. Ramsdell in 1929. Ramsdell maintained that slavery could be profitable only on the very best lands and since these lands, by the late 1850's, had been almost completely settled, slavery would have gradually become more and more decadent until, finally, economic causes would have required emancipation. He pointed out that high cotton prices of the 1850's could not last and, in fact, had already shown evidence of decline by 1860. As good lands were taken up and cotton prices declined, slave prices would drop also and Eastern states would no longer have the Western slave market in which to dispose profitably of excess slaves. In the meantime, with no new land available, more slaves would be on hand than could be used. Owners of large slave forces would find the expense of maintaining them too high to make cotton production by slave labor profitable. Slaves would become an economic handicap and slaveowners would look for a way to free their slaves and thereby relieve themselves of the burden of supporting them.[33]

While Phillips and his followers were amassing a formidable array of economic reasoning and statistical data to prove that slavery was unprofitable both as an economic system (because of its effects on the South) and as a business enterprise (because slaveowners made

[32]Charles Sackett Sydnor, *Slavery in Mississippi* (New York, 1933), 196-200; Charles S. Davis, *The Cotton Kingdom in Alabama* (Montgomery, 1939), 180. In a brief analysis of the economics of slavery during the last decade before the Civil War, James D. Hill concluded that the business of production by slave labor was in general unprofitable. Many planters, he admitted, became rich, "but these cases were more than likely due to peculiar advantages in location, fertility of soil or individual administrative ability; on the whole, in spite of slavery rather than because of it." Hill, "Some Economic Aspects of Slavery, 1850-1860," *South Atlantic Quarterly,* XXVI (April 1927), 161-77.

[33]Charles W. Ramsdell, "The Natural Limits of Slavery Expansion," *Mississippi Valley Historical Review,* XVI (September 1929), 151-71. Ramsdell's conclusion, of course, was that slavery would have disappeared within a generation, and therefore the Civil War had been unnecessary.

little profit), other historians were challenging this thesis on all levels. Some sought to show that Southern backwardness was not the fault of slavery; others stoutly maintained that planters on the whole made very substantial profits. The beginnings of this anti-Phillips or revisionist school can be traced back as far as the first decade of the twentieth century, but most of the revisionist work was done in the period beginning in the 1930's. It is this school which seems to be most active at the present time; nevertheless, there are still strong adherents to the traditional point of view.

The Mississippi planter and historian, Alfred Holt Stone, writing in the first decade of the century, relied heavily on Phillips but came to different conclusions. Stone's central argument was that it was the Negro and not slavery which retarded the ante bellum South. The Negro, according to Stone, was an inferior being incapable of advancing whether free or slave: "The negro was a negro before he was a slave and he remained a negro after he became free. I recall no sound economic argument against slave negro labor per se . . . which is not today equally as sound against free negro labor per se." Had white free labor been used in Southern production, the foundation of Southern economic life would have been sounder. Some form of the plantation system would have undoubtedly developed, "but it would have been based upon free white labor, and would have served as a great training school for the production of small farmers."[34] The innate inferiority of Negroes prevented them from reaching this level.

But the most telling of the earlier blows struck in the revisionist cause were the works of Robert R. Russel and Lewis C. Gray written in the 1930's. Neither sought to reverse completely Phillips' point of view, but both aimed at changing the emphasis of his analysis.

Russel made no effort to deny that the ante bellum Southern economy was backward; he did deny, however, that slavery was responsible. Rather, the South was hamstrung by its "climate, topography, natural resources, location with respect to the North and to Europe, means of transportation, and character of the white population."[35] The fact that population in the North was less

[34]Alfred Holt Stone, "Some Problems of Southern Economic History," *American Historical Review*, XIII (July 1908), 791; Alfred Holt Stone, "The Negro and Agricultural Development," American Academy of Political and Social Science, *Annals*, XXXV (January 1910), 13.

[35]Robert R. Russel, "The General Effects of Slavery upon Southern Economic Progress," *Journal of Southern History*, IV (February 1938), 54.

dispersed led to more concentrated markets for Northern manufacturers and lessened the problems of transportation to and from these markets. Household manufacture was more firmly entrenched in the Northeast from the start, and, as Northwestern agricultural regions opened up, Easterners were forced to leave the countryside—they were no longer able to compete—and were thus available as operatives in industry. In the South, the profitability of staple agriculture and the fact that slaves "were certainly not as well adapted to mechanical employments as to agriculture" prevented the development of this same pattern. The central weakness in the South was not simply that slave labor was used but that it was primarily an area of commercial agriculture. Planters lived on future earnings and borrowed from Northern and British sources, thereby incurring an expense which limited the amount of capital accumulation in the region. Overproduction of the staples forced prices down and cut into profits and, therefore, into savings. But these were phenomena of agricultural production and had little to do with the use of slave labor. Furthermore, the argument that slavery absorbed Southern capital was incorrect: "Slavery did not absorb Southern capital in any direct sense; it affected the distribution of capital within the section. The mere capitalization of the anticipated labor of a particular class did not destroy or diminish any other kind of property."[36]

The central element in Lewis C. Gray's revisionist argument was that slavery was a highly profitable form of business enterprise. Slave labor, when used for staple production, would always supplant free labor because it was cheaper and more efficient. The employer of slave labor had a guaranteed labor supply; women as well as men could be used in the fields; child labor could be used extensively; labor troubles such as strikes and lockouts were unknown. The slaveowner could appropriate every bit of surplus created by the slave over and above bare subsistence. Thus, slaveowners had to give their slaves only just enough to keep them alive; wage laborers could not offer their services for less.[37] The

---

[36] *Ibid.*, 47-52. See also Robert R. Russel, "The Effects of Slavery upon Non-slaveholders in the Ante-Bellum South," *Agricultural History,* XV (April 1941), 112-26, and *Economic Aspects of Southern Sectionalism, 1840-1861* (Urbana, 1924), 55-64.

[37] Lewis Cecil Gray, *History of Agriculture in the Southern United States to 1860* (2 vols., Washington and New York, 1933-1941), I, 448, 462, 470-74. Gray disputed the contention that the planter's need to buy his labor supply was an added expense when figured in terms of the entire life of the slave: "When capitalization was accurately

high prices of slaves in the 1850's, Gray wrote, reflected accurately the profitability of such labor, and it was profitability that accounted for its continued use.[38]

Although Gray disputed the contention that all of the South's ills could be traced to slavery, he did argue that the "ultimate influence" of slavery "upon the economic well-being of the South was pernicious." Slavery was most profitable on the richest and most favorably situated lands; other lands were left to the free population which lived at a subsistence level. This free population provided a very small market and exerted little pressure for the construction of roads, canals, schools, and other necessary social improvements. Because slavery was profitable, all available capital that was accumulated went into expansion of staple production using slave labor and, hence, was unavailable to industry or trade. The South remained, therefore, "a predominantly agricultural country" and was "consequently subject to the disadvantages characteristic" of such an economy. The fundamental disadvantage was the slow accumulation of local capital which further intensified the problems of expansion, diversification, and economic growth. "Hence," he concluded, "we have the near-paradox of an economic institution competitively effective under certain conditions, but essentially regressive in its influence on the socio-economic evolution of the section where it prevailed."[39]

The work of Gray and Russel opened up a double-barreled assault on the Phillips point of view. Russel had questioned the allegation that slavery was the main cause of Southern backwardness, and Gray had disputed the contention that slaveowning was not a profitable business enterprise. Further revisionist work proceeded along these two lines, although most of the succeeding work gave major emphasis to the problem of slavery as a business rather than as an economic system.

---

effected, the series of successive incomes as they became available actually were equivalent to interest and replacement; for interest and replacement would have been allowed for in the relatively low value that the owner paid for the services of the slave, capitalized on a terminable basis." In other words, Gray was arguing that the alleged extra cost in the form of interest and depreciation on the slave as a form of capital investment was not an extra cost at all but was a surplus which could be appropriated by the planter by virtue of his ownership of the slave over the entire period of his life. *Ibid.*, 473-74.

[38]*Ibid.*, 448, 476-77; II, 933-34, 939.

[39]*Ibid.*, 933-34, 940-42.

Thomas P. Govan subjected the bookkeeping methods used by Phillips and his followers to critical scrutiny. The central problem in determining profitability, according to Govan, was simply to decide whether planters made money on their investment. He criticized the work of Phillips, Sydnor, Flanders, and others on two counts: They failed to consider all possible sources of profit in making their calculations, and they considered as an expense an item which should have been considered as part of the profit. Services received from household slaves, food and other provisions grown on the plantation and used by the owner, and the increase in the value of land and slaves must all be considered as part of profit; yet, Govan charged, these items were ignored in figuring income. Furthermore, interest on investment, which Sydnor and others listed as an expense, was, in reality, a profit item. According to the classical economists, profit is made up of interest on investment, payment for supervision, and payment for risk. Accountants usually do not separate the first and last of these, but they do include them in the profit column. When these adjustments in bookkeeping methods are made, Govan concluded, slaveownership emerges as a highly profitable business.[40]

The bookkeeping problem was approached somewhat differently by Robert Worthington Smith. It is a mistake, he insisted, to consider capital investment on the basis of current prices on slaves. While slave prices were extremely high in the 1850's, it would be incorrect to use the appreciated value of slaves owned from an earlier period (or those born and raised on the plantation) as the capital investment in figuring profit. If, Smith concluded, profit is calculated upon the "capital actually invested in slaves" rather than upon current prices, "a very good return seems to have been paid to the majority of owners."[41]

The most all-inclusive revisionist work on the question of American slavery is Kenneth M. Stampp's *The Peculiar Institution,* published in 1956. Disagreeing with Phillips about almost every aspect of slavery in the United States, Stampp differed with him, too, over the economics of slavery. But while Phillips gave major emphasis to the problem of slavery as an economic system, Stampp

[40]Thomas P. Govan, "Was Plantation Slavery Profitable?" *Journal of Southern History,* VIII (November 1942), 513-35.
[41]Robert Worthington Smith, "Was Slavery Unprofitable in the Ante-Bellum South?" *Agricultural History,* XX (January 1946), 62-64.

was mainly concerned with slavery as a business: " . . . allowing for the risks of a laissez-faire economy, did the average ante-bellum slaveholder, over the years, earn a reasonably satisfactory return from his investment?"[42] Stampp's answer was unequivocal: "On both large and small estates, none but the most hopelessly inefficient masters failed to profit from the ownership of slaves." Slave labor was cheaper and could be more fully exploited; this made up for any loss due to inefficiency. Capital invested in slaves was not an added expense but merely a payment in advance for work which would be performed over a period of years. Hidden sources of profit, such as food produced on the plantation, sale of excess slaves, natural increase of slaves, appreciation of land values because of improvements—all, when added to the income from the sale of the staple, served to increase profits.[43] Stampp concluded that there is no evidence that slavery was decadent, no evidence that it would soon have died had not the war brought it to an abrupt end.[44]

Two Harvard economists added their voices to the chorus of revisionist argument in a paper published in 1958. Their purpose, declared Alfred H. Conrad and John R. Meyer, was to take the argument over profitability out of the realm of accounting and,

---

[42]Kenneth M. Stampp, *The Peculiar Institution* (New York, 1956), 390. Stampp denied that slavery kept the planters in debt. This problem arose from poor management and extravagance, a product, not of slavery, but of "the southern culture that required these extravagances." *Ibid.*, 391. The charge that slavery absorbed capital and retarded industrialization was also false, according to Stampp: "It is doubtful . . . that slavery in any decisive way retarded the industrialization of the South. After the African slave trade was legally closed, the southern labor system absorbed little new capital that might have gone into commerce or industry. . . . The domestic slave trade involved no further investment; it merely involved the transfer of a portion of the existing one between individuals and regions." *Ibid.,* 397. Another historian, George R. Woolfolk, in a study attacking what he called the Helper-Phillips thesis, argued that slavery did not freeze great wealth in slaves. On the contrary, he wrote, slave capital was easily converted into liquid capital because of the great facility with which slaves could be sold. Woolfolk, "Cotton Capitalism and Slave Labor in Texas," *Southwestern Social Science Quarterly*, XXXVII (June 1956), 43-52.

[43]Stampp, *Peculiar Institution,* 400-11, 414. It is clear that Stampp relies heavily on Gray, Govan, and Smith. His footnotes give recognition of his debt to these earlier revisionist scholars.

[44]" . . . If the slave-holder's economic self-interest alone were to be consulted, the institution should have been preserved. Nor is there any reason to assume that masters would have found it economically desirable to emancipate their slaves in the foreseeable future." *Ibid.,* 417-18.

instead, measure profitability according to economic concepts.[45] They constructed an economic model of a Southern cotton plantation for the years of 1830 to 1860 and then computed the return on investment on the basis of a Keynesian capital-value formula.[46] Their calculations showed that returns on cotton production varied from 2.2 per cent on low-yield land to 13.0 per cent on very fertile land, with returns of 4½ to 8 per cent encompassing "the majority of ante bellum cotton operations." Profits on the raising and selling of slaves were considered separately. Their calculations for this part of the slave industry showed returns varying from 7.1 per cent to 8.1 per cent depending on the number of children produced. These figures, the authors maintained, showed not only that profits were made in slaveowning, but that this form of investment was as good as an investment elsewhere in the economy. This was true throughout the South and not only on the best lands. Where lands were good, profits came from cotton production; where lands were poor, profits came from the raising and selling of slaves.[47]

Up to this point Conrad and Meyer centered their argument on the question of slavery as a business. They then turned to the broader question of slavery and its effect on the South. Slavery, they concluded, did not hamper Southern economic growth. Available capital was not used for industrialization and diversification simply because it could be more profitably used in agricultural production. The economic problems of the South were the product of an agricultural community and not a result of the existence of slavery.[48]

[45]Alfred H. Conrad and John R. Meyer, "The Economics of Slavery in the Ante Bellum South," *Journal of Political Economy,* LXVI (April 1958), 96.

[46]"Investment returns are properly computed by using the capital-value formula, $y = x_t/(1 + r)^t$, where y is the cost of the investment, x_t is realized return t years hence, and r is the internal rate of return of what Keynes called the marginal efficiency of capital. . . . The criterion for a profitable investment is that the marginal efficiency exceeds the interest rate (in the Keynesian terminology)." *Ibid.,* 98. The authors calculated the longevity of slaves (assuming on the basis of available figures that a 20-year-old field hand had a 30-year life expectancy), the cost of investment (average cost of slaves, land, equipment, and average annual maintence costs over the period, 1830-1860), the annual average yield per hand, and the average annual price for cotton. Using 6 per cent as the rate of return slaveowners could earn in other investments outside of slavery, the authors applied these figures to the formula and solved for r. *Ibid.,* 99-107.

[47]*Ibid.,* 106-107, 109-14, 120-22. Their explanation of how figures were calculated (and the assumptions they were forced to make in the absence of adequate figures) may be found on pp. 106-108.

[48]*Ibid.,* 119-20. A brief article by John E. Moes suggested that the capitalization of

Two recent works, in dealing with the question of profitability, show the influence of Conrad and Meyer's findings. Stanley M. Elkins in his study of slavery wrote that the economists, by dropping accounting methods and substituting "the economic . . . concept of profit" have made a "conceptual breakthrough" on the question of profitability. Paul W. Gates, in his discussion of slavery in *The Farmer's Age,* leaned heavily on Conrad and Meyer's analysis in concluding that slavery was profitable.[49] It is clear, however, that Conrad and Meyer's work will not find universal acceptance. It was almost immediately challenged, briefly but cogently, by Douglas F. Dowd.[50]

More recently another economist, Robert Evans, Jr., has published his findings on the question of profitability. Assuming a classical market, he calculated returns on investments in slave capital on the basis of profits earned through the hiring out of slaves during the three decades before the Civil War. He found that the rate of return on slaves varied from 9.5 per cent to 18.5 per cent, figures which were usually higher than those which could be earned in possible alternate areas of investment.[51]

---

labor "does of itself most probably have a detrimental effect on economic growth." But, Moes wrote, this is a problem only when a society "is dependent upon its own capital resources." Such was not the case in the South, for the section was able to import large amounts of capital, a situation which would tend to overcome the detrimental effects of slavery on economic growth. He concluded by questioning the generally accepted assertion that "investment (and development) in the Ante Bellum [South] lagged behind that of the North." John E. Moes, "The Absorption of Capital in Slave Labor in the Ante-Bellum South and Economic Growth," *American Journal of Economics and Sociology,* XX (October 1961), 535-41.

[49]Stanley M. Elkins, *Slavery* (Chicago, 1959), 234; Paul W. Gates, *The Farmer's Age: Agriculture, 1815-1860 (New York, 1960),* 154-55. Gates also cited as his sources the work of Gray and Stampp, but his argument parallels most closely that of Conrad and Meyer.

[50]Douglas F. Dowd, "The Economics of Slavery in the Ante Bellum South: A Comment," *Journal of Political Economy,* LXVI (October 1958), 440-42.

[51]Robert Evans, Jr., "The Economics of American Negro Slavery, 1830-1860," in National Bureau of Economic Research, *Aspects of Labor Economics* (Princeton, 1962), 185-243. Evans indicated that he used "the net rent received by owners of slaves when they rented them out as the estimate of the income earned by the capital good" (p. 191) and assumed "that the hired slave labor market was classical rather than Keynesian in character . . . " (p. 194*n).* Evans' method and his approach to the problem were immediately attacked by a historian (Thomas P. Govan) and an economist (John E. Moes). See "Comments" by these scholars, *ibid.,* 243-56. Govan wrote that he agreed with Evans' conclusion but added that the economist's evidence had "little relevance to this conclusion" (p. 243).

Almost all the writers whose work has been discussed in these pages, whether economists or historians, have, to one degree or another, influenced the conclusions of writers of more general works, who show some of the same diversity of opinion as do the specialists.[52]

It would be folly to assume that this vexing question will ever be resolved to everyone's satisfaction. In part, the difficulty in arriving at a satisfactory solution stems from varying definitions of the problem. Contemporaries argued vociferously, but they were arguing about two very different things. They could agree that slavery had to be considered in its relation to the Southern economy, but there was no agreement as to the particular issues this consideration involved. Ulrich B. Phillips in his analysis gave major stress to slavery as an economic system, but he also introduced what to him apparently was a secondary question, the profitability of slavery as a business enterprise. It was this question which his followers, and the revisionists as well, have emphasized down to our own day.[53] Thus,

[52]Avery Craven questioned whether slavery could be blamed for Southern backwardness. Southern values and ideals rather than slavery accounted for a lack of diversified economic life in the ante bellum South. "The South often deliberately chose rural backwardness." Avery Craven, *The Coming of the Civil War* (New York, 1942), 90-91. Allan Nevins came to exactly opposite conclusions. The South did not choose rural backwardness, according to Nevins; it was forced upon the section by the institution of slavery, which "discouraged industrialism," kept immigrants from the region, discredited "the labor of the white artisan," and "tied the South to a slovenly and wasteful staple-crop system." Allan Nevins, *Ordeal of the Union* (2 vols., New York, 1947), I, 493-94. Two prominent Southern historians, Francis Butler Simkins and Clement Eaton, tend to straddle the fence in their textbooks. They recognize that the slave system was in many ways disadvantageous to the Southern economy, but they do not put the entire blame for Southern backwardness on the peculiar institution. Climate, improvidence, and, most important, the fact that the South was primarily agricultural must share the blame with slavery, according to these two. Simkins, *A History of the South* (New York, 1953), 129-32; Eaton, *A History of the Old South* (New York, 1949), 273-78. Economic historians seem to be more united in their opinions. Louis M. Hacker argued that only those few planters on the very best land could make money; most could not. Hacker, *The Triumph of American Capitalism* (New York, 1940), 317-21. The authors of current popular economic histories agree in general with this and also agree that slavery was responsible for retarding Southern economic development. Ernest L. Bogart and Donald L. Kemmerer, *Economic History of the American People* (New York, 1947), 386-410; Edward C. Kirkland, *A History of American Economic Life* (New York, 1951), 170-73; Herman E. Kroos, *American Economic Development* (Englewood Cliffs, N. J., 1956), 129-32; Gilbert C. Fite and Jim E. Reese, *An Economic History of the United States* (Boston, 1959), 164-65.

[53]The works of Russel and, in part, Gray are the most noteworthy exceptions to this.

a subtle shift in emphasis has taken place through the years in the discussion of slavery's profitability, a shift which is obvious if one compares not the conclusions but the central problem posed by Phillips early in the century with that considered by Conrad and Meyer several decades later.

Some light at least could be shed on the problem if there could be agreement as to what the problem is. In reality, two distinct topics have been discussed over the years, and they are not necessarily related. At least, their relationship has to be proved before they can be considered related. Even if every slaveowner were able to realize a twenty-five per cent return on his investment, it does not necessarily follow that slavery as a system was economically profitable. The real question is neither one of bookkeeping nor one of economic profit. It is a problem of economic history.

To deal with the question of slavery as an economic system, one must clearly distinguish those elements in the Southern economy which existed because of slavery and those which were unrelated to slavery. Those who argue that Southern backwardness arose, for the most part, because the South was primarily agricultural must first show that this would have been true whether or not the institution of slavery existed. Conversely, those who argue that slavery prevented diversification must prove (1) that economic diversification did take place in nonslave agricultural areas and (2) that it was slavery and not other factors which prevented diversified investment in the South. Furthermore, if slavery is to be called the cause of any given phenomenon in the Southern economy, the exact dynamics of the influence of slavery must be shown. It is not enough to juxtapose the results with the existence of slavery to establish a causal relationship. A final methodological question must be posed: Can the economics of slavery be discussed adequately in purely economic terms?

Some work has already been done along the lines suggested here. Two decades ago Fabien Linden considered the effect of slavery on the development of manufacturing in the prewar South. Treating slavery as a political and social as well as an economic institution, Linden traced the dynamics of the opposition to a move to establish widespread manufacturing establishments in the South in the 1840's.[54] More recently Eugene D. Genovese has, in a similar

[54]Fabien Linden, "Repercussions of Manufacturing in the Ante Bellum South," *North Carolina Historical Review*, XVII (October 1940), 313-31.

manner, investigated the problem of slavery in relation to the home market in the ante bellum South.[55]

A different line of approach has been taken by Douglas Dowd, who made a comparative analysis of economic development in the South and West. Further work in this direction, including comparisons with underdeveloped countries, might yield significant results. Dowd also suggested ways in which the economic question had to be broadened: "The nature and extent of resources are of course meaningless apart from the social context within which they exist."[56]

Certainly new lines of thought and research can be explored. If scholars are mindful of the complexities of the question of profitability, and cognizant of the nature of the work already accomplished, we can expect the writings of the future to increase our knowledge of the South and its peculiar institution. The prospect is of more than academic interest. Not only could further work in this field deepen our understanding of nineteenth-century American economic history. It might also give valuable insights into the dynamics of economic growth and development.

JOHN E. CAIRNES

The Economic Basis of Slavery

John Elliott Cairnes (1823-1875), son of an Irish brewery-owner, was at the time of his death regarded as one of the leading economists of his age. Even today, when doubts as to his originality weigh more heavily than they did formerly, he rates respectful mention in any history of

[55]Eugene D. Genovese, "The Significance of the Slave Plantation for Southern Economic Development," *Journal of Southern History*, XXVIII (November 1962), 422-37.

[56]Douglas F. Dowd, "A Comparative Analysis of Economic Development in the American West and South," *Journal of Economic History*, XVI (December 1956), 558-74.

Selected passages from Chapters II and III of John E. Cairnes, *The Slave Power: Its Character, Career, and Probable Designs: Being an Attempt to Explain the Real Issues Involved in the American Contest* (New York: Carleton, 1862).

economic thought. Like many economists of his day and later, he had great confidence in his ability to arrive at the truth by a process of pure deduction, supplemented by highly selective use of empirical material for illustrative purposes. Although he never visited the United States, and seems to have been familiar with only a handful of works dealing with slavery, the work which established his reputation was his book, *The Slave Power,* in which he undertook to explain, primarily for English readers, the fundamental issues underlying the American Civil War and the nature of the civilization which had grown up in the Southern states. Basic to this explanation was his analysis of the economics of slavery.

Believing as he did that "the course of history is largely determined by the action of economic causes," Cairnes found it natural (in a manner which today we might be inclined to call Marxist) to relate every aspect of Southern life—its political style, its class structure, its expansionism, and so on—to the institution of slavery. For this reason he found it necessary to explain why slavery had become established in the United States, and why it had survived only in the South. Translated into words which economists might use today, his explanation ran in terms of a favorable man/land ratio and the production functions of the great Southern agricultural staples, particularly cotton and tobacco. And he experienced no great difficulty in spelling out how, after the remarkable expansion of the cotton textile industry in England and the invention of Whitney's cotton gin in the United States, cotton production by slave labor had proved profitable to slave-owners.

This, however, was only the start of his analysis. Profitable to slave-owners the system may once have been but it was nevertheless harmful to the wellbeing of the Southern states themselves. Quite apart from the moral effects of slavery, its economic consequences were in the long run certain to be injurious. These consequences stemmed in particular from its effects on the quality of the labor force (what, in a telling phrase, he called the "compulsory ignorance" in which slaves were kept) and on the fertility of the soil. Thus (notice the language of deductive logic) the fact that slavery was profitable at one time did not imply that it was profitable still; the most that could be inferred from the continued existence of the system was that it was self-supporting.

It is quite clear that, in Cairnes' judgment, slavery was inimical to the economic development of the South. On the narrower issue of whether or not, in the years immediately before the Civil War, it was still profitable to the slave-owners, he nowhere commits himself explicitly.

It is worth noting, however, in the last few paragraphs reprinted here, his comments on the division of labor that had developed between the old and the new South, the former specializing in the production of slaves, the latter in the production of cotton. The suggestion here is that, even in the more exhausted soil of the old South, expedients had been found to maintain the profitability of the system.

Published in an American edition in 1862, Cairnes' book attained great popularity in the North, presumably because it offered what seemed to be an objective, scientific validation by an outside analyst of most of the beliefs which Northerners already held about slavery. It also sold widely in England; its demonstration that the economic interests of the South's largest customer coincided with that customer's moral preferences must have been reassuring to many readers.

BEFORE PROCEEDING to an examination of the social and political system which has been reared upon the basis of slavery in North America, it will be desirable to devote some consideration to the institution itself in its industrial aspects. The political tendencies of the Slave Power, as will hereafter be seen, are determined in a principal degree by the economic necessities under which it is placed by its fundamental institution; and in order, therefore, to appreciate the nature of those tendencies, a determination of the conditions requisite for the success of slavery, as an industrial system, becomes indispensable.

The form in which it will be most convenient to discuss this question will be in connexion with the actual position of slavery in the American continent. As is well known, the system formed originally a common feature in all the Anglo-Saxon settlements in that part of the world, existing in the northern no less than the southern colonies, in New England no less than in Virginia. But before much time had elapsed from their original foundation, it became evident that it was destined to occupy very different positions among these rising communities. In the colonies north of Delaware Bay slavery rapidly fell into a subordinate place, and gradually died out; while in those south of that inlet its place in the industrial system became constantly more prominent, until ultimately it has risen to a position of paramount importance in that region, overpowering every rival influence, and moulding all the phenomena of the social state into conformity with its requirements.

The problem, then, which I propose to consider is the cause of this difference in the fortunes of slavery in these different portions of American soil.

* * *

The true causes of the phenomenon will appear if we reflect on the characteristic advantages and disadvantages which attach respectively to slavery and free labour, as productive instruments, in connexion with the external conditions under which these forms of industry came into completion in North America.

The economic advantages of slavery are easily stated: they are all comprised in the fact that the employer of slaves has absolute power over his workmen, and enjoys the disposal of the whole fruit of their labours. Slave labour, therefore, admits of the most complete organization, that is to say, it may be combined on an extensive scale, and directed by a controlling mind to a single end, and its cost can never rise above that which is necessary to maintain the slave in health and strength.

On the other hand, the economical defects of slave labour are very serious. They may be summed up under the three following heads:—it is given reluctantly; it is unskillful; it is wanting in versatility.

It is given reluctantly, and consequently the industry of the slave can only be depended on so long as he is watched. The moment the master's eye is withdrawn, the slave relaxes his efforts. The cost of slave labour will therefore, in great measure, depend on the degree in which the work to be performed admits of the workmen being employed in close proximity to each other. If the work be such that a large gang can be employed with efficiency within a small space, and be thus brought under the eye of a single overseer, the expense of superintendence will be slight; if, on the other hand, the nature of the work requires that the workmen should be dispersed over an extended area, the number of overseers, and therefore, the cost of the labour which requires this supervision, will be proportionately increased. The cost of slave-labour thus varies directly with the degree in which the work to be done requires dispersion of the labourers, and inversely as it admits of their concentration. Further, the work being performed reluctantly, fear is substituted for hope, as the stimulus to exertion. But fear is ill calculated to draw from a labourer all the industry of which he is capable. "Fear," says

Bentham, "leads the labourer to hide his powers, rather than to show them; to remain below, rather than to surpass himself." . . . "By displaying superior capacity, the slave would only raise the measure of his ordinary duties; by a work of supererogation he would only prepare punishment for himself." He therefore seeks, by concealing his powers, to reduce to the lowest the standard of requisition. "His ambition is the reverse of that of the freeman; he seeks to descend in the scale of industry, rather than to ascend."

Secondly, slave labour is unskilful, and this, not only because the slave, having no interest in his work, has no inducement to exert his higher faculties, but because, from the ignorance to which he is of necessity condemned, he is incapable of doing so. In the Slave States of North America, the education of slaves, even in the most rudimentary form, is proscribed by law, and consequently their intelligence is kept uniformly and constantly at the very lowest point. "You can make a nigger work," said an interlocutor in one of Mr. Olmsted's dialogues, "but you cannot make him think." He is therefore unsuited for all branches of industry which require the slightest care, forethought, or dexterity. He cannot be made to co-operate with machinery; he can only be trusted with the coarsest implements; he is incapable of all but the rudest forms of labour.

But further, slave labour is eminently defective in point of versatility. The difficulty of teaching the slave anything is so great, that the only chance of turning his labour to profit is, when he has once learned a lesson, to keep him to that lesson for life. Where slaves, therefore, are employed there can be no variety of production. If tobacco be cultivated, tobacco becomes the sole staple, and tobacco is produced whatever be the state of the market, and whatever be the condition of the soil. This peculiarity of slave-labour, as we shall see, involves some very important consequences.

Such being the character of slave-labour, as an industrial instrument, let us now consider the qualities of the agency with which, in the colonization of North America, it was brought into competition. This was the labour of peasant proprietors, a productive instrument, in its merits and defects, the exact reverse of that with which it was called upon to compete. Thus, the great and almost the sole excellence of slave-labour is, as we have seen, its capacity for organization; and this is precisely the circumstance with respect to which the labour of peasant proprietors is especially defective. In a community of peasant proprietors, each workman labours on his own account, without much reference to what his fellow-workmen are doing. There is no commanding mind to whose guidance the whole labour force will yield obedience, and under whose control it may be directed by skilful combinations to the result which is desired. Nor does this system afford room for classification and economical distribution of a labour force in the same degree as the system of slavery. Under the latter, for example, occupation may be found for a whole family of slaves, according to the capacity of each member, in performing the different operations connected with certain branches of industry—say, the culture of tobacco, in which the women and children may be employed in picking the worms off the plants, or gathering the leaves as they become ripe, while the men are engaged in the more laborious tasks; but a small proprietor, whose children are at school, and whose wife finds enough to occupy her in her domestic duties, can command for all operations, however important or however insignificant, no other labour than his own, or that of his grown-up sons—labour which would be greatly misapplied in performing such manual operations as I have described. His team of horses might be standing idle in the stable, while he was gathering tobacco leaves or picking worms, an arrangement which would render his work exceedingly costly. The system of peasant proprietorship, therefore, does not admit of combination and classification of labour in the same degree as that of slavery. But if in this respect it lies under a disadvantage as compared with its rival, in every other respect it enjoys an immense superiority. The peasant proprietor, appropriating the whole produce of his toil, needs no other stimulus to exertion. Superintendence is here completely dispensed with. The laborer is under the strongest conceivable inducement to put forth, in the furtherance of his task, the full powers of his mind and body; and his mind, instead of being purposely stinted and stupified, is enlightened by education, and aroused by the prospect of reward.

Such are the two productive agencies which came into competition on the soil of North America. If we now turn to the external conditions under which competition took place, we shall, I think, have no difficulty in understanding the success of each respectively in that portion of the Continent in which it did in fact succeed.

The line dividing the Slave from the Free States marks also an important division in the agricultural capabilities of North America. North of this line, the products for which the soil and climate are best adapted are cereal crops, while south of it the prevailing crops are tobacco, rice, cotton, and sugar; and these two classes of crops are broadly distinguished in the methods of culture suitable to each. The cultivation of the one class, of which cotton may be taken as the type, requires for its efficient conduct that labour should be combined and organized on an extensive scale. On the other hand, for the raising of cereal crops this condition is not so essential. Even where labour is abundant and that labour free, the large capitalist does not in this mode of farming appear on the whole to have any preponderating advantage over the small proprietor, who, with his family, cultivates his own farm, as the example of the best cultivated states in Europe proves. Whatever superiority he may have in the power of combining and directing labour seems to be compensated by the greater energy and spirit which the sense of property gives to the exertions of the small proprietor. But there is another essential circumstance in which these two classes of crops differ. A single labourer . . . can cultivate twenty acres of wheat or Indian corn, while he cannot manage more than two of tobacco, or three of cotton. It appears from this that tobacco and cotton fulfil that condition which we saw was essential to the economical employment of slaves—the possibility of working large numbers within a limited space; while wheat and Indian corn, in the cultivation of which the labourers are dispersed over a wide surface, fail in this respect. We thus find that cotton, and the class of crops of which cotton may be taken as the type, favour the employment of slaves in the competition with peasant proprietors in two leading ways: first, they need extensive combination and organization of labour—requirements which slavery is eminently calculated to supply, but in respect to which the labour of peasant proprietors is defective; and secondly, they allow of labour being concentrated, and thus minimize the cardinal evil of slave-labour—the reluctance with which it is yielded. On the other hand, the cultivation of cereal crops, in which extensive combination of labour is not important, and in which the operations of industry are widely diffused, offers none of these advantages for the employment of slaves, while it is remarkably fitted to bring out in the highest degree the especial excellencies of the industry of free proprietors. Owing to these causes it has happened that slavery has been maintained in the Southern States, which favour the growth of tobacco, cotton, and analogous products, while, in the Northern States, of which cereal crops are the great staple, it from an early period declined and has ultimately died out. And in confirmation of this view it may be added that wherever in the Southern States the external conditions are especially favourable to cereal crops, as in parts of Virginia, Kentucky, and Missouri, and along the slopes of the Alleghanies, there slavery has always failed to maintain itself. It is owing to this cause that there now exists in some parts of the South a considerable element of free labouring population.

These consisiderations appear to explain the permanence of slavery in one division of North America, and its disappearance from the other; but there are other conditions essential to the economic success of the institution besides those which have been brought into view in the above comparison, to which it is necessary to advert in order to a right understanding of its true basis. These are high fertility in the soil, and a practically unlimited extent of it.

The necessity of these conditions to slavery will be apparent by reflecting on the unskilfulness and want of versatility in slave labour to which we have already referred.

When the soils are not of good quality cultivation needs to be elaborate; a larger capital is expended; and with the increase of capital the processes become more varied, and the agricultural implements of a finer and more delicate construction. With such implements slaves cannot be trusted, and for such processes they are unfit. It is only, therefore, where the natural fertility of the soil is so great as to compensate for the inferiority of the cultivation, where nature does so much as to leave little for art, and to supersede the necessity of the more difficult contrivances of industry, that slave labour can be turned to profitable account.

Further, slavery, as a permanent system, has need not merely of a fertile soil, but of a practically unlimited extent of it. This arises from the defect of slave labour in point of versatility. As has been already remarked, the difficulty of teaching the slave anything is so great—the result of the compulsory ignorance in which he is kept, combined with want of intelligent interest in his work—that the only chance of rendering his labour profitable is, when he has once learned a lesson, to keep him to that lesson for life. Accordingly where agricultural operations are carried on by slaves the business of each gang is always restricted to the raising of a single product. Whatever crop be best suited to the character of the soil and the nature of slave industry, whether cotton, tobacco, sugar, or rice, that crop is cultivated, and that crop only. Rotation of crops is thus precluded by the conditions of the case. The soil is tasked again and again to yield the same product, and the inevitable result follows. After a short series of years its fertility is completely exhausted, the planter abandons the ground which he has rendered worthless, and passes on to seek in new soils for that fertility under which alone the agencies at his disposal can be profitably employed. . . .

Slave cultivation, therefore, precluding the conditions of rotation of crops or skilful management, tends inevitably to exhaust the land of a country, and consequently requires for its permanent success not merely a fertile soil but a practically unlimited extent of it.

To sum up, then, the conclusions at which we have arrived, the successful maintenance of slavery, as a system of industry, requires the following conditions:—1st. Abundance of fertile soil; and, 2nd. A crop the cultivation of which demands combination and organization of labour on an extensive scale, and admits of its concentration. It is owing to the presence of these conditions that slavery has maintained itself in the Southern States of North America, and to their absence that it has disappeared from the Northern States.

INTERNAL ORGANIZATION OF SLAVE COMMUNITIES

[This] explanation . . . of the success and failure of slavery in different portions of North America resolved itself into the proposition, that in certain cases the institution was found to be economically profitable while it proved unprofitable in others. From this position—the profitableness of slavery under given external conditions—the inference is generally made by those who advocate or look with indulgence on the system, that slavery must be regarded as conducive to at least the material well-being of countries in which these conditions exist; and these conditions being admittedly present in the Slave States of North America, it is concluded that the abolition of slavery in those states would necessarily be attended with a diminution of their wealth, and by consequence, owing to the mode in which the interests of all nations are identified through commerce, with a corresponding injury to the material interests of the rest of the world. In this manner it is attempted to enlist the selfish feelings of mankind in favour of the institution; and it is not impossible that many persons, who would be disposed to condemn it upon moral grounds, are thus led to connive at its existence. It will therefore be desirable, before proceeding further with the investigation of our subject, to ascertain precisely the extent of the admission in favour of the system which is involved in the foregoing explanation of its success.

And, in the first place, it must be remarked that the profitableness which has been attributed to slavery is profitableness estimated exclusively from the point of view of the proprietor of slaves. Profitableness *in this sense* is all that is necessary to account for the introduction and maintenance of the system (which was the problem with which alone we were concerned), since it was with the proprietors that the decision rested. But those who are acquainted with the elementary principles which govern the distribution of wealth, know that the profits of capitalists may be increased by the same process by which the gross revenue of a country is diminished, and that therefore the community as a whole may be impoverished through the very same means by which a portion of its number is enriched. The economic success of slavery, therefore, is perfectly consistent with the supposition that it is prejudicial to the material well-being of the country where it is established. The argument, in short, comes to this: the interests of slave-masters—or rather that which slave-masters believe to be their interests—are no more identical with the interests of the general population in slave countries in the matter of wealth, than in that of morals or politics. That which benefits, or seems to benefit, the one in any of these departments, may injure the other. It follows, therefore, that the economic advantages possessed by slavery, which were the inducement to its original establishment and which cause it still to be upheld, are perfectly compatible with its being an obstacle to the industrial development of the country, and its variance with the best interests, material as well as moral, of its inhabitants.

Further, the profitableness which has been attributed to slavery does not even imply that the system is conducive to the interests (except in the narrowest sense of the word) of the class for whose especial behoof it exists. Individuals and classes may always be assumed to follow their own interests according to their lights and tastes; but that which their lights and tastes point out as their interest will vary with the degree of their intelligence and the character of their civilization. When the intelligence of a class is limited and its civilization low, the view it will take of its interests will be correspondingly narrow and sordid. Extravagant and undue importance will be attached to the mere animal pleasures. A small gain obtained by coarse and obvious methods will be preferred to a great one which requires a recourse to the more refined expedients; and the future well-being of the race will be regarded as of less importance than the aggrandisement of the existing generation.

But our admissions in favour of slavery require still further qualification. The establishment of slavery in the Southern States was accounted for by its superiority in an economic point of view over free labour, in the form in which free labour existed in America at the time when that continent was settled. Now, the superiority of slavery over free labour to which its establishment was originally owing, is by no means to be assumed as still existing in virtue of the fact that slavery is still maintained. Of two systems one may at a given period be more profitable than the other, and may on this account be established, but may afterwards cease to be so, and yet may nevertheless continue to be upheld, either from habit, or from unwillingness to adopt new methods, or from congeniality with tastes which have been formed under its influence. It is a difficult and slow process under all circumstances to alter the industrial system of a country; but the difficulty of exchanging one form of free industry for another is absolutely inappreciable when compared with that which we encounter when we attempt to substitute free for servile institutions. It is therefore quite possible—how far the case is actually so I shall afterwards examine—that the persistent maintenance of the system at the present day may be due less to its economical advantages than to the habits and tastes it may have engendered, and to the enormous difficulty of getting rid of it. Since the settlement of the Southern States a vast change has taken place in the American continent. Free labour, which was then scarce and costly, has now in many of the large towns become superabundant; and it is quite possible that, even with external conditions so favourable to slavery as the southern half of North America undoubtedly presents, free labour would now, on a fair trial, be found more than a match for its antagonist. Such a trial, however, is not possible under the present *régime* of the South. Slavery is in possession of the field, and enjoys all the advantages which possession in such a contest confers.

The concession then in favour of slavery, involved in the explanation given of its definitive establishment in certain portions of North America, amounts to this, that *under certain conditions of soil and climate, cultivation by slaves may for a time yield a larger net revenue than cultivation by certain forms of free labour.* This is all that needs to be assumed to account for the original establishment of slavery. But the maintenance of the institution at the present day does not imply even this quantum of advantage in its favour; since, owing to the immense difficulty of getting rid of it when once established on an extensive scale, the reasons for its continuance (regarding the question from the point of view of the slaveholders) may, where it has once obtained a firm footing, prevail over those for its abolition, even though it be far inferior as a productive instrument to free-labour. The most, therefore, that can be inferred from the existence of the system at the present day is that it is self-supporting.

Having now cleared the ground from the several false inferences with which the economic success of slavery, such as it is, is apt to be surrounded, I proceed to trace the consequences, economic, social, and political, which flow from the institution. . . .

. . . . Slave labour is, from the nature of the case, unskilled labour; and it is evident that this circumstance at once excludes it from the field of manufacturing and mechanical industry. Where a workman is kept in compulsory ignorance, and is, at the same time, without motive for exerting his mental faculties, it is quite impossible that he should take part with efficiency in the difficult and delicate operations which most manufacturing and mechanical processes involve. The care and dexterity which the management of machinery requires is not to be obtained from him, and he would often do more damage in an hour than the produce of his labour for a year would cover. Slavery, therefore, at least in its modern form, has never been, and can never be, employed with success in manufacturing industry. And no less plain is it that it is unsuited to the functions of commerce; for the soul of commerce is the spirit of enterprise, and this is ever found wanting in communities where slavery exists: their prevailing characteristics are subjection to routine and contempt for money-making pursuits. Moreover, the occupations of commerce are absolutely prohibitive of the employment of servile labour. A mercantile marine composed of slaves is a form of industry which the world has not yet seen. Mutinies in mid-ocean and desertions the moment the vessel touched at foreign ports would quickly reduce the force to a cipher.

Slavery, therefore, excluded by these causes from the field of manufactures and commerce, finds its natural career in agriculture; and, from what has been already established respecting the peculiar qualities of slave labour, we may easily divine the form which agricultural industry will assume under a servile *régime*. The single merit of slave labour as an industrial instrument consists, as we have seen, in its capacity for organization—its susceptibility, that is to say, of being adjusted with precision to the kind of work to be done, and of being directed on a comprehensive plan towards some distinctly conceived end. Now to give scope to this quality, the scale on which industry is carried on must be extensive, and, to carry on industry on an extensive scale, large capitals are required. Large capitalists will therefore have, in slave communities, a special and peculiar advantage over small capitalists beyond that which they enjoy in countries where labour is free. But there is another circumstance which renders a considerable capital still more an indispensable condition to the successful conduct of industrial operations in slave countries. A capitalist who employs free labour needs for the support of his labour force a sum sufficient to cover the amount of their wages during the interval which elapses from the commencement of their operations until the sale of the produce which results from them. But the capitalist employing slave labour requires not merely this sum—represented in his case by the food, clothing, and shelter provided for his slaves during the corresponding period—but, in addition to this, a sum sufficient to purchase the fee-simple of his entire slave force. For the conduct of a given business, therefore, it is obvious that the employer of slave labour will require a much larger capital than the employer of free labour. The capital of the one will represent merely the current outlay; while the capital of the other will represent, in addition to this, the future capabilities of the productive instrument. The one will represent the interest, the other the principal and interest, of the labour employed. Owing to these causes large capitals are, relatively to small, more profitable, and are, at the same time, absolutely more required in countries of slave, than in countries of free labour. It happens, however, that capital is in slave countries a particularly scarce commodity, owing partly to the exclusion from such countries of many modes of creating it—manufactures and commerce for example—which are open to free communities, and partly to what is also a consequence of the institution—the unthrifty habits of the upper classes. We arrive therefore at this singular conclusion, that, while large capitals in countries of slave labor enjoy peculiar advantages, and while the aggregate capital needed in them for the conduct of a given amount of industry is greater than in countries where labour is free, capital nevertheless in such countries is exceptionally scarce. From this state of things result two phenomena which may be regarded as typical of industry carried on by slaves—the magnitude of the plantations and the indebtedness of the planters. Wherever negro slavery has prevailed in modern times, these two phenomena will be found to exist. They form the burthen of most of what has been written on our West Indian Islands while under the *régime* of slavery; and they are not less prominently the characteristic features of the industrial system of the Southern States. "Our wealthier planters," says Mr. Clay, "are buying out their poorer neighbours, extending their plantations, and adding to their slave force. The wealthy few, who are able to live on smaller profits, and to give their blasted fields some rest, are thus pushing off the many who are merely independent." At the same time these wealthier planters are, it is well known, very generally in debt, the forthcoming crops being for the most part mortgaged to Northern capitalists, who make the needful advances, and who thus become the instruments by which a considerable proportion of the slave labour of the South is maintained. The tendency of things, therefore, in slave countries is to a very unequal distribution of wealth. The large capitalists, having a steady advantage over their smaller competitors, engross, with the progress of time, a larger and larger proportion of the aggregate wealth of the country, and gradually acquire the control of its collective industry. Meantime, amongst the ascendant class a condition of general indebtedness prevails. . . .

The reader is now in a position to understand the kind of economic success which slavery has achieved. It consists in the rapid extraction from the soil of a country of the most easily obtained portion of its wealth by a process which exhausts the soil, and consigns to waste all the other resources of the country where it is practised. To state the case with more particularity—by proscribing manufactures and commerce, and confining agriculture within narrow bounds, by rendering impossible the rise of a free peasantry, by checking the growth of population—in a word, by blasting every germ from which national well-being and general civilization may spring—at this cost, with the further condition of encroaching, through a reckless system of culture, on the stores designed by Providence for future generations, slavery may undoubtedly for a time be made conducive to the pecuniary gain of the class who keep slaves. Such is the net result of advantage which slavery, as an economic system, is capable of yielding. To the full credit of all that is involved in this admission the institution is fairly entitled. . . .

. . . We have already seen the tendency of slave-labour to exhaust the soil, and the rapidity with which this process proceeds, reducing to the condition of wilderness districts which fifty years before were yet untouched by the hand of cultivation. Now, this would seem to promise that the reign of slavery, if ruinous, should at least be brief, and we might expect that, when the soil had been robbed of its fertility, the destroyer would retire from the region which he had rendered desolate. And such would be the fate of slavery, were it depending exclusively on the soil for its support; but, when trading in human beings is once introduced, a new source of profit is developed for the system, which renders it in a great degree independent of the resources of the soil. It is this, the profit developed by trading in slaves, and this alone, which has enabled slavery in the older Slave States of North America to survive the consequences of its own ravages. In Maryland and Virginia, perhaps also in the Carolinas and Georgia, free institutions would long since have taken the place of slavery, were it not that just as the crisis of the system had arrived, the domestic slave-trade opened a door of escape from a position which had become untenable. The conjuncture was peculiar, and would doubtless by Southern theologians be called providential. The progress of devastation had reached the point at which slave cultivation could no longer sustain itself. A considerable emigration of planters had actually taken place, and the deserted fields were already receiving a new race of settlers from the regions of freedom. The long night of slavery seemed to be passing away, and the dawn of a brighter day to have arrived, when suddenly the auspicious movement was arrested. A vast extension of the territory of the United States, opening new soils to Southern enterprise, exactly coincided with the prohibition of the external slave trade, and both fell in with the crisis in the older States. The result was a sudden and remarkable rise in the price of slaves. The problem of the planters' position was at once solved, and the domestic slave-trade commenced. Slavery had robbed Virginia of the best riches of her soil, but she still had a noble climate—a climate which would fit her admirably for being the breeding place of the South. A division of labour between the old and the new states took place. In the former the soil was extensively exhausted, but the climate was salubrious; in the latter the climate was unfavorable to human life spent in severe toil, but the soil was teeming with riches. The old states therefore undertook the part of breeding and rearing slaves till they attained to physical vigour, and the new that of using up in the development of their virgin resources the physical vigour which had been thus obtained.

It has been contended that the constant drain of slaves must have its effect in diminishing, and ultimately exhausting, the slave population in the states from which it proceeds; and on this ground the domestic slave trade has found advocates amongst persons who profess themselves opposed to slavery in general, as tending to effect its extinction in the older states. But such a view, if sincerely entertained, can only find credit with those who are unacquainted with the laws of population, and it has been amply refuted by the experience of half a century. Far from conducing in the slightest degree to the decline of slavery in the older states, the inter-state traffic has tended directly to establish it, and the slave population of those states has steadily increased under the drain. The single exception to this statement is the State of Delaware, and Delaware is the only one of those states in which the sale or removal of slaves is prohibited by law. The real character of the influence exercised by the internal trade on the breeding states was strikingly shown on the annexation of Texas. That event occurred in 1844. It was followed by a great increase in the demand for slaves for the South, and with what effect on the states which supplied them?—with the effect of a positive increase in their slave population. The slave population of the principal slave-breeding state, Virginia, had declined in the decade previous to the annexation, but at the end of the following decade it was found to have increased. The explanation of this, of course, is perfectly simple. Slaves in the older states being of little value for agricultural purposes, there is no inducement to encourage their increase so long as agriculture is the sole purpose to which they can be turned; but with the increase of the slave trade, their value increases, and they are, therefore, raised in greater numbers.

ULRICH B. PHILLIPS

The Economic Cost of Slaveholding in the Cotton Belt

The selection which follows is probably the most important article ever published on the economics of black slavery in the United States. This is not because many people today agree with it. Quite the contrary: its conclusions are now largely discredited, and it is probably true, as Douglas Dowd suggested in 1957, that the writings of Ulrich B. Phillips should now be regarded as sociological rather than historical materials—"documents, almost, revealing how a partisan of the Lost Cause viewed the evolution of that society." If so, it is not the first time that the histories of one generation have become the documentary materials of the next.

For our purposes, however, the selection has an additional importance. It was this article, published in 1905, that set the terms of reference for the controversy that was to follow. Phillips defined the issues; few later scholars have shifted those issues very much. He stated his conclusions without equivocation; later scholars at least knew what they did not agree with. He set out the evidence that, in his judgment, validated his conclusions, and challenged other historians to show where, if anywhere, he had gone wrong. And he brought together valuable quantitative data, particularly on slave prices; some of it is dubious and incomplete, to be sure, but again and again in later articles you will find Phillips' statistics cited as the best available.

It was, for the time, a good article. It is unfortunate that few people nowadays read anything else that Phillips wrote, and in particular that his treatise on *American Negro Slavery,* published in 1918, is now virtually ignored. The article was one of the first publications of a young scholar; it did not represent Phillips' mature and elaborated thinking on the subject. Chapter XIX of *American Negro Slavery,* for example, is in many ways a better, and certainly a more detailed, discussion of the "business" aspects of slavery than the article. But it is the article that is quoted and referred to, and consequently it is the article that is reprinted here.

Phillips' principal thesis is simply stated. By the 1850s slavery, originally profitable, had become an economic burden on the South—

Reprinted with permission from the *Political Science Quarterly,* XX (June, 1905), 257-275.

an "obstacle to all progress." It was maintained and defended in the South because, though no longer profitable, it was necessary for racial peace. "As soon as the negroes were on hand in large numbers, the problem was to keep their savage instincts from breaking forth . . . the institution of slavery was considered necessary to preserve the peace and to secure the welfare of both races." The white people of the South, in other words, undertook to carry on their own shoulders an economic burden, an institution which retarded their growth in wealth and industry, because they saw no other way to limit the risk of negro uprisings. When federal intervention likely to disturb this necessary institution seemed imminent, they were driven, through "force of circumstances," into secession, as the lesser of two evils.

In his *American Negro Slavery,* Phillips flatly denied the existence of a market-oriented slave-breeding sector in the southern economy, and professed to have found no shred of evidence to support such an assertion. "In the case of slaves," he wrote, "the cost of rearing had no practical bearing upon the market price, for the reason that the owners could not, or at least did not, increase or diminish the production at will." This proposition had important consequences. On the one hand it meant that Phillips parted company, on a question of fact, with J. E. Cairnes and many other critics of slavery and aligned himself with those Southerners who, then and later, repudiated as a slur upon Southern honor the very suggestion that slaves had been systematically bred for sale. On the other hand, it meant that Phillips was able to confine his analysis of profitability to the single issue of whether or not the use of slaves to produce goods (and not their use to produce other slaves) had been profitable. In analyzing slave pricing he likened the slave, not to a piece of capital equipment like a machine, which could be reproduced when it was profitable to do so, but to a mineral deposit which was essentially a free gift of nature, from the point of view of the whole economy, though it might indeed be purchased or leased for a price by private individuals. Fluctuations in the market price of slaves reflected mainly the movement of demand, which in turn reflected "the play of conjectures as to the present value of the total future earnings." Long-run trends in slave prices, however, after the cessation of the external slave trade with Africa, were decisively affected by the failure of supply to respond to the market. In general, according to Phillips, slave prices and cotton prices fluctuated in step with each other. The trend around which the fluctuations took place, however, was downward for cotton, upward for slaves. Thus the planter was, as it were, caught between the closing blades of a pair of scissors. "By the close of the 'fifties," he concluded, "it is fairly certain that no slaveholders but those few whose plantations lay in the most advantageous parts of the cotton and sugar districts and whose managerial ability was exceptionally great were earning anything beyond what would cover their maintenance and carrying charges." Nevertheless, for reasons basically cultural and economic—slavery, said Phillips, was "less a business than a life"—the South could not rid itself of what had become an economic incubus.

In analyzing Phillips' article it may be helpful to distinguish between his argument on the one hand, and what the late Joseph Schumpeter would have called his "vision" on the other. His argument you can appraise by the usual methods of logical analysis and scrutiny of evidence. But his vision, the point of view from which he selected and interpreted evidence, is a non-rational, non-logical matter. You may not care for it; you may not find it personally acceptable; but you have to reckon with it in dealing with a dead historian just as you would in dealing with a living neighbor. Phillips' vision is a vision of the South as victim—as a region and a people trapped by the irreversibility of history into a social system which no longer made economic sense but which could not be gotten rid of. It is, in a sense, a tragic view of history, not common among American historians. There is more to it than just an *apologia* for the South.

His argument is quite another matter. I have no intention here of specifying precisely where the weak points are. That is your responsibility, aided by the later selections in this book. It would be a useful exercise, after reading Phillips' article but before reading the later pieces, to try to lay out with precision the economic model that underlies his reasoning. You will find that only under certain extreme assumptions regarding trends in the productivity of slave labor and in the returns to the other factors of production (e.g. land rents) does his proof of the growing unprofitability of slavery hang together. Merely to show that the price of slaves was rising faster than the price of cotton is not enough. Neither is the fact that planters reinvested profits in expansion, nor the fact that they used northern credit. You must ask yourself what model Phillips is using, and whether the evidence he provides, and the argument he bases on it, proves that plantation slavery had in fact become uneconomic before the Civil War, or indeed whether it even makes such a conclusion plausible.

It is worth noting, in this connection, the way in which Phillips' vision influences his vocabulary and thereby the semantics he uses to make his argument convincing. Observe, for example, his use of the term "monopoly", with reference both to the supply of negroes after the end of the external slave trade and the supply of cotton by the South to England. By any usual definition, it would be difficult to justify its use in either of these contexts, but it does enable Phillips to portray the Southern economy as helplessly at the mercy of "the apparently capricious play of the compound monopoly of cotton and slave labor." Similarly it is hard to see why reinvestment of earnings in plant expansion is referred to as a "vicious circle." If this were so, every prosperous firm in an expanding industry would be victimized by the same vicious process. And some reservations are in order when Phillips describes a planter who bought slaves as investing in a "fictitious form of wealth" while the Yankee shipowner who brought the slaves from Africa is congratulated on making a "genuine profit."

To help us find our way through semantic mazes like this, there is no substitute for rigorous economic analysis. And it is in precisely this area that Phillips is most vulnerable to attack. His position, however, is not as extreme as it has sometimes been represented as being. Does he assert that all uses of slaves were unprofitable by the start of the Civil War? Or only that on the average, or for certain crops, or in certain regions, they were unprofitable? Does he mean "unprofitable" in the sense in which a business is unprofitable when its total costs are greater than its total revenues? Or is he saying, essentially, that the South was locked into a socio-economic matrix which held no potential for growth? If so, does he suggest what alternative path of development would have been preferable? Does he imply that the South, if left alone, would have rid itself of slavery without the Civil War, since by then it was clearly an economic burden? Or does his reference to the need for a "convulsion or crisis of some sort," if slavery were to be disestablished in any region, amount to an admission that the conflict was indeed irrepressible?

APART from mere surface politics, the ante-bellum South is largely an unknown country to American historians. The conditions, the life, the spirit of its people were so different from those which prevailed and still prevail in the North that it is difficult for northern investigators to interpret correctly the facts which they are able to find. From the South itself they have received little assistance; for before the war southerners were content, as a rule, to transmit traditions without writing books and since the war they have been too seriously engrossed in adapting themselves to new conditions to feel any strong impulse towards a scientific reconstruction of the former environment. When the South shall have been interpreted to the world by its own writers, it will be highly useful for students of other sections and other countries to criticise and correct, utilize and supplement the southern historical literature.[1] At the present time, however, the great need seems to be that of interpretation of developments in the South by men who have inherited southern traditions. This consideration will perhaps justify the following incomplete study.

Whether negro slavery was an advantage in the early colonies and whether it became a burden in the later period, and, if so, how the change occurred, and why the people did not relieve themselves of the incubus—these are a few of the fundamental problems to which the student must address himself. The present essay, based on a study of slave prices, deals with the general economic conditions of slaveholding, and shows the great transformation caused by the opening of the cotton belt and the closing of the African slave trade.

As regards the labor supply, the conditions at the outset in the new world of America were unlike those of modern Europe, but similar to those of Asia and Europe in primitive times. The ancient labor problem rose afresh in the plantation colonies, for land was plentiful and free, and men would not work as voluntary wage-earners in other men's employ when they might as readily work for themselves in independence. There was a great demand for labor upon the colonial estates, and when it became clear that freemen would not come and work for hire, a demand developed for servile labor. At first recourse was had to white men and women who bound themselves to serve three or four years to pay for their transportation across the sea, and to English criminals who were sent to the colonies and bound to labor for longer terms, frequently for five or seven years. Indian slaves were tried, but proved useless. Finally the negroes were discovered to be cheap and useful laborers for domestic service and plantation work.

For above half a century after the first negroes were brought to Virginia in 1620, this labor was considered a doubtful experiment;

---

[1] In the study of the economic history of American slavery the writer has enjoyed the collaboration of Dr. Charles McCarthy, of Wisconsin, a keen thinker with a point of view which supplements that of a southerner.

and their numbers increased very slowly until after the beginning of the golden age of the colony toward the end of the reign of Charles II. But the planters learned at length that the negroes could be employed to very good advantage in the plantation system; and after about 1680 the import of slaves grew steadily larger.[2]

In the West Indies the system of plantations worked by slaves had been borrowed by the English settlers from the Spaniards; and when the South Carolina coast was colonized, some of the West India planters immigrated and brought this system with them. In view of the climate and the crops on the Carolina coast, negro slave labor was thought to be a *sine qua non* of successful colonizing. The use of the slaves was confined always to the lowlands, until after Whitney invented the cotton gin; but in the early years of the nineteenth century the rapid opening of the great inland cotton belt created a new and very strong demand for labor. The white farming population already in the uplands was by far too small to do the work; the lowland planters began to move thither with their slaves; the northern and European laboring classes were not attracted by the prospect of working alongside the negroes; and accordingly the demand for labor in the cotton belt was translated into an unprecedented demand for negro slave labor.

Negro slavery was established in the South, as elsewhere, because the white people were seeking their own welfare and comfort. It was maintained for the same economic reason, and also because it was thought to be essential for safety. As soon as the negroes were on hand in large numbers, the problem was to keep their savage instincts from breaking forth, and to utilize them in civilized industry. The plantation system solved the problem of organization, while the discipline and control obtained through the institution of slavery were considered necessary to preserve the peace and to secure the welfare of both races. Private gain and public safety were secured for the time being; but in the long run, as we shall see, these ends were attained at the expense of private and public wealth and of progress.

This peculiar labor system failed to gain strength in the North, because there was there no work which negro slaves could perform with notable profit to their masters. In certain parts of the South the system flourished because the work required was simple, the returns

[2]For statistics of the increase of slaves in Virginia, see J.C. Ballagh, *History of Slavery in Virginia,* pp. 10 to 25, *et passim.*

were large, and the shortcomings of negro slave labor were partially offset by the ease with which it could be organized.

Once developed, the system was of course maintained so long as it appeared profitable to any important part of the community Wherever the immediate profits from slave labor were found to be large, the number of slaves tended to increase, not only through the birth of children, but by importations. Thus the staple-producing areas became "black belts," where most of the labor was done by slaves. With large amounts of capital invested in slaves, the system would be maintained even in times of depression, when the plantations were running at something of a loss; for, just as in a factory, the capital was fixed, and operations could not be stopped without a still greater loss. When property in slaves had become important, the conservative element in politics became devoted, as a rule, to the preservation of this vested interest. The very force of inertia tended to maintain the established system, and a convulsion or crisis of some sort was necessary for its disestablishment in any region.

As a matter of fact it was only in special industries, and only in times of special prosperity, that negro slave labor was of such decided profit as to escape condemnation for its inherent disadvantages. But at certain periods in Virginia and in the lower South, the conditions were unusual: all labor was profitable; hired labor was not to be had so long as land was free; indentured white servants were in various ways unsatisfactory, and negro slaves were therefore found to be of decided profit to their masters. The price of Africans in colonial times was so low that, when crops and prices were good, the labor of those imported repaid their original cost in a few years, and the planters felt a constant temptation to increase their holdings of land and of slaves in the hope of still greater profits.

Thus in Virginia there was a vicious circle: planters bought fresh lands and more slaves to make more tobacco, and with the profits from tobacco they bought more land and slaves to make more tobacco with which to buy yet more land and slaves. The situation in the lower South was similar to that in Virginia, with rice and indigo, or sugar, or in latter times cotton, substituted for tobacco. In either case the process involved a heavy export of wealth in the acquisition of every new laborer. The Yankee skipper had a corresponding circle of his own: he carried rum to Guinea to exchange for slaves, slaves to the plantation colonies to exchange for molasses, molasses to New England to exchange for more rum, and this rum again to

Guinea to exchange for more slaves. The difference was that the Yankee made a genuine profit on every exchange and thriftily laid up his savings, while the southern planter, as a rule, invested all his profits in a fictitious form of wealth and never accumulated a surplus for any other sort of investment.

From an economic point of view the American system of slavery was a system of firmly controlling the unintelligent negro laborers, and of capitalizing the prospective value of the labor of each workman for the whole of his life. An essential feature of that system was the practice of buying and selling the control over the slave's labor, and one of the indexes to the economic situation at any time may be found in the quotations of slave prices.

The slave trade had no particular local home or "exchange," but it extended throughout all the slaveholding districts of America. Though the number and frequency of slave sales was relatively small, the traffic when once developed had many of the features of modern stock or produce markets. It cannot be forgotten, of course, that the slave trade involved questions of humanity and social organization as well as the mere money problem; but from the financial point of view the slave traffic constituted simply an extensive commodity market, where the article dealt in was life-time labor. As in any other market, the operations in the slave trade were controlled by economic laws or tendencies. There were bull influences and bear influences, and occasional speculative campaigns. And when at times the supply was subjected to monopoly control, the prices tended to go wild and disturb the general system of finance in the whole region.

In the general slave market there was constant competition among those wishing to sell, and among those wishing to buy. The volume of the colonial slave trade and the rate of slave prices tended to fluctuate to some extent with the tides of prosperity in the respective staple-producing areas; but during the colonial period the plantations in the different regions were of such varied interests, producing tobacco, rice, indigo, cotton, sugar and coffee, that depression in one of these industries was usually offset, so far as concerned the slave-trader, by high profits in another. Barbadoes was the information station. The slave ships touched there and gathered news of where their "ebony" was to be sold the highest.[3] The Royal African Company had the best system of intelligence,

---

[3]D. McKinnon, *Tour Through the British West Indies*, p. 8.

and about 1770 and 1780 it sold its cargoes at a fairly uniform price of £18 to £22 per head,[4] while the independent traders appear to have obtained from £15 to £25, according to the chances of the market. American-born slaves, when sold, brought higher prices than fresh Africans, because their training in plantation labor and domestic service rendered them more valuable. The prices of the home-raised slaves varied considerably, but so long as the African trade was kept open, the price of field hands of all sorts was kept reasonably near to the price of the savage African imports.

In the very early period the sellers in the slave market were more eager than the buyers, and the prices ranged nearly as low as the cost of purchasing slaves in Africa and transporting them to America; but great prosperity in all the different groups of plantations at the same period soon greatly increased the demand, and the ships in the traffic proving too few, prices rapidly advanced. After this, however, there came a decline in tobacco profits; then the war of revolt from Great Britain depressed all the staple industries simultaneously, and following that the American production of indigo was ruined by foreign competition. Thus in 1790-95 slave prices reached the bottom of a twenty years' decline.[5]

[4] *Virginia Magazine,* iii, 167. Calendar of State Papers, Colonial Series, America and West Indies, 1775-76, p. 155 *et passim.*

[5] The depression of industry in the staple districts toward the close of the eighteenth century is illustrated by several contemporary writers. Samuel DuBose, in his reminiscences of St. Stephen's parish, describes conditions in lowland South Carolina in the period after the close of the American Revolution:

"When peace was restored every planter was in debt. . . . Ruin stared many in the face. Besides, with the exception of rice, the country had no staple crop; for since the bounty, which as colonists they had enjoyed on the export of indigo and naval stores, had been discontinued, these products ceased to have any value, and negroes fell in price. Prime gangs were not unfrequently sold for less than two hundred dollars per head. . . . The people however. . . . were sanguine respecting the future. . . . They strove to reduce their expenses to the lowest possible point; they manufactured clothing for themselves and their slaves; raised abundant supplies of poultry and stock of various kinds, and with these contrived to live in plenty. . . . [At length] the Santee Canal was projected and constructed within their neighborhood. Everyone availed himself of a greater or less extent of this opportunity of hiring their negroes; for men they received thirty and for women twenty pounds sterling per annum, besides their food. At times a thousand laborers were employed on this work, which was seven years in being completed. The enterprise, which was disastrous to those who had embarked in it, rescued a large number of planters from ruin. It was commenced in 1792, and finished in 1800. Two or three years after it had been commenced, a few planters in the neighborhood tried the cultivation of cotton on a small scale, but the progress of this enterprise was slow and irresolute, in

The developments following Whitney's invention of the cotton gin revolutionized the situation. Slave prices entered upon a steady advance, which was quickened by the prohibition of the African trade in 1808. They were then held stationary by the restrictions upon commerce, and were thrown backward by the outbreak of war in 1812. But with the peace of Ghent the results of the new cotton industry and of the cessation of African imports became strikingly manifest. The inland fields of the lower South proved to be peculiarly adapted for the production of cotton. The simplicity of the work and the even distribution of the tasks through the seasons made negro slave labor peculiarly available. With the increasing demand of the world for cotton, there was built up in the South perhaps the greatest staple monopoly the world had ever seen. The result was an enormous demand for slaves in the cotton belt. American ports, however, were now closed to the foreign slave trade. The number of slaves available in America was now fixed, the rate of increase was limited, and the old "tobacco South" had a monopoly of the only supply which could meet the demand of the new "cotton South."

Till 1815 "colonial" conditions prevailed, and the market for slave labor was relatively quiet and steady. In 1815 began the "ante-bellum" régime, in which the whole economy of the South was governed by the apparently capricious play of the compound monopoly of cotton and slave labor. The price of cotton was governed by the American output and its relation to the European demand. And the price of slaves was governed by the profits in

---

consequence of the difficulty of preparing it for market. With the improvement of the gins, the cotton culture increased and was extended, until 1799, when Capt. James Sinkler planted three hundred acres at his plantation Belvidere, on Eutaw Creek, and reaped from each acre two hundred and sixteen pounds, which he sold for from fifty to seventy-five cents per pound." This pamphlet of DuBose's is reprinted in T. G. Thomas' History of the Huguenots in South Carolina, N. Y., 1887, *vide* pp. 66-68. The accuracy of the statements quoted is borne out by the very interesting manuscript records of the Porcher-Ravenel family, which are now in the possession of members of the family at Pinopolis, St. John's parish, Berkeley, S. C.

Virginia conditions are indicated in a letter of George Washington to Alexander Spotswood, Nov. 23, 1794, which is published in the *New York Public Library Bulletin,* vol. ii, pp. 14, 15. Spotswood had written that he intended moving west, and asked advice as to selling his lands and slaves. Washington replied that he believed that before many years had passed slaves would become a very troublesome sort of property, and that, except for his principles against selling negroes, he himself would not by the end of twelve months be possessed of a single one as a slave.

cotton and the relation of the labor demand to the monopolized labor supply.[6]

For an understanding of slaveholding economics, a careful study of the history of slave prices is essential. Prior to the middle of the eighteenth century, the scarcity of data, the changing value of gold, the multiplicity of coinage systems and the use of paper money with irregular depreciations unfortunately present so many obstacles that any effort to determine the fluctuation of slave prices would be of very doubtful success. For the following periods the study is feasible, although under the best of existing circumstances slave prices are hard to collect and hard to compare. The proportion of the slave population on the market at any time was very much smaller than the student of prices could wish for the purpose of his study; and many of the sales which were made are not to be found in the records. The market classification of the slaves was flexible and irregular; and, except in Louisiana, most of the documents in the public archives do not indicate the classification. To make thoroughly accurate comparison of slave prices at different times and places, we should need to know, among other things, the sex, age, strength and nativity of the slaves; the purity or mixture of blood of the negroes, mulattoes, quadroons, mestizoes, *etc;* and their special training or lack of it. For such statistical purposes, however, the records have many shortcomings. In many cases they state simply that the slave Matt or Congo or Martha, belonging to the estate of William Jones, deceased, was sold on the date given to Thomas Smith, for, say, $300, on twelve months' credit. Such an item indicates the sex and states the price, but gives little else. In other instances the slaves are classed as infants, boys, men (or fellows) and old men; girls, wenches and old women. Whole families were often sold as a lot, with no individual quotations given. Women were hardly ever sold separate from their young children. In the dearth of separate sale quotations, any study of the prices of female slaves would have to be based chiefly upon appraisal values, which of course were much less accurate than actual market prices.

The sales made by the professional slave traders were generally recorded each in a bill of sale; but in most of the localities these were not transcribed into the formal books of record, and the originals have mostly disappeared. The majority of the sales of which records are to be found were those of the slaves in the estates

[6]*Cf.* De Toqueville, *Democracy in America,* vol. ii, p. 233.

of deceased persons. These sales were at auction; and except in abnormal cases, which may often be distinguished, they may be taken as fairly representative of slave prices for the time and place.

There was always a great difference between the values of individual slaves. When the average price of negroes ranged about $500, prime field hands brought, say, $1,000, and skilled artisans still more. At that rate, an infant would be valued at about $100, a boy of twelve years and a man of fifty at about $500 each, and a prime wench for field work at $800 or $900.

The most feasible comparison of prices is that of prime field hands, who may be defined as well-grown, able-bodied fellows, with average training and between eighteen and thirty years of age. To find the current price of prime field hands in lists where no classification is given, we take the average of the highest ordinary prices. We ignore any scattering extreme quotations, as applying probably to specially valuable artisans, overseers or domestic servants, and not to field hands. Where ages are given, we take the average of the prices paid for grown fellows too young to have received special training. We leave aside, on the other hand, the exceptionally low quotations as being due to infirmities which exclude the slave from the prime grade. The professional slave traders in the domestic traffic dealt mostly in "likely young fellows and wenches." In the quotations of the sales by these traders, when no details are recorded, we may assume that the average, except for children, will range just a little below the current rate for prime field hands.

In view of all the hindrances, the production of a perfectly accurate table of prices cannot be hoped for, even from the exercise of the utmost care and discrimination. The table which follows is simply an approximation of averages made in a careful study of several thousand quotations in the state of Georgia.[7]

The parallel quotations of cotton prices[8] afford a basis for the

[7]The sources used for this tabulation are the documents in the Georgia state archives and the records of Baldwin, Oglethorpe, Clarke and Troup counties, all lying in the Georgia cotton belt, together with bills of sale in private hands, travelers' accounts, and articles in the newspapers of the period. Instances of sudden rise or fall in slave prices and sales of large and noted estates were often reported in the local press, with comments. There is no printed collection of any large number of slave-price quotations.

[8]The cotton price averages are made from the tables given by E. J. Donnell in his *Chronological and Statistical History of Cotton,* New York, 1872, with the aid of the summaries published by G. L. Watkins, *Production and Price of Cotton for One Hundred Years,* U.S. Department of Agriculture, Washington, 1895.

Year	Average Price of Prime Field Hands	Economic Situation and the Chief Determinant Factors	Average N. Y. Price of Upland Cotton	Years
1755 ...	£55			
1773 ...	60			
1776–1783		War and Depression in Industry and commerce.		
1784 ...	70	Peace and returning prosperity.		
1792 ...	$300	Depression due to Great Britain's attitude toward American commerce.		
1793		Cotton gin invented.		
1800[1] ..	450	. ...	30 cents.	1795–1805
1808		African slave trade prohibited.		
1809 ...	600	Embargo moderates rise in prices.	19 cents.	1805–1810
1813 ...	450	War with Great Britain	12 cents.	1813
1818 ...	1000	Inflation	29 cents.	1816–1818
1819		Financial crisis	16 cents.	1819
1821 ...	700	Recovery from panic	14 cents.	1821
1826 ...	800	Moderate prosperity	15 cents.	1824–1827
1827		Depression.		
1828 ...	700	. ...	10 cents.	1827–1828
1835 ...	900	Flush times	17½ cents.	1835
1837 ...	1300	Inflation—crash	13½ cents.	1837
1839 ...	1000	Cotton crisis	13½ cents.	1839
1840 ...	700	Cotton crisis; acute distress	9 cents.	1840
1844 ...	600	Depression	7½ cents.	1844
1845		Severe depression	5½ cents.	1845
1848 ...	900	Recovery in cotton prices. Texas demand for slaves .	9½ cents.	1847–1848
1851 ...	1050	Prosperity	12 cents.	1851
1853 ...	1200	Expansion of cotton industry and simultaneous rise in tobacco prices.[3]	11 cents.	1850–1860
1859 ...	1650			
1860[2] ..	1800			

[1]The quotations down to this point are lowland quotations. There were very few slaves in the uplands before 1800.

[2]In the later fifties there were numerous local flurries in slave valuations. In central Georgia prime negroes brought $2,000 in 1860, while in western Georgia and central Alabama the prices appear not to have run much above $1,500. For prices in the other parts of the South in that decade, see G. W. Weston, Who are and who may be slaves in the United States, a pamphlet published in 1856. See also Brackett, The Negro in Maryland; Ingle, Southern Sidelights; Hammond, The Cotton Industry, and *De Bow's Review*, vol. xxvi, p. 647.

[3]The rise in tobacco prices and the revival of prosperity in Virginia in this decade tended to diminish the volume of the slave trade and contributed to raising slave prices. *Cf.* W. H. Collins, The Domestic Slave Trade in the Southern States, N. Y., 1904, p. 57.

study of slave-labor capitalization. In examining these quotations it will be noticed that during many brief periods the prices of slaves and cotton rose and fell somewhat in harmony; but that in the whole period under review the price of cotton underwent a heavy net decline, while slave prices had an extremely strong upward movement. The change which took place in the relative slave and cotton prices was really astonishing. In 1800 a prime field hand was worth in the market about 1500 pounds of ginned cotton; in 1809, about 3000 pounds; in 1818, about 3500; in 1826, about 5400; in 1837, about 10,000; in 1845, about 12,000; in 1860, 15,000 to 18,000. In his capacity for work, a prime negro in 1800 was worth nearly or quite as much as a similar slave in 1860; and a pound of cotton in 1860 was not essentially different from a pound of cotton in 1800. But our table shows that within that epoch of three-score years there was an advance of some 1000 or 1200 per cent in the price of slaves as measured in cotton.

The decline in the price of cotton was due in some measure to a lessening of cost, through improvements in cultivating, ginning and marketing. The advance in slave prices was due in part to the increasing intelligence and ability of the negroes and to improvements in the system of directing their work on the plantations, and also in part to the decline in the value of money. But the ten-fold or twelve-fold multiplication of the price of slaves, when quoted in terms of the product of their labor, was too great to be explained except by reference to the severe competition of the planters in selling cotton and in buying slaves. Their system of capitalized labor was out of place in the modern competitive world, and burdened with that system all the competition of the cotton planters was bound to be of a cut-throat nature. In other words, when capital and labor were combined, as in the American slaveholding system, there was an irresistible tendency to overvalue and overcapitalize slave labor, and to carry it to the point where the financial equilibrium was unsafe, and any crisis bankruptcy.

Aside from the expense of food, clothing and shelter, the cost of slave labor for any given period of time was made up of several elements:

(1) Interest upon the capital invested in the slave.

(2) Economic insurance against (a) his death, (b) his illness or accidental injury, and (c) his flight from service.[9] Of course

---

[9]Physicians' and attorneys' fees should perhaps be included under the head of insurance. It may be noted that doctors' charges were generally the same for slaves as

insurance policies were seldom taken out to cover these risks, but the cost of insurance against them must be reckoned in the cost of slave labor for any given period.

(3) The diminishing value of every mature slave by reason of increasing age. Because of the "wear and tear" of his years and his diminishing prospect of life and usefulness, the average slave of fifty-five years of age would be worth only half as much as one of twenty-five years, and after fifty-five the valuation decreased still more rapidly. In computing the cost of any group of slaves it will be necessary to set over against this depreciation the value of the children born; but, on the other hand, the cost by groups would be increased by the need of supporting the disabled negroes who were not in the working gangs.

(4) Taxation assessed upon the capitalized value of the slaves. In the slaveholding region as a whole, in the later ante-bellum period, the total assessed value of slave property was at least as great as that of all the other sorts of property combined.

The rate of slave hire would furnish a good index of the current price of slave labor year by year, if sufficient quotations on a stable basis could be obtained. But on account of the special needs or wishes of the ·parties to the individual bargains, there were such opportunities for higgling the rate in individual cases that the current rate is very elusive. The following averages, computed from a limited number of quotations for the hire of men slaves in middle Georgia, are illustrative: In 1800, $100 per year; in 1816, $110; in 1818, $140; in 1833, $140; in 1836, $155; in 1841, $140; in 1860, $150. These were in most cases the years of maximum quotations in the respective periods. The local fluctuations in short periods were often very pronounced; but in the long run the rate followed a gradual upward movement.

The relation between the price of slaves and the rate of their hire should theoretically have borne, in quiet periods, a definite relation to the rate of interest upon capital; but the truth is that in the matter of slave prices there was, through the whole period after the closing of the African trade, a tendency to "frenzied finance" in the cotton belt. Slave prices were largely controlled by speculation, while slave hire was regulated more largely by the current rate of wages for

---

for white persons. To illustrate how expensive this charge often was, we may cite an instance given in the records of Troup county, Georgia, where Dr. Ware collected from Col. Truitt's estate $130.50 for medicine and daily visits to a negro child, from November 29, 1858, to January 5, 1859.

labor in general. The whole subject of these relations is one for which authentic data are perhaps too scanty to permit of thorough analysis.

Negro slave labor was expensive, not so much because it was unwilling as because it was overcapitalized and inelastic. The negro of himself, by reason of his inherited inaptitude, was inefficient as a self-directing laborer in civilized industry. The whole system of civilized life was novel and artificial to him; and to make him play a valuable part in it, strict guidance and supervision were essential. Without the plantation system, the mass of the negroes would have been an unbearable burden in America; and except in slavery they could never have been utilized, in the beginning, for plantation work. The negro had no love of work for work's sake; and he had little appreciation of future goods when set over against present exemption from toil. That is to say, he lacked the economic motive without which voluntary civilized industry is impossible. It is a mistake to apply the general philosophy of slavery to the American situation without very serious modification.[10] A slave among the Greeks or Romans was generally a relatively civilized person, whose voluntary labor would have been far more productive than his labor under compulsion. But the negro slave was a negro first, last and always, and a slave incidentally. Mr. Cairnes and others make a great mistake when they attribute his inefficiency and expensiveness altogether to the one incident of regulation. Regulation actually remedied in large degree the disadvantages of using negro labor, though it failed to make it as cheap, in most employments, as free white labor would have been. The cotton planter found the negro already a part of the situation. To render him useful, firm regulation was necessary. The forcible control of the negro was in the beginning a necessity, and was not of itself a burden at any time.[11]

In American slaveholding, however, the capitalization of labor-

---

[10]Palgrave's Dictionary of Political Economy contains an excellent article upon slavery, in which it is indicated that harshness and compulsion were not always essential in slave labor; that the motive force was often a sort of feudal devotion to the master; and, further, that negro slave labor was practically essential for developing the resources of the hot malarial swamp regions.

[11]The current rate of hire to-day for negro workmen in agriculture in Georgia is from $8 to $12 per month; but for the year 1904, the state of Georgia leased out its able-bodied convicts at an average rate of $225 per year. When under strict discipline, the average negro even to-day, it appears, is worth twice as much as when left to his own devices.

value and the sale and purchase of labor-control were permanent features; and when the supply was "cornered" it was unavoidable that the price should be bid up to the point of overvaluation[12]. And this brings us to the main economic disadvantage of the system.

In employing free labor, wages are paid from time to time as the work is done, and the employer can count upon receiving from the products of that labor an income which will enable him to continue to pay its wages in the future, while his working capital is left free for other uses. He may invest a portion of his capital in lands and buildings, and use most of the remainder as circulating capital for special purposes, retaining only a small percentage as a reserve fund. But to secure a working force of slaves, the ante-bellum planter had to invest all the capital that he owned or could borrow in the purchase of slaves and lands;[13] for the larger his plantation was, within certain limits, the more economies he could introduce. The temptation was very strong for him to trim down to the lowest possible limit the fund for supplies and reserve. The slaveholding system thus absorbed the planter's earnings; and for such absorption it had unlimited capacity, for the greater the profits of the planters the more slaves they wanted and the higher the slave profits mounted. Individual profits, as fast as made, went into the purchase of labor, and not into modern implements or land improvements.[14]

---

[12]In the periods of high slave prices employers found that slave labor was too expensive to be used with profit except in plantation industry under the most favorable circumstances. Striking proof of this is to be seen in the eager employment, wherever they could be had, of Irish and German immigrants for canal and railway building, ditching and any other labor which might prove injurious to a negro's health and strength. Slaves were growing too dear to be used. W. H. Russell (My Diary North and South, Boston, 1863, p. 272) writing of the Louisiana sugar district in 1860, says: "The labor of ditching, trenching, cleaning the waste lands and hewing down the forests, is generally done by Irish laborers, who travel about the country under contractors, or are engaged by resident gangsmen for the task. Mr. Seal lamented the high prices for this work; but then, as he said, 'It was much better to have Irish do it, who cost nothing to the planter, if they died, than to use up good field hands in such severe employment.'" The documentary evidence in regard to the competition and rather extensive substitution of immigrant labor for that of slaves in the times of high slave prices is quite conclusive, in spite of its fugitive character. Further data may be found in *DeBow's Review,* vol. xi, p. 400; *Harper's Magazine,* vol. vii, pp. 752 *et seq.;* Sir Chas. Lyell, Second Visit to the United States, vol. ii, p. 127; Waddell, Annals of Augusta County, Virginia, pp. 272, 273; and the James River and Kanawha Canal Company's fourth annual report, Richmond, 1839.

[13]*Cf.* F.L. Olmsted, A Journey to Texas, pp. 8-10.

[14]This was lamented by many planters, especially in times of low staple prices. *Cf. Southern Agriculturist,* published at Charleston, 1828, vol. ii, p. 1 *et passim;* and

Circulating capital was at once converted into fixed capital; while for their annual supplies of food, implements and luxuries the planters continued to rely upon their credit with the local merchants, and the local merchants to rely upon their credit with northern merchants and bankers.

Thus there was a never-ending private loss through the continual payment of interest and the enhancement of prices; and, further, there was a continuous public loss by the draining of wealth out of the cotton belt by the slave trade.[15] With the stopping of the African slave trade, the drain of wealth from the lower South was not checked at all, but merely diverted from England and New England to the upper tier of southern states; and there it did little but demoralize industry and postpone to a later generation the agricultural revival.

---

especially an address by Dr. Manly before the Alabama State Agricultural Society, Dec. 7, 1841, published in the *Tuscaloosa Monitor,* April 13, 1842. (File in the Alabama State Department of Archives and History.)

[15]This injurious effect of the slave traffic is strikingly illustrated in the account by a Charleston bookseller, E.S. Thomas, of the misfortunes which befell his business by the reopening of the South Carolina ports to the foreign slave trade in 1803. Thomas had found the business opportunities in Charleston exceedingly good; and for some years he had been annually doubling his capital. But in November, 1803, he had just opened a new importation of fifty thousand volumes, when news came from Columbia that the legislature had opened the ports to the slave trade. "The news had not been five hours in the city," he writes, "before two large British Guineamen, that had been lying on and off the port for several days expecting it, came up to town; and from that day my business began to decline. . . . . . . A great change at once took place in everything. Vessels were fitted out in numbers for the coast of Africa, and as fast as they returned their cargoes were bought up with avidity, not only consuming the large funds that had been accumulating but all that could be procured, and finally exhausting credit and mortgaging the slaves for payment . . . . . . For myself, I was upwards of five years disposing of my large stock, at a sacrifice of more than a half, in all the principal towns, from Augusta, in Georgia, to Boston." E.S. Thomas, Reminiscences, vol. ii, pp. 35, 36.

The same general phenomena were observed in various other parts of the South, as is shown by the following extract from a letter written August 22, 1774, by one John Brown, a citizen of Virginia, to William Preston: "Some time ago you told me that you intended to enter the servant trade, and desire[d] me to tell if there was any encouragement our way for the sale of them. I think there is none, for these reasons: (1) the scarcity of money; (2) servants are plenty and everyone has as many as they want; besides, the country is sunk in debt by them already. If you have not as yet engaged, I think it not prudent for you to do it at the present juncture; you have business enough upon hand, but these things you can better think of than I can." Original MS. in Wisconsin Historical Society, Draper Collection, series QQ, vol. iii, no. 81.

The capitalization of labor lessened its elasticity and its versatility; it tended to fix labor rigidly in one line of employment. There was little or no floating labor in the plantation districts; and the planter was obliged to plan in detail a whole year's work before the year began. If he should plant a larger acreage than his "force" could cultivate and harvest, a part of the crop would have to be abandoned, unless by chance some free negro or stray Irishman could be found for the odd job. As an illustration of the financial hardships which might befall the slaveholder, it may be noted that in 1839 William Lowndes Yancey happened to lose his whole force of slaves through poisoning in the midst of the working season. The disaster involved his absolute ruin as a planter, and forced him to seek some other opening which did not require the possession of capital.[16]

In the operations of cotton production, where fluctuating and highly uncertain returns demanded the greatest flexibility, the slaveholding system was rigid. When by overproduction the price of cotton was depressed, it could be raised again only by curtailing the output in the American cotton belt, which had the monopoly. But the planter, owning cotton lands and slaves trained in the cotton field alone, found it hard to devote his fields with success to other crops or to sell or lease his negroes to any one else, for no one else wanted them for any other purpose than cotton production. In fact, the proportion of the southern resources devoted to cotton production tended always to increase. To diminish the cotton output required the most heroic efforts. As a rule, the chances of heavy gains from cotton planting outweighed those of loss, in the popular estimation; and the strong and constant tendency was to spoil the market by over-supply.

There were uncertain returns in cotton raising, and great risks in slave-owning. The crop might be heavy or light in any year, according to the acreage and the weather, and prices might be away up or away down. A prime slave might be killed by a rattlesnake or crippled in a log-rolling or hanged for murder or spirited away by the underground railroad. All these uncertainties fostered extravagance and speculation.

In the cotton belt inflation and depression followed each other in rapid succession; but the times of prosperity brought less real advantage and periods of depression caused greater hardship in the

[16]G.W. DuBose, *Life of Wm. L. Yancey*, p. 39.

slaveholding South than in any normally organized community. For by the capitalizing of labor, profits were generally absorbed through the purchasing of additional slaves at higher prices, while in time of need the cotton-planter found it impossible to realize upon his investment because his neighbors were involved in the same difficulties which embarrassed him, and when he would sell they could not buy.

When after the peace in 1815 the system of industry and finance of the ante-bellum South had fully developed itself, the South and its leaders were seized in the grip of social and economic forces which were rendered irresistible by the imperious laws of monopoly. The cotton-planters controlled the South, and for some decades they dominated the policy of the federal government; but the cotton-planters themselves were hurried hither and thither by their two inanimate but arbitrary masters, cotton and slavery.

Cotton and slavery were peculiar to the South, and their requirements were often in conflict with the interests and ideas prevailing in the other parts of the United States. As that conflict of interests and sentiments was accentuated, it became apparent that the South was in a congressional minority, likely to be overridden at any time by a northern majority. Ruin was threatening the vested interests and the social order in the South; and the force of circumstances drove the southern politicians into the policy of resistance. To the leaders in the South, with their ever-present view of the possibility of negro uprisings, the regulations of slavery seemed essential for safety and prosperity. And when they found themselves about to become powerless to check any legislation hostile to the established order in the South, they adopted the policy of secession, seeking, as they saw it, the lesser of the evils confronting them.

Because they were blinded by the abolition agitation in the North and other historical developments which we cannot here discuss, most of the later generation of ante-bellum planters could not see that slaveholding was essentially burdensome. But that which was partly hidden from their vision is clear to us to-day. In the great system of southern industry and commerce, working with seeming smoothness, the negro laborers were inefficient in spite of discipline, and slavery was an obstacle to all progress. The system may be likened to an engine, with slavery as its great fly-wheel—a fly-wheel indispensable for safe running at first, perhaps, but later rendered less useful by improvements in the machinery, and finally becoming a burden instead of a benefit. Yet it was retained, because it was still considered essential in securing the adjustment and regular working of the complex mechanism. This great rigid wheel of slavery was so awkward and burdensome that it absorbed the momentum and retarded the movement of the whole machine without rendering any service of great value. The capitalization of labor and the export of earnings in exchange for more workmen, always of a low degree of efficiency, together with the extreme lack of versatility, deprived the South of the natural advantage which the cotton monopoly should have given. To be rid of the capitalization of labor as a part of the slaveholding system was a great requisite for the material progress of the South.

LEWIS C. GRAY

Economic Efficiency and Competitive Advantages of Negro Slavery under the Plantation System

Was slave-owning by the late 1850s generally a losing business? Had slavery become unprofitable to most slave-holders? Was the slave system by that date maintained to prevent negro revolt and secure the racial supremacy of the white man, rather than because the white man was making money out of it? Specifically, was it true, as Phillips had alleged, that by the late 1850s only plantations on the best land and with the most efficient management could show a profit?

Lewis C. Gray, in his massive *History of Agriculture in the Southern United States to 1860,* first published in 1932, found good reason to think otherwise. Black slave labor was not necessarily nor in all circumstances less efficient than white wage labor. With training, the black man was capable of performing most tasks at least as efficiently as the white. Under certain conditions the slave system was more efficient than wage labor and tended to displace it. These conditions obtained in the production of the great Southern agricultural staples.

Selections from Chapter XX of Lewis C. Gray, *History of Agriculture in the Southern United States to 1860* (2 volumes, Washington, D.C., 1933). Reprinted by permission of The Carnegie Institution of Washington.

Labor was scarce in relation to land resources, and the superior stability and predictability of a slave labor force gave it a decided advantage over any possible alternative.

As regards profitability to the slave-owner, Gray saw the problem as essentially simple. An abundance of fertile land in the New World, combined with expanding markets in the Old, meant that the labor force could produce a surplus, in physical and revenue terms, over and above their requirements for subsistance. When this labor force was composed of slaves, the surplus was legally not their property but that of their masters. Part of the surplus had to be spent to pay for equipment and supervision. The remainder—and normally there was a remainder—was income to the slave-owners. Geography, climate, technology, and markets created the "appropriable surplus"; the institutional arrangements of a slave society placed it in the hands of those who owned the slaves.

Gray's style of argument is diffuse and leisurely; his proofs are circumstantial; his language and style are of the nineteenth century. But he is not to be underestimated. In the relatively short passage from his book which is reproduced here you will find, if you take the trouble to look, most of the central elements that have, since he wrote, figured prominently in the debate over the economics of slavery. It is true that his discussion of the "qualities of the Southern plantation Negro" does not show him at his best; a personality profile that rests on an allegedly inherent "mental instability" would not pass the scrutiny of psychologists or anthropologists today. But his analysis of the conditions under which slavery will have a "competitive superiority" over wage labor represented an important advance over anything that had gone before; and significant anticipations of later work can be found in his discussions of the man/land ratio necessary for the emergence of slavery, of the basis of slave pricing, and of the conditions under which large-scale manumission might have taken place. What we begin to find in Gray, in other words, is the systematic use of economic analysis; his work represented an advance primarily because it had better theoretical underpinnings.

There remains, however, the perplexing matter of how the central problem is to be defined. What are we analyzing? Gray's answer is worth arguing over. The essential question, for him, is not whether the South, in some hypothetical alternative universe, would have been better off if its entire population had been made up of white laborers of western European origin working under the wage system, but "whether the South could have employed the African Negro, after he was brought to this country, in any more effective manner." Though the rationale is entirely different, the way the question is phrased is disconcertingly reminiscent of Ulrich B. Phillips. What Gray seems to be saying is that, once Africans were present in this country in substantial numbers, slave-labor staple agriculture was, in the circumstances of the time, the most efficient way of using and maintaining them. *Is* this what Gray is saying? If so, is he correct?

THE TENDENCY for slave labor to displace free labor where conditions were favorable to producing and marketing the staples raises the question as to what economic characteristics gave slavery an advantage over rival systems of labor. The competitive advantages of servitude as compared with slavery . . . were largely inherent in the respective characteristics of the two methods of obtaining and employing labor. It by no means follows that free white labor would be at a similar disadvantage in competition with Negro slavery. The consideration of this question need not involve either the ethical aspects of slavery or its general social and economic advantages and disadvantages from the standpoint of national or sectional welfare.

The discussion of efficiency of Negro slave labor has been befogged by a failure to distinguish between those industrial qualities peculiar to Negro labor and those attributable to the influence of slavery. There has been a tendency to assume that all the laziness and incapacity exhibited by the Negro are ascribable to his status as a slave.[1] This confusion has been largely the outgrowth of the arbitrary assumption that slave labor must be inherently less economic than free labor because slave labor is given grudgingly and half-heartedly, while free labor is spurred by self-interest. Turgot and Adam Smith developed this attitude,[2] and it soon became a commonplace of economic generalization, accepted even by some

[1]For instances, see *Hunt's Merchants' Magazine,* XXVIII, 197; Hammond, M.B., *Cotton Industry,* 94-99; Brown, W.G., *Lower South in American History,* 29. Among those who have kept clear of this confusion are the following: Stone, "Some Problems of Southern Economic History," in *American Historical Review,* XIII, 779 *et seq.;* also Ulrich Bonnell Phillips in various writings on Southern economic history.

[2]Turgot, *Reflections on the Formation and Distribution of Wealth,* 21; Smith, A., *Wealth of Nations,* I, 364; *cf.* for other instances, Roscher, *Principles of Political Economy,* I, Bk. I, Chap. IV; Nicholson, *Principles of Political Economy,* I, 82, 239, 359. For an interesting outline of economic doctrine on slavery, see Phillips, U.B., *American Negro Slavery,* Chap. XVIII.

Southern writers.[3] Francis A. Walker gave the formula an eloquent presentation: "The whip," he wrote, "only stimulates the flesh on which it is laid. It does not reach the parts of the man where lie the springs of action. No brutality of rule can evoke even the whole physical power of a human being."[4] Cairnes recognized three fundamental elements of inefficiency in slave labor: "It is given reluctantly; it is unskillful; it is wanting in versatility."[5]

The two latter points in Cairnes' analysis were probably true enough of the great body of American Negro slaves. They were lacking in skill and versatility judged by the standards of a highly diversified industrial life; but such qualities are not necessarily a severe economic handicap for an extractive economy. John Stuart Mill recognized this point and accepted the classical formula of general inefficiency with some reservations.[6] Mill's caution was also justified by an obstinate fact that had been either disregarded or inadequately explained by exponents of the dogma, namely, the ability shown by slave labor in the West Indies and the South to displace free-labor under certain conditions. Frequently slave labor was very profitable. Adam Smith himself had recognized this fact, but he reconciled it with his general belief in the inefficiency of slave labor by the vague assumption that slave labor was tolerable in certain plantation regions because the sugar and tobacco industries were so intrinsically profitable that they were able to prosper in spite of the inefficiency of slave labor. Smith and others also explained the survival of slavery in certain regions on the ground that climatic conditions excluded the employment of white labor, but Cairnes definitely rejected this explanation as applied to the greater part of the South.[7]

Mill's brief but trenchant discussion, combined with the inductive approach of the German Historical School and the concept of social

---

[3]For instances, see Cooper, *Elements of Political Economy,* 106; Harrison, J.B., *Review of the Slave Question,* 12; Raymond, *Comparative Economy of Free and Slave Labor in Agriculture,* 12. For a contrary statement, see Ruffin, *Diary,* II, No. 430, p. 596 (Manuscripts, Library of Congress).

[4]*Wages Question,* 73.

[5]*The Slave Power,* 39. His analysis was quoted with approval by others. For instances, see Fawcett, *Manual of Political Economy,* 312; Seligman, *Principles of Economics,* 158.

[6]*Principles of Political Economy,* I, 294-300.

[7]Smith, A., *Wealth of Nations,* I, 365; Cairnes, *The Slave Power,* 34-36.

evolution, had the effect of introducing an element of relativity into the consideration of the economics of slavery.[8] The admission that Negro slave labor might be as efficient as free white labor under certain economic conditions gradually became fruitful in leading to some discussion of the nature of these conditions. A number of writers have reached the conclusion that these are: (1) a one-crop system, permitting the routinizing of operations; (2) crops requiring year-round employment of labor, thus preventing slave owners from suffering loss through idleness of labor, a loss mainly borne by the laborer himself under the wage system; (3) crops permitting employment of a large amount of labor on a small amount of land, thus simplifying the problem of supervision. Conversely, it has been assumed that Negro slave labor is not effective in general farming or in non-agricultural operations.[9] This tendency of thought has also laid special stress on the relationship of population to land and has led to the conclusion that slavery tends to prosper where population is sparse, and inevitably becomes decadent with increasing population density.[10] These conclusions will require later analysis.

One essential fallacy of Smith and his followers was in assuming that if slave labor be less efficient in terms of physical performance than free labor, the former must thereby be "dearer." The two things are not necessarily identical. Even though white labor be superior to Negro slave labor in economic skill and adaptability, it is conceivable that the superior cheapness of the Negro slave might result in enabling his master to overbid white labor in competition for land or to undersell it in disposal of products. As early as 1803 Jean Baptiste Say had pointed out that the owner of a slave was in a position to deprive him of all but subsistence, and this fact, he argued, explained the large profits of San Domingo planters.[11] Adam Smith himself had recognized the fact that the slave might be

[8]A notable contribution to this general point of view is made by Nieboer, *Slavery as an Industrial System.*

[9]For instances, see Simons, *Social Forces in American History,* 223; Cairnes, *The Slave Power,* 42; Fawcett, *Manual of Political Economy,* 313-316.

[10]This point of view was foreshadowed in the discussion by Roscher *(Principles of Political Economy,* I, Chap. IV), J.S. Mill *(Principles of Political Economy,* I, 294-300), and Cairnes *(The Slave Power,* 44-46). For modern formulation under the influence of the evolutionary concept, see Loria, *Economic Synthesis,* 95-99; Simons, *Social Forces in American History,* 236, 262; Seligman, *Principles of Economics,* 157-161; Hadley, *Economics,* 27-29.

[11]*Treatise on Political Economy,* I, 215-217.

compelled to work for bare subsistence, but he swept it aside with the general argument that slave labor was dear because inefficient through lack of inducement.[12]

Say's significant point was not followed out in subsequent discussions of the competitive power of slavery, although occasionally admitted as a fact.[13] Generally the two points of view have been inextricably confused. Thus, Hodgson, who undertook to refute Say's point, argued that if slave labor were cheaper than free labor it should hire for less, whereas he presented certain selected statistics to prove that the hire of slave labor was greater.[14] It would appear rather strange, however, that the less productive and efficient labor would hire for more, and therefore Hodgson's argument proved too much. He and others discussed the relative cost of the two forms of labor and showed slave labor to be the more expensive by including interest and depreciation on capital value in costs through confusing phenomena growing out of the capitalization of a surplus over costs with the actual costs of utilizing labor.[15] Still others, for instance, James Raymond, while admitting that slaves were given a coarser and cheaper kind of subsistence, believed they made up for this by greater wastefulness in using it.[16]

It is desirable to consider these various theories in the light of the facts.

SOME CHARACTERISTICS OF NEGRO SLAVE LABOR IN THE SOUTH

The relative efficiency of the Negro slave can be considered without reference to the responsibility of slavery for making him what he was, and also without reference to the vexed question of his capacity for progress or for the assimilation of culture, a problem whose solution depends upon further development of anthropological science.[17]

---

[12] *Wealth of Nations,* I, 82.

[13] Gibson, *Human Economics,* 93; Cairnes, *The Slave Power,* 39.

[14] Letter to Say, on the comparative expense of free and slave labor, reprinted in *Remarks during a Journey through North America,* 297-299.

[15] *Ibid.,* 291-299; Cooper, *Elements of Political Economy,* 107. For discussion of the significance of capitalization in the case of slaves, see below, p. 473.

[16] *Comparative Economy of Free and Slave Labor,* 13.

[17] See Tucker, G., *Letters from Virginia,* 73-103; Hoffman, *Race Traits and Tendencies*

Southern slaves were by no means racially homogeneous. Not only were they of various degrees of mixture between blacks and whites, but also of different African stocks, some of them probably not Negroid, being offshoots from Bantu or Fulah stock.[18] Before the suppression of the slave trade planters distinguished shrewdly these ethnic differences, appraising their characteristic qualities at commercial values.[19] On the other hand, the social environment tended to reduce them to a uniform psychic plane, for the majority lived under similar surroundings.

Many of the qualities of the Southern plantation Negro were common to other races. Uncontrolled by inhibitions that hedge in civilized societies, the plantation Negro was credulous and superstitious—the natural prey of the charlatan and the quack. The primitive Negro was characterized by a peculiarly unstable mental life. His anger and hatred lacked the sustained character of similar moods of the American Indians. In courage he was not wanting, but it was of the passional variety, proceeding from wild bursts of rage or jealousy. Rarely did he exhibit a love of wild daring or quiet self-control in face of danger. Frequently, however, he manifested a stolidity with regard to impending punishment which was the product of primitive insensibility. His so-called cowardice was partly an outgrowth of habitual inferiority, which was as much the result of circumstances as the attitude of domination among the whites; and his consciousness of the superiority of his master amounted to an obsession which made it easy for a determined white man to control a hundred Negroes.[20] The primitive Negro's volubility and mendacity, the tendency to licentiousness, the

---

of the American Negro; Tillinghast, *The Negro in Africa and America,* especially Pt. I, Chaps. IV-VI.

[18]Stone, "Mulatto Factor in the Race Problem," in *Atlantic Monthly,* XCI, 658-662; Thomas , W.H., *American Negro,* "Foreword," p. xix, and p. 175.

[19]*Practical Rules for the Management and Medical Treatment of Negro Slaves in the Sugar Colonies,* Pt. I, Chap. I; Edwards, *British West Indies,* II, 60-76; Major, "With the Spanish Records of West Florida," in Historical Society of East and West Baton Rouge, *Proceedings,* II, 63; *cf. Southern Planter,* II, 40; Wallace, D.D., *Henry Laurens,* 76.

[20]*Cf.* especially Thomas, W.H., *American Negro,* 60, 127; Bruce, P.A., *Plantation Negro as a Freeman,* 76 *et seq.;* Stone, "Mulatto Factor in the Race Problem," in *Atlantic Monthly,* XCI, 658 *et seq.;* Winston, "Relation of the Whites to the Negroes," in *Annals of the American Academy,* XVIII, 105-108.

emotional volatility—the quick transitions from hysterical joy and wild gaiety to despondency—these qualities were also as much manifestations of mental instability as of an unorganized mental life and undeveloped ethical consciousness.[21]

This mental instability of plantation Negroes—the impulsiveness and immediacy of action, incapacity for constant and controlled attention, and lack of constructive power and continuous effort toward remote ends—was the foundation of their incapacity for self-direction, and accounts for their frequent failures as independent farmers and for the unfortunate immediate results of emancipation in the South and the West Indies.[22] These failures are not necessarily prophetic, but they confirm the belief of the majority of proslavery writers, shared by some antislavery writers, that the Negro was not ready for complete self-direction.[23]

The same qualities that incapacitated Negroes for industrial autonomy also impaired somewhat their efficiency as agricultural laborers. There is abundant testimony concerning their carelessness, wastefulness, improvidence, and unreliability. A writer in the *American Farmer* said:[24]

> There is, perhaps, not in Nature a more heedless, thoughtless human being than a Virginia field negro. With no care upon his mind, with warm clothing and plenty of food, under a good master, he is far the happier man of the two. His maxim is, "Come day, go day, God send Sunday."

Olmsted was impressed with repeated instances of waste and carelessness—especially in regions where plantation organization was least well developed. He mentions, for instance, the following observations:[25]

---

[21]Thomas, W.H., *American Negro,* 111, 118-120, 177-197; Dyer, "Some Types in Dixie-Land," in *Cosmopolitan,* XXII, 235-246.

[22]Hoffman, *Race Traits and Tendencies of the American Negro,* Chap. VI; Banks, *Economics of Land Tenure in Georgia,* 72-77; Hammond, M.B., *Cotton Industry,* 189-191; Kelsey, *Negro Farmer,* Chaps. IV-VI; Phillips, U.B., "Economics of the Plantation," in *South Atlantic Quarterly,* II, 231-236.

[23]Among the antislavery writers who were strong disbelievers in immediate emancipation were Captain Basil Hall, Sir Charles Lyell, and Frederick Law Olmsted.

[24]1 series, XV (1833-4), p. 139; *cf. Farmer and Planter,* V, 230.

[25]*Seaboard Slave States,* II, 114-116.

Gates left open and bars left down, against standing orders; rails removed from fences by the negroes, as was conjectured, to kindle their fires with; mules lamed, and implements broken, by careless usage; a flat-boat, carelessly secured, going adrift on the river; men ordered to cart rails for a new fence, depositing them so that a double expense of labor would be required to lay them, more than would have been needed if they had been placed, as they might almost easily have been, by a slight exercise of forethought; men ordered to fill up holes made by alligators or craw-fish in an important embankment, discovered to have merely patched over the outside, having taken pains only to make it *appear* that they had executed their task— not having been overlooked while doing it, by a driver; men, not having performed duties that were entrusted to them, making statements which their owner was obliged to receive as sufficient excuse, though, he told me, he felt assured they were false—all going to show habitual carelessness, indolence, and mere eye-service.

Unquestionably Olmsted exaggerated the responsibility of slavery for these characteristics, which are frequently displayed by free Negro laborers working for themselves. It is further probable that a part of the carelessness and shiftlessness observed by Olmsted and others resulted from the lax supervision and easy-going spirit of interior regions where the economy was not predominantly commercial. Even Olmsted was impressed with the steadiness, strength, and effectiveness of Negro labor under systematic direction in the capitalistic cotton plantations of the Southwest.[26] A number of British travellers were similarly impressed with the skill and precision of plantation laborers in field work and compared them with hired laborers to the disadvantage of the latter.[27]

Various discussions of the industrial capacity and efficiency of Negro slaves have failed to allow for the progress made by them during the ante bellum period. The great body of Negroes came to America ignorant savages. Care was requisite to prevent them from injuring themselves with the implements employed. It was necessary to teach them the simplest operations with hand tools and

[26]*Ibid.,* 114; *idem, Cotton Kingdom,* 1, 13, 89, 118-136; *idem, Journey in the Back Country,* 432.

[27]See, for instance, Mallet, *Cotton,* 181; Wray, "Culture and Preparation of Cotton," in Royal Society of Arts, *Journal,* VII, 79.

to instruct them in the elementary methods of living—how to cook, put on their clothing, and care for their houses. They had yet to learn the language and the ethics of civilization.[28] While the majority had no opportunity to acquire industrial experience beyond routine tasks of field husbandry, before the Revolution, as we have noted, Negroes were displacing indentured servants in various handicrafts. In time a large part of the handicraft work in Southern cities was carried on by slaves.[29] Under competent supervision the Negro acquired peculiar skill in picking and hoeing cotton and other simple routine operations of field labor.[30]

Negroes developed special skill in using the plow, in cradling, threshing, stripping tobacco, and in the care of livestock. There was notable progress after the close of the colonial period in the acreage of the various crops per hand.[31] Much of this, of course, reflected increased employment of horse-drawn implements, development of more effective implements, and more efficient methods of plantation organization and management; but part of this progress reflected the advance in personal efficiency, intelligence, and experience of slaves. Thus, Simons has divided the decennial statistics of total production of the South from 1800 to 1860 inclusive by the total slave population for each decennial year respectively with the following results:[32]

1800	$16.10	1840	$37.11
1810	19.50	1850	43.51
1820	24.63	1860	51.90
1830	22.00		

These statistics, of course, disregard a good many things such as changes in price levels, influence of improved implements, and decline in domestic industries. The attribution of the entire Southern product to the slaves irrespective of the relative part produced by

[28]Robin, *Voyages,* III, 170; *De Bow's Review,* VIII, 234; *Southern Cultivator,* XVI, 234.

[29]*South Carolina Gazette and General Advertiser* (Charleston), Nov. 29-Dec. 2, 1783; *Maryland Gazette* (Annapolis), June 5, 1755; *Virginia Independent Chronicle* (Richmond), Nov. 21, 1787; *Gazette of the State of South Carolina* (Charleston), Jan. 1, 1784; *Columbian Mirror and Alexandria Gazette* (Virginia), June 15, 1793; *Virginia Gazette* (Williamsburg, Purdie ed.), Mar. 17, 1775.

[30]See below, p. 702.

[31]For specific figures, see pp. 707, 731, 737, 743.

[32]*Social Forces in American History,* 232.

white labor is another source of possible error, even in the indication of trends. Nevertheless, the more than threefold increase in sixty years is probably not without considerable significance as an indication of progress in the efficiency of slave labor, in connection with the general progress in agricultural technique.

COMPARATIVE EFFICIENCY OF NEGRO SLAVES

Even in the colonial period a number of contemporary estimates indicate that the productivity of Negro slaves was approximately as great as that of white hands. According to Rochefoucauld, a Negro could cultivate 2½ acres of tobacco, with an average product of 1,000 pounds per acre.[33] In the latter part of the seventeenth century white laborers in Delaware made from 2,000 to 3,000 pounds each.[34] Parkinson, who certainly did not come to America with any prepossession in favor of slave labor, declared:[35]

> Notwithstanding the many irregularities to which these negroes subject their master, it is allowed that they are the best servants in America, . . . There are many reasons for it; They bear the heat of the sun much better than any white man, and are more dexterous with the hoe, and at all planting business. In pulling corn, I observed the black men to be much more expert than any white man, and so in everything appertaining to planting.

Colonel Landon Carter asserted, "Those few servants that we have don't do as much as the poorest slaves we have."[36] Washington, however, expressed the opinion that "Blacks are capable of much labour, but having (I am speaking generally) no ambition to establish a *good* name, they are too regardless of a *bad* one, and of course require more of the master's eye than the former"—that is, white laborers.[37] After the close of the colonial period there is evidence that for unskilled labor the Negro was not even absolutely inferior to white labor. Occasionally planters and other employers expressed their preference for Negroes as compared with

[33] *Travels,* III, 169.
[34] Read, *Some Leaves from the Early History of Delaware and Maryland* (Pamphlet read before the Delaware Historical Society, Sept. 24, 1868), p. 2.
[35] *Tour,* II, 420.
[36] *Diary* (William and Mary Quarterly, XX), 182.
[37] *Letters on Agriculture,* 61.

unskilled Irish and Italian laborers. In 1842 the contractors of the James River Canal considered one Negro "equal to two Irishmen."[38] White laborers were sometimes notably inefficient. In 1838 a writer, speaking of conditions in northern Virginia, declared:[39]

> There is to the common laborer in this country every temptation to idleness. . . . How can it be expected that he will remain stationary with his employer at $100 or $150 a year, when for twenty, he can buy an old horse and second-hand cart, or steal them, and after begging his way to Illinois or Wisconsin, can squat on a quarter section of land.

Judging also by relative farm wages paid free laborers and hired slaves, the superiority of white laborers was not sufficiently great to lead to a very notable difference in the valuation of the services of the two classes of labor. About 1791, in Virginia, a white farm laborer for a year cost from £10 to £15 and board. The labor of a Negro slave commanded from £8 to £12 and board.[40] In 1796 William Strickland reported that the usual price paid in Virginia for male slaves hired for farm labor was £9 per year and board and clothing. Unusually strong Negroes employed in digging the James River Canal had been paid for at the rate of £11 5s. each. Their maintenance and clothing were estimated at the same amount. Strickland estimated the annual cost of slave labor to the hirer, including maintenance, was £18 or about 1 shilling 2 pence per working day. In Maryland the service of a free black might be had for 1 shilling per day and of whites for 1 shilling 6 pence, but these items included no clothing and no obligation for medical attendance and loss of time through illness.[41] About 1849 hire of Negro male slaves in Tatnall County, Georgia, was $80, and of women $40, the marked difference probably due to their employment in lumbering. White men were hired for $10 per month, but received no clothing and assumed the risk of illness or other incapacity.[42] In 1857

---

[38]Dew, *Review of the Debate of the Virginia Legislature of 1831 and 1832,* p. 126; Buckingham, *Slave States of America,* II, 112; Olmsted, F. L., *Journey through Texas,* 32; *American Farmer,* 1 series, X (1828-9), p. 273; Holmes, G. K., *Wages of Farm Labor* (U. S., Dept. Agric., Bur. of Statistics, *Bulletin 99),* pp. 14, 18, 22; *Southern Planter,* II, 36.

[39]*Farmers' Register,* V, 747; *Farmer and Gardener,* IV, 409.

[40]Washington, Letters on Agriculture, 61.

[41]*Report to the [British] Board of Agriculture* (Farmers' Register, III), 207.

[42]White, G., *Statistics of Georgia,* 535.

able-bodied male field hands were being hired out in Maryland for $120 to $150 per year besides board. Common Irish laborers received $1 per day throughout the year and boarded themselves, besides losing their wages when not working. Near Burlington, Vermont, farm laborers were hired by the year at $150 and board at the employer's table. In the Genessee valley wages were $16 a month for eight months and $12 a month for the other four.[43] In these cases, of course, the hand would lose his time in case of protracted illness.

VARIOUS CONCLUSIONS CONCERNING EFFICIENCY OF NEGRO SLAVES

Many contemporary writers, including some of proslavery sympathies, assumed that slave labor was intrinsically uneconomical as compared with free labor in general farming.[44] Yet, in the physical operations of general farming slaves frequently displayed considerable skill. A contemporary writer asserted, "In the use of the axe, hoe, scythe and cradle, or driving and training teams, the practiced Negro of Georgia is surpassed by few white men I ever saw."[45] It was admitted by some observers that slaves could cultivate as large an acreage of corn or wheat per hand as could a free laborer.[46] Even in the care of livestock it was possible to find reliable individual Negroes to whom these functions could be entrusted. The inferiority of Negro slave labor in general farming was not due to the incapacity of the Negro to perform the manual operations involved, most of which, in that period when farm machinery was but little employed, were not more complex than in producing the staples. Indeed, general farming with slave labor at times proved successful. Where it was unprofitable, this was due mainly to three conditions: (1) A larger amount of supervision per unit of labor was required than in less diversified forms of agriculture, which is also true when free Negro or white labor is employed; (2) In a number of regions general farming was severely handicapped for lack of a home market; (3) The competitive superiority of cotton and sugar enabled planters employing virgin soils to offer

[43]Russell, R., *North America, Its Agriculture and Climate,* 135-137.
[44]*Farmers' Register,* I, 39.
[45]*Southern Cultivator,* VI, 67; *cf. De Bow's Review,* IX, 422.
[46]Russell, R., *North America, Its Agriculture and Climate,* 140-142.

higher prices for slaves than could be afforded in general farming.[47]

Much of the contemporary opinion of antislavery critics concerning the intrinsic inefficiency of Negro slavery was due to attributing to slavery such characteristics of Southern agriculture as soil wastage, extensive methods of cultivation, and the one-crop system. As already noted, these practices were attributable mainly to a sparse labor supply in proportion to land resources and to the superiority of the South for the production of certain great staples. The assertion made by a Southerner that "an *improving* system of agriculture cannot be carried on by slaves" was amply disproved in certain regions and periods.[48]

The dogma was frequently put forward that Negro slaves could not be trusted with the use of machinery, and it was held that this would forever deter the development of manufacturing in the South. Some Southerners were also convinced of this, and occasionally were pessimistic as to the successful operation of farm machinery by slaves.[49] The fact that the great majority of Negroes had had little or no mechanical training was no proof that they were incapable of learning.

About 1818 a Negro slave of Fauquier County, Virginia, was reported to have invented a machine for cutting corn and at the same time preparing the land for a subsequent crop.[50] The readiness with which innumerable members of the race in recent years have adapted themselves to the mysteries of the gas engine in automobile repair work, to the use of farm machinery, and to various other mechanical employments indicates the fallacy of these assumptions. Before the Civil War Negro slaves had demonstrated their ability to operate factory machinery.[51]

The essential question is not whether the South would have been better off if its entire population had been made up of white laborers of western European origin working under the wages system; but whether the South could have employed the African Negro, after he was brought to this country, in any more effective manner; and more than this, why the Negro slave, in spite of the alleged inferiority of

[47]See below, p. 477.
[48]Harrison, J. B., *Review of the Slave Question,* 10; Fawcett, *Manual of Political Economy,* 317. See above, p. 447.
[49]Harrison, J. B., *Review of the Slave Question,* 11.
[50]*Niles' Weekly Register,* XV, 80.
[51]See below, p. 934.

slavery as a method of stimulating exertion, was able to displace the economy of free small farmers.

For one thing, considering the characteristic immediacy of the primitive Negro, it is probable that the rewards and punishments of the plantation system were more powerful stimuli than the rewards of industry would have been for him under a system of free labor. By no means were all slaves sullen, wretched, and driven cattle, working only under the lash.[52] On the smaller plantations, especially, they felt an interest in the affairs of the plantation, and their advice was not infrequently asked by the master. In many cases they took pride in the master's wealth and prosperity, tacitly accepting the position of inferiority and subordination—a position that probably caused them little sorrow.[53]

Slavery as an industrial system possessed certain positive advantages even as compared with the system of wage labor. From the standpoint of the employer, slavery provided a stable labor supply. Barring ordinary accidents and sickness, the laborer's services were always available—an important advantage in large-scale farming.[54] There was possibly a certain degree of economic inelasticity in the supply of labor, particularly at harvest time, when there was little surplus labor except children;[55] and slave labor flowed less readily than free labor to the type of employment promising greatest economic opportunity,[56] due partly to lack of diversity in the Negro's economic experience, partly to the difficulties in transferring the capital values of the slave's labor.[57] As compared with serfdom, however, slavery possessed the manifest advantage that the laborer could be moved to the point of greatest productive advantage, while the serf was bound to a particular manor.[58] It was found practicable to employ slave women in field labor, as well as men, while throughout America custom did not ordinarily sanction

[52]The insensibility of many primitive races to the ignominy of slavery was pointed out with many illustrations by Roscher in 1854. *Principles of Political Economy,* I, Chap. IV, Sec. LXIX.

[53]*Southern Agriculturist,* III, 601; *De Bow's Review,* XXV, 53; Lyell, *Second Visit to the United States,* II, 78-82.

[54]For presentation of this point of view, see *Southern Planter,* I, 138, 157; Ruffin, "Slavery and Free Labor Defined and Compared," in *ibid.,* XIX, 731; *De Bow's Review,* VIII, 71; *Hunt's Merchants' Magazine,* XXIX, 327.

[55]Hildreth makes much of this disadvantage. *Despotism in America,* 119.

[56]Raymond, *Comparative Economy of Free and Slave Labor,* 3-6.

[57]See below, p. 474.

[58]Phillips, U. B. *American Negro Slavery,* 346.

the employment of white women in the fields. Furthermore, it was practicable to use child labor from a comparatively early age in such activities as worming and suckering tobacco and picking cotton.[59] Slavery involved no problem of unemployment, and the system bred no lockouts, blacklists, and strikes.

ECONOMIC ASPECTS OF MAINTAINING THE STOCK OF SLAVES

Although normally there was a considerable surplus over current costs of subsistence in employing the labor of healthy field hands, this does not demonstrate the existence of a lifetime surplus—that is, a total return from the entire labor of the slaves in excess of the lifetime costs of maintaining them. When slaves were obtained by importation, it was customary generally to bring in adults, but this source of supply became comparatively unimportant after the prohibition of the slave trade. It became necessary, therefore, to depend largely on rearing slaves from birth to working age, as well as to maintain those who were sick or disabled by accident or old age.

The question of the profitableness of rearing slaves to working age was not without some connection with the costs and possibilities of importation. In the West Indies, for instance, some planters accepted the principle that it was "cheaper to purchase a negro than to breed one up."[60] Humboldt asserts that in Cuba he heard "discussed with the greatest coolness, the question whether it was better for the proprietor not to overwork his slaves, and consequently have to replace them with less frequency, or whether he should get all he could out of them in a few years, and thus have to purchase newly imported Africans more frequently."[61] For the British West Indies, during the colonial period, estimates of the net annual decrease of the slave stock to be replaced by importation ranged from 4 to 7 per cent.[62] However, West Indian conditions in this regard were essen-

---

[59]Russell, R., *North America, Its Agriculture and Climate*, 142.

[60]Pinckard, *Notes on the West Indies*, II, 465; *Practical Rules for the Management and Medical Treatment of Negro Slaves in the Sugar Colonies*, 18, 130.

[61]*Cuba*, 227.

[62]Report of the Committee of the Jamaica Assembly on the Sugar Trade, in Edwards, *British West Indies*, II, 490; Benezet, *Guinea and the Slave Trade*, 72; Burke, Edm., *European Settlements in America*, II, 124-126; *American Husbandry*, II, 138.

tially different from conditions in the South. The West Indies were nearer the source of supply, and consequently newly imported slaves came somewhat cheaper.[63] On account of density of population and high price of land the cost of rearing slaves to maturity was very much greater than in the South. Finally, the heavy labors of sugar planting made adult male slaves in the West Indies more economical than women and children, and there tended to be a preference for importing males, resulting in a large disproportion in numbers of the sexes.[64] Apologists for the slavery system in the Islands lay emphasis on this third cause of depreciation in slave stocks. Antislavery writers allege a deliberate policy of working slaves to death because of cheapness of importation.

There is some evidence that so long as the slave trade to the American Continent was open, there was a tendency in the rice district of South Carolina and the sugar region of Louisiana toward a policy of relying largely on importation, although profitableness of importation, as compared with maintaining the slave stock by natural means, was relatively less than in the West Indies.[65] In the latter part of the ante bellum period there were well managed rice estates where there was a considerable net annual increase;[66] but they were probably exceptional. Normally rice planters barely maintained their slave stock, and to do so required good management.[67] This was due less to mistreatment or overwork than to insalubrity of conditions of work in the rice swamps.[68] In the neighboring sea-island cotton plantations, where conditions of labor were far more healthful, there was a normal annual increase of 4 to 8 per cent.[69] In short-staple cotton and tobacco regions the increase of slave stock was regarded as an important source of plantation income, but estimates of rate of increase are conflicting. Jefferson thought 4 per cent was the normal rate in Virginia.[70] Forty years

[63]See above, p. 368.

[64]Edwards, *British West Indies*, II, 113. See also Humboldt, *Cuba*, 213-215.

[65]*Southern Cultivator*, VII, 69; Flint, *Geography and History of the Western States*, I, 527; *American Husbandry*, I, 394, 407; Stokes, *Constitution of the British Colonies*, 414.

[66]Olmsted, F. L., *Seaboard Slave States*, II, 46; *De Bow's Review*, XIV, 70; *Southern Cultivator*, XVI, 273; *Hunt's Merchants' Magazine*, XV, 378.

[67]Phillips, U. B., *Plantation and Frontier*, I, 148; Russell, R., *Culture of Carolina Rice*, 11.

[68]Hewatt, *South Carolina and Georgia*, I, 159; Hall, B., *Travels in North America*, III, 188; Russell, R., *North America, Its Agriculture and Climate*, 179.

[69]*Cf.* statement of Colonel Allston, in *De Bow's Review*, XVI, 594.

[70]Washington, *Letters on Agriculture*, 70.

later Edmund Ruffin estimated the rate at 7 to 10 per cent.[71] This estimate, however, probably allowed for appreciation in value. In 1838 a writer discussing conditions in Amherst and Nelson counties, Virginia, estimated the average increase at only 3 per cent a year; but it was not unusual, even in the lower South, to count on an annual increase of 5 per cent.[72]

Although the net increase of slave stock was an important item in plantation income and profits, especially in the border States, merely rearing slaves for sale was not profitable, since increase would constitute by itself only a very moderate interest on capital, with no allowance whatever for costs of maintenance. Consequently it did not pay to keep a larger force than was needed to cultivate the land.[73] In fact, about 1835, when agriculture in Virginia and Maryland was just recovering from a long depression, it did not appear feasible to earn a reasonable return on invested capital from increase of slave stock plus the proceeds from hiring their labor to others, nor from its employment by the owner, except under very efficient management.[74]

INFLUENCE OF CAPITALIZATION ON COMPETITIVE STRENGTH OF SLAVE LABOR

The actual basis of the competitive power of Negro slavery was greatly obscured by capitalization, for the prospective series of annual incomes from the ownership of a slave were capitalized on the same principle as a terminable annuity or any other terminable use-bearer. In the case of the slave the process of capitalization involved more obscurity than for bonds or other contractually predetermined income, for it was necessary to anticipate future earnings. As compared with land, the valuation of the slave involved the uncertainties of loss by sudden death or incapacity for labor through disability. Although the actuarial risk presumably was discounted in the purchase price of slaves, the possibility of loss by death was a considerable element in the risks of the individual planter. The risk was greater for small than for large planters, and this fact, accentuated by the rising prices of slaves, appears to have

[71]*Essay on Calcareous Manures*, 73.

[72]*Farmers' Register*, V, 8; *De Bow's Review*, VII, 437; XVI, 594; Russell, W. H., *My Diary North and South*, I, 397; *Hunt's Merchants' Magazine*, XV, 379; XXXI, 640.

[73]Russell, R., *North America, Its Agriculture and Climate*, 136.

[74]For discussion and illustration, see *Farmers' Register*, II, 253.

been one of the reasons for the concentration of slave ownership that occurred just before the Civil War.[75] In the last two decades before the Civil War insurance companies were beginning to insure the lives of slaves,[76] but it is doubtful if there was a widespread tendency for planters to avail themselves of this form of protection.

About the period of the Revolutionary War slaves were reported to be capitalized at 4 to 6 times the average annual hire.[77] In 1791 Jefferson estimated the ratio at 5 to 1. In Missouri, just before the Civil War, the rates of hire by the year averaged about 14 per cent of capital values in the case of male slaves and about 6 per cent for female slaves.[78]

As already noted, the question of the relative competitive advantages of slave labor and of free labor was confused from time to time by a tendency to assume that the interest and replacement fund calculated at a certain rate on the capital value of the slave was an extra cost which the employer of free labor did not have to assume, representing therefore a special and notable disadvantage in the case of slave labor. Such an assumption, however, was the reflection of incorrect economic analysis. When capitalization was accurately effected, the series of successive incomes as they became available actually were equivalent to interest and replacement; for interest and replacement would have been allowed for in the relatively low value that the owner paid for the services of the slave, capitalized on a terminable basis. In short, the process of capitalization obscures the fact that the so-called interest on investment and the replacement fund constitute actually the surplus over cost of maintenance appropriable from the ownership of the slave.[79]

Of course, in a process of valuation involving anticipation of the future, actual income and capitalized future income are likely to involve serious discrepancies, not only in individual cases, but even at times over large areas. Many farmers do not figure carefully interest earned on their investment.[80] Furthermore, the individual operator might make the services of the slave earn more through

---

[75]*De Bow's Review*, XXV, 489.

[76]*Ibid.*, IV, 275; X, 241; XIV, advertisement; Brackett, *The Negro in Maryland*, 91.

[77]Schoepf, *Travels in the Confederation*, II, 148.

[78]Trexler, *Slavery in Missouri*, 31.

[79]In considering the rent of mines the present writer has previously discussed this point—that both the so-called rent and the royalty, or replacement fund, are parts of the same thing, namely the economic rent, or appropriable surplus. "Rent under the Assumption of Exhaustability," in *Quarterly Journal of Economics*, XXVIII, 481.

[80]Ware, *Notes on Political Economy*, 102.

good management or less through poor management than had been allowed for in the process of market valuation.

PRINCIPAL BASIS OF THE COMPETITIVE SUPERIORITY OF SLAVE LABOR

An understanding of the reasons for the competitive superiority of slave labor as compared with free labor in regions favorable to the commercial production of staples rests on a comparatively simple basis. In the New World, with its abundance of fertile land, labor, when employed with a reasonable degree of efficiency, could produce a volume of physical goods larger than the bare requisites of its subsistence from birth to death. The owner of the slave had legally appropriated his services for life, and therefore was in a position to appropriate the surplus above the requisites of subsistence. Of course, land, equipment, and supervision were necessary to employ this labor productively, but these requisites exist also in the employment of free labor. The physical surplus might disappear for a time on account of crop failure and price fluctuations might also cause the value surplus to vanish for short periods, but normally there was both a physical and a value surplus for the full lifetime of the slave, which was appropriable by reason of the institution of slavery.

It was this appropriable surplus that gave slave labor under plantation organization an irresistible ability to displace free labor, whether hired or engaged in production on family-sized farms. Substantially, the minimum level of competition in the case of slave labor was bare subsistence. The planter was able, if necessary, to produce at price levels that left little more than the expense of maintaining the slave. White labor could bid no lower. As a matter of fact, however, the basis of competition rarely reached so low a level. There were extensive areas of fertile land where white labor could find an outlet for its energies without coming into acute competition with slave labor. Where free white labor did come into direct competition with slave labor in the South there resulted the process of geographical segregation already pointed out. The possession of areas suitable to the marketing of products was of vital importance to the owner of slaves, for otherwise he could enjoy the surplus product of their labor only in the form of a food surplus, which it was impossible to consume, or in an excess of personal services. In competition for the locations favorable to commercial agriculture the planter was able, if necessary, to pay a portion of the annual value of the slave or its capitalized equivalent as a premium to outbid free labor in the acquisition of land.

RELATION OF THE ECONOMY OF SLAVE LABOR TO THE SUPPLY OF LAND

Had no restrictions been placed on the slave trade the supply of slaves might ultimately have become so great that the value of their product would have barely exceeded the cost of maintaining slaves. This might have resulted either from the law of diminishing returns due to scarcity of land, or to depression in the prices of products due to overproduction. In his *Political Economy of Slavery* Edmund Ruffin recognized the former possibility.[81] Tucker concluded that slavery would tend to become economically moribund when the density of population reached 66 per square mile.[82]

Loria has developed a similar doctrine in a little different form, as follows: When land is abundant and the number of slaves relatively few, slavery as an economic institution is in the ascendant. The *peculium* of slaves—that is, the property they are able to accumulate out of their allowance or other sources—will then be generous, but the masters will advance the value of the slave to the point where the slave is not able to accumulate enough to purchase his liberty. On the other hand, as the supply of slaves becomes very great in relation to productive opportunities the slave's peculium will be very much less ample, but values will fall in still greater proportion and the slave will be able to purchase his freedom.[83]

Professor Loria's interpretation, however, appears to be merely an involved method of recognizing the conclusion that diminishing returns from increasing numbers might reduce the surplus above subsistence to a negligible point and render the ownership of slaves a profitless responsibility. To speak of the masters raising the prices of slaves with the purpose of preventing them from purchasing their freedom out of the peculium may serve the purposes of a philosophy of exploitation. The fact is that in the South the peculium itself was rarely large enough to suffice for the purpose of purchasing the slave's freedom, although there were individual instances of this.

[81]P. 6.
[82]*Progress of the United States,* 112.
[83]*Economic Synthesis,* 95-99.

Increasing numbers and the pressure of land scarcity could have lowered the peculium but little. On the other hand, the value of slaves was not subject to arbitrary action, but reflected the surplus from the employment of slave labor as evaluated under conditions of market competition.

It is conceivable, of course, that the operation of the law of diminishing returns might be greatly postponed through development of industrialism. If this tendency had occurred it is probable that the emancipation of the slave would have resulted, because freedom would have provided conditions more favorable to initiative and the exercise of intelligence. Under such conditions, as some economists have recognized, the slave's productivity would have become so much greater, when allowed to shift for himself, that he could have paid his master the equivalent of his earnings as a slave and obtained enough above this to accumulate the means of purchasing his freedom.[84]

The belief, however, that in 1860 slavery in the South was on the point of being "strangled for lack of room to expand"[85] is a wholly mistaken interpretation of actual conditions. The plantation system was not seriously limited by scarcity of land. It had utilized only a small fraction of the available land area.[86] The most fertile and easily available soils may have been occupied, but there was an extensive area remaining, a considerable part of which has been brought into cultivation since 1860. Before the Civil War railways were rapidly opening up new fertile areas to plantation agriculture. Far from being a decrepit institution, the economic motives for the continuance of slavery from the standpoint of the employer were never so strong as in the years just preceding the Civil War.

The argument that slavery was becoming unprofitable just before the Civil War has been presented by Professor U. B. Phillips from another standpoint. While recognizing clearly that the value of the slave was largely the result of a capitalization of net earnings, he argues that speculation had carried slave prices beyond the point at which slaves could be profitably employed except under the most favorable conditions. He points to the fact that cotton was very much lower in 1860 than it had been in the third and fourth decades,

[84]Hadley, *Economics*, 35.

[85]Simons, *Social Forces in American History,* 236, 262; *cf.* Seligman, *Principles of Economics,* 157-161.

[86]See below, pp. 640-642.

while the value of slaves was very much higher. It is easily possible, however, to derive a mistaken conclusion from this fact. Professor Phillips appears to defend the position that the movement toward overcapitalization was permanent, resulting in a steadily growing tendency for plantation agriculture to become unprofitable.[87] Achille Loria also accepts and elaborates this interpretation.[88] The present writer does not agree with this conclusion. Overexpansion of market prices of slaves, land, bonds, or other income-bearers in relation to net earnings, as a result of speculation, is at most only a temporary phenomenon. Expansion and contraction of slave prices occurred several times during the ante bellum period in relation to variations in the prices of the great Southern staple, cotton.[89] Moreover, as compared with earlier periods, prices of cotton should be considered in relation to the fact that in the interval from 1794 to 1860 there was a considerable reduction in cost of producing cotton.[90] It is not improbable, also, that slave prices in the earlier period had not completely risen to the point justified by the enormous profits that contemporary accounts describe; for slaves had not come to have the scarcity value later arising from restriction of the trade, whereas demand for cotton increased for a time very rapidly, giving rise to prices far in excess of even the high costs of production.[91] There is no apparent reason why high market values of slaves should be a permanent cause for unprofitable plantation economy. Had such a condition prevailed for a considerable period, affecting the profits of a great majority of those who were actively demanding slaves, this demand must ultimately have declined, and with it the excessive values. It must be remembered, however, that the active demand which tended to enhance the prices of slaves came from those planters who were making large profits and who sought to expand their slaveholdings on the basis of these profits.[92]

[87]"Economic Cost of Slaveholding in the Cotton Belt," in *Political Science Quarterly*, XX, 257-275.

[88]*Economic Synthesis*, 97.

[89]See below, pp. 665-667.

[90]See Chap. XXX.

[91]See below, p. 681.

[92]For contemporary accounts attesting the high profits made by planters, both in the earlier and in the later periods, see Gilmer, G. R., *First Settlers of Upper Georgia*, 165; Flint, *Geography and History of the Western States*, 506; Ingraham, *Sunny South*, 298.

ROBERT R. RUSSEL

The General Effects of Slavery upon Southern Economic Progress

We turn now to a seminal article by Robert R. Russel, a modern American historian, who in 1938 undertook to reappraise some of the beliefs about slavery and the economic development of the South which, by the time he wrote, had become common currency. You will notice immediately that Russel is not concerned only or even primarily with the narrow issue of the profitability of slavery. His interest is in the effects of the institution, and in particular the ways in which it may have retarded or limited the economic development of the region.

To the extent that these alleged effects were adverse, you can, if you wish, call them the "costs" of slavery; but you must remember that this is a metaphorical use of the word and that these are not the kind of costs that an accountant would introduce into a calculation of profitability. They may, nevertheless, be very relevant if you want to estimate whether or not the slave-labor economy of the South would have survived and flourished, if the Civil War had not intervened, or if you want to "set the record straight" about what slavery meant, in the long run, to the society that nurtured and defended it, whether or not it was a profitable system in the short run. The issues involved in an inquiry of this sort are more complex and harder to quantify than in a narrowly-limited analysis of profitability.

Before turning to the content and argument of Russel's article, however, let us look for a moment at one additional complexity that had been introduced since Ulrich B. Phillips first presented his case. When Phillips in 1905 tried to show that plantation slavery had become unprofitable by the late 1850s, he rested most of his argument on a demonstration that the price trends for cotton and for slaves had moved in opposite directions, squeezing between them the planter's profit margin. Having disposed (as he thought) of that issue, he then tried to show how slavery, in ways other than mere profitability, had tended to retard Southern economic progress. Here, however, his arguments showed much less originality and in fact hardly represented an advance over the ideas of J. E. Cairnes, for whose work he professed

---

From *The Journal of Southern History,* IV (February, 1938), 34-54. Copyright 1938 by the Southern Historical Association. Reprinted by permission of the Managing Editor.

to have little respect. For example, we may well doubt whether Cairnes, who was after all a competent economist, would have written as Phillips did of "an irresistible tendency to overvalue and overcapitalize slave labor." In discussing the limitations of the black slave labor force, Phillips could speak of the "inherited inaptitude" of the negro, while Cairnes would go no further than to refer to the compulsory ignorance in which the slave was kept. And it is a fair question whether Cairnes, who knew his Ireland, could have regarded it as uniquely characteristic of American negroes that they "had no love of work for work's sake" and were therefore devoid of "the economic motive without which no voluntary civilized industry is possible." In these respects and others Phillips' analysis of precisely why slavery retarded the economic development of the South, if indeed it did, leaves one dissatisfied.

In his *American Negro Slavery,* however, Phillips added a new dimension to the argument which did not appear in his 1905 article but which was to play a significant role in later discussion. This was contained in his allusion—it was little more—to the idea that by the late 1850s the slave-cotton economy of the South had reached its natural limits, beyond which it would not have spread, even had it been politically and legally permitted to do so. As he expressed it: "On the one hand virtually all the territory on the continent climatically available for the staples was by the middle of the nineteenth century already incorporated into slaveholding states; on the other hand, had new areas been available the chief effects of their exploitation would have been to heighten the prices of slaves and lower the prices of crops." Geographic expansion would have aggravated the economic problems of the South, not relieved them; by the same line of argument, since virtually all the area geographically suited for slave-labor cotton production was already in use for that purpose, there was little risk that the slave system could have spread farther West.

This argument was carried considerably farther in a well-known article written by Charles Ramsdell and published under the title, "The Natural Limits of Slavery Expansion," in the *Mississippi Valley Historical Review* in September, 1929 (Volume 16, pages 151-171). Most of the article is an exercise in economic geography and bears little direct relationship to the issue which concerns us here: the profitability of slavery. But the line of descent from Phillips' theories is clear, and so is its bearing on the visceral issue that underlies much of this discussion. Was the Civil War unnecessary? Would slavery have disappeared without it? If Phillips was to be believed, slavery was not only unprofitable in the late 1850s, but was widely recognized in the South itself as being a drag on material progress. And now Ramsdell, elaborating on one of Phillips' *obiter dicta,* was prepared to claim that by 1860 slavery had no place to go. It had reached its natural and impassable limits. Unprofitable in the regions where it was already established, it would have been unworkable, if tried, elsewhere—even on the cheap and fertile cotton lands of the Texas plains. Ramsdell's concluding paragraph is worth quoting at length:

> . . . it seems evident that slavery had about reached its zenith by 1860 and must shortly have begun to decline, for the economic forces which carried it into the region west of the Mississippi had about reached their maximum effectiveness. It could not go forward in any direction and it was losing ground along its northern border. A cumbersome and expensive system, it could show profits only as long as it could find plenty of rich land to cultivate and the world would take the product of its crude labor at a good price. It had reached its limits in both profits and lands. The free farmers in the North who dreaded its further spread had nothing to fear. Even those who wished it destroyed had only to wait a little while—perhaps a generation, probably less. It was summarily destroyed at a frightful cost to the whole country and one third of the nation was impoverished for forty years. One is tempted at this point to reflections upon what has long passed for statesmanship on both sides of that long dead issue. But I have not the heart to indulge them.

Those who say that war in general is stupid and unnecessary, and particular wars particularly so, are usually on firm ground. But Ramsdell was saying more than this: he was saying that slavery was a disappearing institution by 1860, and his evidence for this assertion, in so far as it was not based on matters of climate, soil types, and so on, rested upon Phillips' supposed demonstration that slavery, even in those regions in which it was already established in 1860, was unprofitable and inimical to economic development. His 1929 article represented perhaps the high water mark in acceptance of this view. Reconsideration of the argument and reexamination of the evidence was overdue.

Robert Russel's article, "The General Effects of Slavery upon Southern Economic Progress," shows this reconsideration and reexamination well under way by 1938. Particularly noteworthy is Russel's consistent refusal to take the easy way out and explain every feature which differentiated the South from the North and the West by reference to slavery. Farming practices, readiness to adopt mechanization, attitudes to manual and menial labor, savings and investment propensities—in each of these respects Russel finds it possible to admit cultural differentiation without granting to slavery more than incidental or contributory causal significance. In his analysis of Southern population trends, and of migration into and out of the South, this tactic pays large dividends. But in analyzing the reasons for the absence of substantial economic diversification in the South, and for a supposedly low rate of capital accumulation in that region, its effectiveness is somewhat less clear.

Regarding these latter problems, note how Russel approaches his analysis. He refers to a question which, he says, has caused historians much trouble: To what extent, if at all, was slavery responsible for the comparative dearth of economic opportunities in the South? Here we are faced with what has all the earmarks of a fair question—one with enough fat on it to supply a dozen doctoral dissertations. But how do we know that there was in fact a "comparative dearth of economic opportunities" in the South? Russel says there was, because he has already used this dearth to explain why most European immigrants headed for New York and the upper midwest. This is, however, hardly equivalent to demonstrating the fact of its existence, and Russel immediately finds it necessary to add the qualification that, for the population as a whole, there was no such dearth in Southern agriculture. The "thing to be explained" reduces, in fact, to the observation that manufacturing industry was relatively slow to develop in the South. This in turn, after briefly referring to the dispersion of Southern markets and the limitations of the South in terms of industrial raw materials and waterpower sites, Russel finally ascribes to two causes: the continued profitability of staple agriculture, and the fact that slave labor was not as well adapted to "mechanical employments" as to agriculture. This conclusion amounts to saying that the comparative advantage of the South, given its natural resources and the fact that slaves made up the bulk of its labor force, lay in staple agriculture, and that specialization in that line of activity represented a rational allocation of resources. But this, obviously, requires a solid demonstration that staple agriculture, particularly in cotton, was in fact still profitable; and it is in any case a long way from proving a dearth of economic opportunities.

Similar difficulties arise in connection with Russel's treatment of capital accumulation. Once again we must ask ourselves whether the problem has been correctly stated. To what extent was slavery in the

South responsible for "a dearth of capital for investment"? A fair question again, it seems; but did the dearth exist? No direct evidence is offered. To say that capital would have been diverted from agriculture or would have flowed in from the outside if the South had offered "exceptional opportunities" is to say nothing a prudent man would care to deny, in the absence of an operational definition of "exceptional." And an allegation that Southern planters "did not save as much for investment as might logically be expected of them" is surely a rather insubstantial charge. What we need to know is whether there were investment opportunities in the South, known to contemporaries, that would have been profitable at the going rate of return on capital, but which failed to attract investment, either from Southerners or from outside. These and other ambiguities in an otherwise keenly critical discussion result from inadequate specification of the underlying model and imprecise identification of the relevant variables.

Note, in conclusion, that Russel's concept of profitability refers, as did Phillips', only to the use of slaves in producing goods. This becomes clear in his discussion of the "absorption of capital" argument. Here we are given a two-region trade model in which Virginians rear slaves and sell them to Mississippi cotton planters. The production of slaves, however, unlike the production of cotton, is not carried on as a business, and the supply is price-inelastic. " . . . the supply of slaves was not adjusted to demand and prices were normally considerably in excess of costs of production." Consequently the Virginians earned above-normal profits (or is this the wrong word in the circumstances?) from their slave-breeding operations, and used these profits to subsidize their worn-out tobacco plantations. The model is ingenious: worth noting are the twin assumptions that the supply of slaves was not responsive to market demand, and that the slave-breeding sector did earn large profits.

MANY WRITERS have made sweeping generalizations as to the effects, allegedly injurious, of Negro slavery upon the economic progress of the South. It is believed that many time-honored generalizations about the subject are incorrect. The economics of slavery as expounded by the abolitionists, especially the English economist, J. E. Cairnes,[1] seemed to triumph on the battlefield. Such views have subsequently been accepted too implicitly not only in the

---

[1] J. E. Cairnes, *The Slave Power: Its Character, Career, and Probable Designs* (New York, 1862).

North but even in the South.[2] It is proposed to examine anew several widely-accepted generalizations.

Slavery is still being blamed for the wasteful and unscientific methods of farming practiced in the South before the Civil War. The authors of two popular college textbooks in the economic history of the United States both quote a table of statistics found in Ezra C. Seaman's *Essays on the Progress of Nations,* published in 1868, which compares the "free" and "slave" states in respect to number of acres of improved and unimproved land in farms in 1860 and the total value and the average value per acre of farm lands. The comparison shows inferiority of the slave states in all respects; and the writers leave the impression that slavery was the cause.[3] One author says:

> A second condition which made slavery possible and profitable was an abundance of new land. . . . If land anywhere became scarce and dear, slavery tended to disappear. Intensive and scientific methods of farming were seldom possible under the indifferent and wasteful slave system. Consequently, the colonial method was persisted in, of cropping a tract of land until it was exhausted and then moving on to a fresh piece.[4]

As a matter of fact, "skinning" the soil was practiced in all sections of the country. It was as common in most districts of the North as it was in the South. It was at least as common in the small-farm belts of the South as in the plantation districts. The preponderant reason was the same everywhere, namely, the cheap-

[2]The writer's quarrel is principally with general history and history textbooks, especially economic texts. Of the latter, Edward C. Kirkland, *A History of American Economic Life* (New York, 1932), is excepted, although it is believed that some of his conclusions require modification. Among the more detailed accounts which have greatly influenced recent textbooks are M. B. Hammond, *The Cotton Industry: An Essay in American Economic History* (New York, 1897), which is very critical of slavery, and the various works of Ulrich B. Phillips, especially *American Negro Slavery* (New York, 1918), and *Life and Labor in the Old South* (Boston, 1929). Those familiar with these works will readily recognize the differences between the conclusions reached in this article and the conclusions of the scholars named. The writer has great respect for the treatment of slavery in Lewis C. Gray, *History of Agriculture in the Southern United States to 1860,* 2 vols. (Washington, 1933), and agrees with most of it, but cannot accept his interpretation of several important matters.

[3]Ernest L. Bogart, *Economic History of the American People* (New York, 1935), 456; Harold U. Faulkner, *American Economic History* (New York, 1935), 391.

[4]Bogart, *Economic History of the American People,* 455.

ness of land. It was cheaper to acquire and clear a new farm of virgin soil than it was to restore, or even maintain, the fertility of the old. Contributory reasons were inertness and ignorance; but the want of initiative and knowledge was not as great among planters as among small farmers. The best farming in the South was done by planters,[5] many of whom took keen interest in agricultural reform and experimental methods[6] and farmed in an intensive manner.[7] In general, however, before the Civil War, it was only in the vicinity of cities, where land became dear by reason of its demand for special purposes, such as dairying and truck gardening, that much attention was given to manuring, fertilizing, and crop rotation. Speaking by and large, Southern soils—except rich bottom lands—wore out more rapidly than Northern. Cotton did not exhaust the soil as rapidly as grain crops; tobacco was hard on the soil.[8] But the land is nearly everywhere rolling or hilly, the soil is generally lighter than in the North, the greater part of the section lacks good native grasses, which would check erosion on lands retired from cultivation, and there are more heavy, dashing rains. Consequently there was much more soil erosion in the South.[9]

There was nothing inherent in slavery that prevented the adoption of more scientific methods of agriculture.[10] A planter could direct his slaves to spread manure, cotton seed, or marl, to plow horizon-

[5]Avery O. Craven, *Soil Exhaustion as a Factor in the Agricultural History of Virginia and Maryland, 1606-1860,* in University of Illinois *Studies in the Social Sciences,* XIII, No. 1 (Urbana, 1925), 86-91, and *passim.* W. H. Russell told of a great sugar plantation which was "better tilled than the finest patch in all the Lothians." *My Diary North and South* (New York, 1863), 103.

[6]Craven, *Soil Exhaustion,* 86-121, 134-44; *id.,* "The Agricultural Reformers of the Ante-Bellum South," in *American Historical Review* (New York, 1895-), XXXIII (1926), 302-14; Gray, *History of Agriculture in the Southern United States,* II, 779-92.

[7]Gray, *History of Agriculture in the Southern United States,* I, 447, 449.

[8]Hammond, *Cotton Industry,* 45, 79; Eugene W. Hilgard, *Report on the Geology and Agriculture of the State of Mississippi* (Jackson, 1860), 242; Craven, *Soil Exhaustion,* 32-33.

[9]R. O. E. Davis, *Soil Erosion in the South* (United States Department of Agriculture, *Bulletin No. 180* [Washington, 1915]), 8, 17-20; Craven, *Soil Exhaustion,* 27-39, 162.

[10]Cf. Craven, *Soil Exhaustion,* 162-64; and Gray, *History of Agriculture in the Southern United States,* I, 445-48; II, 940. Rosser H. Taylor, *Slaveholding in North Carolina: An Economic View* (Chapel Hill, 1926), 43, believes that slavery may have contributed to the clearing of new fields instead of improving old ones "as it was convenient to employ slaves in winter in clearing new fields." Phillips (ed.), *Plantation and Frontier, 1649-1863,* Vols. I and II in John R. Commons (ed.), *A*

tally on the hillsides, to avoid shallow tillage, and to pile brush in incipient gullies. The small farmer might do such things himself, but he was less likely to do them than the planter was to have them done.

Slavery may have retarded the adoption of improved agricultural machinery. At any rate, the proposition is true that employers will hesitate to entrust expensive and complicated machinery to careless, irresponsible, and incompetent workmen. On the other hand, large farmers, other things being equal, are abler and more likely to adopt improved machinery than small farmers. The small farmers of the South certainly made no better record in this regard than the planters. Cotton growers were not slow to adopt the cotton gin, one of the most revolutionary pieces of agricultural machinery in our history. Sugar-making machinery was complicated and expensive. Southern planters adopted the various improvements in the plow as the improved plows could be had. They rapidly substituted horses and mules for the slow-moving oxen when they were found to be better adapted to their purposes. In fact, the ox was displaced more slowly in New England than in other sections of the country, including the South.[11]

There is only a modicum of truth in the assertion, which still finds its way into print, that slavery inspired a contempt for physical labor among the white people of the South, and thereby rendered the section a great economic disservice. Slavery, or the presence of Negroes, which was the result of slavery, may properly be credited with responsibility for the idea universally prevalent in districts with considerable black population that whites must not perform *menial* services, that is, such personal services for others as cooking,

---

Documentary History of American Industrial Society, 10 vols. (Cleveland, 1910), I, 93, states that in the piedmont region the frequent need of clearing new fields disturbed the plantation routine and enabled small planters to hold their own against large. Taylor, *Slaveholding in North Carolina,* 81, states that the practice of paying overseers by allowing them a share of the crop "was criticized on the ground that it was rapidly producing deterioration of the soil." Craven, *Soil Exhaustion,* 38, believes the criticism valid, and so does Gray, *History of Agriculture in the Southern United States,* I, 448.

[11]Perhaps the principal reason for delaying subsitution in various localities was the lack of sufficient grain for feed, without which horses and mules could not do much hard work. There were other reasons for delay, however. See Percy W. Bidwell and J. L. Falconer, *History of Agriculture in the Northern United States, 1620-1860* (Washington, 1925), 111-13, 243, 403-405; Gray, *History of Agriculture in the Southern United States,* II, 851-52.

washing, scrubbing, and attendance as maids or valets.[12] Originally, perhaps, whites shunned the performance of such services simply because of their menial character. Because whites shunned them, they were the more readily assigned to Negroes; and the more blacks were thus employed, the more odious to whites such tasks became. But, although slavery may have excluded whites from menial services, it does not follow that whites were deprived of productive employment on that account.

Slavery and Negroes may also have bred the idea in slaveholding regions that people who could afford to own or hire servants should not perform their own domestic tasks, much as generations of low wages for household servants in England have established the idea that no woman of the middle class or above may do her own housework, at least not without a servant or two about for the sake of appearances. It was indeed true that families in slaveholding regions began to employ domestic servants at a lower income level than was the case in nonslaveholding districts. In so far as slavery was responsible for this, the institution rendered the South an economic disservice to the extent that it caused a greater degree of idleness than existed among similar classes in other sections— provided that such leisure is not to be considered economically desirable. But it should not be overlooked, in this connection, that mistresses on all but the largest plantations had heavy responsibilities in supervising servants in various household manufactures, in looking after the sick, in teaching the children, and in many other concerns.

There was no stigma attached in the South in slavery days to the performance of manual labor, as distinguished from menial, or of any other sort of labor not considered menial.[13] There were

[12]The line was often finely and strangely drawn. A Virginia farmer told Frederick L. Olmsted that he did not know that white farm laborers were particular about working with Negroes, but no white man would ever do certain kinds of work, such as taking care of cattle or getting water or wood for use in the house. If one should ask a white man to do such work, he would get mad and reply that he was no "nigger." Poor white girls never hired out to do servants' work, but they would help another white woman with her sewing and quilting and take wages for it. There were some "very respectable ladies" that would go out to sew. *The Cotton Kingdom*, 2 vols. (New York, 1861), I, 82.

[13]In the South considerable point was made of this distinction between menial and manual labor. In the North the word *menial* was not so commonly used, either as adjective or noun.

situations, however, in which whites would not work with slaves, just as now there are situations in which whites will not work with Negroes. White wage earners, except perhaps immigrants who had not yet learned to draw the line, would not labor on a plantation under an overseer. They would, however, work with slaves if there was some evident distinction in tasks or status. A white farmer and his sons had no repugnance to working along with their own or hired slaves at any task required on the farm. White hired men, too, would work with the farmer and his slaves. A farmer's wife and daughters might not work in the fields with slaves, but the women folk of nonslaveholding whites were about as likely to work in the fields as were Northern women similarly circumstanced. In both sections, as in England, women were withdrawn from the fields as standards of living rose. An overseer on a plantation was not supposed to do physical labor, even if so inclined; to do so, it was thought, and no doubt correctly, would be detrimental to discipline. A foreman who had charge of a small group of slaves on a farm or a small plantation—and there were many such—was expected to work along with the slaves. A large planter and his sons might not engage in physical labor; to do so would lower them in the esteem of their neighbors and slaves. It is difficult to say whether slavery was responsible for this pleasing fancy or only made it more possible to humor it. English country gentlemen and their sons likewise eschewed manual labor, and Northern mill-owners did not as a rule send their sons into the mills as hands. Furthermore, even planters who employed overseers usually had their time well-occupied with the management of their plantations, and their management was economically more productive than wielding the plow or hoe would have been.

The same situation obtained in the cities and towns of the South. In factories, mills, and shops, and about the wharves, white laborers, free Negroes, and slaves, sometimes of both sexes, worked side by side, usually, but not always, with some distinction of tasks. Frequently the whites objected to working with Negroes and sought to have them excluded from certain employments, but never successfully. The opposition arose partly from race prejudice and partly from dislike of Negro competition. In the North, where Negro laborers were relatively few, the opposition of whites to Negro competition was more effective. It would seem unlikely that many whites were deprived of useful employment by their disinclination to work with Negroes or to labor at certain tasks commonly performed by slaves.[14]

Southern people in general were more inclined than those in the East and Northwest to dislike physical labor, especially heavy physical labor, and to seek "white-collar" jobs or to live by their wits. The evidence on this point is overwhelming. But it does not follow that slavery was the cause of this difference. A similar variance in other places and in other times has commonly been explained by differences in temperature, humidity, ease of making a living, eating and drinking habits, general health, cultural antecedents, and social organization.[15] If such explanations are valid for other places and other times, they are equally valid for the United States in slavery times.

A more difficult question with regard to the general economic effects of slavery is whether or not the institution retarded the growth of population of the slaveholding states. If so, it was a grievous fault; for economic history shows that increase in population in a region has been conducive to the development of improved means of transportation, the commercialization of agriculture and manufactures, and the extension of the factory system— developments which, with all their evils, have contributed to economic progress.

At the close of the colonial period the six commonwealths which continued to permit slavery and to colonize new "slave" territory, that is, Delaware, Maryland, Virginia, the two Carolinas, and Georgia, together with Louisiana, Florida, and Texas, had a slightly greater population than the seven states to the north which shortly

---

[14]The last four paragraphs are based upon numerous but widely scattered scraps of evidence gleaned from a variety of sources, especially *De Bow's Review* (New Orleans, 1846-1880); the various works of Olmsted dealing with the South; and Phillips (ed.), *Plantation and Frontier*, I, II. Considerable evidence is presented in an uncritical manner in Charles H. Wesley, *Negro Labor in the United States, 1850-1925: A Study in American Economic History* (New York, 1927), Chap. III. Particular statements made above are confirmed by Kathleen Bruce, *Virginia Iron Manufacture in the Slave Era* (New York, 1930), Chap. VI; Ivan E. McDougle, "Slavery in Kentucky, 1792-1865," in *Journal of Negro History* (Lancaster, Pa., 1932-), III (1934), 296; Alfred H. Stone, "Free Contract Labor in the Ante-Bellum South," in *The South in the Building of the Nation,* 12 vols. (Richmond, 1909), V, 142.

[15]The influence of such factors in the case of the poor whites is well described by Paul H. Buck, "The Poor Whites in the Ante-Bellum South," in *American Historical Review,* XXXI (1925), 41-55.

became "free." In 1860 there were eighteen free and fifteen slave states. According to the census for that year the former had a population of 18,800,527, the latter, 12,315,374. Wherein lies the explanation? We can not now detect any differences in the birth and death rates of the two sections.

For one thing, the number of people of Southern birth who migrated to the North was much greater than the number of people of Northern birth who moved to the South. In 1850 there were 608,626 people of Southern birth living in free states and only 199,672 people born in free states residing in the South. The corresponding numbers for 1860 were 713,527 and 371,421.[16] In 1860 there were, by careful estimate, about 800,000 more people of Southern birth and parentage living in free territory than there were people of Northern stock living in slaveholding regions. This accounts, then, for approximately 1,600,000 of the 6,500,000 disparity in population between sections.

This large net loss to the South in intersectional migration, in turn, is to be explained almost wholly by the circumstances of the westward movement of population during the period and the various conditions and political maneuvers that determined which of the new states beyond the mountains should be free and which slave. The old story of thousands of small farmers from the South fleeing across the Ohio River to escape slavery is almost pure fiction.[17] People from the older states moved west with various motives, the principal one being the acquisition of land. They usually followed the most available routes. Before the railroads were built, great numbers of people from Virginia and Maryland went up the Potomac Valley, crossed over to the Ohio River, using the Cumberland National Road after it had been built, floated down the Ohio, and eventually found homes in Kentucky and the southern parts of Ohio, Indiana, and Illinois, or beyond the Mississippi in Missouri, Arkansas and Iowa. Many other people from Maryland, Virginia, and North Carolina crossed the Blue Ridge by various routes, picked up the trail in the Great Valley, and followed it down into Tennessee or turned off and went through Cumberland Gap into Kentucky. Thousands of Kentuckians and Tennesseeans in turn, of the first, second, or later generations, moved on west or northwest

---

[16]*Compendium of the Seventh Census of the United States,* 1850, pp. 116 ff.; *Eighth Census of the United States, 1860, Population,* 616 ff. The District of Columbia is included with the South.

[17]Taylor, *Slaveholding in North Carolina,* 56-58.

into southern Indiana, southern Illinois, Missouri, Arkansas, and, in less numbers, into Iowa and southwestern Wisconsin. Only slaveholders who wished to take their slaves with them were debarred from choosing a location north of the Ohio; scores of slaveholders, in fact, did take their slaves into Indiana and Illinois under life or other long-term indentures permitted by the early laws.[18] Of the 608,626 natives of the South living in 1850 in free states, 505,096 resided in the four states of Ohio, Indiana, Illinois, and Iowa, and of the latter number 462,088 had been born in Virginia, Maryland, North Carolina, Kentucky, and Tennessee. The corresponding numbers for 1860 were 713,527, 530,843, and 481, 322, respectively.

Many thousands of people from Pennsylvania and, to a less extent, from New York and New Jersey, crossed to the Ohio River, floated down that stream, and eventually settled on the left bank in Kentucky or crossed the Mississippi into Missouri. Other thousands settled first on the right bank of the Ohio, and then later, they or their children moved on into Kentucky or, especially, Missouri. Of the 371,421 people born in free states but living in 1860 in slave states, 208,059 were to be found in Missouri and Kentucky. Northerners certainly did not shun Missouri. In 1860 there were 166,620 people living there who had been born on free soil and 274,572 who had been born in other slave states. There was also a large interchange of population across the line between Pennsylvania and New Jersey on the one side and Virginia, Maryland, and Delaware on the other; 49,827 people born north of the line were living south of it in 1860, and 50,958 born south of it were living on the other side. There was much less exchange of population between New England and the Great Lakes region on the one hand and the Lower South on the other. But such exchange did occur. Thousands of Yankees undeterred by slavery went south to farm, work in mills, run steamboats, buy cotton, sell merchandise, teach school, and fill all manner of other jobs which became available. There were many more Northerners scattered about the Lower South than there were people from the latter region residing in the Upper North. In 1860 there were 12,549 natives of New England living in the seven cotton states and only 2,169 people from the cotton states to be found in New England.

The other important cause of the disparity of population between

[18]John B. McMaster, *A History of the People of the United States from the Revolution to the Civil War*, 8 vols. (New York, 1883-1913), III, 526-28; V, 187.

the North and the South in 1860 was the fact that the former had received much the greater share of the foreign immigration. In 1860 there were 3,582,999 people of foreign birth living in free states and the territories and only 553,176 in the slave states. In 1850 the numbers had been 1,900,325 and 310,514. Why did not the slave states get a larger share of the immigrants? The blame has often been unjustly placed upon slavery.

Most of the immigrants in ante-bellum days, as since, landed at New York City, for that was the principal terminus of the trans-Atlantic packet lines and, after their advent, the steamship lines. Many remained in New York; the majority scattered to various parts of the country. Most numerous among the immigrants after 1845 (about the time the tide of immigration set in strongly) were the Irish. They were poor and sought work for wages. They found it chiefly in the cities and factory towns and in railroad and canal construction. The cities and mill towns were mainly in the East, and the railroads and canals were being built mostly there and in the Northwest. A considerable number of Irishmen found work building Southern railroads and many were employed at the wharves of New Orleans and other Southern towns. They showed no great prejudice against slavery or against Negroes.

Next most numerous among immigrants were Germans. They usually had more means than the Irish, and a larger proportion of them went to the growing Northwest, acquired land, and grew grain and raised livestock. They undoubtedly disliked slavery. But they would have preferred the Northwest even if slavery had not been in the picture. There they could get excellent land at the minimum government price located in districts which were being rapidly opened to markets by the building of railroads. They could practice a type of farming more like that of the old country. And acclimation was less difficult than in the South. Thousands of Germans went to the quasi-slave state of Missouri where land and farming were quite like those of states of the Northwest. And a considerable number were lured to the rich, cheap lands of Texas to grow cotton and grain.[19] Few of them acquired slaves, partly because they disliked slavery and partly because they could not afford to purchase them.

It would seem, then, to be a safe conclusion that neither slavery nor the presence of Negroes was in any direct sense responsible for

---

[19] Albert B. Faust, *The German Element in the United States,* 2 vols. (Boston, 1909), I, 490-501; Olmsted, *Cotton Kingdom,* II, 96, 262-66.

the failure of the slaveholding states as a whole to grow as rapidly in population as the free states as a whole between 1790 and 1860. No doubt thousands of individuals were deterred from going South by race prejudice, dislike of slavery, or a disinclination to compete with slaves for jobs. But, since so many others were undeterred by such motives and considerations, it is reasonable to suppose that, if economic opportunities had been great enough, people would have come in greater numbers from the North and from Europe to seize upon them.[20]

This conclusion is further justified by events which have occurred since slavery was abolished. The percentage of immigrants locating in the South has been even less than it was in slavery days. For example, in 1890 only 8.3 per cent of the foreign born of this country lived in the South whereas 13.4 per cent had lived there in 1860. Now it is possible that it has been the presence of the Negro, a resultant of slavery, which has repelled. But it is highly probable that it has been the comparative lack of economic opportunities in the South, still suffering from the ravages of war for much of the period.[21] Many whites and blacks have gone North to get jobs, especially during the great boom prior to 1929. Moreover, the presence of Negroes has not kept Northerners out of particular localities or particular occupations in the South where opportunities have called.

The conclusion just stated brings up another question which has caused historians much trouble, namely, to what extent, if at all, was slavery responsible for the comparative dearth of economic opportunities in the South which, in turn, kept the population from growing more rapidly? In agriculture slavery reduced opportunities somewhat for nonslaveholding whites but not for the population as a whole. Because of it the white farm population was probably less than it would otherwise have been, but the total farm population was greater. And, be it noted, when writers say that slavery retarded the growth of the population of the South, they mean total population, not white population only.

The story is briefly this: The staple crops of the South gave the incentive for men of enterprise to engage in large-scale agriculture. Land was plentiful and cheap. The labor problem was more difficult. People of good-enough quality would not work for low-enough wages, in large-enough numbers, and with sufficient regularity in a

---

[20]Cf. Emory Q. Hawk, *Economic History of the South* (New York, 1934), 220-21.
[21]Gray, *History of Agriculture in the Southern United States,* II, 940.

country where it was so easy to get land and farm independently. The solution was first found in indentured servants, and the earliest plantations were developed with that class of labor. As time passed Negro slaves were preferred, great numbers were imported, they throve, and multiplied, and many farmers developed into planters.[22]

Although a time did not arrive when more than about one third of the agricultural population of the South, including the Negroes, lived on plantations as distinguished from small farms,[23] the great bulk of the staple crops came to be produced on plantations—all the sugar and rice, most of the tobacco, and at least three fourths of the cotton. There were several reasons for this.[24] In the production of sugar and rice, which required considerable capital, small farmers could not compete with planters and were crowded out. The competitive advantages of the plantation in the growing of cotton and tobacco were not so great, if, indeed, there were any. But planters held slaves for the primary purpose of producing staples for market; they would not have kept slaves had it not been for this motive. Small farmers, on the contrary, were under no particular urge to engage in commercialized agriculture. They might make a better living by doing general or subsistence farming. Slaves were better adapted to tᴎᴄ routine of the plantation than they were to the more varied tasks of general farming with considerable household manufacturing. Also, as a class, the planters were more enterprising and they were better managers than the small farmers; the more ambitious and capable of the small farmers were likely to graduate into the planter class. So planters got the better lands, near enough to transportation facilities to justify staple agriculture, while small farmers had cheaper, but not necessarily poorer, lands more remote from the routes of commerce and followed a more self-sufficing economy or, if they remained in the plantation belts, lived on the poorer lands and practiced a more general agriculture than their planter neighbors.

If slavery had not existed in the South and, consequently, there

[22]The subject of this paragraph has been amplified and more thoroughly reasoned in Robert R. Russel, "The Economic History of Negro Slavery in the United States," in *Agricultural History* (Chicago, Baltimore, 1927-), XI (1937), 308-21.

[23]The percentage depends upon where the line is drawn between the plantation and the farm. If the minimum number of slaves on a plantation be arbitrarily set at ten, about 30 per cent of the farm population resided on plantations in 1850. Cf. Gray, *History of Agriculture in the Southern United States,* I, 482, 529.

[24]These reasons are developed at greater length in an unpublished paper by the writer on "The Effects of Slavery upon Non-Slaveholders in the Ante-Bellum South."

had been few or no plantations, it is reasonable to presume that the lands which were in fact in plantations would have been held by the more capable small farmers, who would have raised staples although in somewhat smaller quantities than they were actually produced. In that case the white farm population of the South would have been greater than it actually was, but not as great as the actual farm population, both white and black.

But immigrants into the North after 1790 went largely into nonagricultural occupations. To what extent, if at all, was slavery responsible for the backwardness of the South in other lines of economic development than agriculture? Manufacturing may be selected for consideration since, next to agriculture, it is the most fundamental industry.

Even in colonial times the Southern commonwealths did less manufacturing in proportion to population than did the Northern. In the middle period, as the industrial revolution proceeded, the South did a smaller and smaller percentage of the nation's manufacturing. In 1860 the capital invested in manufacturing in the South was only 9.5 per cent of the capital so invested in the entire country; and the number of hands employed was only 8.4 per cent of the nation's total. Moreover, nearly one half of Southern manufactures consisted of flour and grist, lumber, and turpentine, products of simple operations.

A number of reasons may be advanced to account for the industrial backwardness of the South, few of which have much relevance to slavery. In colonial times in the tidewater region, the continued and anticipated profits of staple agriculture, together with the superior adaptability of slaves thereto, made it unnecessary and unprofitable to do much household and shop manufacturing. In the Northern colonies and the back country of the South, the lack of markets for agricultural products constrained the people to do more manufacturing. A combination of factors—the abundance of white pine, water power near the sea, the demand for ships and boats for the fisheries and the carrying trade, markets for lumber in the same regions where the fish were marketed—caused lumbering and shipbuilding to be concentrated largely along the New England coast. In a similar fashion other special factors caused various other branches of manufacturing to be more or less concentrated in the North.

When the Industrial Revolution reached the United States, population was comparatively sparse in the South, distances were great, and means of transportation poor. The poorer whites afforded little demand for manufactured goods. Neither did the slaves, but the masters, who exploited their labor, presumably compensated for them in this regard. So markets were too dispersed and inadequate to encourage large-scale manufacturing. The population of the East was more compact and, therefore, transportation facilities could be provided at lower cost. The purchasing power of the people was greater.

The streams of the South were less manageable for power than were those of the East. Southern power sites were relatively inaccessible to natural avenues of transportation; in New England, especially, considerable power was available very near the sea.

The principal Southern raw material, cotton, was not at all bulky and would stand transportation to distant markets. The humid atmosphere of the New England seaboard was advantageous to cotton mills. For lumbering the North possessed much the same advantages over the South in the middle period that it had possessed in the colonial. Even before coal came to be used in smelting, parts of Pennsylvania had an advantage over other regions of the country in ironmaking by reason of the juxtaposition of wood, ore, and limestone in localities near navigable rivers or other means of transportation. When coal superseded charcoal the advantage of Pennsylvania was enhanced. To illustrate, in the days of charcoal furnaces a considerable secondary iron industry was developed in Richmond, Virginia, which used pig iron smelted in the back country and brought down the James River. After smelting with anthracite was well developed in eastern Pennsylvania, about 1850, the Richmond iron works procured their pig iron there and the back country furnaces died out.[25] The principal iron ore field of the South, near present Birmingham, Alabama, was in ante-bellum days all but inaccessible. The Pittsburgh field, by way of contrast, lay at the head of a magnificent system of inland waterways transportation. After railroads penetrated northern Georgia, northern Alabama, and eastern Tennessee, during the fifties, numbers of small furnaces and foundries sprang up, but they could not compete with those of Pennsylvania except in the local markets.

In the East, where there had been more household and shop industry, and much manufacturing done under the "putting out" system, there were more laborers to be diverted to mills and

[25]Bruce, *Virginia Iron Manufacture in the Slave Era*, 275-78.

factories when they came in. The opening of improved means of communication with the fine farming regions of western New York and the Northwest brought destructive competition to Eastern agriculture, released still more men, women, and children to become mill hands, and supplied them with food and raw materials. In the South the continued profitableness of staple agriculture prevented slaveowners from turning to manufacturing or diverting their slaves thereto. Although slaves were frequently used successfully in mills, factories, and shops, in fact in practically every mechanical pursuit, they were certainly not as well adapted to mechanical employments as to agriculture.[26] It was difficult to transform the small, independent, self-sufficing farmers of the South into urban wage earners.

Capital for industry in the East had come from the profits of merchandising and shipping as well as from the profits of industry. In the South there was no considerable source of capital outside manufacturing itself. The profits of agriculture, such as they were, were absorbed in expanding agriculture and providing facilities for transportation. If the section had offered exceptional opportunities, capital and labor would have been diverted from agriculture or would have flowed in from the outside, but such was not the case. Once the North had gained a good start upon the South in manufacturing, it became harder for the latter to make progress. For then infant industries in the South would have to get started in the face of unrestricted competition from firmly established industries in the North.[27]

Of the various reasons enumerated for the backwardness of the South in manufacturing, only one relates directly to slavery. Slave labor was not so well adapted to manufacturing as to agriculture, and, therefore, other things being equal, slaveowners preferred to keep their slaves engaged in the latter. A second reason for which slavery has frequently been blamed may relate indirectly to the institution, namely, a dearth of capital for investment. It becomes

[26]There was much discussion of this point in the South about 1845-1852. The consensus was about as stated here. *Ibid.,* Chap. VI; Wesley, *Negro Labor in the United States,* Chap. I; Phillips, *American Negro Slavery,* 375-78; Robert R. Russel, *Economic Aspects of Southern Sectionalism, 1840-1861,* University of Illinois *Studies in the Social Sciences,* XI, No. 1, Pts. I, II (1923), 41, 54.

[27]The reasons for the backwardness of the South in manufacturing are described in greater detail in Victor S. Clark, "Manufactures," in *The South in the Building of the Nation,* V, 299-335; Russel, *Economic Aspects of Southern Sectionalism,* 54-64; Gray, *History of Agriculture in the Southern United States,* II, 931-36.

necessary, therefore, to ascertain what effects, if any, slavery had upon saving and investment in the South.

Slavery, as we have seen, made possible the development of large-scale farming. By all the rules of economic history the planters should have saved much for investment in further productive enterprises; it is the people with the larger incomes who do most of the saving for investment. The planters did save. They saved more than their small-farmer neighbors did. They saved enough to keep expanding their agricultural operations. They provided much of the capital for internal improvements and other productive undertakings. But the fact remains that they did not save as much for investment as might logically be expected of them.

Many of the planters, especially those of old families, did not have steady habits and frugal instincts. They often had visions of grandeur inherited from spacious colonial days and reinforced by real or fancied descent from English aristocracy.[28] At any rate, planters who were making money, and often those who were losing it,[29] lived well. They built big houses. Their habitations were literally overrun by domestic servants. They bought luxuries. Those with the largest incomes frequently spent their substance at Northern watering places or in European travel. How slavery could have been responsible for these enlarged views it is impossible to see, except, of course, that it was slavery that made it possible to indulge them.

Again, planters' savings were diminished by the almost universal practice of living and operating not upon the income from the preceding crop but upon the anticipated income from the next crop; that is, they lived largely upon advances received from their factors upon contemplated or growing crops as security. These advances cost dearly. They cost not only interest but also the reduced prices which they occasioned, for the markets were frequently glutted and prices depressed because so many planters were under the necessity of selling their crops as soon as harvested in order to pay their debts. This practice of obtaining advances upon anticipated crops would not have prevented, it might even have facilitated, the accumulation of capital in the South, if the advances had been made by Southern men. But they were not. They were made in the last analysis by

[28]Thomas J. Wertenbaker has thoroughly discredited the old idea that Virginia was largely settled by cavaliers. *Patrician and Plebian in Virginia, or the Origin and Development of the Social Classes of the Old Dominion* (Charlottesville, 1910); *id., The Planters of Colonial Virginia* (Princeton, 1922).

[29]Taylor, *Slaveholding in North Carolina*, 95-96.

Northern or British firms.[30] Even if the planter eschewed advances from his cotton factor, the result was much the same, for in that case he bought supplies on long credit from his merchant who in turn had bought them on long credit from Northern jobbers or wholesalers. It would be difficult to name anything more efficacious in preventing the accumulation of capital than eight, ten, or fifteen per cent interest, often compounded.

This system of advances was caused partly by the lack of habits of thrift, already bemoaned. Its principal cause was the speculative character of a commercialized agriculture with distant markets. A farmer who produces for market is always under strong temptation to borrow money, get more land and hands, and put out a larger acreage, because there is always the possibility of raising a bumper crop and selling it at top prices. Nature is not consistent. There is always the prospect in any community of having a big crop while there is a total or partial failure elsewhere, with consequent high prices and big income for those who dwell in the favored community. Farmers gamble on the big year.[31] Such speculation has by no means been confined to slaveowners and cotton growers. It has been as evident in nonslaveholding regions as in slaveholding—the wheat belt for instance. Slavery only made it possible for some farmers to gamble on a bigger scale.

Another thing, closely related to the factor just mentioned, which militated against the accumulation of capital in the South was the occasional overproduction of staples. Within a few decades after the invention of the gin, the cotton states were producing over three fourths of the cotton sold in the world's markets. A big crop in the South sent the price down, a small crop sent it up. It happened more than once that a smaller crop of cotton at a high price brought in a larger aggregate amount to the growers than a large crop at a low price. But constant pleas to grow less cotton and more corn fell on deaf ears. In the cases of tobacco, sugar, and rice, the American crop was such a small part of the world's total that its quantity had comparatively little effect on world prices, and, therefore, there could be overproduction in the South, considered alone, only in the sense that labor and capital might more profitably have been directed into other channels. A chief reason for the overproduction of staples, when it occurred, was the speculative character of

[30]Alfred H. Stone, "The Cotton Factorage System of the Southern States," in *American Historical Review,* XX (1915), 557-65; Hammond, *Cotton Industry,* 108 ff.; Russel, *Economic Aspects of Southern Sectionalism,* 100-107.

[31]Cf. Hammond, *Cotton Industry,* 109; Olmsted, *Cotton Kingdom,* II, 49.

commercialized agriculture just noted. Slavery did not supply the urge to speculate, but it made speculation possible on a larger scale and thus contributed to overproduction. In general, of course, it was to the advantage of the South to produce great crops of cotton and other staples. Occasional overproduction was preferable to consistent underproduction. And without slavery there would have been consistent underproduction during the period under consideration.

It has frequently been stated that slavery "absorbed" capital in the South which otherwise might have been used in productive enterprises.[32] Such a statement needs much qualification if it is not to be misleading. While the foreign slave trade lasted, part of the profits of Southern industry went to Yankee skippers, English lords, Dahomey chiefs, etc., in exchange for slaves. Thus capital which might have been used to build sawmills or ships or for other productive purposes in the South was "fixed" in the form of slaves. Capital could not be taken out of the South by the internal or domestic slave trade, however. To illustrate, suppose Mississippi cotton planters, out of the profits of the industry, bought Virginia slaves. The slaves would still be in the South and presumably capable of paying for themselves and providing a reasonable profit on the investment. The savings of the planters would still be in the South also, although in Virginia instead of Mississippi, and, presumably, could be invested in factories, railroads, and other productive enterprises. They in turn might attract labor from the North or from Europe. Suppose, however, the Mississippi planters were able to hire free-born Virginians to come down and work their plantations and, instead of buying slaves, invested their savings in sawmills in their own state, employing workers attracted from the North or from Europe to operate the sawmills. The South as a whole would lose no laborers and no savings in this case, but Virginia would have been to the trouble and expense of rearing workers until they had reached maturity only to see them go away to contribute to the prosperity of another state. Thus slavery did not absorb Southern capital in any direct sense; it affected the distribution of capital within the section. The mere capitalization of the anticipated labor of a particular class did not destroy or diminish any other kind of property.[33]

---

[32]For example, Phillips seems to have said this. *American Negro Slavery,* 395-99; *id.,* "The Economic Cost of Slaveholding in the Cotton Belt," in *Political Science Quarterly* (New York, 1886-), XX (1905), 271-75.

[33]Gray, *History of Agriculture in the Southern United States,* I, 460, has put this point very clearly.

But in an indirect way slavery may have had the effect of absorbing capital nevertheless. Take the case of the Virginia tobacco planters and the Mississippi cotton planters again. The Virginians probably received considerably more for their slaves than they had invested in rearing them, for the supply of slaves was not adjusted to demand and prices were normally considerably in excess of costs of production. And probably, instead of investing their profits in productive enterprises, the Virginians used them for living expenses, not having produced enough on their worn-out tobacco plantations to maintain their accustomed style of living. Thus as a consequence of slavery the profitable cotton industry of Mississippi might be carrying along the incubus of an unprofitable tobacco industry in Virginia or at least enabling tobacco planters there to live in a style not justified by their earned incomes.[34] Under a free-labor system this would hardly have been possible. But, on the other hand, if it had not been for slavery, cotton growers of Mississippi might not have had any savings to invest.

In conclusion, the importance of Negro slavery as a factor determining the character and extent of the economic development of the South has been greatly overestimated. It brought a racial element into the population which would not otherwise have been represented in any considerable numbers. The importation of slaves and the increase of the Negro population gave the South a larger total population, at any date, than it otherwise would have had, but no doubt retarded the growth of the white population. Slavery made possible the widespread development of the plantation system of farming and, thereby, gave a great impetus to the growing of the various Southern staples. This was beneficial to the South as a whole, although there was occasional overproduction, to which slavery contributed. Slavery may have retarded the diversification of Southern industry. It was conducive to the accumulation of capital on the whole, although it had the serious disadvantage of permitting more productive districts to contribute to the livelihood of the people of less productive regions. But compared with such great economic factors as climate, topography, natural resources, location with respect to the North and to Europe, means of

[34]For similar views of contemporaries of slavery, see Frederick L. Olmsted, *A Journey in the Back Country* (New York, 1861), 325; Cairnes, *Slave Power*, 72-76. See, also, Taylor, *Slaveholding in North Carolina,* 66. Edmund Ruffin of Virginia, another contemporary, held a contrary view. See "The Effects of High Prices of Slaves," in *De Bow's Review,* XXVI (1859), 647-57.

transportation, and character of the white population, Negro slavery was of lesser consequence in determining the general course of Southern economic development.

THOMAS P. GOVAN
Was Plantation Slavery Profitable?

Historians differ in their attitudes to hypothetical history—the kind of history that asks "What would have happened if . . . ?" Conventionally regarded as a practice of doubtful morality, its attractions to the intellect and the imagination are nevertheless so seductive that the most respectable practitioners of the craft are not infrequently caught *in flagrante delicto.* A good example is the article by Ramsdell already mentioned, in which the author clearly asserts that *if* the Civil War had not occurred, slavery would not in any case have survived for long. And logicians will tell you that *every* statement of necessary causation in history—of the type "A (and not C or D or E or F) caused B"—contains within itself the hypothetical and counterfactual proposition, "If A had not happened, B would not have happened either."

What has this to do with our inquiry into the profitability of slavery? Here, at first glance, it might appear that we are dealing with a simple question of fact, and nothing hypothetical at all. Did slave-owning planters make profits or did they not? Granted that we may have to deal with some matters of definition involving mainly what we are going to call certain items in an accounting statement, and granted that we may have difficulty in getting all the information we need, we are nevertheless surely dealing with an empirical issue and not with an imaginary universe of things that might have been.

Thomas P. Govan, in the selection which follows, starts in precisely this straight-forward manner. Was slave labor as profitable to the planter as free labor would have been? This is an interesting question for speculation, perhaps, but not a question that can be answered. Were the planters of the Old South making money from their

From *The Journal of Southern History*, VIII, Number 4 (November, 1942), 515-535. Copyright 1942 by the Southern Historical Association. Reprinted by permission of the Managing Editor.

operations? Here is a question of a different sort, one the historian can tackle. And in this style Govan proceeds, setting himself the modest goal of indicating on which side of the issue the truth probably lies.

In the process he accomplishes a great deal that needed to be done. There are none of the broad statements and categorical judgments of a Cairnes or a Phillips, none of the gloomy speculations of a Ramsdell. In contrast, here for the first time in our survey we are shown actual plantation records, as well as data from the manuscript returns for the 1850 and 1860 censuses. We are given a brief but informative guide to the mazes of actuarial accounting, to the theory of profit, and to the differences between what an accountant, a businessman, and an economist mean by the word—as well as what a planter probably meant by it. We are shown how seemingly slight differences in definition and procedure could result in strikingly variant estimates of a plantation's profits. And, finally, we are given a sober appraisal of the findings, concluding with the judgment that, on balance, the evidence suggests that slave-labor plantations in the Old South did indeed make profits "in the ordinary business sense of the term."

All this is well and good. And it is hardly fair to fault a man for not doing something he never intended to do in the first place. It was no part of Govan's plan in this article to speculate upon whether or not specialization in the production of agricultural staples by slave labor represented a rational allocation of scarce resources in the South. Nor was it his intention to judge whether or not, in terms of the rate and direction of economic development in the South, the slave-cotton complex exercised a positive or a negative influence. Questions such as these could hardly have been approached, far less answered, without resort to precisely the kind of hypothetical theorizing that Govan wished to avoid.

Between the hypothetical and the real, the possible and the actual, there is, however, no clear boundary but only an uncertain margin. And we are sometimes reminded of this in disconcerting ways. What is the value of that kind of capital asset we call a slave? His current market price? No so, says the accountant; that figure fluctuates from day to day in response to all sorts of random influences, and it would be impossible for me on that basis to judge whether the operation was really profitable. Should we use his cost, then, less depreciation (or plus appreciation)? Better, if you know the proper rate of depreciation; at least this lets the accountant set a definite figure in his books. But what the slave is really worth (and here speaks the economist) is surely what he will produce for you, over and above the cost of maintaining him, as long as he is able to produce anything. There is, of course, one complication. What you need to know is the present value of that stream of net future earnings, and to find that out you have to know what one dollar "x" years from now is worth today. In other words, you need the proper interest rate.

The interest rate in this capital-valuation formula is the rate at which we discount the future, looking at it from the standpoint of the present. Economists, as well as anthropologists, have long recognized that individuals and cultures differ in their rate of time discount. For practical purposes economists usually assume that a good approximation to the figure we need is the current market rate of interest on securities of similar risk and maturity. This amounts to saying that, when we value a capital asset, we include in our calculation a figure representing what one dollar would earn if invested in comparable alternative uses.

Already the hypothetical "if" enters our discussion. But it rates more than just a toehold. When is it sensible to purchase a capital asset? Obviously, when its rate of return is equal to or greater than the rate of return on other possible investments of similar risk (assuming that you think it worth your while to invest at all and not keep your money in the form of cash). Involved here is a comparison between what your money would earn if invested in the particular form contemplated and what it would earn if invested in other possible ways. This is a comparison between hypothetical alternatives. And there is no way of avoiding such comparisons, since they are inescapably part of any decision involving the future.

One final step: When is a particular use of capital profitable? Let us set aside for the moment the professional conventions of the accountant and face the question squarely. A particular way of using capital is profitable when the rate of return realized from that use, compared to its cost, is not less than the rate which could be realized in alternative uses, compared to their costs. One could equally well say "economically rational" instead of "profitable", since the rule is just as applicable to economic systems that do not recognize the existence of profits as it is to our own. It is a rule for the sensible allocation of scarce resources among alternative uses. This is why it is the way an economist will always approach the problem, even if it makes him talk in ways which accountants and businessmen find unusual.

The question you should ask yourself is simply this: Is it possible to find out whether or not slavery was profitable merely by examining evidence on the uses to which slaves were in fact put and the money that was in fact made out of these uses? In an accounting or business sense, it certainly is, if we may leave aside for the moment all questions of the availability of evidence. But in an economic sense it probably is not, because the question an economist wants to ask is really not at all a question about how an entrepreneur kept his books and figured out his costs and revenues, but a question about resource allocation. Did the capital invested in slaves earn, in the late 1850s, a rate of return at least as great as it would have earned in alternative uses? If the answer is affirmative, then investment in slaves represented an economically rational use of scarce capital and was "profitable" in that sense. If negative, then the total volume of output would have been greater if the capital had been used in other ways, and its use in the form of slaves was in that sense "unprofitable."

This, however, was not the question that Thomas Govan set out to tackle. His point of view was that of the professional historian, concerned to appraise and weigh evidence and to judge where, on balance, the truth lay. From this point of view, a good historical question is one that can be answered from the available evidence. Govan's central question was of this sort: he asked himself whether the preponderance of historical evidence supported a belief that the operation of a slave-labor plantation was profitable as a business enterprise. The question is a limited one. It covers much less than all one might like to know about the economics of slavery. But it has the two great virtues of being precise and of being answerable.

THE DEBATE over the profitableness of slavery has been going on, in one form or another, for almost one hundred and fifty years.[1] It is, perhaps, too late for a definitive settlement of the question because of the destruction of so much of the evidence, but there can be an attempt at a reconciliation of the conflicting conclusions of the various students who have written about it.

The argument, too frequently, has been concerned with the question of whether or not slave labor was as profitable as free? Or, could a planter who made money with slaves have made more if he had employed free workers? These are interesting questions for speculation, but hardly more, because materials for a comparison do not exist. An experiment to test their truth or falsity probably could not have been made in the ante-bellum South where slavery appears

[1]Research on this article was made possible through grants from the Julius Rosenwald Fund and the Social Science Research Council.

to have been not so much an economic system as a social order to permit two unlike peoples to live together.[2] At least it does not seem to have been tried. Comparisons between free labor farms in the North and West and slave plantations of the South are of little value because of the widely varying climatic conditions, the nature of the crops, and other circumstances. Similarly profits of a plantation before and after emancipation could hardly be compared because of the vastly different conditions in the two periods.

But if the question is narrowed to the particular one of whether the planters of the Old South were making money from their operations, there is still no agreement to be found among the writers on southern agriculture. Ulrich B. Phillips concluded that by the close of the 1850's it was "fairly certain that no slaveholders but those few whose plantations lay in the most advantageous parts of the cotton and sugar districts and whose managerial ability was exceptionally great were earning anything beyond what would cover their maintenance and carrying charges."[3] Lewis C. Gray, expressly denying Phillips's conclusion, wrote, "Far from being a decrepit institution, the economic motives for the continuance of slavery from the standpoint of the employer were never so strong as in the years just preceding the Civil War."[4]

The same contradictions are to be found among ante-bellum observers. Solon Robinson, the noted agricultural reformer, published a report of his observations at the plantation of Colonel L. M. Williams of Society Hill, South Carolina. The profits of the plantation, according to this statement, were very low. But the editor of the Columbia *South Carolinian,* in complete disagreement, took the same figures and proved that the profits were very large.

Robinson, in his statement, valued the plantation's 4,200 acres (2,700 of which were in cultivation) at $63,000 or $15 per acre; 254 slaves at $88,900 or $350 each; and other assets including livestock, plantation tools, and equipment at $8,502; making a total of $160,402. Expenses amounted to $17,894.48 and included the

[2]E. Merton Coulter (ed.), Ulrich B. Phillips, *The Course of the South to Secession, An Interpretation* (New York, 1939), 152; Dwight L. Dumond, *Antislavery Origins of the Civil War in the United States* (Ann Arbor, 1939), 52; Clement Eaton, *Freedom of Thought in the Old South* (Durham, 1940), 174-75; Ralph H. Gabriel, *The Course of American Democratic Thought* (New York, 1940), 108-109.

[3]Ulrich B. Phillips, *American Negro Slavery* (New York, 1918), 391-92.

[4]Lewis C. Gray, *History of Agriculture in the Southern United States to 1860, 2* vols. (Washington, 1933), I, 476.

following: interest at 7 per cent on the investment in land, slaves, and livestock (but not on the investment in tools and equipment), totaling $11,103; taxes on slaves and land; medical care; wages of three overseers; average expenditures for iron, tools, and equipment (the equivalent of depreciation); shoes, hats, and clothing; molasses, tobacco, and salt; and freight, commission, and other costs of selling and shipping cotton. The plantation produced 331,136 pounds of cotton. Its income from other sources amounted to $2,430 so that the average cost of a pound of cotton was 4.07 cents. Had this cotton sold at 6 cents, Robinson concluded, the profits would have been $1,973.68, at 7 cents, $5,385.04, which was about what it brought, being a little more than 3 per cent.[5]

The editor of the *South Carolinian,* however, completely rejected Robinson's conclusions. First he protested against the uniform valuation of all land at $15 per acre when 1,500 acres were not in cultivation. The plantation did not need more than 750 acres of unimproved land for wood lot, grazing, etc., so that the remaining 750 acres were not, according to the writer, a legitimate part of the plantation. This reduced the real capital by $11,250 to $150,152. "But," continued the editor:

> the most glaring inconsistency which our agricultural tourist exhibits in calculating the profits of a business investment, is in adding the item of interest upon capital as expense. A person investing money in any enterprise is justly considered to be doing a fair business if he makes a small percentage over interest and expenses; and the statement which Mr. Robinson furnishes of Col. Williams's plantation, only proves that our fellow-citizen makes about 12½ per cent. on his capital, and too with the price of cotton placed as low as six cents *in Charleston*— for freight and commission are included in the table of "expenses."
>
> . . . we deny the principle of adding interest on capital, as part of the expenses, when the object is to find out the profits upon that capital. . . . Mr. Robinson calculates interest upon the cost of the stock of the plantation, which is obviously fallacious and deceptive,

[5]James D. B. De Bow, *The Industrial Resources, etc., of the Southern and Western States,* 3 vols., (New Orleans, 1853), I, 161-64; D. Lee, "Cotton," in *Report of the Commissioner of Patents for the Year, 1849,* Part II, *Agriculture* (Washington, 1850), 307-13; Ralph B. Flanders, *Plantation Slavery in Georgia* (Chapel Hill, 1933), 221-22. There are several errors of calculation in the various reprintings of Robinson's report which account for the discrepancies in the figures used by different writers quoted here and subsequently.

where its natural increase must amount to more than the interest. . . . He omits to add to the income of the plantation the natural increase of the labor employed thereon—an item which is always prominent in the planter's calculation, and which would unquestionably amount to 5 or 6 per cent. per annum upon their original cost. And . . . he has certainly neglected the increased value arising from the yearly improvement of a well cultivated plantation. . . . The result then, according to our views, will be as follows:

Capital invested, $150,152.00
Income of the farm

331,136 lbs. cotton, at 6 cents	$19,868.16
Bacon and other provisions	2,430.00
Increase of negroes, say 5 per cent., set down as capital $89,000	4,495.00
	26,793.16
The annual expenses of the farm, as itemized by Mr. Robinson, a full estimate, including freight and commission,	6,791.48
Net profit of capital invested	$20,001.68

These profits amount to over *thirteen per cent per annum* over all expenses—the *Charleston* price of cotton being only put down at 6 cents. Suppose the crop averaged eight cents in Charleston, as it would do at the present time, the profits would be $26,614.40, or nearly 18 per cent.[6]

Thus, two contemporary observers, using essentially the same figures, arrive at quite different results. One said profit for the year was only $1,973.68, while the other was equally certain that it was $20,001.68. Paradoxically, both were essentially correct, because each meant something different when he wrote of profit. "Perhaps no term or concept in economic discussion is used with a more bewildering variety of well established meanings than profit," Frank H. Knight, a modern economist, has stated.[7]

---

[6]De Bow, *Industrial Resources,* I, 163-64. Dr. D. Lee also questioned the validity of Robinson's calculations, saying: "The above estimates are defective and erroneous. . . . No allowance is made . . . for the increase in number and value of the slaves in the course of a year. If this is not equal to 7 per cent. on an average, it is to 3½ per cent., and sometimes reaches 8 or 10 per cent."

[7]Frank H. Knight, "Profit," in *Encyclopedia of the Social Sciences,* 15 vols. (New York, 1930-35), XII, 480-87.

Solon Robinson, probably following the definition of Jean-Baptiste Say,[8] the French nineteenth-century economist, apparently considered profit as mere wages of management. Almost all classical economists "recognized at least three elements in the income of the capitalist entrepreneur: one a payment for the bare use of the capital (equal to the interest rate); a second element representing payment for the entrepreneur's activities as manager; and a third connected in a rather vague way with the carrying of the risks or hazards of the enterprise." Most of them, however, continued to apply the term profit to the combination of the three elements of the proprietor's income. But Say insisted "on a separation between profit and interest and the treatment of profit as a species of wage."[9]

The editor of the *South Carolinian,* however, was not writing of economic profit. He was writing as an ordinary businessman or farmer according to the most generally accepted definition of profit, that of accounting. To him, the entire net income of the proprietor, after the deduction of all expenses, including depreciation and loss of value of assets, was profit.

Unfortunately, Robinson does not seem to have completely realized the meaning of his profit figure. He acted upon the definition of profit as wages of management, deducting interest upon investment as a cost of doing business, but he then assumed that there was a relation between the profit figure and the planter's investment. Actually there was no connection between the two. And when Robinson said that if the cotton were sold at seven cents, the profit would be $5,385.04, or about 3 per cent on the investment, he was merely saying that Colonel Williams' wages for managing the plantation were the equivalent of a 3 per cent return on his capital. The total income of Colonel Williams from the plantation during the year, by Robinson's statement, was $16,488.04, a 7 per cent return on his investment, or $11,103, plus $5,385.04, wages for management.

If this deduction or charge for "interest on investment" had been

[8]Jean-Baptiste Say apparently was widely read and very influential in the United States. His *A Treatise on Political Economy or the Production, Distribution, and Consumption of Wealth* was highly recommended by Thomas Jefferson, who edited the work for American publication in 1817. Five editions were printed and sold between 1817 and 1834, when the sixth edition was issued. Subsequently there was a new American edition in 1855. See Richard Hofstadter, "Parrington and the Jeffersonian Tradition," in *Journal of the History of Ideas* (New York, 1940-), II (1941), 396-97.

[9]Knight, "Profit," in *Encyclopaedia of the Social Sciences,* XII, 481.

called "profit on investment," which would be equally accurate, Robinson's statement would not have been so completely misinterpreted by one modern student, who, in his rewriting of it, said, "The *cash expenditures* totalled $17,879.48, and included the following: interest on capital at 7 per cent."[10] This interest, it must be repeated, was not an expenditure of the planter, but was part of his income.

Most of the modern historians who deny the profitableness of slavery seem to confuse profit, as defined by Say and those who follow him, with the ordinary conception of profit used by businessmen and farmers. None of these historians, so far as can be ascertained from their studies, have used the rather elaborate statistics in the census of 1850 and 1860; or, at least, they have made no attempt to reconcile the conflict between their low estimates of profit from plantation operation and the overwhelming indication of a large increase of wealth in the South between 1850 and 1860.

Selected figures[11] for thirteen of the slave states, excluding rather arbitrarily Missouri and Delaware, show this increase very clearly:

	1850	1860
Number of farms	508,680	665,417
Total improved acres in farms	51,451,040	67,478,629
Average improved acres in farms	101.15	101.41
Total unimproved acres in farms	118,612,338	156,996,549
Average unimproved acres per farm	233.32	235.94
Average size of farms	334.47	337.35
Total cash value of farms	$1,035,544,075.	$2,288,179,125.
Average cash value of farms	$2,035.75	$3,438.71
True value of real and personal property	$2,809.875,462.	$6,245,129,163.
True value of real and personal property per capita—whites and free Negroes	$490.49	$878.08
Total number of slaveholders	326,054	358,728
Total number of slaves	3,110,652	3,833,782
Average number of slaves per slaveholder	9.54	10.69

[10]Flanders, *Plantation Slavery in Georgia,* 221. Italics mine.

[11]Compiled from: James D. B. De Bow, *Statistical View of the United States . . .- Being a Compendium of the Seventh Census* (Washington, 1854), 82, 95, 169; *The Seventh Census of the United States, 1850* (Washington, 1853), xxxiii; *The Eighth Census of the United States, 1860,* 4 vols. (Washington, 1864-1866), II, *Agriculture* (1864), vii, 222, 247-48; Joseph C. D. Kennedy, *Preliminary Report on the Eighth Census, 1860* (Washington, 1862), 195.

Many objections to these figures can be raised. They were collected by the marshals of the various districts and many of them may be inaccurate. Some of these figures lump slaveholders and nonslaveholders together, while others combine rural and urban wealth without distinction. Nevertheless, they are the most complete and accurate now available. Fortunately, however, the manuscript returns of individuals for 1850 and 1860 have in many instances been preserved. From these Dr. Herbert Weaver has studied the individual fortunes of five hundred persons engaged in agriculture in Jefferson and Jones counties, Mississippi. Two hundred and three of these men were nonslaveholders, and the remainder slaveholders, in 1850. In reporting the results of his investigation, he stated:

> The only items checked were number of slaves, amount of improved and unimproved land owned, and the value of farms. By thus tracing individuals through a ten year period, the great prosperity enjoyed by all groups was established beyond all doubt. In practically every case there was an increase in every column. Slaveholdings, if they were slaveholders, showed a decided upward trend, and numerous nonslaveholders were found to own slaves in 1860. . . . Landholding increased . . . , but . . . it seems that the value of the land increased more than the acreage. A part of this was certainly due to a general increase in valuation of land, but the increase was too great to be attributed entirely to that fact. A great part of the increase in value represented increased acreage and improvements. Landholdings increased by about fifty per cent throughout the state, but the value of farms increased more than three fold.[12]

These figures from the census reports and the manuscript returns do not prove that slavery on southern plantations was profitable in its last decade but they do indicate this conclusion strongly enough to place the burden of proof upon those who deny that planters were making profits. Ulrich B. Phillips did not present any direct evidence on this problem but merely stated his own belief that slavery probably was not profitable in the late 1850's. He did not bear this out by citing figures based upon the actual experience of plantation owners, or upon contemporary estimates in newspapers or periodicals. Apparently his principal interest was not in the profits of the plan-

---

[12]Herbert Weaver, "The Agricultural Population of Mississippi, 1850-1860" (Ph.D. dissertation, Vanderbilt University, 1941), 121-25.

tation owner but in comparing the cost of slave and free labor.[13]

The most complete and comprehensive attempt to estimate the profits of plantation slavery is to be found in *Slavery in Mississippi* (1933) by Charles S. Sydnor. In this he has prepared a profit and loss statement, based on average figures from a large number of plantations, which indicates a very small rate of return for plantation owners and advances Professor Sydnor's doubt of the profitableness of slavery. This statement, however, is open to so many objections and questions that a detailed and critical analysis seems appropriate. In his statement, Professor Sydnor said:

The chief source of income would be from cotton. Probably thirty of the fifty negroes worked in the field. If those produced $5\frac{3}{4}$ bales each, there would be a total of 158 bales which, at ten cents a pound, would be worth $6,320.00

The expenses of the plantation would be as follows: 50 negroes at $600 each (in the late 'fifties the price was higher) represented an investment of $30,000. Calculating interest at 6 per cent, this amounted to $1,800.00

At least an equal amount should be added for depreciation in slave property by accidents, deaths, old age, etc. 1,800.00

As the average hand worked about twelve acres, 600 acres would be ample for pastures and woodland as well as fields. Allowing $10 per acre, the investment in land at 6 per cent interest involved a yearly carriage charge of 360.00

and it ordinarily depreciated at the rate of at least three per cent a year in value 180.00

Annual hire of an overseer, at least 300.00

Purchases from New Orleans or elsewhere of negro clothing, miscellaneous plantation supplies, etc. 1,000.00

Without including various miscellaneous expenditures, such as the purchase of corn and pork, of which few plantations produced enough, the total of the expenses and interest charges was $5,440.00

Profit of the planter . . . . 880.00[14]

---

[13]Phillips, *American Negro Slavery*, 344-401; *id.*, "The Economic Cost of Slaveholding," in *Political Science Quarterly* (New York, 1886-), XX (1905), 257-75.

[14]Charles S. Sydnor, *Slavery in Mississippi* (New York, 1933), 195-202. The income figure was not printed in the statement.

From these figures Louis Hacker, in the *Triumph of American Capitalism* (1940), drew the conclusion that the hypothetical planter made only 2 per cent on his invested capital. By the same reasoning a man who lent money at 5 per cent would show a loss of 1 per cent because of the deduction of 6 per cent interest on investment.

Professor Sydnor, himself, understood that "interest on investment" was not an actual expense of the planter, because, as he said, the planter "was, of course, free to spend the interest on his investment in negroes and land, and this was the item that caused the profits from Mississippi plantations to appear high." He also stated that "the $880 might be considered the wages of the planter for managing the enterprise,"[15] but he never recognized that, according to many economists and the generally accepted definition of accountants and businessmen, profit is a combination of this interest on investment and wages for management.

Other objections must be made to the statement. In the chapter "Profitableness of Slavery," Professor Sydnor wrote, "Cotton, however, was not the only source of profit. A planter who barely made expenses by the sale of cotton might find his estate yearly increasing in value by the rearing of young negroes."[16] This certainly seems true because there was a steady natural increase in the slave population during the entire ante-bellum period. In addition, the price of slaves tended generally upward except in years of financial crisis. Nevertheless, in his own estimate of plantation income, Professor Sydnor did' not take this increase in value into account. Instead he deducted, as an expense, $1,800 "for depreciation in slave property by accidents, deaths, old age, etc." It hardly seems correct to consider a working force which not only reproduced itself but increased in number, skill, and price, as a source of expense to the planter.

Similarly the expense figure of depreciation of land seems difficult to justify. At 3 per cent a year the land would be almost valueless after thirty-three years. But Mississippi land is still growing cotton. Unquestionably almost every crop takes something out of the land. But with equal certainty it can be said that the yearly work of the slaves, preparing the soil, ditching the fields, and clearing additional acres, aided fertility and increased value. This sometimes necessitated a cash expenditure for fertilizer or equip-

[15]*Ibid.,* 197.
[16]*Ibid.,* 198

ment, which would be a just charge to plantation expense; but it seems impossible now, with our limited and inadequate knowledge, to be certain whether there was a net gain or loss in value of land from the yearly plantation activity.

Professor Sydnor's estimate of the value of the planter's investment in land and slaves may also be questioned, because he seems to have assumed that the value of an asset is its market value at the particular moment.[17] Prices, however, are the result of so many complex and unascertainable factors that they rarely can be taken as the equivalent of actual value. It is only under ideal circumstances that classical economists accept price as equal to value, and most other economists look on price as one of the evidences of value, not its exact expression.

Neither can the accountant accept this, because it would mean that assets fluctuate in value annually, which would introduce into the profit and loss statement a variable figure unrelated to the activities of the particular enterprise. A profit or loss (the equivalent of an increase or decrease in value of an asset) is usually not considered by an accountant until it has been realized. Prices rise and fall for various reasons, and if these "paper" profits or losses from the unrealized increase or decrease of the market price of an asset were accepted as real, the actual profit or loss from operations during the accounting period would be obscured. For this reason an accountant usually values an asset at its cost, less depreciation, and not at its current market price.

Most of the land and slaves in the South did not change hands after 1849 and consequently the market price in the 1850's had little or nothing to do with their cost. Certainly a majority of the slaves had been reared by their owners, and their capital value as an asset was the cost of their rearing. There is no exact statistical information concerning the cost of rearing the slave, but it hardly could

---

[17]In another place Professor Sydnor says, "Since a fall in price of two dollars a slave would cause a drop of nearly a million dollars in the capital value of the slaves in the State, the profitableness of the institution depended largely on the price of slaves." This statement would not be accepted by an economist or an accountant, unless the owner was in the business of rearing slaves for sale, which few planters were; but, regardless of that, it has not even been considered by Professor Sydnor himself. If a fall in the price of slaves would result in a loss to the planter, then, in logic at least, an increase in price would give a profit to the planter. The price of slaves, according to Phillips, increased almost every year in the 1850's, but this profit, by Dr. Sydnor's own definition, is not included in the statement of plantation income. *Ibid.,* 201.

have amounted to Professor Sydnor's figure of $600, which was based on market price in the early 1850's. This arbitrary capitalization of all slaves at the current market price introduces another element of uncertainty into the statement—again because of the deduction of "interest on investment." For if investment increases each year, with the rise in the price of slaves, the deduction from profit of "interest on investment" is also larger. Consequently the planter shows a decrease instead of an increase in profit from the raised capital value of his assets.

This "interest on investment," some economists say, is a cost of doing business, to others it is a part of profit; and there is also disagreement about how it is to be figured and what rate is to be charged. Some define it as the current rate of return. If it is, no entrepreneur, according to theory, could be expected to make more without attracting competitive capital into the same enterprise. It is also a virtually impossible task to ascertain the current rate of return during this period. Others say it is the current rate of interest on borrowed money. But this figure fluctuated widely with various individuals and sections of the South, and the information upon which to base an average is lacking. Still others insist that it is the so-called "pure" interest rate, the one yielded by the safest investment, but this would be more difficult to ascertain than either of the others. Phillips recommended that such a charge be made in figuring the cost of slave labor, but he made no estimate as to what the rate should be. Sydnor who used 6 per cent and Robinson who used 7 per cent are alike in that they gave no reasons for their respective choices.

This difficulty in arriving at a satisfactory figure is one of the reasons why the financial accountant makes no use of interest on investment.[18] Another is the technical impossibility of handling a

---

[18]There is a serious debate among cost accountants as to whether interest on investment has a proper place in that limited and specialized field of accounting. Some argue, as does Ulrich B. Phillips in his analysis of the cost of slave labor, "that the provision of capital is a necessary expense of a business just as is rent, insurance, or wages, and that it should be treated in the same manner as these expenses." But the majority seem to believe that the return on capital is not an expense but a profit, and the business world is accustomed so to consider it. As a result, to treat interest on investment as a cost of operation would produce financial statements which are misleading. William B. Lawrence, *Cost Accounting* (New York, 1925), 312-13; Roy B. Kester, *Advanced Accounting* (New York, 1933), 515-17; Phillips, "Economic Cost of Slaveholding," in *loc. cit.,* 268-69. Some cost accountants insist that interest on investment should be included "in order to determine what would be a fair profit in

deduction from profit that is neither an expenditure nor the decrease in value of an asset. But the chief argument against its use, is that it gives no information. It is merely the separation of the proprietor's income into two parts, interest upon investment, and profit above that interest. This is of little or no importance to the owner or the accountant, and of interest only to the economist who, in reality, is forced to guess as to the proper apportionment between the two.

If these objections to Professor Sydnor's statement are valid, the hypothetical planter seems to be somewhat better off. The results from his operations would be something like this:

Income from Cotton		$6,320.00
Expenses:		
Annual hire of overseer	$ 300.00	
Plantation supplies	1,000.00	1,300.00
Gross profit		5,020.00

This is the total of the money income and expenditure, though it was stated that no provision had been made for "miscellaneous expenditures such as the purchase of corn and pork, of which few plantations produced enough," and no consideration has been given to the various selling and transportation charges such as freight, insurance, packing costs, and factor's commissions.

It is not, however, a complete statement of the financial condition of the plantation, but it is almost all that can be known with any certainty. If the increase or decrease in value of assets is taken into consideration, so many approximations have to be used that the resulting figures are virtually without meaning. Each acre of land would have to be valued separately; its original cost ascertained; the loss of fertility from the year's crop, the increase in fertility from the year's work, and expenditures for fertilizer and equipment, would have to be balanced against each other; and the resulting figure be

---

a given case," or "to determine whether it is better to manufacture or to buy goods in the open market, and whether it is better policy to manufacture by means of expensive machinery and other equipment or by manual labor." But even these suggest a technical arrangement whereby interest on investment is charged as a manufacturing expense to get manufacturing cost, but is then removed from the books before the net profit is arrived at, so that interest on investment is not shown in the financial statement at all. Jerome Lee Nicholson and John F. D. Rohrback, *Cost Accounting* (New York, 1919), 139-40; Kester, *Advanced Accounting,* 140.

shown as income or expense, as the case might be. Obviously this could not be done with any degree of accuracy. Each slave would then have to be valued on the basis of his cost—the cost of rearing him to work age if born on the plantation, or his original purchase price—his physical condition, age, experience, and special training; and a balance struck as to his increase or decrease in value during the particular year. The totals of these increases or decreases in value would have to be added to or taken away from another figure which would show the net gain or loss from births and deaths of slaves. Only in this way could an accurate figure for a particular plantation be ascertained.

Most of this, however, is hypothetical, and cannot be ascertained from surviving records. It was seldom taken into consideration by the planters themselves who usually were content with the simplest records and figured profits or losses on the basis of cash income and expenditure. They, like the modern accountant, businessman, and farmer, considered their entire net income as profit, and made no attempt to divide it, according to classical theory, into interest on investment, wages of management, and compensation for risk.

If attention is turned to the actual results of plantation operations as they are to be found in some surviving account books and papers, and in reports of contemporary newspapers and periodicals, no consistent pattern of profits is to be found. Cotton, rice, and tobacco, the staples of the South, were such speculative crops that there were wide variations in profit from plantation to plantation, and from year to year. For instance, in 1846-1847 on an Alabama plantation owned jointly by Mrs. R. Brown and Franklin H. Elmore, working 108 slaves and having an estimated value of $70,000, the profits from the sale of 199 bales of cotton were $7,352.40, or 10.5 per cent, with no direct superintendence by either of the proprietors.[19] On the other hand, Farish Carter, one of the most successful Georgia planters, in 1851 made profits of $1,530 on a plantation valued at $150,000. This was a return of only 1 1/4 per cent on his investment.[20] In neither of these statements was credit taken or deduction made for the increase or decrease in value of slaves, the depreciation or appreciation of land, or any other intangible item.

[19]Gilmer & Company, Montgomery, to Franklin H. Elmore, Charleston, March 18, 1847, in Franklin H. Elmore MSS. (Division of Manuscripts, Library of Congress).
[20]Flanders, *Plantation Slavery in Georgia,* 222-23.

Published estimates of the cost of growing cotton and of profits of plantations must be accepted with caution, particularly in the late 1840's and 1850's. During these years the merchants of Liverpool and the manufacturers of Manchester were protesting against the American monopoly of cotton production. The Cotton Supply Association was organized in Manchester with the openly avowed purpose of breaking the American domination of cotton supply by encouraging its growth in the colonies of the empire. Southern cotton growers and merchants, frightened by the possibility of increased competition, attempted to prove that the price of cotton was too low rather than too high, and that the profits from cotton planting had been grossly overstated.

One of these, who acknowledged his purpose, estimated that the gross profits from raising cotton on a well-equipped plantation with 100 slaves and valued at $100,000 would amount only to $1,750 with cotton selling at five cents a pound. But this, according to the writer, did not include anything "for the support of the planter . . . nor . . . to meet those contingent and incidental losses and costs . . . as the loss of servants from epidemics, the loss of *whole teams* from diseases, the frequent accidents to gins and houses from fire, losses from overflows, breaking of levees, &c."[21] Another, writing in the *Soil of the South,* also said that the profits of cotton planting were overestimated, but was forced to admit that "there are more fortunes made at planting than at any other business." His explanation of the paradox was that it was "attributable not to the supposed fact that there is more money made at the business than any other, but because planters are, as a class, more economical, and live more at home than any other." He estimated that the average cost of raising 2,000 pounds of ginned cotton was $160.16, or slightly over 8 cents a pound, but included, as part of cost, 7 per cent profit on the investment in slaves, land, and mules, or $105.76.[22]

One of the longest and most detailed records of a plantation which has been preserved is that of Hopeton on the Altamaha River in Glynn County, Georgia. This plantation was established before the War of 1812 by John Couper, a Scotsman, and remained in his possession until January 1, 1827. In a letter summarizing the results under his ownership, he said:

[21]De Bow, *Industrial Resources,* I, 150-52.
[22]"The Cost of a pound of Cotton," in *De Bow's Review* (New Orleans, 1846-1880), XVIII (1855), 468-70.

You know I commenced planting without capital. Of course had to go in debt and 8 per cent compound interest I found to be the real perpetual motion. Though tolerable successful sometimes, yet I had sad reverses—Embargo, non-intercourse & War—interfered with my prospects, whilst interest progressed—My loss of 60 prime effective negroes—carried off by the Enemy—lessened my annual income full $15,000—to supply their places *in part* I bt. 120 slaves for which I paid an average of 450$. Crops were not favorable. In the year 1824—I had *matured* a crop of 600 Bales cotton—which would have produced $90,000—This was lost in 12 hours by hurricane. In 1825 I again nearly lost my crop by caterpillar. Cotton then sunk in price, without any prospect of improvement. Lands were reduced to $^1/_3$ of their value. Slaves to 250 or 200. In short I saw no hope of paying my debts and retaining my property—& tho not pushed—I thought best during my life to meet the storm. So to make a long story short—Mr. Hamilton being my principal creditor—on his agreeing to pay what other debts I owed—I surrendered to him all my property, debt, and dues of every description in a lump without valuation—except my lands on St. Simons and one hundred slaves—So on the 1st day of January 1827 I was thrown on the world without a dollar to support my people and family—Am glad to get off so well. Even though at a reasonable valuation the property I surrendered, was more than sufficient to pay my debts, yet had it been brought to a forced sale, it might have done less. I am satisfied and relieved from much anxiety. By this event neither my standing in society—nor my mode of living have suffered any change.[23]

This reads as a confession of failure, but though John Couper suffered many grievous misfortunes, he had, by his own statement, begun planting without capital, and ended, after paying all his debts, with a plantation and 100 slaves, worth from fifty to a hundred thousand dollars. He had also, with a large family, lived in luxurious surroundings during most of the period, which is certainly no slight return from a lifetime devoted to planting.

John Couper had turned Hopeton over to his principal creditor, James Hamilton, a Scots merchant, and Hamilton in turn sold half of the plantation and 380 slaves to James H. Couper, son of John, for $137,000 to be paid over a period of fifteen years at 6 per cent interest. Couper was to have the entire management for which he

[23]John Couper, St. Simon's, to James Couper, Scotland, May 24, 1828, in John Couper MSS. (Southern Collection, University of North Carolina).

was to receive $2,000 per year, the run of the plantation, and half the profits.[24] This arrangement continued until January 1, 1841, when Couper, to clear himself of debt, turned back his interest in the plantation to the Hamilton estate. After this, until 1852, Couper continued to manage the plantation for the estate. During the entire period of his management of the plantation from 1827 to 1852, he kept elaborate records of all phases of plantation operations including detailed financial information concerning receipts and expenditures.[25]

From these records it is possible to establish year by year the cost value of the investment in the plantation, the gross and net sales, expenditures, and net profit. As the rate of profit varied widely from year to year it has seemed clearer to present the results in tabular form.

Year	Capital	Gross Sales	Net Sales	Expenses	Profit	Rate of Profit
1827	$274,000.00	ns	$4,367.19$\frac{1}{2}$	$12,239.56$\frac{1}{4}$	$7,871.76$\frac{3}{4}$[26]	
1828	294,895.22	ns	15,043.50	6,924.93	8,118.57	2.7%
1829	298,014.40	ns	11,707.08	9,021.95	2,685.13	.9
1830	298,014.40	ns	15,235.55	12,730.26	2,505.29	.8
1831	298,046.40	ns	22,482.34	16,949.10	5,533.24	1.85
1832	300,126.65	ns	17,030.23	10,910.86	6,119.37	2
1833	302,617.07	ns	22,016.37	10,937.07	11,079.30	3.6
1834	302,617.07	ns	20,609.24	9,918.72	10,690.52	3.5
1835	302,617.07	ns	26,897.48	11,857.64	15,039.84	4.9
1836	302,617.07	ns	31.977.27	8,452.16	23,525.11	7.7
1837	302,617.07	ns	45,970.72	9,868.87	36,101.85	11.9[27]
1838	302,617.07	ns	35.889.13	12,939.44	22,949.69	7.2
1839	302,617.07	$38,484.06	36,199.90	10,022.71	26,177.19	8
1840	302,617.07	26,476.34	24,228.01	11,276.11	12,951.90	4.2

The profits during these years were not large except in the years when the income from crops was supplemented by the hire of slaves to work on the Brunswick Canal. But the figures alone do not give the complete story.

[24]*Ibid.*
[25]Hopeton Plantation Records (Southern Collection, University of North Carolina).
[26]Deficit.
[27]In the three years 1837-1839, inclusive, the income of the plantation was increased by hire of slaves to the contractors building the Brunswick Canal: 1837, $19,208.51; 1838, $15,010.75; 1839, $7,250.49.

As soon as James Couper took over the management of the plantation he began an experiment in sugar raising which turned out unsuccessfully. This not only caused an expenditure of $22,443.82 for machinery in the first six years but also diverted a part of the labor force from other crops. This was not a foolish or reckless experiment, because sugar planters, under not unsimilar conditions in Louisiana, were making great fortunes, but it, apparently, was chiefly responsible for the low profits in the first few years.

As the plantation was turned back to the established crops, rice and sea-island cotton, the rate of profit began to increase to a more satisfactory figure. The statement of plantation expenses also appears to contain a substantial amount—the exact figure cannot be ascertained—for the personal and household expenses of Couper and his family.[28] It is to be remembered that as part of his compensation for management he had the use of house servants, horses, and boats, as well as produce for his table from his plantation. This was no inconsiderable item if the report of Sir Charles Lyell was correct. He visited the plantation in 1845 when conditions were probably the same as between 1827 and 1840. He described the separate villa maintained for Couper and his family on nearby St. Simon's Island, the library containing "Audubon's Birds, Michaud's Forest Trees, and other costly works on natural history," and then added:

> Much has been said in praise of the hospitality of the southern planter, but they alone who have traveled in the southern states can appreciate the perfect ease and politeness with which a stranger is made to feel himself at home. Horses, carriages, boats, servants, are all at his disposal. Even his little comforts are thought of, and everything is done as heartily and naturally as if no obligations were conferred. . . .
>
> The landed proprietors here visit each other in the style of English country gentlemen, sometimes dining out with their families and returning at night, or, if the distance be great, remaining to sleep and coming home the next morning. A considerable part of their food is derived from the produce of the land; but, as the houses are usually distant from large towns, they keep large stores of groceries and of

[28]Hopeton Plantation Records. Couper seems to have kept exact records of his income and expenditures, but his financial statements have not been preserved. In some instances it has been difficult to decide whether a given item should be charged as an expense or considered an increase of capital. It is not believed, however, that there were enough of these to affect the figures given above in any substantial way.

clothing, as is the custom in country houses in some parts of Scotland.[29]

These were real profits and must be considered, even if it is not possible to set a figure for them. At the same time the plantation was increasing, not decreasing, in value. No charge for depreciation on lands, or slaves, or other capital assets, was placed on Couper's books. He had not even written off as loss the cost of the unsuccessful experiment in sugar, but there was no need to. The year by year increase in value of the plantation more than offset these losses.

When Couper turned back his half interest in the plantation to the Hamilton estate on January 1, 1841, three commissioners were appointed by the Superior Court of Glynn County. These commissioners estimated the value of the plantation to be $381,425, or an increase over original cost and additional investment of $78,807.93. This represented a net gain in value of 26 per cent in fourteen years. This estimate, apparently, was too high for Couper and the trustees of the estate, and the actual transfer of title was made at a book value of $342,481.88. The increase in value was $39,864.81, or 13 per cent.[30]

During the twelve years from 1840 to 1852 the plantation was owned by the Hamilton estate but managed by Couper, at a salary of $5,000 a year for ten years and $6,000 a year for two. The same arrangement in regard to household expenses that had been true during the first period appears also to have been in effect during the second and must be remembered in connection with the actual figures of profits. The 1840's were probably the worst decade, economically, in the agricultural history of the ante-bellum South, but the results of Couper's management, after deduction of his and the overseers' salaries were as follows:

Year	Capital	Gross Sales	Net Sales	Expenses	Profit	Rate of Profit
1841	$347,481.88	$30,470.58	$27,974.83	$16,821.98	$11,152.85	3.2%
1842	344,681.88	18,905.86	17,232.27	15,752.97	1,479.30	.43
1843	344,681.88	23,392.47	20,770.26	13,240.05	7,530.21	2.2
1844	344,181.88	30,411.03	27,699.58	17,259.71	10,439.87	3
1845	344,181.88	26,370.14	24.436.28	13,120.11	11,316.17	3.3

[29]Sir Charles Lyell, *A Second Visit to the United States of North America,* 2 vols. (New York, 1849), I, 244-46, 253, 254-55.

[30]Hopeton Plantation Records.

Year	Capital	Gross Sales	Net Sales	Expenses	Profit	Rate of Profit
1846	344,181.88	41,161.97	37,602.85	13,685.68	23,917.17	6.9
1847	343,617.56	29,893.75	27,335.05	14,914.55	12,420.50	3.6
1848	343,617.56	30,807.12	27,810.52	16,397.00	11,413.52	3.3
1849	340.017.56	36,988.17	33,280.75	15,341.87	17,938.88	5.3
1850	342,017.56	35,795.48	32,571.73	16,583.30	15,988.43	4.7
1851	349,474.60	29,587.54	26,603.62	17,627.43	8,976.19	2.6
1852	349,474.60	39,761.40	35.268.04	17,938.93	17,329.11	5[31]

The changes in capital from year to year were the result principally of purchases and sales of land and slaves. Land to the value of $8,789.58 was purchased, while $2,057.56 was received from sales of land, during the twenty-six years. In the same period seven additional slaves were bought and twenty sold. The land evidently had increased in fertility because the crops were larger and produced more income in the later years than in the earlier. The slave record for the plantation has not been located. But Sir Charles Lyell gave indirect evidence of an increase in the number of slaves when he wrote that in 1845 there were 500 at Hopeton, or an increase of 120 from the original 380.[32]

Another plantation for which an extensive record has been preserved is Gowrie, owned by Louis Manigault and located on the Savannah River. The sole money crop was rice. The original value of the plantation was $40,000, and on it were 220 acres of cleared ground, 80 acres uncleared, a fine rice mill, and 50 slaves. The plantation was gradually increased in size until finally it had 638 acres in cultivation, and from time to time additional slaves were purchased. The average value of the plantation during the first six years was approximately $42,115. Net proceeds of the crops of these years were $43,750, total expenses were $12,000, which made the average profit $5,095 a year or 12 per cent on the investment.[33]

There is a gap of sixteen years in the records; then for six years there is a detailed account of all receipts and expenditures. Manigault's investment, through the purchase of additional land and slaves, had increased to approximately $80,000 by 1857. The gross

[31]*Ibid.*

[32]Lyell, *Second Visit*, I, 261-62.

[33]Statement of Louis Manigault, no date, pasted on flyleaf of "Statement of Sales—Gowrie Plantation—Savannah River," in Manigault Plantation Records (Southern Collection, University of North Carolina).

sales of rice for the six years from 1855 to 1861 were $103,739.55. Selling costs for the same period were $22,964.73, making net sales $80,774.82. Plantation expenses totaled $22,135.84, leaving as total net profits for six years, $58,638.98, or an average annual profit of $9,766.49. This amounted to a 12.2 per cent return upon the capital invested in the plantation.[34] The profits from Gowrie were much higher than those from Hopeton. This may be accounted for in part by the difference in the years which the records cover, but probably more because Manigault did not make his home on the plantation, and no household expenses are included in the statement of plantation expenditures. It is certain, however, that Manigault did not consider these last six years to be extraordinarily successful ones. On the contrary he believed them to be particularly difficult.

The plantation had suffered epidemics of cholera in 1852 and 1854 in which twenty slaves, including "many of our *very best* hands," had died. There had been a destructive freshet in 1852, and a hurricane on September 8, 1854, both of which not only injured the standing crops but also strewed the entire plantation with loose rice "to the vast injury" of succeeding crops. Manigault's experienced overseer died in December, 1855, and it was not until April 8, 1859, that another capable man was employed. The overseers in the interim neglected the plantation and the slaves, and it took a year for the new overseer to repair injuries done by his predecessors.

This was satisfactory to the owner, who, in writing his report of operations during 1859-1860, said:

> Mr. Capers has not made a large crop but he says it was much on a/c of the bad condition in which he found the plantation, & I believe him, I am satisfied thus far with him, feeling that he has had no chance. We have bought two new Mules this winter, working in all six mules. During the past winter Mr. Capers has done much work. He has cut a new Canal through two squares, on the upper portion of the plantation, which I think will be of service. We have for the first time used the double horse ploughs, turning the lands much deeper than previously.

In spite of all these difficulties and neglect the land evidently had not deteriorated. The average production for the six years from 1833 to 1838 was 374 barrels of clean rice, while during the six years from 1855 to 1861 the crop averaged 843 barrels. There was,

---

[34]Manigault Plantation Records.

as said above, an increase in acreage devoted to rice from 220 to 638, or 190 per cent, but there was also an increase in production from a low of 220 barrels in 1833 to a high of 995 barrels in 1856, or 397 per cent.[35]

The plantation lost thirty-eight slaves in three cholera epidemics in 1834, 1852, and 1854, which forced Manigault to purchase forty-six slaves, between 1833 and 1861, in addition to the original fifty. This makes a total of ninety-six slaves brought to or purchased for the plantation; but there still were ninety-seven slaves on the plantation in 1857, the last year in which there is a record of the number of slaves. Consequently, it is not correct to charge any of this additional investment in slaves to expense. All that happened was that the natural increase in number and value was wiped out by the epidemics and the plantation neither made nor lost money on its working force.[36]

A third plantation for which there is record of capital, expense, and profits, is that of James H. Hammond of South Carolina, also on the Savannah River. Early in the 1850's Hammond offered his plantation, which he valued at $163,750, for sale. The plantation according to this offer consisted of the following:

1. 150 Negroes who shall constitute 80 task or effective hands and only 2 to 3 non-effective $80,000.00
2. 6300 acres . . . excluding . . . the Silverton Residence & tract of 280 acres & on the other side the Marsh & 1000 or 1500 acres as it may be, but including about 3000 acres of cleared land in good order—650 of it drained land—all except about 100 acres well marled, with mills, landing, etc. @ $12 per acre   75,600.00
3. 6000 bushels corn—60,000 pds. fodder   3,500.00
4. 30 mules & horse under 12 years mostly under 9 years   3,000.00
5. 5 fair Plantation Waggons. 3 ox carts. 4 Horse carts. 30 sets of gears. 60 ploughs, etc.   1,000.00
6. 100 head of hogs @ 1.50 & 40 head Cattle all ½ to Ayreshire with full blood bull and 10 oxen @ 10.00   650.00

          $163,750.00[37]

The detailed records of income and expenditure on Hammond's

[35] *Ibid.*

[36] *Ibid.*

[37] Memorandum initialed J. H. H., no date, but probably 1852, in James H. Hammond MSS. (Division of Manuscripts, Library of Congress).

plantation do not appear to have been preserved but there is a memorandum in his papers which gives exact information for the five-year period from 1849 to 1853. During these years the total income from the sale of cotton, corn, rice, and fodder was $81,088.83. Plantation expenses amounted to $27,019.37, leaving a profit of $54,069.46, or an average annual profit of $10,813.89. Accepting his offer of sale as the total value of his investment, though its original cost to him probably was much less, Hammond had an average net annual return of 6.66 per cent.[38]

Unlike most planters, Hammond kept a separate record of his family expenses apart from the plantation records. In the same five years these expenses amounted to $31,913.55, which, if deducted from profits, gives him an annual net income over all expenses, business and personal, of $4,431.18, or 2.7 per cent.[39]

There seems to be no more justification for a depreciation charge against land or slaves on this plantation than there was at Gowrie or Hopeton, because, at least in Hammond's opinion, the plantation was gaining, not losing value. In 1859 he again wrote out an offer of sale, but this time he asked $175,000 and included only 140 Negroes comprising 70 full hands, 5,500 acres of land, fewer horses, mules, cattle, and pigs, and less corn and fodder.[40]

The records of these three plantations have been presented, not because they are considered to be typical of the plantation system, but merely because, through accident, they have been preserved in more detail than most others. Each was larger than the average plantation in the South, and all three were located in the older part of the South, where, incidentally, by common report, profits were lower than in the newer districts. They do indicate, however, that year after year, during periods of financial crisis or prosperity, some plantations were making profits in the ordinary business sense of the term, and were increasing, not decreasing in value.

The evidence from these plantations, together with the overwhelming evidence of increase in wealth found in the census reports and in Herbert Weaver's study of the individual returns in two counties of Mississippi, all seem to point in a single direction. And that is to the tentative conclusion that the students who have stated that slavery was profitable are more nearly correct than those who deny its profitableness.

[38]Undated, unsigned memorandum in Hammond's writing, *ibid.*
[39]*Ibid.*
[40]Offer of Sale, July 19, 1859, *ibid.*

ALFRED H. CONRAD and JOHN R. MEYER
The Economics of Slavery in the Antebellum South

Economic history as a recognized academic discipline is not yet one hundred years old and in its brief life span it has experienced few revolutions. Indeed, for most of the time there has not been much of an orthodoxy to revolt against. During the past two decades, however, there has been a sense of excitement and movement in the profession. This has been associated mostly with the rise of what has come to be called the "new" economic history. Some of the identifying characteristics of this approach are reliance wherever possible on quantitative evidence, the use of economic theory to generate hypotheses, and the use of econometric techniques to test the fit of hypotheses to data. Pioneering in the development of these methods has been a highly creative group of young economic historians, most of them trained primarily as economists in the graduate school curricula of the 1950s and 1960s. In a sense, indeed, this revolution in economic history, if it deserves the term, is a spillover effect from the more basic revolution in economics itself that is associated with the rise of econometrics in the mid-1950s.

It is to be expected that when new tools come to hand, curious people will want to find out what they can do with them. Many of the early examples of the new economic history show precisely this interest in the potentials of technique. The problems tackled were not at first novel; neither were many of the findings. A not uncommon reaction among economic historians of the older school was a mild puzzlement that anyone should go to so much trouble to prove what was already known. But this was to miss the point. The interest was less in what was demonstrated than in the method of demonstration.

The selection which follows, the well-known article on the economics of slavery by Alfred Conrad and John Meyer, is an early (though by no means the first) example of the new economic history. Written when both authors were junior faculty members at Harvard, it should be read, to be fully appreciated, in conjunction with their essay on methodology, published at roughly the same time under the title, "Economic Theory, Statistical Inference, and Economic History." This latter article presents explicitly the logical and philosophical framework which is left largely implicit in the analysis of slavery. Enough is said in the first few pages of the slavery article, however, to leave little room for doubt as to where the authors' primary interests lay. Indeed they state quite clearly that their purpose is to measure a quantity not measured before and, in so doing, to illustrate a number of methodological points concerning the ways in which statistics and economic theory can be useful to historians. One way to approach the article, in other words, is to think of it primarily as an exercise in technique—in the application of numerical and econometric analysis to problems of explanation in history. It was certainly not intended as an attempt to distill the complex institution of black slavery into the narrow dimensions of a formula, as some later critics apparently thought.

This is not to say that the authors were unaware of the broader dimensions of their theme, and in several passages they refer to these in suggestive terms, noting for example its possible relevance to "the near-slavery existing today in many highly agricultural, underindustrialized lands," to an understanding of the "underlying economic motivations" of a slave system and the type of political structure likely to accompany it, and in their concluding paragraphs to the familiar stereotype of the Civil War as an "unnecessary war." Whether their analysis was, in and of itself, adequate to sustain the burden of these weightier issues is a question to which we shall return.

The strictly technical presentation and analysis of the central issue are carried out with a clarity and expertise that make earlier discussions of the profitablity of slavery seem fuzzy-minded in comparison. Note in particular the unambiguous way in which the slave system, for the purpose of this discussion, is defined. The authors set up a two-commodity, two-region trading system. In one region the production function relates inputs of slaves to the production of agricultural staples (of which cotton is taken as the prototype); in the other, to the production of new slaves. We have noticed before in these readings occasional reference to slave-breeding as a possible source of earnings supplementary to slave-labor agriculture, particularly in the Old South; here this use of slaves to produce other slaves as "intermediate goods" is made an essential part of the income-creating activities under examination, with important implications for the findings. Clearly this requires, on the one hand, a demonstration that systematic slave-breeding for profit was in fact carried on—a proposition much disputed—and, on the other, an estimate of the rate of return on capital invested in the slave-breeding sector. Also required—a point perhaps not so obvious to non-economists—was a demonstration that efficient markets existed for trade between the two sectors, or in other words that there was a smoothly-working process for the allocation of new slaves and the setting of slave prices. It is interesting to observe how the authors handle these vital but touchy issues. Their proof of the existence of specialized slave-breeding areas rests, for example, only partly on citations of reputable testimony, the historian's conventional method. Principal reliance is placed on analysis of the age structure of the slave populations in the slave-breeding and slave-importing areas, and upon evidence that the price differential between female and male slaves was greater when they were hired for field work than when they were purchased outright, this differential reflecting, as the authors concisely express it, the ability of female slaves to "generate capital gains" for their owners when purchased.

The authors' major conclusions have, since the publication of their original article, become well known and are now cited in many textbooks as the accepted truth. Slavery was, in the antebellum years, an "economically viable institution" in virtually all areas of the South. Efficient methods for producing new slaves, for marketing them, and for allocating them among alternative uses did exist. Rates of return on capital invested in prime field hands typically varied between 4.5 and 6.5 percent, but could be as high as 12 or 13 percent or as low as 2 to 4 percent, depending on the fertility of the soil and on the amount of capital equipment the slave had to work with. For female slaves used both for field work and for breeding, rates of return on the capital invested tended to be higher, ranging from 8.1 percent for a mother who bore ten children to 7.1 percent for a mother with five marketable offspring. If the capital invested in slaves had been withdrawn from that use and invested in other ways in the pre-Civil War American economy, it would probably have earned not less than 4.5 to 5 percent and not more than 8 percent, with 6 percent being the most probable figure. Slavery, in consequence, paid about as well as any alternative use to which slave capital might have been put.

In the long run less interest attaches to these particular numerical findings than to the procedures by which they were obtained. The estimates themselves were certain to be revised as other scholars reexamined the evidence and experimented with other techniques of computation; but the methodology was the new thing, and it is to the methods, rather than the particular conclusions, that your critical attention should be directed. It is clear that at many points in their analysis Conrad and Meyer relied heavily on estimates that were essentially "best guesses." It is one of the great virtues of the techniques they used that these guesses are made explicit: the cards are on the table. The central questions the critical reader must ask himself are two. First, are the guesses in fact the best that can be made? And second, how sensitive are the authors' conclusions to corrections in the guesses? For example, it is clear that the findings rely heavily on estimates of the average life span of slaves, the age distribution of the slave population, the number of children a female slave produced during her life, the infant mortality rate among slave children, how much time a female slave lost from field work through pregnancy, and how many male or female children she bore. In other words we require, but do not possess, quite detailed demographic information on the black slave population. How sensitive are the results to errors in these demographic estimates? The same kind of question can be raised about the interest rate estimates. Just as the authors perforce admit that their assumptions about slave natality rates are assumptions "more about what was achievable than about actual happenings," so they are frank to say that determination of the correct interest rate to use for discounting purposes is very difficult, since the conceptually correct rate requires us to assume "circumstances contrary to fact."

Note in conclusion one characteristic of the article that, to some critics, has seemed typical also of other examples of the new economic history. The task the authors set themselves is, in essence, a very strictly delimited one: the measurement of the rate of return on capital invested in slaves. But the implications drawn from this measurement, or suggested by it, are much broader. It is perhaps no great extension to say that such a measurement enables us to gauge the efficiency of the slave-based economy, since comparison of rates of return on capital is a recognized way of comparing the efficiency with which this scarce resource is used. But we wander somewhat farther afield when we begin to speak of slavery as a "maintainable form of organization" and as an "economically viable institution." Similarly, the comments offered by Conrad and Meyer in the concluding sections of their paper do not in fact imply any belief on their part that slavery either retarded or accelerated the economic development of the South. But those who understood them to be saying that slavery, because it was profitable, cannot have retarded Southern economic development, were perhaps guilty of a pardonable misunderstanding. It is necessary, in short, to give full weight to all the qualifications and caveats with which the authors hedged around their conclusions. What Conrad and Meyer showed to be the case was that, on the average, capital invested in slave-labor Southern agriculture paid about as well as it would have if invested elsewhere in the American economy in the same period. This is consistent with theoretical expectations, assuming a national market for capital, mobility of capital between alternative uses, reasonably good information on relative rates of return, and the normal tendency for competition to equalize rates of return on investments of comparable risk and maturity. Regarding the relation between slavery and economic development, the authors' final position was agnostic: their findings did not suggest that slavery, "from the strict economic standpoint," was a deterrent to industrial development.

I. OBJECTIVES AND METHODS

THE OUTSTANDING economic characteristics of southern agriculture before the Civil War were a high degree of specialization and virtually exclusive reliance on a slave labor force. Large-scale, commercial dependence upon slave labor was to distinguish the antebellum South not only from other regions in its own time but from all regions at all other times in American agricultural history. Because of this unique historical status, antebellum southern agriculture has been a subject for special historical attention. Above all else, attention has been focused upon the proposition that, even without external intervention, slavery would have toppled of its own weight. This allegation has its source in the assertions of slave inefficiency to be found in the writings of men who lived with slavery: American or English liberals like G. M. Weston, H. R. Helper, or J. E. Cairnes and southern slaveowners who, in a religious, self-righteous age, could find every motive for the protection of the slave system except that it was personally profitable. The argument is to be found most strongly stated in the work of later southern historians, especially C. W. Ramsdell and U. B. Phillips, who take the position that the Civil War, far from being an irrepressible conflict, was an unnecessary blood bath. They argue that slavery had reached its natural limits and that it was cumbersome and inefficient and, probably within less than a generation, would have destroyed itself. To the question why emancipation was not resorted to, they reply that slavery was for the southerners an important (and evidently expensive) duty, part of their "unending task of race discipline." On the other side, Lewis Gray and Kenneth Stampp have strongly contested this view, contending that southern plantation agriculture was at least as remunerative an economic activity as most other business enterprises in the young republic.

The evidence employed in this debate has been provided by the few, usually fragmentary, accounting records that have come down to us from pre-Civil War plantation activities. The opposing parties have arranged and rearranged the data in accordance with various standard and sometimes imaginary accounting conventions. Indeed, the debate over the value of the different constituent pieces of information reconstructs in embryo much of the historical development of American accounting practices. Virtually all the standard accounting valuation problems have been discussed with relation to the slave question, including the role and meaning of depreciation, the nature and accountability of interest charges, and the validity of distinctions between profits and payments of managerial wages. Still, despite the fact that the problem is ostensibly one in economic history, no attempt has ever been made to measure the profitability of slavery according to the economic (as opposed to accounting) concept of profitability. This study is an attempt to fill that void.

Specifically, we shall attempt to measure the profitability of southern slave operations in terms of modern capital theory. In doing so, we shall illustrate the ways in which economic theory might be used in ordering and organizing historical facts. An additional methodological point is also made evident by this exercise, namely, how the very simple statistical concepts of range and central tendency as applied to frequency distributions of data can be employed in interpreting or moderating inferences from historical facts.[1]

In executing these tasks, we must ask, first, what is it we are talking about? and, second, can we say anything that can be proved or disproved? For example, we must ask what the slave economy was. Was it cotton culture? Was it cotton and sugar and tobacco? Was it all the antebellum southern agriculture? In answering, we shall define slavery in terms of two production functions. One function relates inputs of Negro slaves (and the materials required to maintain the slaves) to the production of the southern staple crops, particularly cotton. The second function describes the production of the intermediate good, slave labor—slave-breeding, to use an emotionally charged term which has affected, even determined, most of the historical conclusions about this problem.

[1]A more thorough presentation of these methodological views was given in Chapter 1.

What do we mean by "inefficiency"? Essentially, we shall mean a comparison of the return from the use of this form of capital—Negro slaves—with the returns being earned on other capital assets at the time. Thus we mean to consider whether the slave system was being dragged down of its own weight, whether the allocation of resources was impaired by the rigidity of capitalized labor supply, whether southern capital was misused or indeed drawn away to the North, and finally, whether slavery must inevitably have declined from an inability of the slave force to reproduce itself.

The hypothesis that slavery was an efficient, maintainable form of economic organization is not a new one, of course. Nor are we, by one hundred years at least, among the first to conclude that Negro slavery was profitable in the antebellum South. What we do believe to be novel, however, is our approach. Postulating that American Negro slavery was characterized by two production functions, we argue that an efficient system developed in which those regions best suited to the production of cotton (and the other important staples) specialized in agricultural production, while the less productive land continued to produce slaves, exporting the increase to the staple-crop areas. It is this structure that we are examining.

We propose to test the hypothesis by putting appropriate values on the variables in the production functions and computing any present value over cost created by the stream of income over the lifetime of the slave. These returns must, of course, be shown to be at least equal to those earnable elsewhere in the American economy at the time. It is further necessary to show that appropriate slave markets existed to make regional specialization in slave-breeding possible and that slavery did not necessarily imply the disappearance or misallocation of capital. Evidence on the ability of the slave force to maintain itself numerically will be had as a corollary result. To accomplish all these assessments, it is necessary to obtain data on slave prices and cotton prices, the average output of male field hands and field wenches, the life-expectancy of Negroes born in slavery, the cost of maintaining slaves during infancy and other nonproductive periods, and finally, the net reproduction rate and the demographic composition of the slave population in the breeding and using areas.

Looked upon simply as a staple-commodity agriculture, the southern system must appear to have been burdened—possibly even to have been on the verge of collapse—under the weight of areas of inefficient, unprofitable farming. We submit that this view is in error and that the error arises from the failure to recognize that an agricultural system dependent upon slavery can be defined operationally only in terms of the production function for both the final good—in our case, cotton—and the production function for the intermediate good—Negro slaves. Considered operationally, in terms of a neoclassical two-region, two-commodity trade system, it must be seen that a slave system produces labor as an intermediate good. The profitability of the system cannot be decided without considering the system's ability to produce chattel labor efficiently.

There are also nonhistorical reasons for taking up once again the economics of antebellum southern slavery. A detailed re-evaluation of the profits of plantation slavery in the American South might help us evaluate the possibilities, first, that the near-slavery existing today in many highly agricultural, underindustrialized lands is an institution that can be expected to disappear automatically or, second, that dislodging it will require substantial governmental pressure or interference. These are, of course, often key policy questions in former colonial countries that are just beginning to develop modern industrial economies.

The possible relevance of the American experience in this connection increases, moreover, as the underlying economic motivations of a slave system are analyzed and established. This happens primarily because, once these motives are recognized, it becomes possible better to understand and predict the political structures that will accompany slavery. In other words, the interrelationships between certain economic and political goals of slavery can be better understood once the underlying economic factors are understood.

II. THE ECONOMIC RETURNS ON SLAVEHOLDING

From the standpoint of the entrepreneur making an investment in slaves, the basic problems involved in determining profitability are analytically the same as those met in determining the returns from any other kind of capital investment. The acquisition of a slave represented the tying-up of capital in what has appropriately been called a roundabout method of production. Like the purchase of any capital, a slave purchase was made in the anticipation of gaining higher returns than are available from less time-consuming or capital-using methods. This model is perhaps particularly applicable in the slave case, because slave investments, like the forests or wine cellars of classic capital theory, produced a natural increase with the passage of time.

Longevity of Slaves. Slave longevity corresponds, of course, to the period for which a slave investment was made. We shall limit attention here to the purchase of twenty-year-old Negroes in the immediate pre-Civil War era and shall deal only with the typical or median life-expectancy for this group. These limits greatly simplify the problem and still include the vast majority of relevant cases.

Investment returns can be computed by using the capital-value formula, $y = x_t/(1+r)^t$, where y is the present value of the investment, x_t is realized net return t years hence, and r is the interest rate.[2] (As an alternative, the internal rate of return can be calculated by setting y equal to the cost of the investment and solving the equation for r; such a procedure is not quite as appropriate in some cases as the present value procedure, but for completeness and ease of comparison, results using both methods are reported subsequently.) When returns are realized over a number of years, the total present value of the capital can be found by simple summation in this formula. The criterion for a profitable investment is that the present value exceeds the current cost of the investment or that the ratio of the present value to cost exceeds unity; this ratio will be subsequently referred to as the "benefit-cost ratio." From this statement of the problem, it is obvious that the following information is needed to determine the profitability of slaveholding from the slaveholder's point of view: *(a)* the longevity of slaves, *(b)* the costs of slaves and any necessary accompanying capital investments, *(c)* the interest rate, and *(d)* the annual returns from slave production activities, defined to include both field labor and procreation. We shall consider each of these in turn and then put the pieces together to determine the approximate profitability of slave investments.

There is a scarcity of good longevity data for the period, but it is known that in 1850 Negroes lived just about as long as whites in the two states for which acceptable data are available. The available figures are given in Table 1. Doubt exists about the quality of these

[2]Computation of present value in this way is preferable to the usual accounting procedure of recording net profit rates on total plantation investment in slaves, land, and durable equipment because of the reproductive character and the limited durability of slave investments. Clearly, the same characteristics do not apply to nondepreciable investments in land. A nondepreciable investment in agricultural land is, however, quite rare.

Table 1 Expectation of Life at Birth in Years for White and Colored
Males, United States, 1850*

State	White	Colored
Massachusetts	38.3	39.75
Maryland	41.8	38.47
Louisiana		28.89

*Reported in L. I. Dublin, A. J. Lotka, and M. Spiegelman, *Length of Life* (New York: Ronald Press Co., 1949) p. 54, where the source is given as the L. W. Meech table based on the records of the 1850 Census and first published in J. C. G. Kennedy, *The Seventh Census—Report of the Superintendent of the Census, Dec. 1, 1852* (Washington, D.C., 1853), p. 13. The Maryland colored data are for slaves only; the Louisiana, for slaves and free together.

estimates because they show Negroes in New England expecting a longer life than whites. This is not the case today, nor was it the case in 1900, when the first good data became available. Also, Negroes appear in this table to have had a longer life-expectancy in 1850 than they had fifty years later. Although surprising, this may be perfectly correct. Negroes could have received better care under slavery than in freedom because the plantation owners had an economic interest in keeping Negroes alive. Furthermore, the Negro in the period after emancipation generally lacked the means to participate equally in the new medical advances, in contrast to his position of roughly equal medical care in the period before 1860.

Life-expectation at birth does not tell us much, of course, about the expectation of a twenty-year-old man. Actually, there are no data on Negro life-expectancy at different age levels in the prewar period except for some imperfect estimates made by Sydnor for Mississippi slaves.[3] Using the average reported age at death of those over the age of twenty who died in 1850, he estimated a life-expectancy of twenty-two years for a twenty-year-old Mississippi slave. This figure is probably low for two reasons. First, the estimating procedure tells more about life-expectancy in the years preceding 1850 than after, unless we make the dubious assumption that there was no advance in medical and dietary knowledge around the middle of the last century. Second, estimates from deaths reported at the end of ten-year intervals and averaged back over the decade would tend to underestimate life-spans at the younger ages. Doubts about the quality of the Sydnor data are born out by consideration of the Massachusetts life-expectancy of 40.1 years for twenty-year-old males, white and Negro, in 1850.[4] Looking back

[3]Charles S. Sydnor, "Life Span of Mississippi Slaves," *American Historical Review*, XXXV (April, 1930), 556-74.
[4]L. I. Dublin, A. J. Lotka, and M. Spiegelman, *Length of Life* (New York: Ronald

at the data in Table 1, there is no reason to expect twenty-year-old Massachusetts Negroes to have a lower life-expectancy than Massachusetts whites, though both clearly lived longer than southern Negroes of the period. Taking all these factors into account, an estimate of thirty to thirty-five years of life-expectancy seems most plausible for twenty-year-old Negroes working as prime cotton hands on southern plantations in the period 1830-50, and a thirty-year life-expectancy will generally be used in the succeeding calculations.

Cost of the Capital Investment. The capital investment in plantation operations included both slaves and the land and equipment on which they worked. The price of slaves fluctuated widely, being subject to the waves of speculation in cotton. The price also depended, among other things, upon the age, sex, disposition, degree of training, and condition of the slave. In order to hold these variables roughly constant, the present analysis is confined to eighteen- to twenty-year-old prime field hands and wenches. Some summary data on slave prices were compiled by U. B. Phillips on the basis of available market quotations, bills of transactions, and reports of sales in most of the important slave markets of Georgia. His estimates of the best averages for several years between 1828 and 1860 are presented in Table 2. On the basis of these data it would appear that both the median and the mean price for prime field hands were in the range of from $900 to $950 in the period 1830-50. Because of the substantial price increases in the last antebellum decade, these averages would run substantially higher for the entire slave period after 1830—specifically, between $1,000 and $1,200. Since the prices of field wenches usually averaged about $100-$150 less than those of hands, they were probably in a range of $800-$850 in the years 1830-50 and between $900 and $1,100 for the entire period 1830-60. (Phillips' averages are substantially confirmed by the detailed tabulation of slave transactions shown in Table A of the appendix to this chapter. This is a reasonably

---

Press Co., 1949), p. 51. It is worth noting that there is general agreement that labor on the rice and sugar plantations was sufficiently more arduous to reduce Negro longevity in such locations. Therefore the Louisiana estimates are probably inordinately pessimistic, and the Maryland figures are better estimates of conditions prevailing on the cotton plantations. This, in turn, means that the thirty-to thirty-five-year estimates used below are, if anything, a little conservative or too low.

Table 2 Estimated Average Slave Prices in Georgia, Selected Years, 1828–60

Year	Average Price of Prime Field Hands
1828	$ 700
1835	900
1837	1,300
1839	1,000
1840	700
1844	600
1848	900
1851	1,050
1853	1,200
1859	1,650
1860	1,800

Source: U. B. Phillips, "The Economic Cost of Slaveholding in the Cotton Belt," *Political Science Quarterly*, XX , No. 2 (1905), 267.

exhaustive list of such transactions as reported in the standard references on antebellum southern agriculture.)

By far the most important nonslave capital was the investment in land. Since the land values varied widely, depending on the quality of the soil and the type of agriculture pursued, attention is confined to cotton culture. The range in cotton-land prices in the period 1830-50 was fairly well bracketed by the $6 per acre paid for poor upland pine land in Alabama and the $35-$40 per acre paid for cleared Mississippi alluvium. Such a range even encompassed the costs of new lands in the Southwest. Although such land was obtained for a nominal original cost, the usual costs of clearing, draining, and otherwise preparing for cultivation, plus the transportation of slaves and supplies, amounted to $20-$30 per acre. There was also variation in the number of acres needed per hand. Counting garden land and woodlots, as well as productive fields, the usual number of acres per field hand was between 15 and 35, the exact figure depending primarily on the quality of the land. This meant an original land investment per hand of somewhere between $90 and $14,000, with $180-$600 bracketing the vast majority of instances.

The price per acre also was related to the durability of the land. Cotton lands lasted between ten and forty years, depending upon original quality and fertilization. In the land-rich, labor-scarce economy of the nineteenth-century United States, fertilization was a rare practice. Furthermore, planters had a choice between operating less capital intensively on low-durability land or more capital intensively on high-durability land. For example, poor Alabama pine land might be expected to last ten years and require 30-35 acres per hand; this meant that $180-$210 had to be reinvested every ten years to utilize the slave force properly. Assuming thirty-year slave longevity and an 8 per cent interest rate, the present value of the land investment for one slave's lifetime was $302-$350 for an upland-pine operation. On the alluvium, by contrast, the land would typically outlast the slave in usefulness; assuming, though, that both lasted the same number of years and that 16 acres of cleared and 10 of uncleared land (at $10 per acre) were used per hand, a total investment of $660 per hand is indicated. This difference in value of the land investment was presumably a function of different yields. At any rate, the typical case was probably halfway between these two, involving a land investment of about $450 per hand.

Similar problems arise in estimating the investment in plows, gins, wagons, cabins, and miscellaneous implements. Such investments ran about $25 per hand in original outlay and had to be renewed every fifteen years. This gives a total present value per hand in such items (again on the assumption of thirty-year slave longevity and 8 per cent interest) of about $33. A small investment was required in work horses and oxen, but in this case the stock was likely to be self-replenishing, reducing the costs to interest on the investment at most. Putting all these capital costs together indicates that $1,400-$1,450 was a fair approximation of the typical or average total investment per male slave in terms of present values. The range ran from $1,250 to $1,650.

Interest Rate. Determining the relevant rate of interest—the rate with which the cotton-slave returns must be discounted or compared—is perhaps empirically the easiest and conceptually the most difficult of the tasks in computing the economic returns on slave investments. While there is a relative abundance of data on interest rates in this period, none corresponds exactly to the desired rate. Probably the most relevant rate of interest would be that which plantation owners or other investors in southern agriculture could have earned on their money in other pursuits if slavery had gone out of existence. This is difficult to estimate on historical evidence, since it assumes circumstances contrary to fact. A close substitute might be earnings on other investments that were *least* dependent upon cotton and southern agriculture. Given the importance of cotton in the American economy prior to the Civil War and the general interdependence of economic systems, even in an economy as primitive as that of the United States in the first half of the nineteenth century, it is difficult to find any conceptually correct figures. The figures that follow are offered in complete recognition of their fallibility, yet they are probably as good as are available.

In the contemporary chronicles southerners and northerners alike considered 6-8 per cent a reasonable rate of return and a reasonable asking price for loans. Figures in this range are repeated over and over again. These figures also are consistent with reported rates charged on prime commercial paper and other debt instruments in the principal money markets before 1860, as shown in Table 3.[5]

Table 3 *Average Annual Interest Rates on Prime Commercial Paper from 1831 to 1860*

	New York*	Boston		New York*	Boston
1831	5.1	6.5	1849	10.0	12.0
1832	5.3	6.5	1850	8.0	7.5
1833	6.9	6.0	1851	9.7	7.0
1834	14.6	14.5	1852	6.6	6.0
1835	7.0	5.0	1853	10.2	10.7
1836	18.4	20.3	1854	10.4	12.0
1837	14.1	6.0	1855	8.9	7.0
1838	9.0	7.0	1856	8.9	10.0
1839	13.2	9.0	1857	12.9	9.0
1840	7.8	6.0	1858	5.0	4.5
1841	6.9	6.0	1859	6.8	7.0
1842	8.1	7.8	1860	7.0	6.0
1843	4.5	3.0	1861	6.5	
1844	4.9	5.0	1862	5.8	
1845	6.0	6.0	1863	5.0	
1846	8.3	8.0	1864	6.0	
1847	9.6	6.0	1865	7.6	
1848	15.1	15.0			

Sources: *New York data:* Federal Reserve Bank of New York, *Monthly Review,* March 1, 1921, p. 3. The figures are also reproduced in A. O. Greef, *The Commercial Paper House in the United States* (Cambridge, Mass: Harvard University Press, 1938), p. 79. *Boston data:* Joseph G. Martin, *One Hundred Years' History of the Boston Stock and Money Markets* (Boston: The Author, 1898), pp. 52–53.
*Two-name sixty-ninety-day paper.
†"First class three to six months, bankable paper." The rate reported is either one sustained for a major portion of the year or an arithmetic average.

[5]In confirmation of these figures, Lance E. Davis, who is now completing a study of New England financial intermediaries (the essentials of which can be found in his Ph.D. dissertation on deposit in the Johns Hopkins University Library), reports that these New England firms consistently realized less than 6 per cent on three-signature

Similarly, rates on New York Stock Exchange call loans, New England municipal issues, and rail debentures, shown in Table 4, fall for the most part within, or below, this same 6-8 per cent range. While the average annual rates fluctuated widely in the years between 1830 and 1850 and the distribution of rates is skewed, the central tendency was clearly close to the 6-8 per cent range. Specifically, the New York average was 9.2 per cent, the median was 8.0, and the mode was between 6.0 and 7.0 per cent.

Table 4 Yields on Various Economic Activities, 1857–65

Year	New England Municipal Bond Yields (January Index Numbers)	Call Money Rates at the New York Stock Exchange (Arithmetic Average of Months)	Railroad Bond Yields (January Average for All Railroads)
1857	5.2	9.3	8.1
1858	5.3	4.2	8.7
1859	4.8	5.4	7.4
1860	4.8	6.0	7.5
1861	4.9	5.8	7.4
1862	5.2	5.2	7.5
1863	4.4	6.2	5.6
1864	4.7	6.6	6.0
1865	5.2	6.2	6.2

Source: Frederick R. Macaulay, *The Movements of Interest Rates, Bond Yields and Stock Prices in the United States since 1856* (New York: National Bureau of Economic Research, 1938), pp. A172–A173 and A34–A38.

The interest rates for the Civil War years, although they lie outside the slavery period of this investigation, may be conceptually the most pertinent figures in Tables 3 and 4. The Civil War rates represent an approximation of what investment returns in the North might have been in the prewar period under complete divorce from the plantation economy—but only an approximation because many other structural changes took place concomitantly with the with-

---

prime commercial paper in the period before 1840; from 1840 to 1860, however, almost all loans were made at 6 per cent, which was the legal maximum under Massachusetts usury laws. He estimates that these intermediaries realized an over-all return of between 6 and 7 per cent in the period 1840-60 on their total investment: 6 per cent on the debt and 7-8 per cent on equity.

drawal of the southern cotton economy. A most significant change was that the Lincoln administration adopted the very essence of Keynesian expansionary fiscal policies. It simultaneously ran a large deficit budget and closed the economy with high tariffs and buy-American clauses in government contracts. On the supply side of the money market, the war meant that the southern withdrawal was consummated without any flow of capital out of slavery and into other ventures. Consequently, returns on northern investments unquestionably remained higher than they would have been if southern cotton had been withdrawn without offsetting government action and with a flow of southern capital into northern money markets. Of course, there might have been compensatory government action even without the war. and the loss of southern funds was at least partially offset by the loss of southern opportunities. Still, the 6-7 per cent average returns realized in the period 1860-65 can be viewed as indicative of at least what might have been achieved in the United States in the absence of cotton investment opportunities.

The realization on short-term, high-quality commercial paper might normally be expected to be below the realization on longer-term investments of the type represented by ownership of a cotton plantation. However, in the period 1840-60 banking practices were rather lax and potentially or actually inflationary, as indicated by the recurrent financial panics of the time. Such unstable financial conditions may have given equity a premium that it might otherwise not have enjoyed. Furthermore, the existence of well-established slave and real estate markets made most plantation investments highly negotiable, thereby reducing the time commitment in such investments. There are some reports available on the realizable returns on longer-term investments; for example, Table 4 presents the rates at which some municipal and railroad development bonds were floated in the prewar period. In addition, Davis reports returns of 16.76 per cent on total capital stock in the 1844-48 period and 5.75 per cent in the 1848-53 period for nine of the larger and more prosperous Massachusetts textile firms.[6]

From these many disparate sources it seems safe to estimate that a wholesale withdrawal of capital from slave operations in southern

[6]Lance E. Davis, "Sources of Industrial Finance: The American Textile Industry," *Explorations in Entrepreneurial History,* IX (April, 1957), 201. The figures are based on the companies' financial records to be found at the Baker Library of the Harvard Graduate School of Business Administration.

agriculture would not have depressed marginal investment returns in the prewar United States economy much below 4.5-5 per cent. Similarly, it seems safe to conclude that the withdrawn capital could not have been expected to earn returns much in excess of 8 per cent. Between these high and low estimates, a return of 6 per cent seems the most probable.

Annual Return. The appropriate annual-return figure to enter as the numerator in the capital equation is the net return on current account, or the difference between gross sales and all out-of-pocket expenses. The expense deduction is limited to out-of-pocket expenses, since all the book charges that complicate the usual accounting procedures are taken into account in the process of constructing the capital cost estimate.

Estimates of plantation expenses have been taken primarily from three excellent, exhaustive records of the available material: J. L. Watkins' *The Cost of Cotton Production,* Lewis C. Gray's *History of Agriculture in the Southern United States to 1860,* and Kenneth Stampp's *The Peculiar Institution.*[7] A reasonably thorough check of

Table 5 *Typical Annual Out-of-Pocket Costs of Maintaining and Working Prime Field Hands on Southern Plantations in the Period 1840–60*

A. Food and clothing	
(1) Out-of-pocket costs where most food was produced on plantation and most clothing was hand-sewn	$ 2.50—$ 3.46
(2) Cash costs if purchased	$25.00—$40.00
(3) Out-of-pocket costs where some ready-made clothing and meat, fish, and other food "delicacies" were purchased	$ 7.00—$10.00
B. Medical care	$ 1.50—$ 2.00
C. Taxes	$ 0.39—$ 1.20
D. Supervision	$ 5.00—$15.00
Total, based on means of the estimates above and option (3) under A	$20.00—$21.00

Principal sources: J. L. Watkins, *The Cost of Cotton Production* (United States Department of Agriculture, Division of Statistics, Miscellaneous Series, Bull. 16 [Washington, D.C.: Government Printing Office, 1899]); Lewis C. Gray, *History of Agriculture in the Southern United States to 1860* (Washington D.C.: Carnegie Institution, 1933), pp. 529–67; Kenneth Stampp, *The Peculiar Institution* (New York: A. A. Knopf, Inc., 1956), chaps. vi, vii, and ix.

[7]These three secondary sources carefully and consistently record the estimates available from three, basic types of primary material. Gray's *History of Agriculture in the Southern United States to 1860* (Washington, D.C., 1933), esp. pp. 529–67, covers

these secondary sources against some primary sources and against one another for consistency indicates that these surveys have been reliably and accurately made. A digest of the estimates is presented in Table 5. The figure of $20-$21 annual out-of-pocket slave maintenance costs is used in subsequent calculations, being subtracted from the annual gross return figures on slave activities.

For a male field hand, returns depended on sales of products realized from his field labor; in the case of a female hand, an addition must be made for the returns realized on the labor and sale of her children. These basically different production functions for the two sexes must be treated separately.

For the male field hand, limited to the returns on his field labor, the gross proceeds depended on the price of cotton and the quantity of his annual output. The output, in turn, was crucially dependent on the quality of the land on which the slave was employed and, to a much lesser degree, upon the quality and amount of capital goods with which he was equipped. The figures in Table 6 illustrate possible variations in productivity per hand. These estimates agree with frequent statements in contemporary journals that in the

Table 6 Reported Yields per Prime Field Hand

Location	Year	Bales per Hand	Source
South Carolina coastal	1849	4½	Watkins
Mississippi (De Soto County)	1849	4	Watkins
Unidentified	1844	7	Watkins
Alabama (Cherokee County)	1855	4	Watkins
Mississippi (Vicksburg area)	1855	8	Watkins
New Southwest land	1850's	5	Gray, p. 912
South Carolina upland	1852	3	Gray, p. 912
Texas	1859	10	Stampp, p. 408
Arkansas River	1859	7	Stampp, p. 408

the cost estimates intermittently reported in the principal agricultural and business journals read by the planters and traders: *DeBow's Review, Farmers' Register, Farmer and Planter, Southern Planter, Southern Agriculturist,* and *Hunt's Merchants' Magazine.* Watkins' *The Cost of Cotton Production* (U.S. Department of Agriculture, Miscellaneous Series, Bull. 16 [Washington, D.C., 1899]) includes the estimates recorded in the Patent Office and the Commissioner of Patents' *Annual Reports,* especially for the years 1844, 1849, 1850, 1852, 1854, and 1855. Stampp's *The Peculiar Institution* (New York, 1956), esp. chaps. vi, vii, and ix, reports the estimates available from diaries and individual plantation records still in existence.

typical case a prime field hand could be expected to raise from 3.5 to 4 bales per year. The maximum seems to have been 7-8 bales on the best lands, and 2-3 bales was the minimum on the poorest land.

The relevant price of cotton for valuing these yields would be the net price realized at the farm (in order that price and cost data be comparable). This means that export prices at the major ports must be adjusted downward by the amount of freight, insurance, storage, drayage, and factor's commission charges that were properly chargeable to the planter. Gray estimates that these costs generally ran between $2.50 and $4.00 per bale. Somewhat more detailed information is presented by Watkins, whose findings are summarized in Table 7. The Gray and the Watkins findings are fully compatible, and a marketing cost of from 0.7 to 0.8 cent per pound appears to be properly deductible from the export price in determining the price f.o.b. farm.

Table 7 *Cotton Marketing Costs per Bale Chargeable to Planters in 1840*

	At Mobile	At Charleston
Freight in	$1.50*	$1.25†
Drayage	0.125	0.13
Weighing	0.125	0.06
Storage (1 month)	0.20	0.24
Insurance (1 month)	‡	0.25
Factor's commission (2–2.5 per cent)	0.80	0.60–1.61
Total per bale	$2.75	$3.03§
Total cents per pound	0.69	0.76§

Source: Watkins, *op. cit.,* pp. 38, 39.
* By river.
† From Columbia.
‡ Not reported. Note that the higher (Charleston) figures have been used in the profit computations to follow.
& Assuming $1.10 factor's commission.
| Four hundred pounds to a bale.

The export price of cotton fluctuated widely over the period, as can be seen from Table 8. New Orleans cotton prices averaged almost 50 per cent higher in the thirties and fifties than in the depressed forties. Even in the forties, however, the export price level was sufficient to insure an average net farm price of not much less than 6.5 cents. Since prices at any given port were usually equal

Table 8 Weighted Yearly Average Prices of Short-Staple Cotton (Usually Louisiana or Mississippi Middling or Second Grade) at New Orleans for the Crop Years 1830–60

Year	Price	Year	Price	Year	Price
1830	8.4	1840	9.1	1850	11.7
1831	9.0	1841	7.8	1851	7.4
1832	10.0	1842	5.7	1852	9.1
1833	11.2	1843	7.5	1853	8.8
1834	15.5	1844	5.5	1854	8.4
1835	15.2	1845	6.8	1855	9.1
1836	13.3	1846	9.9	1856	12.4
1837	9.0	1847	7.0	1857	11.2
1838	12.4	1848	5.8	1858	11.5
1839	7.9	1849	10.8	1859	10.8
				1860	11.1
Decade average price	11.2		7.6		11.2

Source: Gray, op. cit., Table 41, pp. 1027–29.

to the Liverpool price minus ocean shipping rates, the New York and Mobile prices were generally somewhat higher. Taking all this into consideration, 7-8 cents seems a realistic and conservative estimate of the average realized farm price for the whole period.

These price, productivity, and capital cost estimates can be combined to estimate the actual profitability of investments in male slave labor for cotton production. In lieu of a single computation, several cases involving different capital outlays, yields per hand, and realized farm prices have been constructed; the results are given in Table 9.[8] Cases 1,2, and 3 are the most typical; cases 4,5, and 6 represent the situation on somewhat better land. These first six cases, with benefit-cost ratios almost invariably above unity, at 4 and 6 per cent interest rates and internal rates of 4, 5, and 8 per cent,

[8]No allowance has been made in these computations for the expenses of maintaining slaves in their dotage. This does not appear to be a serious omission. Generally speaking, slaves were considered to be virtually fully productive in field labor until reaching their fifty-fifth year—which corresponds to the average life-expectancy on the purchase of a twenty-year-old slave. Furthermore, the direct out-of-pocket costs of simply maintaining a slave were only $10-$15, figures considerably below productive value in field work. Given the possibility of specialized use of older labor in such occupations as gardening, nursery operations, and supervision, it seems doubtful that many slaves lived long enough to be economic drains on current account.

encompass the majority of antebellum cotton plantation operations. Cases 7, 8, and 9 represent the minimum of profitability, or what might be expected on poor upland pine country or the worked-out lands of the eastern seaboard. Operations on these lands were apparently profitable only if money could be borrowed at 4 per cent or if income could be supplemented by breeding slaves. By contrast, cases 10, 11, and 12 show the upper range of profitability realized on the best lands of the new Southwest, the Mississippi alluvium, and the better South Carolina and Alabama plantations.[9] These were quite obviously highly profitable by any standards.

Table 9 Realized Returns on Prime Field Hands under Various Hypothesized Conditions

Case	Present Value of Capital Outlay per Hand	Yield per Hand (Bales)	Average Net Farm Price (Cents)	Benefit/Cost Ratios @4%	@6%	@8%	Approximate Internal Rate of Return (Per Cent)
1	$1,350–$1,400	3³/₄	7	1.07	0.85	0.70	4.5
2	$1,350–$1,400	3³/₄	8	1.26	1.00	0.82	5.2
3	$1,350–$1,400	3³/₄	9	1.45	1.15	0.95	6.5
4	$1,600	4¹/₂	7	1.15	0.91	0.74	5.0
5	$1,600	4¹/₂	8	1.34	1.07	0.87	7.0
6	$1,600	4¹/₂	9	1.54	1.22	1.00	8.0
7	$1,250–$1,300	3	7	0.87	0.69	0.55	2.2
8	$1,250–$1,300	3	8	1.00	0.82	0.67	3.9
9	$1,250–$1,300	3	9	1.19	0.95	0.78	5.4
10	$1,700	7	7	1.79	1.43	1.16	10.0
11	$1,700	7	8	2.08	1.65	1.35	12.0
12	$1,700	7	9	2.36	1.88	1.53	13.0

The calculations in Table 9 pertain to estimates of potential returns for the relatively simple production activities of prime field hands. With the female hand or prime field wench the situation is much more complex; in addition to her own field productivity, the field productivity of her children and the returns realized on their sale must be evaluated. Also, the extra cost of maintaining the

[9]A purist might ask how different returns can be realized in what is ostensibly the same type of economic activity in a relatively competitive industry. The question overlooks the fact that it took a much larger initial outlay to attain productive situations like those in cases 10-12. This is all the more true, since the capital outlay in these cases would be concentrated at the start of the undertaking, while in cases 7-9 some of the outlay would be delayed ten or fifteen years until the land lost fertility.

children and the maternity and nursery costs associated with their births must be counted.

To simplify the calculations in this rather complex situation, the following assumptions are useful:

1. Each prime field wench produced five to ten marketable children during her lifetime. (The computations for the ten-child or upper-limit case are shown in Table 10, while those for the lower limit of five children are shown in Table 11.) Furthermore, successful pregnancies were spaced two years apart. It must be recognized that these figures represent assumptions more about what was achievable than about actual happenings. Slave infant mortality data are too poor to permit inferences about the latter.

2. The prime field wench was one-half to two-thirds as productive as a prime field hand when she was actually at work in the field. This estimate is based on the fact that, when prime field hands and wenches were hired out, the hiring rate on the latter was usually one-half to two-thirds the hiring rate on the former. Thus, it is assumed that the market hiring rate reflects the relative productivity of the two sexes. On the assumption that wenches in late pregnancy were not for hire, adjustment also must be made for the time lost by the female during the pregnancy and postnatal periods. It is assumed here that three months' productive field time was lost for each successful pregnancy; the entire deduction has been made in the year in which the successful birth took place, despite the fact that it would probably be more realistic to assume that one month and a half was lost on each unsuccessful as well as each successful pregnancy. This allowance for "lost time" is probably too generous, since the only births that really cost any important productive field time were those occurring during the peak agriculture seasons, planting and picking times.

3. The wench's children became productive in field labor at age six, with the males becoming self-sustaining by age nine (that is, they then earned the adult maintenance charge of $20 per year), while females became self-sustaining by age thirteen. This can be represented by letting the male productivity go up $5 every year between ages six and nine and letting female productivity increase by $2.50 for every year between the ages of six and thirteen. These rates are in keeping with the previously stated principle that females were roughly half as productive in field labor as males. After reaching a self-sustaining status at these ages, it is further assumed that the children's productivity continued to rise linearly until they

reached their full adult productivity to age eighteen; thus, male productivity is assumed to rise $10 per year between ages nine and eighteen and female productivity $5 per year between ages thirteen and eighteen.

4. The typical wench had as many male as female children. For purposes of computation, the productivity, sales price, and other data for children of the two sexes have been averaged. For example, the final sales price of a typical child is assumed to be $875, halfway between the average price of $825 for prime field wenches and the average price of $925 for prime field hands.

5. Nursery costs were about $50 per successful pregnancy.

Using these assumptions, hypothetical annual returns for a typical prime field wench can be determined; such calculations are shown in Tables 10 and 11. In constructing these tables, it was assumed that the prime field wench and her children worked on land that returned 3.75 bales of cotton per year for every prime male hand employed; that is, the land is slightly below average fertility. Also, a 7.5-cent net farm price for cotton has been used. The first successful pregnancy has been assumed to occur in the second year after the prime field wench is purchased; further successful pregnancies occur at regular two-year intervals. The children were sold at age eighteen, and the annual maintenance cost per child was assessed at the rate of $10 per year for children between ages one and six, $15 per year for seven- to twelve-year-olds, and $20 per year, the full adult maintenance cost, for those age thirteen and over. The maternity costs have been included in the annual charge for the children's upkeep; similarly, the $16 decline every other year for the first few years in the wench's own field returns represents the allowance for time lost because of pregnancy. Benefit-cost ratios and rates of returns were computed on the streams of net returns shown in the far right-hand columns of the tables on the assumption that the total investment in the prime field wench, land, and equipment was between $1,200 and $1,300, figures which would appear to be very good averages. A benefit-cost ratio of 1.62 at a 6 per cent interest rate and an internal rate of return of 8.1 per cent were obtained for the mother bearing ten children; a ratio of 1.23 and a return of 7.1 per cent were estimated for the mother with five children.

These returns are somewhat higher than those calculated for the prime field hands. A proper working of the market mechanism would suggest that the attainable returns on the two sexes should be

Table 10 Annual Returns on a Prime Field Wench Investment (Working on Land Which Yielded 3.75 Bales per Prime Male Field Hand, Assuming a 7.5-Cent Net Farm Price for Cotton and Ten "Salable" Children Born to Every Wench)

Year from Purchase Date	Personal Field Returns	Child Field Returns	Child Sale Returns	Personal Upkeep	Child Upkeep	Net Returns
1	$56			$20		$ 36
2	40			20	$ 50	−30
3	56			20	10	26
4	40			20	60	−40
5	56			20	20	16
6	40			20	70	−50
7	56			20	30	6
8	40	$ 3.75		20	80	−56.25
9	56	7.50		20	45	−1.50
10	40	15.00		20	95	−50.00
11	56	22.50		20	60	−1.50
12	40	37.50		20	110	−52.50
13	56	52.50		20	75	13.50
14	40	75.00		20	130	−35.00
15	56	97.50		20	95	47.50
16	40	127.50		20	150	−2.50
17	56	157.50		20	115	78.50
18	40	195.00		20	165	55.00
19	56	232.50		20	130	134.30
20	40	195.00	$875	20	170	920.00
21	56	232.50		20	130	138.50
22	56	195.00	875	20	120	986.00
23	56	232.50		20	120	148.50
24	56	195.00	875	20	110	996.00
25	56	232.50		20	110	158.00
26	56	195.00	875	20	100	1,006.00
27	56	232.50		20	100	168.00
28	56	187.50	875	20	90	1,008.50
29	56	225.00		20	90	171.00
30	56	180.00	875	20	80	1,011.00
31		210.00			80	130.00
32		157.50	875		60	972.50
33		180.00			60	120.00
34		120.00	875		40	955.00
35		135.00			40	95.00
36		67.50	875		20	922.50
37		75.00			20	55.00
38			875			875.00

Table 11 Annual Returns on a Prime Field Wench Investment (Working on Land Which Yielded 3.75 Bales per Prime Male Field Hand, Assuming a 7.5-Cent Net Farm Price for Cotton and Five "Salable" Children Born to Every Wench)

Year from Purchase Date	Personal Field Returns	Child Field Returns	Child Sale Returns	Personal Upkeep	Child Upkeep	Net Returns
1	$56			$20		$ 36
2	40			20	$50	—30
3	56			20	10	26
4	40			20	60	—40
5	56			20	20	16
6	40			20	70	—50
7	56			20	30	6
8	40	$ 3.75		20	80	—56.25
9	56	7.50		20	45	—1.50
10	40	15.00		20	95	—50.00
11	56	22.50		20	60	—1.50
12	56	37.50		20	60	13.50
13	56	52.50		20	65	23.50
14	56	75.00		20	65	46.00
15	56	97.50		20	75	58.50
16	56	127.50		20	75	88.50
17	56	157.50		20	85	108.50
18	56	191.25		20	85	142.25
19	56	225.00		20	90	171.00
20	56	180.00	$875	20	75	1,016.00
21	56	210.00		20	75	171.00
22	56	157.50	875	20	60	1,008.50
23	56	180.00		20	60	156.00
24	56	120.00	875	20	40	991.00
25	56	135.00		20	40	131.00
26	56	67.50	875	20	20	958.50
27	56	75.00		20	20	91.00
28	56		875	20		911.00
29	56			20		36.00
30	56			20		36.00

approximately equal. That is, the sales price differential between males and females should be such that the rate of return on the two types of investment turns out to be roughly equal in the typical case.

The higher rate of return for the females might be explained, however, in several different ways. First, it may have taken a somewhat higher return on the females to attract capital investment into that type of productive activity. Slave-breeding and slave-trading were not generally considered to be high or noble types of activity for a southern gentleman. Indeed, many plantation owners would stoop to considerable subterfuge to disguise engagement in any part of the slave-trade or breeding operations Second, the investment in the female was a longer-term affair than with the male; from Tables 10 and 11 it is apparent that the bulk of the returns on a female were realized twenty or more years after the investment was made, when the children had grown to marketable ages. To the extent that more distant developments are more uncertain, investments in female slaves could be expected to demand a higher return. Finally, the over-all average price of prime field wenches quoted from Phillips may be too low for proven "childbearers"; as is evident from Table A of the appendix to this chapter and contemporary comments, a female who had proved herself fertile was worth more than a female who had yet to bear her first child.

But these qualifications do not change the principal conclusion that slavery was apparently about as remunerative as alternative employments to which slave capital might have been put. Large or excessive returns were clearly limited to a few fortunate planters, but apparently none suffered excessively either. This general sharing in the prosperity was more or less guaranteed, moreover, if proper market mechanisms existed so that slaves could be bred and reared on the poorest of land and then be sold to those owning the best. Slavery in the immediate antebellum years was, therefore, an economically viable institution in virtually all areas of the South as long as slaves could be expeditiously and economically transferred from one sector to another.

III. REPRODUCTION, ALLOCATION, AND SLAVE MARKETS

It thus remains to be determined whether an efficient supply mechanism—efficient in both its generative and its allocative functions—existed in the antebellum South. That the slave force might reproduce itself was not sufficient; there must also have been a capital market capable of getting the labor to the areas where production was expanding if slavery was to be profitable. The several arguments that, together, form the orthodox opposition to the present hypothesis are as follows (in every case accompanied by a citation as a talisman against any possible charge that we are setting up straw men):[10] (i) slaves are notoriously inefficient and unwilling workers; (ii) slave property, unlike wage labor, must be supported in the years before and after the slave is economically productive; (iii) slaveholding absorbed plantation earnings; (iv) slave economies are constantly threatened by decline because they cannot in general maintain the number of slaves; and (v) capitalization of the labor force inhibits the efficient allocation of labor.

The first and second of these arguments are implicitly tested in the computation of the rate of return on slave capital. We are not concerned with the efficiency per se, however that might be measured, or with the efficiency of slaves as opposed to free white laborers. The more sophisticated version of this efficiency argument—that slave ineptness forced the planters to use a particularly wasteful form of agriculture—is probably untestable because of the difficulties of identification when impetus or motives are being considered. It might be suggested as a partial answer however, that extensive farming was not peculiarly a characteristic of slave agriculture or even of plantation cotton culture. It was common to all North American colonial agriculture and, as late as the end of the nineteenth century, was reputed to be characteristic of farming in the Northwest wheat lands. It is, generally, a salient feature of agriculture when labor is scarce relative to land.[11] But, insofar as slaves were inefficient, the inefficiency must be reflected in the returns computed in our model. Similarly, the costs of maintaining slaves in infancy and dotage are accounted for in our cost of production.

The third argument—that the South lost from the payment of interest and the constant enhancement of slave prices (and therefore overcapitalization of the labor force)—rests in part upon two

---

[10](i) J. E. Cairnes, *The Slave Power* (New York: Follett Foster & Co., 1863), pp. 44-50; F. L. Olmsted. *The Cotton Kingdom* (New York: Mason Bros., (1861), pp. 100-110 (1953 ed.; New York: A. A. Knopf); W. A. Lewis, *Theory of Economic Growth* (Homewood, Ill.: Richard D. Irwin, Inc., 1955), pp. 107-8; (ii) U. B. Phillips, *Life and Labor in the Old South* (Boston: Little, Brown & Co., 1935), pp. 174-75; (iii) U. B. Phillips, "The Economic Cost of Slaveholding in the Cotton-Belt," *Political Science Quarterly,* XX (1905), 257-75; (iv) Lewis, *op. cit.,* pp. 111-13; (v) J. S. Duesenberry, "Some Aspects of the Theory of Economic Development," *Explorations in Entrepreneurial History,* III (1950), 9. This is, of course, intended only as a list of examples, chosen on the grounds that they are particularly well stated.

[11] M. B. Hammond, *The Cotton Industry* (New York, 1897), p. 82. See also *United States Patent Office Report (Agriculture), 1852* (Washington, D.C., 1853), p. 374.

misapprehensions, attributable to U. B. Phillips: (1) that capitalization involves a net loss through the payment of interest and (2) that slaves were, somehow, a fictitious form of wealth. We have already shown that slave capital earned returns at least equal to those earned by other contemporary forms of capital. For the overcapitalization part of the argument, it remains to be shown that slave prices did not run away from cotton values.

The last two of the assertions state the negative of our principal secondary hypothesis, which is that an efficient market system existed for the supply of slaves to the rapidly growing cotton industry of the Southwest through transfer from the exhausted land of the Old South. It will be shown that the slave population, in all but the Louisiana sugar area, more than reproduced itself. It will also be shown the border states were not depleted to provide for western needs, since only the natural increase was exported. Finally, avoiding the emotion-wracked testimony of the time, we will attempt to demonstrate the existence of regional specialization and an efficient market by comparing the demographic composition of the cotton and border states and by examining the price behavior in the market for Negro slaves.

Reproduction of the Slave Labor Force. The history of slavery is full of examples of slave economies that could not reproduce their population and collapsed because of a failure of supply. Frequently, as in the Roman case, the supply was dependent upon a steady flow of military prisoners. The Augustan peace and the stabilization of the borders of the empire are credited with the decline of Roman slavery for this reason. Similarly, the labor supply in the Caribbean sugar islands could be maintained only by importation. It is generally argued that slavery disappeared from Jamaica, not because of abolition in 1834, but because of the inability of the slave population to reproduce itself once the slave trade had been closed.

By contrast, the antebellum cotton-slave economy of the southern states managed to maintain and allocate its labor supply by a system of regional specialization that produced slaves on the worn-out land of the Old South and the border states for export to the high-yield cotton land of the Mississippi and Red River valleys. For the whole nation the Negro rate of increase in the six decades before the Civil War was only slightly below the rate for the white population; for most of the period the slave rate was very much above that for free Negroes. In the South the disparity between Negro and white rates of increase favors the Negro; considering the relative rates of immigration of whites and Negroes after the first decade of the nineteenth century, the discrepancy in natural increase is even more striking. The evidence in Table 12 does not admit of any doubt that the slave population was capable of producing a steady supply of labor for the plantation economy.[12]

TABLE 12 *Percentage Decennial Increase in White and Negro Population, 1790-1860*

Census Year	Total	White	Increase During Preceding Ten Years		
			Negro		
			Total	Slave	Free
1800	35.1	35.8	32.3	28.1	82.2
1810	36.4	36.1	37.5	33.1	71.9
1820	33.1	34.2	28.6	29.1	25.3
1830	33.5	33.9	31.4	30.6	36.8
1840	32.7	34.7	23.4	23.8	20.9
1850	35.9	37.7	26.6	28.8	12.5
1860	35.6	37.7	22.1	23.4	12.3

Source: Bureau of the Census, *Negro Population in the United States, 1790-1915* (Washington, D.C., 1918), Tables 2 (chap. ii) and 1 (chap. v) and pp. 25 and 53. The sharp declines in the rate of increase for slaves in the decades ending in 1840 and 1860 probably reflect the generation cycle following the increase in importations, mostly of mature Negroes, in the years just prior to 1803.

Slave Markets and Allocation. The more important issue, however, is whether or not the slave force could be allocated efficiently. The natural rate of increase was more than sufficient in the Old South to meet the needs of agriculture in the region, but in the West it was less than sufficient to meet the demands for increased cotton production. By direct export and by the migration of planters with their work forces, the eastern areas supplied the needs of the Southwest. In every decade before the Civil War the increase of slaves in the cotton states was much above, and in the Atlantic and border states much below, the rate of increase for the whole slave population. Indeed, in the decades ending in 1840 and 1860 the net rate of population increase in the Old South was only slightly above the level sufficient to maintain the population at a constant level, 4.5 per cent and 7.1 per cent (see Table 13). From 1790 to 1850 the increase of slaves in the Atlantic states was just 2 per cent per annum, while in the Gulf states (including Florida),

[12]See Bureau of the Census, *Negro Population in the United States, 1790-1915* (Washington, D.C., 1918); Gray, *op. cit.,* chap. xxviii; Cairnes, *op. cit.,* chap. iv; E. Halle, *Baumwollproduktion und Pflanzungswirtschaft* (Leipzig, 1897), Vol. I, Book III, 5.3.

TABLE 13 Percentage Rate of Population Increase, by Race, in the Cotton and Border States, 1790-1860

Decade Ending	Cotton States* White	Cotton States* Negro	Border States† White	Border States† Negro
1800	42.9	47.4	27.9	24.4
1810	37.5	61.3	23.5	23.4
1820	38.8	48.0	19.5	15.5
1830	40.0	46.8	19.0	14.0
1840	31.3	37.6	21.1	4.5
1850	34.1	35.6	34.5	11.0
1860	27.6	29.0	39.2	7.1

Source: Ernst von Halle, *Baumwollproduktion und Pflanzungswirtschaft in den Nordamerikanischen Sud-staaten* (Leipzig, 1897, p. 132. His sources were Tucker, *Progress of the United States* (to 1840), *Census of Population* (1850 and after), and H. Gannett, *Statistics of the Negroes in the United States.*
*North Carolina, South Carolina, Georgia, Florida, Alabama, Mississippi, Louisiana, Texas, Arkansas, and Tennessee.
†Delaware, Maryland, District of Columbia, Virginia, West Virginia, Kentucky, and Missouri.

Arkansas, and Tennessee the rate was 18 per cent per annum. A rough but probably conservative estimate of the export from the selling states between 1820 and 1860 is given by W. H. Collins. Taking the difference between the average natural increase and the actual rate in the selling states, Collins arrived at the following estimates:[13]

1820-30	124,000
1830-40	265,000
1840-50	146,000
1850-60	207,000

Collins estimated that at least three-fifths of the removals from the border states were due to emigration to the Southwest rather than to export. While this has little bearing upon the issue of allocative efficiency, it does have significance for the corollary assertion that the slaveowners of the border states, consciously or unconsciously, were engaged in a specialized breeding operation,

[13]W. H. Collins, *The Domestic Slave Trade of the Southern States* (New York, 1904), chap. iii. In the first decade the selling states include Virginia, Maryland, Delaware, North Carolina, Kentucky, and the District of Columbia; the buying states are assumed to be South Carolina, Georgia, Alabama, Mississippi, Tennessee, and Missouri. In 1830, Florida and, in 1850, Texas were added to the buying group. Tennessee, Missouri, and North Carolina are very uncertain assignments, since these states were far from homogeneous slave-marketing areas; some parts imported, while other parts exported, during the period (cf. Halle, *op. cit.*, pp. 282 ff., and Frederic Bancroft, *Slave Trading in the Old South* [Baltimore: J. H. Furst, 1931], chap. xviii, for similar estimates, consistent with those given by Collins).

producing chattel labor for the growing Southwest. In 1836 the *Virginia Times* estimated that, "of the number of slaves exported [from Virginia], not more than one-third have been sold, the others being carried by their masters, who have removed."[14] Ruffin supposed that the annual sale in 1859 "already exceed in number all the increase in slaves in Virginia by procreation."[15] Bancroft goes beyond these estimates and states that "in the 'fifties, when the extreme prejudice against the interstate traders had abated and their inadequate supplies were eagerly purchased, fully 70 per cent of the slaves removed from the Atlantic and the border slave states to the Southwest were taken after purchase or with a view to sale, that is, were the objects of slave-trading."[16] Whatever the accuracy of these several estimates, which range from two-fifths to four-fifths of total exports of slaves from the border and the Atlantic states, it is clear that sales of slaves provided an important capital gain for the exporting states. There is ample documentary evidence that planters in the Old South were aware of this, that some welcomed it and depended upon it, and that others were fearful of its effect upon the agriculture of the area and upon the tenability of slavery. Some spoke frankly about Virginia as a "breeding state," though the reply to such allegations was generally an indignant denial. Whether systematically bred or not, the natural increase of the slave force was an important, probably the most important, product of the more exhausted soil of the Old South.

The existence of such specialization is evident in the demographic composition of the cotton and breeding areas and in the price behavior in the markets for slaves. Table 14 demonstrates that the selling states contained, in 1850 and 1860, a greater proportion of children under fifteen years and a substantially greater proportion of slaves above the age of fifty than did the buying states. While the disproportions are not great enough to characterize the selling states as a great nursery, the age composition is in the direction which our hypothesis would lead one to expect. The relationship between the prices of men and women in the slave market, when compared with the ratio of hiring rates for male and female field hands, gives an even stronger indication that the superior usefulness of females of

[14]Quoted in *Slavery and the Internal Slave Trade in the United States of North America* (London, 1841) (by the Executive Committee of the American Anti-Slavery Society), p. 13. On the same page the authors assert that four-fifths or more of the slaves brought into the buying states were supplied by the internal slave trade.

[15]Edmund Ruffin, *DeBow's Review,* XXVI (1859), 650.

[16]Bancroft, *op. cit.,* p. 398.

breeding age was economically recognized. The relative hiring rates for men and women in 1860, shown in Table 15, can be taken as a measure of their relative values in the field.[17]

TABLE 14 Slave Population by Age

		(Per Cent)				
		1860			1850	
Age (Years)	Total	Selling States*	Buying States†	Total	Selling States*	Buying States†
Under 15	44.8	45.6	43.8	44.9	45.6	44.3
15–19	11.4	11.5	11.4	11.1	11.3	11.0
20–29	17.6	16.5	18.9	18.0	17.0	18.9
30–39	11.7	10.7	11.8	11.3	10.5	12.1
20–49	36.4	34.4	38.1	36.4	34.6	38.1
50 and over	7.5	8.5	6.7	7.5	8.5	6.6

Source: J. C. G. Kennedy, *Population of the United States in 1860* (Washington, D.C., 1864), "Classified Population," Tables No. 1, by state; J. D. B. DeBow, *Statistical View of the United States, . . . Being a Compendium of the Seventh Census* (Washington, D.C., 1854), Part II, Table LXXXII, pp. 89–90.
*Virginia, Maryland, Delaware, South Carolina, Missouri, Kentucky, District of Columbia.
†Georgia, Alabama, Mississippi, Florida, Texas, Louisiana.
Note.—The exclusion of Tennessee and North Carolina is explained in n. 14. Missouri was included with the selling group because of its apparent net selling position in this period.

To be compared to these rates are the purchase prices of male and female slaves in the same markets in 1859 and 1860. Purchase prices should reflect the relative usefulness of the sexes for field work. More than this, however, if there is any additional value to slave women—for breeding purposes, presumably—there should be a premium in the form of a narrower price differential than is found in the hiring rates. The prices shown in Table 16 are taken from Table A in the Appendix. Whenever possible, 1860 is used; wherever necessary, 1859. Table 16 includes age designations and, when available, a description of the grade or class represented in the average price.[18] This evidence is a striking confirmation of the validity of the model. In every case but one, the purchase price differential is

[17]The rates are quoted in Hammond, *op. cit.,* p. 90, from *Report of the Commissioner of Agriculture, 1866* (Washington, D.C., 1867), p. 416. Three Virginia newspaper quotations in G. M. Weston, *Who Are and Who May Be Slaves in the United States* (undated pamphlet), give ratios ranging between 2 and 2.5, supporting Hammond's estimate. There is a possible overestimate in these ratios, if they are to be used to infer relative usefulness in the field, since some allowance was probably made for time lost for delivery by pregnant females. No evidence has been found on this point, however.

[18]With one exception—the South Carolina, 1860, comparison—the pairings are taken from single sales. In addition, the pairings are made, as far as possible, with slaves of apparently comparable quality. The Virginia and Mississippi quotations are from average-price listings and are probably most useful for present purposes.

TABLE 15 Annual Hiring Rates for Male and Female Slaves
(Including Rations and Clothing), by States, 1860

State	Men	Women	Ratio (Men:Women)
Virginia	$105	$ 46	2.28
North Carolina	110	49	2.25
South Carolina	103	55	1.87
Georgia	124	75	1.65
Florida	139	80	1.74
Alabama	138	89	1.55
Mississippi	166	100	1.66
Louisiana	171	120	1.43
Texas	166	109	1.52
Arkansas	170	108	1.57
Tennessee	121	63	1.92

narrower than the hiring-rate differential. The price structure clearly reflects the added value of females due to their ability to generate capital gains. It is especially interesting in this regard to note that the price ratios in Virginia and South Carolina, the two breeding states represented in the list, show practically no differential. This evidence clearly shows that the Old South recognized in the market the value of its function as the slave-breeding area for the cotton-raising West.

"Overcapitalization" of the Labor Force. The aspect of slave economics that causes the most confusion and outright error is that which relates to the capitalization, and, in the antebellum southern case, the presumed overcapitalization of slave labor. Phillips speaks of an "irresistible tendency to overvalue and overcapitalize" and argues that slaveholding had an unlimited capacity for absorbing the planters' earnings through the continual payment of interest and the enhancement of prices. For the Cotton Belt this was presumably aggregated into a continuous public drain of wealth, first, to England and New England and, later, to the upper South.[19] Moreover, a series of writers from Max Weber down to the most recent theorists of economic growth have argued that capitalization tends to rigidify

[19]Phillips, "The Economic Cost of Slaveholding in the Cotton-Belt," *op. cit.,* pp. 271 ff.

TABLE 16 Selected Prices of Male and Female Slaves, 1859 and 1860

State (Year)	Age	Condition	Male Price	Female Price	Ratio
Virginia (1859)	17–20	Best	$1,350–$1,425	$1,275–$1,325	1.07
South Carolina		Prime	$1,325		}1.03
		Wench		$1,283	
South Carolina		Field hand	$1,555		}.91
(1859)		Girl		$1,705	
Georgia	21	Best field hand	$1,900		}.88
	17	(9 mo. inf.)		[$2,150]	
Georgia (1859)		Prime, young	$1,300		}
		Cotton hand,			}1.04
		houseservant		$1,250	
Alabama (1859)	19		$1,635		}1.37
	18, 18, 8			$1,193	
Mississippi		No. 1 field	$1,625	$1,450	1.12
		hand			
Texas	21,15		$2,015	$1,635	1.23
Texas (1859)	17,14		$1,527	$1,403	1.09

the pattern of employment. "Free labor is necessary to make free transfers of labor possible. A production organization cannot be very flexible if it has to engage in the purchase or sale of slaves every time it changes its output."[20] But this is really a question of how good the market is; no one, after all, claims that manufacturing is made suicidally inflexible by the fact that expanding sectors must buy the capitalized future earnings of machinery. There are three issues to be distinguished in this argument: first, the alleged tendency toward overcapitalization; second, the inflexibility of chattel labor and the difficulty of allocating it, geographically and industrially; and third, the loss of wealth.

First, was the southerner his own victim in an endless speculative inflation of slave prices? The assertion of an irresistible tendency to overvalue and overcapitalize must mean that he was so trapped, if it means anything. Phillips answered the question by comparing the price of cotton with the price of prime field hands, year by year. He found, or believed he found, a permanent movement toward overcapitalization inherent in American slaveholding. But speculative overexpansion is capable of reversal; from the inflation of 1837 to the bottom of the depression in 1845, slave prices fell as sharply as

[20]Duesenberry, *loc. cit.*

cotton prices. If the rise from that lower turning point is a demonstration of speculative mania, it was a mania solidly based on the increase in the value of the crop per hand, owing to the concentration of production in more fertile areas, the greater efficiency of the American-born slaves, lowered transportation costs, and the development of new high-yield varieties of cotton from the fourth decade of the century on.[21] Finally, the choice of the initial period in Phillips' analysis exaggerates the decline in cotton prices relative to the price of slaves. At the turn of the century the demand for cotton was increasing rapidly, supporting remarkably high prices, while the unrestricted African slave trade kept domestic slave prices well below the level that might be expected in view of the level of profits. Table 17 and Chart 1 demonstrate the relationships among slave prices, cotton prices, and the value of cotton output per slave (of field-work age, ten to fifty-four). Several things become clear in this comparison. To begin, the relationship between slave and cotton prices is significant for Phillips' purposes only if there is no increase in productivity. While he is struck by the fact that slave prices rose more rapidly than did cotton prices in the long upswing starting in the early 1840's, it is equally striking to observe that (New Orleans) slave prices rose about one and one-half times between the low point in 1843-45 to 1860, while values of cotton production per hand rose more than three times from the low in 1842. This was recognized in the *New Orleans Daily Crescent* in 1860, as follows:

> Nor do we agree with our contemporaries who argue that a speculative demand is the unsubstantial basis of the advance in the price of slaves. . . . It is our impression that the great demand for slaves in the Southwest will keep up the prices as it caused their advance in the first place, and that the rates are not a cent above the real value of the laborer who is to be engaged in tilling the fertile lands of a section of the country which yields the planter nearly double the crop that the fields of the Atlantic States do.[22]

Furthermore, it would appear that slave prices fluctuated less than did cotton prices. This and the less clear-cut lag of the slave prices make it difficult to accept the image of unwary planters helplessly

---

[21]Gray, *op. cit.,* chap. xxx; *DeBow's Review,* XVIII (1855), 332-34; Hammond, *op. cit.,* pp. 76-77, 113-19; T. P. Kettell, *Southern Wealth and Northern Profits* (New York, 1860), p. 48.

[22]Quoted in Phillips, *Life and Labor in the Old South,* p. 180. Having quoted this, Phillips, without offering any evidence, asserts: "But surely a peak was being shaped, whose farther side must have been a steep descent, whether in time of peace or war."

Chart 1 Slave Population and Prices and the Value of Cotton Production, 1802-60.

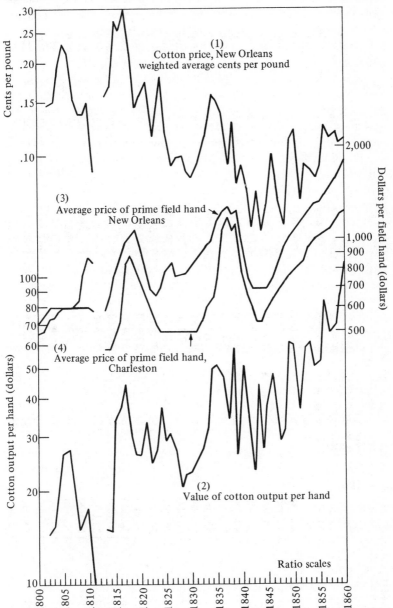

(1)
Cotton price, New Orleans
weighted average cents per pound

(3)
Average price of prime field hand
New Orleans

(4)
Average price of prime field hand,
Charleston

(2)
Value of cotton output per hand

Ratio scales

Sources: (1), (2), (3): see Table 17; (4): estimated visually from graph in U. B. Phillips, *Life and Labor in the Old South*, p. 177.

TABLE 17 Value of Cotton Production and Slave Population, 1802-60, New Orleans Prices

Year	Crop (Thousands of Pounds)	Average Price (Cents per Pound)	Value (Thousands)	No. of Slaves, Aged 10-54 Years*	Crop Value per Slave	Price of Prime Field Hand	Crop Value per Hand per Dollar Slave Price
1802	55,000	0.147	$ 8,085	550,708	$ 14.68	$ 600	.02
1803	60,000	.150	9,000	568,932	15.82	600	.03
1804	65,000	.196	12,740	587,157	21.70	600	.04
1805	70,000	.233	16,310	605,381	26.94	600	.05
1806	80,000	.218	17,440	623,606	27.97	600	.05
1807	80,000	.164	13,120	641,831	20.44	600	.03
1808	75,000	.136	10,200	660,055	15.45	640	.02
1809	82,000	.136	11,152	678,280	16.44	780	.02
1810	85,000	.147	12,495	696,505	17.94	900	.02
1811	80,000	.089	7,120	717,376	9.93	860	.01
1813	75,000	.155	11,625	759,118	15.31	600	.03
1814	70,000	.169	11,830	779,989	15.17	650	.02
1815	100,000	.273	27,300	800,860	34.09	765	.05
1816	124,000	.254	31,496	821,731	38.33	880	.04
1817	130,000	.298	38,740	842,602	45.98	1,000	.05
1818	125,000	.215	26,875	863,473	31.12	1,050	.03
1819	167,000	.143	23,881	884,344	27.00	1,100	.03
1820	160,000	.152	24,320	905,215	26.88	970	.03
1821	180,000	.174	31,320	933,517	33.55	810	.04
1822	210,000	.115	24,150	961,818	25.11	700	.04
1823	185,000	.145	26,825	990,120	27.04	670	.04
1824	215,000	.179	38,485	1,018,421	37.99	700	.05

TABLE 17 (continued)

Year							
1825	255,000	.119	30,345	1,046,723	28.99	800	.04
1826	350,000	.093	32,550	1,075,024	30.28	840	.04
1827	316,900	.097	30,739	1,103,326	27.86	770	.04
1828	241,399	.098	23,657	1,131,627	20.91	770	.03
1829	296,812	.089	26,416	1,159,929	22.77	770	.03
1830	331,150	.084	27,817	1,208,034	23.03	810	.03
1831	354,247	.090	31,882	1,247,489	25.56	860	.03
1832	355,492	.100	35,549	1,275,061	27.88	900	.03
1833	374,653	.112	41,961	1,302,633	32.21	960	.03
1834	437,558	.155	67,821	1,330,206	50.99	1,000	.05
1835	460,338	.152	69,971	1,357,778	51.53	1,150	.05
1836	507,550	.133	67,504	1,385,350	46.79	1,250	.04
1837	539,669	.090	48,510	1,412,923	34.38	1,300	.03
1838	682,767	.124	84,663	1,440,495	58.77	1,220	.05
1839	501,708	.079	39,635	1,468,067	27.00	1,240	.02
1840	834,111	.091	75,904	1,507,779	50.34	1,020	.05
1841	644,172	.078	50,245	1,568,022	32.04	870	.04
1842	668,379	.057	38,098	1,611,269	23.65	750	.03
1843	972,960	.075	72,972	1,654,516	44.11	700	.06
1844	836,529	.055	46,009	1,697,762	27.10	700	.04
1845	993,719	.068	67,573	1,741,009	38.81	700	.06
1846	863,321	.099	85,469	1,784,256	47.90	750	.06
1847	766,599	.070	53,662	1,827,503	29.36	850	.04
1848	1,017,391	.058	59,009	1,870,750	31.54	950	.03
1849	1,249,985	.108	134,998	1,913,996	70.53	1,030	.07
1850	1,001,165	.117	117,136	1,979,059	59.19	1,100	.05

TABLE 17 (continued)

1851	1,021,048	.074	75,558	2,034,482	37.14	1,150	.03
1852	1,338,061	.091	121,764	2,080,554	58.53	1,200	.05
1853	1,496,302	.088	131,675	2,126,626	61.92	1,250	.05
1854	1,322,241	.084	111,068	2,172,698	51.12	1,310	.04
1855	1,294,463	.091	117,796	2,218,770	53.09	1,350	.04
1856	1,535,334	.124	190,381	2,264,843	84.06	1,420	.06
1857	1,373,619	.112	153,845	2,310,915	66.57	1,490	.05
1858	1,439,744	.115	165,571	2,356,988	70.25	1,580	.04
1859	1,796,455	.108	194,017	2,403,060	80.74	1,690	.05
1860	2,241,056	0.111	$248,757	2,460,648	$101.09	$1,800	.06

Source: *Crops:* Computed from the data on number of bales and average weight of bales in James L. Watkins, *Production and Price of Cotton for One Hundred Years* (U.S. Department of Agriculture, Miscellaneous Series, Bull. 9 [Washington, D.C. 1895]). *Price:* Gray, *op. cit.*, Table 41: "Weighted Yearly Averages and Monthly Prices in Cents per Pound of Short-Staple Cotton at New Orleans for the Crop Years 1802-1860." *Slaves:* Bureau of the Census, *Negro Population in the United States, 1790-1915,* "Slave and Free Colored Population at Each Census by Sections and Southern Divisions: 1790-1860," p. 55, and "Negro Population in Years Specified, Classified by Sex and Age Periods: 1830-1910," p. 166. *Slave prices:* Estimated visually from the chart "Approximate Prices of Prime Field Hands in Hundred of Dollars per Head: . . . at New Orleans . . . ," in U. B. Philips, *Life and Labor in the Old South* (Boston, 1935), p. 177.

*To estimate the slave population in the intercensal years, the increase over each decade was divided into equal parts and assigned to each year in the decade. The proportion of Negroes in the field-work age brackets (between the ages of ten and fifty-four) was .641 in 1860, .635 in 1850, .621 in 1810, and .610 in 1830. The census-year proportions at the beginning and end of each decade were averaged for use in the intervening years. For the years before 1830, an estimate of .60 was used. There is no implication that we have measured the number of field hands, but it should be noted that the range .60-.65 brackets several contemporary estimates of the proportion of the slave population employed in cotton agriculture (see, e.g., P. A. Morse, "Southern Slavery and the Cotton Trade," *De Bow's Review,* XXIII [1857], 475-82).

exposing themselves in a market dominated by speculators. It would make more sense to argue simply that the rising trend of slave prices coupled with a growing slave population is, in and of itself, strong evidence of the profitability of slavery.

The Efficiency of Allocation. The second point relates to geographic allocation and, to a lesser extent, to the mobility of the slave labor force among crops. The slave prices in all regions move very closely with cotton prices and products per hand. It is clear, too, that the eastern prices move directly with the cotton-area slave prices, although in the last two decades the rate of increase of prices fell behind in the breeding area. If the market were extremely imperfect and the transfer between the breeding and consuming states inefficient, in contradiction to our hypothesis, then there should be much less evidence of regional arbitrage than is found here. In response to the western demand, Virginia and the other eastern states shipped their natural increase to the cotton areas. Indeed, it is frequently argued that the transfer was too efficient and that the Old South was being continuously depressed by the high price of labor occasioned by western demand. Edmund Ruffin, particularly, took this position and argued that slave trade could not bring profits to Virginia but could result only in the paralysis of her industry. If true, this argument would be supported empirically by increasing real estate values on the western lands and decreasing values in the Atlantic and border states. That is, the chain of high cotton profits—high slave prices—increased cost of farming in the Old South should have depressed land prices in the latter area. Emigration, by reducing demand, should have meant more downward pressure. The only influence that operated in the direction of maintaining the value of land in the older states was the profit to be had from the increase and sale of slaves. Indeed, in 1850 and 1860 the value per acre of farm land and buildings in the border states was $7.18 and $12.33 and, in the lower South for the same two census years, $4.99 and $8.54. Undoubtedly, the western cotton land earned a considerable rent in farming over the older land. It was this rent that maintained the flow of migration to the Cotton Belt. But that migration depended upon and supported the prosperity of the breeding states. It also is not clear that slavery was able to continue only by skinning the topsoil and moving on, leaving exhausted land and low slave and land value in its wake. Quite the contrary, the evidence can plausibly be interpreted as indicating a unified, specialized economy in which the settlers on the naturally superior western lands (superior even before the deterioration of the older regions by single-crop cultivation of tobacco and cotton) were able to bid slave labor away from general farming and to make wholesale abandonment of the older areas unnecessary, if indeed there had ever been such a necessity.

Slavery and Southern Economic Growth. Finally, there are two economic arguments about slavery and potential southern growth to be considered. The assertion that slavery per se was inimical to economic growth rests in part upon the alleged inefficiency of slave labor in industrial pursuits and in part upon the loss of capital that might otherwise have gone into industrialization and diversification.

The inefficiency argument is not supported very securely. There were slaves employed in cotton factories throughout the South. Slaves were used in the coal mines and in the North Carolina lumbering operations. In the ironworks at Richmond and on the Cumberland River, slaves comprised a majority of the labor force. Southern railroads were largely built by southern slaves. Crop diversification, or the failure to achieve diversification, appears to have been a problem of entrepreneurship rather than of the difficulties of training slaves. In the face of the demand for cotton and the profits to be had from specializing in this single crop, it is hardly difficult to explain the single-minded concentration of the planter.[23]

In what ways was slavery allegedly responsible for the drain of capital from the South? The lack of diversification, to the extent of a failure even to provide basic supplies, made necessary the import of much food and virtually all manufactured articles from the North. But half of this assertion, the argument that laid the responsibility for the single-crop culture upon slavery, has been found questionable already.

The major avenues by which wealth is said to have been drained from the cotton states were the excessive use of credit (through dependence upon factors' services) and the "absorption" of capital in slaves. Good crop years bring the temptation to expand production; bad years do not bring any release from the factors. But resort to factoring is characteristic of speculative, commercial agriculture,

[23]See Robert R. Russel, *Economic Aspects of Southern Sectionalism, 1840-1861* (Urbana, Ill., 1924), esp. pp. 54-64, and "Slavery and Southern Economic Progress," *Journal of Southern History,* IV (February, 1938), 34-54. See also Gray, *op. cit.,* pp. 458-61, 940-42, and Hammond, *op. cit.,* pp. 40-44, 94-96.

whether or not the labor force is organized in slavery. It is also frequently argued that slavery gave southern planters a taste for extravagant, wasteful display, causing the notorious lack of thrift and the relative lack of economic development, compared to that experienced in the North and West. This is a doubtful inference, at best. Slavery did not make the cavalier any more than slavery invented speculation in cotton. However, insofar as successful slave management required military posture and discipline, the southerner's expensive image of himself as a *grand seigneur* was encouraged. It is beyond the scope of this paper to offer hypotheses about the reasons for the relative degrees of entrepreneurship in Charleston and Boston; in this context it is sufficient to state that slavery per se does not seem to have been responsible for the excessive reliance upon factoring and external sources of credit.[24]

There remains only the absorption of capital in slaves to set the responsibility for lack of growth in the South upon the peculiar institution. Earnings that might have gone out of the South to bring in investment goods were fixed in the form of chattel labor. For the early years, during the external slave trade, there is some plausibility to this argument, though it is difficult to see how the capitalization of an income stream, excellent by contemporary standards, can be said to count as a loss of wealth. In the later years there was, except to the extent that northern or English bankers drew off the interest, a redistribution of wealth only within the slave states: from the cotton lands back to the less profitable field agriculture of the older section. And, to the extent that the old planting aristocracy used the profits to maintain the real or fancied magnificence of the preceding century, capital was absorbed. But, as Russel pointed out, slavery also made the profits in the cotton fields and the resultant demand for eastern hands. We are left with the conclusion that, except insofar as it made speculation in cotton possible on a grander scale than would otherwise have been the case and thereby weakened whatever pressure there might have been for diversification, capitalization of the labor force did not of itself operate against southern development.

[24]Hammond, *op. cit.,* pp. 107-12; Russel, *op. cit.,* pp. 49 ff.; M. B. Hammond, "Agricultural Credit and Crop Mortgages," in *The South in the Building of the Nation* (Richmond, Va., 1909), V, 457-61; Alfred H. Stone, "The Cotton Factorage System of the Southern States," *American Historical Review,* XX (1915), 557-65. For an excellent discussion of the seigneurial impediments to entrepreneurship see W. J. Cash, *The Mind of the South* (New York, 1941), pp. 42-70.

IV. CONCLUSION

In sum, it seems doubtful that the South was forced by bad statesmanship into an unnecessary war to protect a system that must soon have disappeared because it was economically unsound. This is a romantic hypothesis, which will not stand against the facts.

On the basis of the computation of the returns to capital in our model of the antebellum southern economy and the demonstration of the efficiency of the regional specialization, the following conclusions are offered.

1. Slavery was profitable to the whole South, the continuing demand for labor in the Cotton Belt ensuring returns to the breeding operation on the less productive land in the seaboard and border states. The breeding returns were necessary, however, to make the plantation operations on the poorer lands as profitable as alternative contemporary economic activities in the United States. The failure of southern agriculture on these poorer lands in the postbellum period is probably attributable, in the main, to the loss of these capital gains on breeding and not, as is so often suggested, to either the relative inefficiency of the tenant system that replaced the plantations or the soil damage resulting from war operations. These factors were unquestionably contributing elements to the difficulties of postbellum southern agriculture, but they were of relatively small quantitative importance compared with the elimination of slave-breeding returns.

2. There was nothing necessarily self-destructive about the profits of the slave economy. Neither the overcapitalization argument nor the assertion that slavery must have collapsed because the slaves would not reproduce themselves is tenable. Slave prices did not outpace productivity, and the regional slave price structure would imply a workable transfer mechanism rather than the contrary.

3. Continued expansion of slave territory was both possible and, to some extent, necessary. The maintenance of profits in the Old South depended upon the expansion, extensive or intensive, of slave agriculture into the Southwest. This is sufficient to explain the interest of the Old South in secession and does away with the necessity to fall back upon arguments of statesmanship or quixotism to explain the willingness to fight for the peculiar institution.

4. The available productive surplus from slavery might have been used for economic development or, as in some totalitarian regimes

of this century, for militarism. In spite of this good omen for development, southern investment and industrialization lagged. It is hard to explain this lag except on the social ground that entrepreneurship could not take root in the South or on the economic ground that the South did not really own the system but merely operated it. Furthermore, the American experience clearly suggests that slavery is not, from the strict economic standpoint, a deterrent to industrial development and that its elimination may take more than the workings of "inexorable economic forces." Although profitability cannot be offered as a sufficient guaranty of the continuity of southern slavery, the converse argument that slavery must have destroyed itself can no longer rest upon allegations of unprofitability or upon assumptions about the impossibility of maintaining and allocating a slave labor force. To the extent, moreover, that profitability is a necessary condition for the continuation of a private business institution in a free-enterprise society, slavery was not untenable in the antebellum American South. Indeed, economic forces often may work toward the continuation of a slave system, so that the elimination of slavery may depend upon the adoption of harsh political measures. Certainly that was the American experience.

DOUGLAS F. DOWD

The Economics of Slavery in the Antebellum South: A Comment

Of the many critiques of the Conrad and Meyer analysis, that by Douglas Dowd of Cornell University is presented here for two reasons. First, it was made immediately after Conrad and Meyer concluded the presentation of their paper at the joint Economic History Association - National Bureau of Economic Research conference in Williamstown, Massachusetts, in September, 1957, and therefore may be taken as representing the initial reactions of a concerned scholar. And secondly, it typifies a line of criticism which has shown remarkable durability

Reprinted from the *Journal of Political Economy,* October 1958, by permission of the University of Chicago Press. Copyright 1958 by the University of Chicago Press.

since then—one which Conrad and Meyer have tried to answer on more than one occasion, but which apparently will not die.

What is the essence of Dowd's objection? The estimates and calculations which, as Conrad and Meyer saw the matter, made up the substance of their analysis? Not at all. What Dowd takes exception to are, first, the philosophical presuppositions with which Conrad and Meyer approached their problems, and secondly, the broader implications of their study for Southern history, for slavery, and for an understanding of economic development in general. The issues which concerned him bore, to Conrad and Meyer, only a marginal relationship to what they had tried to do. But the issues which Conrad and Meyer regarded as central seemed to Dowd little more than an academic exercise in computation unless and until their relationship to the broader concerns of historians was brought out into the open.

Conrad and Meyer had proceeded by isolating their problem. Their central concern was to measure an economic quantity; the farthest they had been willing to go in generalizing about slavery and economic development was to say that, judging from American experience and looking at the matter "from the strict economic standpoint," slavery did not seem to have been a deterrent. The whole tenor of their analysis, as of their later defenses, was to insist that they were doing what economists are trained and qualified to do—that is, to analyze the economic aspects of human behavior. They did not deny that slavery, like most other human institutions, had other aspects, equally deserving of investigation; but that was not their business. They did not question that the South's willingness to fight for its peculiar institution might conceivably be explained on non-economic grounds; they merely said that the economic explanation seemed sufficient and, that being so, it was not necessary to "fall back upon" other lines of reasoning.

And in doing this they were, of course, doing what modern social science in the United States, modelling itself on the natural sciences, has consistently tried to do. They were specialists, tackling a specialized problem. Their goals were precision, accuracy, and verifiability. They had defined their problem clearly and set up a simple and operational explanatory model. Their evidence and the ways in which they had made their estimates were out in the open for everyone to inspect. It was all perfectly straight-forward. Who could take exception?

As it turned out, a surprisingly large number of people could take exception, though few expressed the bases for their reactions as clearly and persuasively as Dowd. What was at issue was a matter of profound importance, and not for historians and economists alone. In a phrase, it was the nature, methods, and responsibilities of social science. To compress Dowd's remarks any further than they were already compressed in this brief Comment would be unfair, but it is surely clear that what he is rejecting is the compartmentalization, specialization, and fragmentation characteristic of the social sciences as they are organized in North America today. What he is pleading for is an approach which tries to see problems whole. What he is repudiating is the practice by which a single, specialized discipline, having analyzed a complex human problem to its own satisfaction and within its own definitional limits, then presumes to claim that nothing more need be done. None of this should be difficult for today's generation of students to understand.

Historians are particularly wary of the over-simplifications to which these practices often lead; their training and temperament make it hard for them to forget the terrible complexity of the real world. It is probably true that most people who responded favorably to Douglas Dowd's criticisms had been trained as historians, while those who thought his objections irrelevant or obscurantist were, by training, economists. But to say this is already to over-simplify; the division is not between two academic professions and two graduate curricula but between two views of how we should grapple with the confusions of human behavior. Do we isolate and simplify, tackle one thing at a time, build our models in the full knowledge that of course they are over-simplifications but nevertheless pin our hopes to them as the best bet for getting precision and verifiability in our conclusions? Or do we set the interrelatedness of things in the very forefront of our vision and determine that, if we do theorize, we will use only theories that do no violence to the complexity of the evidence—even if this means sacrificing some of the seductive preciseness that other methods seem to offer?

It is easy to caricature these points of view, particularly when discussing them in the abstract. The best way to grasp their implications is probably to see them brought to bear on a single issue, as we do here. To most of Dowd's criticisms Conrad and Meyer found it easy to frame what seemed, in their terms at least, an adequate defense. In their short Reply (not reprinted here) they readily admitted as a matter of principle the interrelations between the "social" and the "economic" in the process of economic development, but insisted that this was not the issue they had been concerned with. In the same way they admitted that, if one asked (for example) *why* slave-plantation profits had not been effectively used for development in the South, an answer might possibly be found in psychology "or even metaphysics," but their analysis provided no such answer, since its purpose had been entirely different. The substance of their reply is summed up in two sentences: "Dowd may feel that our definition of economics is too strict. But he should not, on that ground, reread the hypotheses and conclusions in the light of what he thinks ought to be tested."

But in a sense this was the heart of the matter. Were Conrad and Meyer asking the right questions? What are the "right" questions to ask about slavery? How do you know? It is always frustrating (and sometimes more than that), when you have just done something rather difficult, to be told that maybe you should have done something else; but one of the functions of a critic is to raise exactly that sort of issue. Most of Dowd's criticisms were not the sort that could be quickly answered, for they had their origin in a philosophy of intellectual inquiry and a theory of historical development quite different from those that underlay the work of the economists he criticized. Perhaps, without distortion, we can phrase the difficulty in words rather different from those he himself used. The apparatus of modern economic analysis was developed to aid us in understanding how highly commercialized economies function. To achieve rigor and precision, it assumes as a necessary simplification a state of affairs in which people act according to economically rational rules. When this apparatus is applied to historically-real societies in which behavior follows other rules and is guided by other norms, this simplification must be borne in mind. Southern slave-based society, as Dowd understood it, was of this type. Southern planters were indeed businessmen; they were much interested in profits; what set them apart from Northern businessmen was their inclination to take with the utmost seriousness those "non-economic" matters that stemmed from slavery. This was a society, in other words, in which business and profit-seeking had no autonomous sanction but rather were kept subservient to the over-riding necessity of maintaining the dominant position of the white man. How much sense did it make to analyze a society like this as if it had been run to maximize profits? About as much sense for the historian of Southern slavery as it would be for the foreign policy advisor concerned with the "third world" countries of today. In neither case can the primacy of economic goals be safely taken for granted. Are there then limits to the applicability of economic analysis? Are the categories and concepts of economic theory timeless, applicable to all periods of history and all types of society? Or are they historically and culturally conditioned, applicable to some problems and periods but not, without extensive modification, to others?

MESSRS. CONRAD AND MEYER have undertaken to re-examine the question of the economics of slavery in the antebellum South "and on the basis of the computation of the returns to capital in [their] model of the antebellum southern economy and the demonstration of the efficiency of regional specialization" to draw conclusions about the profitability of slavery, the viability of the slave system, the importance of slavery to the southern economic system (as measured by "the interest of the Old South in secession"), and the relationship of slavery to the economic development of the South. In varying degrees, I find myself at odds with their conclusions on all these matters, but my differences are sharpest with their views on the relationship between slavery and economic development, and it is this question that I shall emphasize here. My disagreements are both methodological and substantive.

The authors have undertaken a careful, useful, and imaginative ordering of the facts relevant to the profitability of slavery in the antebellum South. Had they stopped there, I should have no comment to make. But they also direct their attention, however briefly, to the broader implications of slavery. Brief though their qualitative conclusions may be, I am disturbed lest they go unchallenged. My essential criticisms are (1) that the breadth of their conclusions is not supported by the narrowness of their investigation and (2) that their conclusions concerning slavery and economic development are wrong.

There is every reason to welcome an attempt such as theirs—an attempt by the economist to explore the past to shed light on current questions. But, when he does so, the economist must also recognize that he is then wandering through a forest, not, as in conventional economics, examining a potted plant. This is particularly true when examining the nature and impact of as complex an institution as slavery in America. There is every reason why contemporary economists should be vitally concerned with questions of economic development, for there are of course many questions involved in economic development programs which only economists can answer. But this does not mean that the historical process of economic development—or of stagnation—can be explained solely or even primarily in economic terms, that economic institutions and processes are the outcome of or have their impact solely or even primarily upon economic affairs; it does not mean that one can meaningfully separate out the "social" from the "economic" meaning of a particular institution, for the "two" are in a continuous state of interaction. This is clearly true of slavery in the South, and my objection to the Conrad-Meyer position is that they do not seem to have recognized it.

The authors contend that "the available productive surplus from slavery might have been used for economic development or, as in totalitarian regimes in this century, for militarism. In spite of this good omen for development, southern investment and industrialization lagged. It is hard to explain this except on the social ground that entrepreneurship could not take root in the South or on the economic ground that the South did not really own the system but merely operated it." It was not only entrepreneurship that could not take root in the South; it was the basic elements of a capitalist society that could not take root. I do not think I am alone in believing that slavery and all that it entailed was fundamental in inhibiting industrial capitalism—and economic growth—in the South. Whether slavery is looked upon as a "social" or as an "economic" institution is, for present purposes, irrelevant. The "available productive surplus from slavery" could not exist apart from the social milieu required for the maintenance of slavery. If profits were made from the slave system, it was at a price: the domination of southern society by the slave issue. This in turn meant the suppression of that kind of social rationality which has been, for better or for worse, associated with the development of industrial capitalism.

Conrad and Meyer have read widely in the literature of slavery, and they must surely be aware of the pervasive impact of such an institution on the society in which it exists. This was certainly true of ancient Greece and Rome. It was true a fortiori of the antebellum South, because the institution of slavery was then, in the Western world, an anachronism. The authors argue as though slavery were merely another, more manipulable, form of labor; as though it were, one might say, institutionally neutral. And, working essentially within the methodology of neoclassical economics (with time allowed in occasionally), they have analyzed the "economic" meaning of slavery as though they were analyzing the representative firm in the long run (or even, at times, in the short run).

The authors' argument may be reduced to this: *either* slavery was profitable *or* it was a deterrent to economic development. My contention is that it was a deterrent to economic growth despite the fact of its profitability. The point may perhaps be made by asking a question: When Indian economic planners estimate that a proposed project will be profitable, do they thereupon assume that it will contribute to the economic development of India? In short, "economics" should be concerned with more than profitability, particularly short-run profitability.

Apparently impounded in *ceteris paribus* are what I have long thought were some accepted implications of slavery in the South: (1) an economy of (virtually) no markets, based as it was on a labor force isolated from the system of exchange, "paid" little and in kind if Negro, dominantly self-sufficient if white; (2) a society whose consumption-savings standards were seigneurial, with implications for both capital accumulation and persistent indebtedness; (3) a society whose notions of status elevated the aristocratic agrarian and denigrated the mercantile-industrial pursuits.

There was nothing "irrational" or controversial about the introduction of slavery in Colonial America. Nor was there anything irrational about its continuation and expansion after the cotton gin. But slavery had, by then, become a matter of heated debate, even and perhaps particularly in the South. Southern society up until about 1820 had not yet hardened into the Cotton Kingdom; the economy was still relatively diversified (more so than during the rest of the century), and the society was still relatively fluid. During and after the twenties, cotton became king, and slavery became the *sine qua non* of the economic well-being of the South as a region. But the economic well-being of the South must be defined as having meaning for a small percentage of the southern population. A society whose wealth is derived from plantation economy does not tend, as does an industrial society, to push its prosperity down through all layers of the population (albeit, in the latter case, in waves of diminishing force). If southern society was to be firmly cemented to the institution of slavery and a plantation economy, an ideology had to be developed to buttress that which was materially inimical to the well-being of the mass of the people. That is, an essentially irrational ideology had to dominate the mind of the South (in Cash's apt phrase), or the Old South would be destroyed by internal and external pressures.

But taking the United States in the early nineteenth century, with all that connotes in terms of social, political, religious, and economic institutions and attitudes—a belief in social mobility and human rights, political democracy, the Christian ethic, economic individualism, and so on—what did the American in the South have to "do" with his mentality, his beliefs, his conscience, his behavior (to mention only these) in order to allow, let alone enforce, the enslavement of human beings? All this, in a world which was self-consciously giving up the institution; in a nation which was leading the rest of the world in the development of democratic institutions and demonstrating the productive power (for that time and place, at least) of economic individualism; in a section which yielded to none in its expressed dedication to the word of God and the rights of man. For the southerner to convert himself to beliefs and behavior which would support and comport with slavery required a concentration so intense that all else became secondary—including the process of capital accumulation. Does economic development take place when economic questions are in the realm of the after-thought?

Who would be inclined to use the term "capitalist" to describe the owners of southern wealth? Apart from a William Gregg here and there, southern capital was *planter* capital. Planters were of course interested in profits; so were medieval "businessmen" (as jarring a term as "southern capitalists"). But neither group approached the question of capital accumulation in the sense in which the northern manufacturer did. In the South, slaves were never *just,* or even most importantly, capital, any more than a Cadillac car is just, or even most importantly, transportation to the modern American. This was true because slaves *were* slaves, a fact of such enormity in America at that time that it could be accommodated only by dedicating southern society to its perpetuation. And this meant that economic development was relegated to the back of the mind of the southerner, big or small.

If all this sounds too vague, perhaps too psychological or even metaphysical, it is partly because the requisite elaboration and specification would go beyond the limits of a "comment"; but it is partly because the process of economic development does not appear to be reducible to the neat categories of conventional economics.

YASUKICHI YASUBA

The Profitability and Viability of Plantation Slavery in the United States

Alfred Conrad once remarked that, although the paper he and John Meyer wrote on the profitability of slavery was intended to dispose of the issue, in fact it seemed to set off a new round of controversy and argument. Much of the explanation for this paradoxical outcome lay in the characteristic already mentioned: their article suggested, or seemed to imply, generalizations much broader than the restricted issue that was its stated focus. But another part of the explanation lay in the fact that the article invited confirmation by other methods and elaboration along other lines. For a controversy that had already been going on for so long, it was remarkable that so much interest could still be aroused.

Yasukichi Yasuba of Kyoto University, in the article which follows, concentrates on two related issues: the appropriate definition of profitability; and the relation of profitability to viability. The latter term is not defined explicitly by Yasuba, but he clearly intends it to have the same meaning as "economic viability" in the Conrad and Meyer article. In that context it was used almost synonymously with economic profitability (see above, page 157). Having shown that slavery was about as profitable a use for capital as any other available at the time, the authors concluded that the institution was "economically viable," provided only that slaves could be efficiently transferred from surplus to deficit areas. But they used the phrase only once, and it did not figure prominently in their conclusions.

On a common-sense basis, an institution may be called economically viable if it enjoys an inflow of income adequate to maintain its capital stock and to keep the factors of production it requires from being attracted away into other uses. If it is not economically viable, it will go out of existence for economic reasons within a period of time the length of which we should, in principle, be able to specify. To say that an institution is economically viable is not, of course, the same thing as saying that it will in fact survive, far less that it ought to. When Conrad and Meyer almost casually referred to Southern slavery as economically viable, they presumably meant only to state in different

From *The Economic Studies Quarterly*, XII (September, 1961), 60-67. Reprinted by permission of the author, the editors, and the publisher, *Toyo Keizai Shinpo Sha* (The Oriental Economist, Ltd).

words their central conclusion that they had found no economic reason why slavery should not have continued to exist.

When, however, we extend the use of the concept of economic viability from a particular economic sector to a whole society, it takes on an aura of meaning that transcends a strict definition of profitability. One might speculate, for example, as to whether the society in question enjoyed a flow of income large enough to finance an adequate level of political or military "protection costs", to use Frederic C. Lane's suggestive phrase. If one were thinking along those lines, a proof that slave capital earned eight or ten percent a year would hardly be tantamount to proving that the slave society was economically viable. Similarly, if a particular political subdivision of a country were growing in income per capita at a rate of only one percent a year, while the rest of the country enjoyed a rate of five percent, would we want to call its regional economy economically viable, even though every industry existing within its borders at that time were earning a rate of return on capital equal to the national average? It is not difficult, in short, to think of situations in which it would not make much sense to equate economic viability with economic profitability; and perhaps for that reason the discussion of economic viability has been replete with confusion.

In Yasuba's terminology, economic viability depends solely on economic profitability. Hence the importance of a correct definition of economic profitability and of distinguishing it from the accountant's concept. He criticizes Stampp for failing to make this distinction; and he faults Conrad and Meyer for basing their concept of profitability on the market price of slaves instead of the costs of reproducing them. To compare the discounted present value of a slave's future earnings with that slave's current price, he says, tells us nothing more than whether the market is properly doing its job; the proper comparison is with the slave's cost of reproduction, or how much it cost to replace him. It is interesting to observe that this criticism depends for its validity upon an assertion made by U.B. Phillips: that the supply of slaves was largely independent of their price. If this were not so, it would make no difference whether estimates of the rate of return on slave capital were based on market prices or on costs of slave-rearing, for any discrepancy between the two would be quickly wiped out by an appropriate adjustment of supply. Conrad and Meyer had based their estimates upon the proposition that the supply schedule did adjust quite rapidly to changes in the profitability of slave ownership. The major difference between Yasuba's approach and that of Conrad and Meyer seems to hinge on this point, although there are other differences in detail.

If, in the antebellum period, the supply of slaves was largely independent of the price they brought on the market, the supply schedule of slaves would be price-inelastic and would move to the right only slowly as the natural increase of the slave population made more labor available. An increasing demand for slaves (a shift of the demand schedule to the right) would then lead to an upward, downward, or horizontal trend in slave prices, the slope of the trend line depending on the relative movements and shapes of the two schedules. Now, a slave's price, if the market is functioning efficiently, represents the discounted value of his net future earnings. Any discrepancy between the price of a slave and his costs of reproduction would then represent the economic rent to be derived from slave ownership—the difference between the income you could get from the slave, and what it cost to replace him. If we can measure the size of this economic rent component—the degree to which slave prices exceeded the cost of rearing slaves—we have a sensitive measure of the profitability of slavery. If this differential between prices and reproduction costs grew over time, it would indicate that slavery was becoming increasingly profitable and that capital invested in slaves was earning a rate of return larger than the market rate of interest. Or, at least, this would be so if it were safe to assume that prices were not influenced by "non-economic factors" and that the adjustment of prices to net returns was immediate.

As with the Conrad and Meyer article, much of the interest of Yasuba's analysis lies, for the economist, in the techniques used and their theoretical rationale. His empirical findings are easily summarized. Over the whole forty-year period preceding the Civil War the trend of capitalized rents was strongly upward, whether calculated in current or in deflated dollars. Only in one brief sub-period, covering the depressed years of the late 1830s and early 1840s, was the trend downward, and even in this period most of the decline in current dollar figures was offset by a decline in prices. As the nation neared the brink of civil war, the average amount of capitalized rent in slave prices was rising rapidly. These estimates, in short, provide no support, for a belief that slavery was becoming unprofitable. Judged by the test of profitability, the slave-labor economy of the South was economically viable over the whole antebellum period and was becoming increasingly so as the period drew to a close.

WHETHER OR NOT slavery in the ante-bellum South was profitable for planters has been the subject of dispute for a long time. Contemporary slave owners, economists and politicians have offered evidence to support both sides of the argument. Some suggested that it was profitable to hold slaves because their physical inefficiency was more than compensated by their cheapness. Many others, however, insisted that slavery was an economic burden for planters and continued to exist only for non-economic reasons. Later historians were also divided on this matter. Most influential among the pessimists was Ulrich B. Phillips who, upon examination of numerous testimonies by planters as well as the records of the prices of cotton and slaves, reached the conclusion that "by the close of the 'fifties it is fairly certain that no slave-holders but those few whose plantations lay in the most advantageous parts of the cotton and sugar districts and whose managerial ability was exceptionally great were earning anything beyond what would cover their maintenance and carrying charges."[1] On the other hand, such writers as L. C. Gray, Thomas P. Govan and Robert Worthington Smith, computing the rate of return directly from the plantation account books, found that slavery was profitable for planters.[2]

Writers differed as to the meaning and interpretation of "profitability." Some were simply curious to know "whether planters of the Old South were making money from their operations."[3] Others went further and drew inferences concerning the economic viability of the system. A number of them reasoned that slavery was an economic burden for planters and it would eventually have toppled of its own weight without external intervention. They argued that Southerners defended their peculiar institution partly because they feared the social and political consequences which would ensue from emancipation and partly because they were blinded by the abolition agitation in the North.[4]

[1]Ulrich Bonnell Phillips, *American Negro Slavery,* New York: Peter Smith, 1952, pp. 391-392.

[2]Lewis Cecil Gray, *History of Agriculture in the Southern United States to 1860,* Washington: Carnegie Institute of Washington, 1930, Vol. I, pp. 462-480.

Thomas P. Govan, "Was Plantation Slavery Profitable?" *The Journal of Southern History,* Vol. VIII, No. 4 (November 1942).

Robert Worthington Smith, "Was Slavery Unprofitable in the Ante-Bellum South?" *Agricultural History,* Vol. XX, No. 1 (January 1946).

[3]Govan, *op. cit.,* p. 514.

[4]Ulrich B. Phillips, "The Economic Cost of Slave-Holding," *Political Science Quarterly,* Vol. XX, No. 2 (June 1905), p. 275.

On the other hand some of those who found that slavery was profitable viewed their findings as disproving the hypothesis that slavery was not a viable institution. Two of the most recent studies along this line can be found in Stampp's *The Peculiar Institution*[5] and Conrad and Meyer's "The Economics of Slavery in the Ante Bellum South."[6] In this paper, first, it will be pointed out that these two studies, like others before them, failed to define the concept of profitability correctly in relation to the question of viability of slavery. Then, an appropriate measure of profitability will be suggested and, according to it, it will be concluded that slavery was an economically viable institution on the eve of the Civil War.

Stampp: Accountant's Concept of Profitability. There is a slight, but conceptually important, difference between the profitability measure of Stampp and that of Conrad and Meyer. By profitability Stampp meant a rate of return on the original value of the investment in the plantation. In other words, his initial question was, "allowing for the risks of a laissez-faire economy, did the average ante-bellum slave-holder, over the years, earn a reasonably satisfactory return from his investment?"[7] This is an accountant's concept and as such it cannot be criticized. However, when Stampp went on and reasoned that "during the last ante-bellum decade slavery was still justifying itself economically"[8] he had crossed a line which he should not have crossed. For accountant's profitability is not necessarily identical with economic profitability, and economic viability depends solely on the latter.

To demonstrate the inadequacy of the accountant's concept in this respect, let us examine hypothetical cases of three planters who used land of the same quality and whose managerial abilities were identical. The first planter bought all his slaves in 1841, the second in 1845, and the third in 1849. The price of a prime field hand was

---

Ralph Betts Flanders, *Plantation Slavery in Georgia,* Chapel Hill: The University of North Carolina Press, 1933, pp. 227-228, 231.

Charles Sackett Sydnor, *Slavery in Mississippi,* New York: Appleton-Century, 1933, p. 202.

[5]Kenneth M. Stampp, *The Peculiar Institution,* New York: Alfred A. Knopf, 1956, pp. 383-418.

[6]Alfred H. Conrad and John R. Meyer, "The Economics of Slavery in the Ante Bellum South," *The Journal of Political Economy,* Vol. LXVI, No. 2 (April 1958).

[7]Stampp, *op. cit.,* p. 390.

[8]*Ibid.,* p. 408.

highest in 1841 and lowest in 1845. If the rate of return in 1849 for the third planter was equal to what might be got from alternative investments, the rate of return for the first planter must have been less than adequate and that for the second planter more than adequate. Following Stampp's reasoning we have to say that, "if the slave-holder's economic self-interest alone were to be consulted, the institution should have been preserved"[9] for the second and third planters, and it should have been abolished for the benefit of the first planter!

Conrad and Meyer: The Rate of Return Based on Costs Inclusive of Rent. Conrad and Meyer set out to test the hypothesis "that slavery in the South must have fallen before very long *because* it was unprofitable."[10] Naturally, they tried to "measure the profitability of slavery according to the economic (as opposed to accounting) concept of profitability."[11]

From scattered data for the period 1830-60 they chose those values which seemed to show central tendencies for the life-expectancy and price of slaves, the costs of other capital investments, the market rate of interest, out-of-pocket costs, productivity, the price of cotton, and other relevant variables. Since there were definite upward trends in most variables, the method resulted, roughly speaking, in choosing average values for the period around 1845-50. For this model, Conrad and Meyer computed the marginal efficiency of slave capital, *valuing slaves at the market price.*[12] The marginal efficiency turned out to be as high as in alternative investments, whereupon Conrad and Meyer rejected the above hypothesis.

The capital costs of slaves which are to be equated with the present value of the future stream of income in the equation of marginal efficiency of capital are determined by the nature of the problem at hand. If one is interested in the profitability of slave

---

[9]*Ibid.,* p. 414.

[10]Alfred H. Conrad and John R. Meyer, "Reply: The Economics of Slavery in the Ante Bellum South," *The Journal of Political Economy,* Vol. LXVI, No. 5 (October 1958), p. 443.

[11]Conrad and Meyer, "The Economics of Slavery in the Ante Bellum South," p. 96.

[12]It may be noted that Stampp's measure of profitability, when it is applied to newly acquired slaves, gives approximately the same result as that of Conrad and Meyer, although Stampp did not use the fancier formula for the marginal efficiency of capital. Therefore, the criticism in this section applies also to Stampp.

capital *in a particular industry,* say rice cultivation, in which only a fraction of the total slave population is used, the market price of a slave is the costs to be used in the calculation of profitability. A lower (than ordinary) rate of return based on the current price of slaves would then suggest the downfall of slave-using rice cultivation. Again, if one is interested in the profitability of slave capital *in a section* of the South, the Conrad and Meyer method would be meaningful for the same reason.

As a matter of fact, much of the confusion in the past seems to have stemmed from identifying the profitability of the slave system as a whole with the profitability of slave capital in certain regions or in certain uses. It was probably true that, in the 1850's, in such trades as canal and railway building, ditching and tobacco processing, free workers were cheaper than slaves.[13] It was also true that in the eastern and northern section of the South, the rate of return based on the current price of slaves was below the market rate of interest, or the rate of return from the alternative uses of capital.[14] These facts were the omens of the decline of the use of slaves in these trades and sections, but they had nothing to do with the future of slavery as a whole.

If one is interested in the viability of slavery as a whole, the costs which are to be equated with the present value of the future stream of income are not the price of slaves but the costs of reproduction of the capital, that is, the costs of rearing slaves. In the case of ordinary reproducible capital goods, a discrepancy between costs and price does not last long. For whenever the reproduction costs of a particular kind of capital good become smaller than its price, its supply will increase until the equality is restored. A movement in the opposite direction will take place, when the costs are above the price. Ever since the prohibition of the slave trade, however, the supply of slaves was largely independent of their price[15] and, hence, the discrepancy continued to exist. Indeed, as we shall see presently, towards the end of the period a large part of the price of slaves

[13]Phillips, "The Economic Cost of Slave-Holding," p. 271.
Do., Life and Labor in the Old South, Boston: Little, Brown & Co., 1929, p. 187.

[14]Phillips, *American Negro Slavery,* p. 391. Stampp, *op. cit.,* p. 411. Of course, if we compute the rate of return on the original costs of investment as Stampp did, it may turn out to have been "adequate" in the Upper South where most slave-owners bought their slaves when the prices were much lower. But this should not have prevented the slave-owners from liquidating their investment, if profitability on the market value of slaves was lower than the interest rate.

[15]Phillips, *Life and Labor in the Old South,* p. 174.

was capitalized rent. Conrad and Meyer computed their rate of return on the basis of costs inclusive of this rent. Thus, what they actually proved was not the profitability of *the slave system* but rather the fact that the price of slaves did not show any significant over- or under-capitalization of annual net returns.

A downward shift of the demand schedule for cotton may have taken place a few years earlier. Or, an innovation in production method may have reduced the incidental costs some time before. Whatever changes had happened in the past in the marginal net revenue product must have been largely absorbed by the adjustment in the price of slaves. The internal rate of return based on the market value of slaves has always to remain more or less equal to the market rate of interest and thus cannot reveal anything even about the past performance of slavery, not to speak of the future.

A rate of return (on the market value of investment) lower than the market rate of interest is not impossible, if the rate of return is computed, as is done by Conrad and Meyer, from current statistics. For example, there may actually be a lag in the adjustment of the slave price behind the change in marginal net revenue product. In that case a lower rate of return would indicate a decline of slavery. On the other hand, the price of slaves, instead of lagging behind a past change, may anticipate a future change in marginal net revenue product and, if so, a lower rate of return would indicate a strengthening of the position of slavery. When there has been a persistent long-run trend, the latter interpretation would seem to be a more convincing one. Still another possibility is that non-economic factors, for instance, prestige value attached to slave holding, cause a lower rate of return to persist. If that is the case, there is no reason to expect the downfall of slavery because of the lower rate of return.

The Capitalized Rent in the Price of Slaves in the Ante-Bellum South. Some writers, including Stampp and Conrad and Meyer, have suggested movements of the price of slaves as another measure of the position of slavery. Stampp, for example, noted that "in the final analysis, the high valuation of Negro labor during the 1850's was the best and most direct evidence of the continued profitability of slavery."[16] This argument is much more sensible than the one behind the use of the internal rate of return based on costs

---

[16]Stampp, *op. cit.*, p. 414.

inclusive of rent; but it, too, has a serious defect in that it fails to take account of changes in the costs of rearing slaves. If the costs of rearing had increased by more than the price of slaves, it would hardly be justifiable to say that the profitability of slavery increased.

The correct statement to make is: If the portion of the price of slaves which represents capitalized rent was increasing, it is a sign of the increased profitability of slavery. To say that capitalized rent was positive is the same thing as to say that the rate of return based on the reproduction costs of slaves was above the market rate of interest, provided that non-economic factors did not affect the determination of the price and there was no lag nor anticipation in capitalization. Conrad and Meyer showed that these conditions were satisfied in the ante-bellum South. Therefore, to see if slavery in the ante-bellum South was viable, either the rate of return based on the reproduction costs of slaves or the amount of the capitalized rent in the market price of slaves may be examined. Here we chose to estimate the latter because it is simpler to compute.

As a starting point we shall compute capitalized rent for the model of plantation economy presented by Conrad and Meyer with two modifications. First, infant mortality should be introduced into the model. Although the available data may be poor, it seems better to use them than to neglect them. From four records of infant mortality, cited by Stampp,[17] which include altogether some 300 live births, the ratios of the number of those who died within one year and of those who died between ages one and four to the number of survivors can be estimated. And then, assuming that the first group died at the end of the first year and the second at the end of the third, expected gross costs for "breeding" an adult slave compounded at the interest rate of six per cent[18] and cumulated up to the nineteenth year, when the slave became a prime field hand, can be calculated. They are $728.[19]

---

[17]Stampp, *op. cit.*, p. 320.

[18]6% seems to be the appropriate discount rate for this period. Cf. Conrad and Meyer, *op. cit.*, p. 103.

[19]The ratio, p_1, of the number of those who died within one year to the number of those who survived into adulthood was 0.396; and the ratio, p_2, of the number of those who died between the ages one and four to the number of survivors was 0.156. The costs per death within one year, compounded up to the nineteenth year, c_1, were $188; the cumulated costs per slave who died between ages one and four, c_2, were $240; and, finally, the cumulated costs per survivor, c_3, were $616. The gross costs for breeding an adult slave successfully were $p_1 c_1 + p_2 c_2 + c_3 = \$728$.

Secondly, the incidental capital costs in employing slave children, which were neglected by Conrad and Meyer, should be taken into account. In order to avoid the difficulty arising from the difference between the total life of an asset and the length of the time during which it was used, we may assume that the slave owners rented land and capital goods for employing child labor. Rental is computed on an assumption that land and capital goods maintained the same efficiency throughout their lives, or alternatively, that a capital-mix which consists evenly of capital goods of all ages was rented. Annual rent for Alabama pine land which cost $195 and lasted ten years would be $26. Rent for Mississippi alluvium with a thirty-year life and costing $660 would be $48. Taking the arithmetic mean, we get $37. Rental of other capital goods would be $3, making the total incidental capital costs per adult slave per year $40.[20]

According to Conrad and Meyer, slaves started to be productive at age six. The male slave's gross earning, starting from $5, went up $5 every year between ages six and nine, and $10 yearly after that until it reached the full adult productivity of $110 per year at age eighteen. The female slave's gross earning was half as much as that of male slaves.[21] The average gross earning for male and female slaves was $3.75 at age six, $15 at age nine and then went up $7.50 yearly until it reached $82.50 at age eighteen. Therefore, cumulated gross earnings of a slave child averaged for male and female amounted to $637 in terms of the present value in the nineteenth year. If we assume that the ratio of the incidental capital costs to the gross earning was the same for all ages, the present value of the total incidental capital costs would be $309, so that the net value of pre-adult work was $328. Subtracting this amount from the gross rearing costs of $728, we get the average (male-female) net costs of rearing an adult slave of $400. The average price of male and female slaves at age eighteen was $875.[22] Therefore, the part which capitalized rent represented in this price was $475.

The capitalized rent for a prime field hand and that for a prime field wench can be computed in the same manner from the Conrad and Meyer model. Deducting from the price of $925 the net rearing

---

[20]*Ibid.*, pp. 100-101. Annual rent is computed in the following way:

If x represents annual rent; c, the price of an asset; i, the market rate of interest; and n, the life of the asset, then $c = \sum_{t=1}^{n} \dfrac{x}{(1 + i)^t}$ $\therefore x = \dfrac{i(1 + i)^n}{(1 + i)^n - 1} \cdot c$

[21]*Ibid.*, p. 107.

[22]*Ibid.*, pp. 100, 108.

costs of $188, we obtain a capitalized rent for a prime field hand in the amount of $737. Similarly, the capitalized rent for a prime field wench can be shown to have been $213.[23]

If we compute the rate of return on the net costs of rearing rather than on the price of slaves, it will be much higher than the market rate of interest. Therefore, on the basis of the capitalized rent or the rate of return based on the rearing costs of slaves, there is no evidence that slavery would have collapsed for any economic reason.

The Trend of Capitalized Rent, 1821-1860. Since Conrad and Meyer used averages over a period in which most variables showed upward trends, their model represented, roughly speaking, the period around 1845-50. It may, therefore, be suspected that the capitalized rent computed above is significantly different from the figure for the end of the 1850's—some ten years later. Moreover, the capitalized rent, though it explains the increase in the slave labor force, does not tell whether or not the position of slavery was strengthened. Hoping to shed some light on these problems, we shall proceed to ascertain the trend of capitalized rent in the price of a prime field hand over a period of forty years prior to the Civil War.

Because of the lack of sufficient information, we have to make several auxiliary assumptions. First, we divide the period 1821-60 into eight 5-year subperiods and assume that the Conrad and Meyer model represents subperiod 1846-50. Secondly, we assume incidental capital costs to be proportionate to the gross earnings from cotton, which is determined by multiplying the 1846-50 figures by the quinquennial average index of crop value per slave (with 1846-50 as the base year). This index is computed from Table 17 in the Conrad and Meyer article. The value of time lost by pregnancy is also multiplied by the index of crop value per slave.

Gross rearing costs other than the value of time lost by pregnancy are estimated on an assumption that it is proportionate to the cost of living index. For the latter G. R. Taylor's wholesale price index of commodities other than South Carolina export staples at Charleston is used.[24] The index for 1818-42 is linked with that for 1843-61 by

[23]Cf. *Ibid.,* pp. 107-108.

[24]George Rogers Taylor, "Wholesale Commodity Prices at Charleston, South Carolina, 1796-1861," *Journal of Economic and Business History,* Vol. IV, No. 4 (1932), pp. 874, 876.

using the unweighted average of price relative of corn and wheat in Virginia for 1842 and 1843.[25] Corn and flour are the most important items in Taylor's non-export staples, each occupying 20% of the total weight in the 1843-61 series.[26]

The prices of slaves are taken from Table 17 in the Conrad and Meyer article. The arithmetic mean of the prices of a prime field hand for 1846-50 is $936 as against the model price of $925. In order to adjust for the discrepancy, every value of the model is multiplied by 936/925. Thus, for the period 1846-50 the gross rearing costs were $737, the net income from child labor was $546, and the net rearing costs, therefore, were $191. Deducting this from the price of $936, we obtain a capitalized rent in the amount of $745.

Finally, it is assumed that there was no change in the long-term interest rate and in infant mortality over the whole period.

Capitalized rent is computed both in current and constant (1846-50) dollars. Taylor's wholesale price index of all commodities at Charleston is used as a deflator. As above, the 1818-42 index is linked to the 1843-61 index by utilizing several commodity series. In addition to corn and wheat in Virginia, rice and cotton at Charleston[27] and sugar at New Orleans[28] are taken into account. In the 1843-61 series rice and cotton account for all of the export staples group, and sugar for 36% of the imports group. The weight of each of -three major groups, which Taylor failed to indicate in his article, is estimated from his index by solving a set of simultaneous equations. Thus, in linking, the following weights are used:

Corn	14.6
Wheat	14.5
Cotton	37.4
Rice	6.6
Sugar	26.9
	100.0

The result is shown in Table 1 and Chart 1. An upward trend is clear both in current values and in real values. As expected,

[25]Gray, *op. cit.,* Vol. II, p. 1039.
[26]Taylor, *op. cit.,* p. 869.
[27]*Ibid.,* p. 870.
[28]Gray, *op. cit.,* p. 1034.

Table 1 Capitalized Rent in the Price of a Male Slave, Age Eighteen

	(1) Average Price of a Slave	(2) Gross Rearing Costs	(3) Net Income from Child Labor	(4) Capitalized Rent in Current Dollars (1)−(2)+(3)	(5) All Commodity Price Index (1846–50=100)	(6) Capitalized Rent in (1846–50) Constant Dollars (4)÷(5)
1821–25	$736	$657	$349	$428	$128	$334
1826–30	792	614	286	464	105	442
1831–35	974	671	431	734	113	650
1836–40	1,206	848	497	855	128	668
1841–45	744	591	379	532	91	585
1846–50	936	737	546	745	100	745
1851–55	1,252	807	600	1,045	108	968
1856–60	1,596	938	922	1,580	121	1,306

fluctuations are somewhat damped in the real series, making the upward trend still easier to be seen.

Conclusion. Of course, the numerical values of the capitalized rent cannot be taken too seriously. It is hoped that further inquiries into

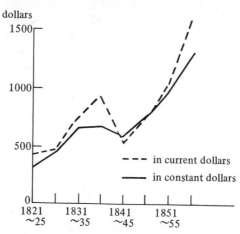

Chart 1 *Capitalized Rent in the Price of a Male Slave, Age Eighteen*

primary data may shed more light on its level and trend. It seems unlikely, however, that the upward trend will be reversed. Thus, in the Ante Bellum South, slavery steadily strengthened its economic position. Extrapolation of the trend line is quite another problem and we admit that it would be hardly legitimate. In order to make a satisfactory forecast, we should need information about the probable changes in the factors which determine the level of the capitalized rent. At the present stage, therefore, only two things can be said in conclusion. First, the trend of the capitalized rent from 1821 to 1860 does not reveal any indication of an imminent downfall of slavery. Second, even if a reversal of the trend had been "around the corner", it would have been difficult to wipe out quickly the large capitalized rent that existed in the late 1850's.

ROBERT EVANS, JR.
The Viability of Slavery

For Yasuba, economic profitability implied economic viability. But is this always so? Can viability be sensibly distinguished from profitability? And is this a useful distinction to make?

These thorny questions were explored by Robert Evans, Jr., in a lengthy analysis presented to a National Bureau of Economic Research conference on labor economics in 1961. From his presentation we reproduce here only the relatively short section which deals explicitly with the viability of the slave-labor economy. It should be emphasized that most of Evans' analysis was concerned with other matters. The bulk of his paper is a recomputation of the rate of return on capital invested in slaves, or precisely the same issue as that on which Conrad and Meyer had focussed. His technique, however, is significantly different. Conrad and Meyer estimated the annual return on slave capital as a residual, by subtracting from gross sales all out-of-pocket expenses—an entirely correct procedure, but one which had led to much argument over whether or not they had selected the right values for the many revenue and expense variables they had had to estimate (yield per field hand, cotton prices, marketing costs, food and clothing, medical care, and so on). Evans bases his estimates on figures of the net rent received by owners of slaves when they rented them out: that is, on the yearly hire of slaves whose employer was not their owner. The hiring-out of slaves in this way, while by no means uncommon, was not the predominant practice, but this does not affect the utility of Evans' figures, if one can assume that they are a good sample of all slave hires. The net rent of a slave provides a measure of the net income that could be earned from the ownership of that particular type of capital asset. And this measurement can be made, moreover, directly from market data, rather than having to be estimated as a residual. The procedure is precisely analogous to that involved if we were to estimate the rate of return on capital invested in automobile ownership from the rental charges of automobile rental agencies.

There are other differences from the Conrad and Meyer approach, of

From "The Economics of American Negro Slavery, 1830-1860," by Robert Evans, Jr. in *Aspects of Labor Economics* (Copyright © 1962 by National Bureau of Economic Research), published by Princeton University Press, pp. 221-227. Reprinted by permission of Princeton University Press.

a less basic nature. Evans, for example, with a slight gain in realism, introduces slave death rates explicitly into his calculation of the rate of return, instead of working from the median life expectancy of twenty-year-old slaves at the time of purchase, as had Conrad and Meyer. He differs from Conrad and Meyer, both practically and conceptually, in his view of the correct alternative rate of return to use when judging whether or not investment in slaves paid as well as other available forms of investment. Conrad and Meyer argued that the correct alternative was the rate of return that Southern capitalists could have earned if slavery had gone out of existence, and with this in mind used a variety of interest rate series, most of them relating to returns on investments and loans in the North—investments, in other words, that were *least* dependent upon cotton and Southern agriculture. Evans, in contrast, prefers to use the rate of return on capital invested in Southern railroads, on the grounds that there were serious imperfections in the national capital market and that the relevant rate is that which Southerners might have earned in the South, if investment in slaves had not been open to them. These variations in concepts and procedures did not in fact result in substantial variation in the results. Evans suggests that the alternative rate of return may have been about 6 to 10 percent in the years 1830 through 1860; Conrad and Meyer had set their "most probable" figure at 6 percent. Evans' calculations yield a rate of return on twenty- to fifty-year-old male slaves that varied between 10.3 and 12.0 percent per year in the Lower South in the decade of the 1850s, and from 9.5 to 13.8 percent in the Upper South. Even after making reasonable allowance for errors of estimation, rates like these were at least equal to the rate of return being earned on other forms of capital.

Evans' position on the viability issue is stated unambiguously at an early point in his article. He departs markedly from Yasuba's position and, by implication, from that of Conrad and Meyer. ". . . . the determination of the return to slaveholding," he writes, "while of interest because of the widespread uncertainty concerning its magnitude is of little value in answering the more relevant question whether the industry was viable. The viability can be estimated by ascertaining whether it exhibited characteristics of a declining industry." And what are these characteristics? Not a rate of return on capital lower than the market rate; unless the capital market was seriously imperfect, these rates would be equal, even though the industry was declining. Capital values adjust to expected returns. More relevant would be a declining demand for the unique capital employed (slaves), a declining rate of production of that unique capital, and a declining demand for the specialized intermediate goods (female slaves) used to produce that unique capital. Is there evidence that the slave-labor economy of the South before the Civil War exhibited any such characteristics as these?

Yasuba, in his concluding paragraph, had alluded to issues of this kind. Pointing out that it would be invalid to extrapolate the trend of his capitalized rent series beyond the 1850s, he had nevertheless argued that, even if at some later date the upward trend had reversed, it would have taken considerable time to wipe out the large capitalized rent that existed in the late 1850s. By implication, therefore, if not by direct statement, he had concluded that slavery was not a declining industry in the 1850s. Similarly Conrad and Meyer, though the main thrust of their analysis had been directed at an estimate of the going rate of return on slave-ownership, had not been so naive as to argue that a satisfactory rate of profit in the antebellum years *in itself* gave assurance that such a rate would continue thereafter. Evans, however, was the first investigator to make this complex problem a central issue.

Evans' line of analysis impels him to concentrate on demand conditions—the demand for slaves in general, for slave labor relative to wage labor, and for female slaves relative to male slaves—and on the impact of these demand factors on the production of slaves (i.e., on the slave birth rate). Significantly, he assumes that the short-run supply schedule for slaves was completely inelastic. This enables him to interpret changes in slave prices as indicators of changes in demand conditions alone. He finds no evidence of falling demand such as would be characteristic of a declining industry. Lack of evidence leaves it uncertain whether slave birth rates rose or fell, or whether the demand for females to be used as "breeders" increased relative to the demand for males; but there is some suggestion of a relative rise in the demand for women as childbearers in the late 1850s.

An intriguing suggestion closes Evans' analysis. Is it conceivable, he asks, that slaves, if given access to credit or an opportunity to accumulate savings from part-time employment, would have purchased their freedom from their masters and extinguished the slave economy in that way? If so, was it a viable economy? The idea invites elaboration (and received it at the hands of John E. Moes in a "Comment" on Evans' paper). There are grounds for believing that the productivity of slaves would have been higher if they had been given the opportunity to earn their freedom; such an increment in productivity in itself might have been sufficient to compensate the slave-holder financially for the capital loss he would sustain on manumission. In any event, slaves might well have been willing to pay a price to purchase their freedom higher than the price their owner could expect to get for them in any normal market. If so, large-scale manumission would have made some people better off and left nobody worse off. If such a situation is indeed conceivable (whether or not historically probable), it raises serious questions whether the slave economy can really be said to have been economically viable, even though the rate of profit was satisfactory and even though there were no signs of slackening demand. If non-economic considerations had not intervened, the economic self-interest of both parties—master and slave—would have led to liquidation of the system.

It is an interesting question for speculative minds to entertain. What it leaves out of account are precisely the issues of power and racial dominance that Dowd and others have emphasized. Large-scale manumission could not have been carried out without revolutionizing the very social structure that the controlling groups in the South were dedicated to preserving. A society cannot truly free its slaves without giving them a measure of power. If an economy functions only by denying its human factors of production this power—and in particular the power to withhold their labor if they wish—should we call it viable?

FAVORABLE RATES of return for investors in slaves provide an answer to a major historical question, that of slave profitability. They do not answer what, to the economist, is the more relevant question, that of the viability of slavery. Viability is more relevant because theory predicts that investors will be induced to shift out of a declining industry because of capital losses on capital goods completely specialized to that industry rather than because of rates of return which are lower than market rates. Consequently, in attempting to assess the position and role of the slave industry in the United States just before the Civil War, one is primarily interested in the viability of the system and in data that suggest the probability that holders of slave capital would sustain substantial and continuing capital losses within the decision period of the average investor. Such data must be limited by the ex-ante knowledge of 1856 through 1860 and not by the ex-post knowledge of the present-day investigator.

A variety of political events of the period bear on the question of viability. Their usefulness is impaired because it is not clear exactly what their economic implications were. The controversy over new slave states may have meant that the industry was viable only if it could expand geographically; it may have been almost entirely related to the balance of political power in the Senate. The agitation for the re-opening of the foreign slave trade may have been because the industry was viable only if new slaves could be procured more cheaply, or that the industry was very viable and an increased supply of slaves was desired to limit the windfall capital gains to current owners. The movement by some slave states to prohibit manumission[1] and to allow free Negroes to become slaves may have indicated that too many slaves were being freed for economic reasons, or it may have meant that there was little concern over the power to manumit and that the laws were passed to reassure abolitionists that the South was not going to give up slavery. No attempt will be made to evaluate the implications of these events. Conclusions on viability will be drawn from information that appears to be less subject to a variety of interpretations.

Before discussing data, let us consider briefly some of the characteristics of an industry that is either nonviable or on the verge of becoming nonviable. Such an industry should exhibit some or all of the following: (1) a relative decline in the demand for its product; (2) a decline in the demand for the specialized capital used in the production of the industry's product; (3) a declining rate of production of the specialized capital used in the industry; (4) a declining demand for the specialized capital used in the industry which supplies specialized capital to the declining industry. In the case of a nonviable slave industry, one should observe a decline in the demand for the labor services of slaves relative to the demand for the labor services of free men, a decline in the demand for slave capital, a falling slave birth rate, and a decline in the demand for female slaves relative to male slaves.

Because of the capital nature of the industry, one can assume that changes in the price of slaves result from shifts of the short-run demand curve along a completely inelastic short-run supply curve. (The ratio per year of new male slaves fifteen to sixty years of age to the average number of male slaves fifteen to sixty years of age is 0.022 for the period 1850 to 1860.) Therefore, in the following

---

[1]Mississippi changed its laws in 1857 to prohibit manumission under any circumstances. (Sydnor, *Slavery in Mississippi,* p. 236.) A similar law went into effect in Maryland in 1860 (Jeffrey R. Bracket, *The Negro in Maryland,* Johns Hopkins University Press, 1889, p. 171). Many states passed laws just before the Civil War to allow free Negroes to become slaves (Gray, *History of Agriculture,* Vol. I, p. 527).

discussion, shifts in prices of labor services and of the capital good are presumed to illustrate the demand conditions facing the industry.

The demand for the labor services of slaves relative to the demand for the labor services of free men did not appear to be declining in the late 1850's. In the Lower South the average hire for male slaves in 1856 through 1860 was 17 per cent greater than it was in 1851 through 1855. In the Upper South the average hires in 1856 through 1860 and 1851 through 1855 were essentially equal. In the Lower South the median hire rose 25 per cent and in the Upper South it rose 8 per cent between these two periods.[2] The Virginia and Tennessee Railroad paid an average of $135.00[3] for its hired slaves in 1854 and $149.00 in 1857.[4] The Richmond and Danville Railroad paid $135.00[5] in 1855 and $139.00[6] in 1860. The Central Railroad and Banking Company of Georgia reported that the price of hire in 1859 was 20 per cent higher than it had been in 1858.[7] The ratio of slave wages to white wages in the Navy Shipyard at Gosport, Virginia, was the same in July 1860 as it had been in November 1854.[8] In Columbia, South Carolina, wage increases received in 1856-57 were, for white stone cutters 20 per cent, for white carpenters 12 per cent, and for hired slave laborers 8 per cent.[9]

There appears to have been a strong rightward shift in the demand curve for slaves as capital goods in the period 1850 through 1860. The nominal increase in the price of prime male field hands in the Lower South was 72 per cent between 1850 and 1860. The deflated (by New Orleans wholesale price index)[10] price increase was 68 per

[2]White wages also rose in these periods.

[3]Annual Reports, Commonwealth of Virginia, 1853-54, p. 806.

[4]*Tenth Annual Report of the Virginia and Tennessee Railroad,* Library of the Bureau of Railway Economics, Association of American Railroads, pp. 210-212.

[5]*Proceedings and Annual Reports of the Richmond and Danville Railroad,* Library of the Bureau of Railway Economics, 1856, p. 30.

[6]*Ibid.,* 1860.

[7]*Reports of the Central Railroad and Banking Company of Georgia,* No. 20-32, Library of the Bureau of Railway Economics, p. 148.

[8]National Archives, Washington, United States Navy Bureau of Yards and Docks, Payrolls of Mechanics and Labors. . . . Gosport, Virginia, November 1854 and July 1860.

[9]State House Construction Payrolls, South Carolina State Archives, Columbia, Negroes, April 1856, Whites, July 1856 and January 1857.

[10]Arthur H. Cole, *Wholesale Commodity Prices in the United States: 1700-1861,* Cambridge, Harvard University Press, 1938, p. 178, Table 93.

cent. In the Upper South the nominal increase was 62 or 112 per cent, depending upon which estimate of the 1860 Upper South price is used. The deflated (by Charleston wholesale price index)[11] price increases were 50 and 98 per cent.

The average increase in price of twelve railroad stocks on the Boston Stock Market between 1850 and 1860 was 13 per cent. The stock of the Hartford and New Haven Railroad increased in price 17 per cent between 1850 and 1860, and paid a higher dividend rate than any other railroad on the Boston market for that period.[12]

Some students of slavery, in later times as well as in the contemporary period, felt that the increase in slave prices was purely speculative in character. The editor of the *New Orleans Daily Crescent* disagreed with the speculative argument: "It is our impression that the great demand for slaves in the Southwest will keep up the prices as it has caused their advance in the first place, and that the rates are not a cent above the real value of the laborer."[13] One study of the marginal value productivity supports the editor's position.[14]

Whether the slave birth rate (Table 1) was a function of the price of slaves is not known, but it is not important because census data are inconclusive about the rate's increase or decrease between 1850 and 1860. It is not clear whether the demand for females rose relative to that of males. One would expect that a proved "breeder" would command a premium in the market relative to her unproved sister and that one could estimate the relative male-female demand

TABLE 1 *Slave Birth Rates*

(per cent)	*Number of:*			
	Children Aged 0 Divided by Females Aged 15–44		*Children Aged 0 to 4 or 5 Divided by Females Aged 15–44*	
	1850	*1860*	*1850*	*1860*
Upper South	0.120	0.134	0.163	0.158
Lower South	0.102	0.119	0.150	0.139
All South	0.115	0.131	0.154	0.151

Source: Figures for 1850 are from DeBow, *Statistical View . . . , pp.* 88–89; *for 1860 from The Eighth Census,* pp. 594–595. The ratio of females 40–44 years old to those 40–49 years was estimated from figures in DeBow, p. 104.

[11]*Ibid.,* p. 168, Table 80.
[12]Martin, *One Hundred Years' History . . . ,*pp. 145-149.
[13]Phillips, *Life and Labor in the Old South,* p. 180.
[14]Conrad and Meyer, "The Economics of Slavery . . . ," p.117.

by movements in the "breeder" premium. Despite the number of words written about a premium price for "breeders," no clear-cut evidence of a premium has been presented.[15] One can still obtain some indication of the demand for women in their role as childbearers by observing the ratio of female to male price over a period of years (Table 2). Table 2 suggests that the demand for women as childbearers, if anything, was rising in the latter years of slavery.[16]

Table 2 Ratio of Female to Male Slave Prices

Market	Date	Ratio	Market	Date	Ratio
Richmond	Mar. 1842	0.78	Richmond	July 1859	.91
Richmond	Oct. 1842	.84	Mobile	Oct. 1859	.86
Richmond	Nov. 1844	.78	Richmond	Nov. 1859	.91
Richmond	Feb. 1847	.75	Richmond	Dec. 1859	.93
Richmond	Nov. 1848	.83	Mobile	Dec. 1859	.91
Richmond	Dec. 1848	.82	New Orleans	Dec. 1859	.91
Richmond	Nov. 1849	.87	Mobile	Jan. 1860	.88
Richmond	Jan. 1858	.85	New Orleans	Jan. 1860	.89
Richmond	Dec. 1858	.86	Richmond	June, 1860	.87
Richmond	Jan. 1859	.88	Richmond	July, 1860	.89
Richmond	Feb. 1859	.86			

Source: Each ratio is computed from information from a single source. The observations for 1842, 1844, 1848, December 1858, and December 1859 appear to originate from the Dickinson Company of Richmond. All the collections cited are in the Duke University Library, Durham, North Carolina. Data for 1842 and 1844 are from the William Weaver papers for those years; for 1848 and December 1858, from the letters of Joseph Dickinson; for 1847 from the letters of John E. Dennis. The remainder of the data are from the letters of William A. J. Finney.

In addition to examining slavery in terms of the usual economic criteria of a declining industry, one other aspect of the slave industry must be examined. Because its capital goods are human rather than inanimate, they might be more valuable to the individual slave than to any other owner. It would, therefore, have been

[15]Conrad and Meyer (p. 110) speak of a higher average price for proved childbearers as evident in the figures in their Appendix A. Examination of these data for 1859 and 1860 reveals that the premium is dependent upon a specific assumption concerning the ages of the children sold with their mothers.

[16]If demand was increasing, then there is little danger that the system was nonviable because one could not afford to raise slaves at the current prices. While a more direct test of this fact would be desirable, it has not been attempted because it would involve estimates of variables about which little is known. I have made a few rough calculations based upon average number of children per woman (census figure), death rates for women and children, etc. and it appears that, as one would expect, rates of return on female slaveholding are equal to those obtained for male slaveholding.

possible for the industry to be viable by all the usual economic criteria, and yet have been nonviable because the slaves, if given the opportunity, would have purchased the industry out of existence.

The rates of manumission in the period 1850 through 1860 suggest that this special form of nonviability was not present. The census estimated that there were 3,000 manumissions in the 1860 census year and that about 20,000 had been manumitted between 1850 and 1860.[17] Compared to the annual increase in the slave population, these rates of manumission are quite small—about one-tenth of the increase in the male slave population fifteen to sixty years of age in the same period. It has been suggested that self-purchase reached its peak in the industrialized cities.[18] At its peak it was not very large.[19] Between 1831 and 1860, 592 Negroes were manumitted in Richmond and Petersburg, Virginia.[20] About 296 of these manumissions may have been promoted or instigated by Negroes.[21] Perhaps a majority of the 296 were cases of self-purchase. At a maximum then, the number of manumissions by self-purchase in a period of thirty years is equal to about 5.8 per cent of the number of male slaves fifteen to sixty years of age in these two cities in 1850,[22] to 5.2 per cent of the number of slaves employed in factories in Richmond in 1846,[23] and 4.7 per cent of the number employed in 1856.[24]

Thus it would appear that the slave industry did not exhibit characteristics of a nonviable industry about to wither and die under the impact of adverse economic forces, but rather gave every indication in its latter years of being a strong and growing industry.

[17] *The Eighth Census,* p.xv.

[18] Sumner Eliot Matison, "Manumission by Purchase," *Journal of Negro History,* April, 1948, pp. 146-167.

[19] That it was not larger is probably in great part because the majority of slaves who earned extra money for themselves spent it for pleasure. Eaton, *Slave-Hiring in the Upper South,* p. 669. The reader interested in this aspect of the system should consult Stanley M. Elkins, *Slavery,* University of Chicago Press, 1959.

[20] Luther Porter Jackson, "Free Negro Labor and Property Holding in Virginia, 1830-1860" (Unpublished Ph.D. dissertation, University of Chicago), p. 240. Much of the material in this dissertation has been published in book form.

[21] *Ibid.,* p. 227.

[22] DeBow, *Statistical View* . . . , p. 398.

[23] Jackson, *Free Negro Labor* . . . , p. 71.

[24] *Ibid.*

EDWARD SARAYDAR and RICHARD SUTCH

The Profitability of Ante Bellum Slavery

The work of Yasuba and Evans represented one line of development from the Conrad and Meyer analysis: the checking of the results by alternative methods. But what if one were to follow the same method as Conrad and Meyer had, only using better data? How sensitive were their results to improvements or modifications in the factual information used?

This was the question raised by Edward Saraydar in 1964, when he published his "Note on the Profitability of Ante Bellum Slavery" in the *Southern Economic Journal*. He set himself the same problem as had Conrad and Meyer: calculate the internal rate of return on capital invested in slave-labor cotton production. But at several critical points he inserted into the calculation quantitative data which he judged to be superior; and in one important respect he claimed that he had found reason to believe that the Conrad and Meyer results were statistically biased. The outcome was a finding that the principal conclusion of the Conrad and Meyer analysis was "quite possibly erroneous."

This kind of critique is immensely valuable, and immensely laborious, since it requires you to return to the original sources and recalculate the basic estimates to be inserted into the rate-of-return formula. Much easier, of course, if you can find some gross error or inconsistency in the analysis, or some relevant factor omitted, or if you can allege (as some did) that it was all irrelevant to the really important issues anyway. A man who subjects the work he is criticizing to the kind of step-by-step dissection exemplified in Saraydar's critique is really paying it the highest compliment.

The principal points on which Saraydar takes issue with Conrad and Meyer are easily identified. He accepts, though not without reservations, their estimate of slave life-expectancy. He uses approximately the same figure for the average price of a prime field hand. But he raises by a significant margin the estimate of the necessary ancillary investment in land and farm implements, and the figure for maintenance and supervisory costs. On the product or income side of the calculation, a problem of major significance is introduced in connec-

---

This and the next article by Richard Sutch are from *The Southern Economic Journal*, XXX (April 1964), 325-332 and XXXI (April 1965), 365-377. Copyright 1963 and 1964 by *The Southern Economic Journal*. Reprinted by permission of the Editor and the authors.

tion with the estimates of slave productivity. Conrad and Meyer, when estimating the out-of-pocket costs of maintaining field hands, had assumed that they were dealing with plantations where most of the provisions, clothing, and so on for the slaves were produced on the plantation and did not have to be purchased from outside sources. Their typical plantation, in other words, was more or less self-sufficient, at least as far as the provisioning of the labor force was concerned. Did their estimates of productivity refer to the same sort of plantation? If so, obviously the slave labor force would have had to spend some of its time furnishing the supplies necessary for its own maintenance. A figure purporting to measure how much cotton this labor force could produce, *if it produced nothing else,* would clearly be too high. Were the Conrad and Meyer productivity or "yield" estimates of this type? A complex series of comparisons with later data on cotton production leads Saraydar to conclude that the Conrad and Meyer yield estimates cannot have referred to self-sufficient plantations, as did their expense estimates. Consequently the figures used for average yields (from 2 to 3 bales per hand per year on the poorest land, from 7 to 8 on the best) were biased upwards. Saraydar's own calculation gives yield estimates varying from 2.0 bales on very poor land to 3.6 bales on the best alluvial soils. These revised figures, in conjunction with an average price for cotton of 8 cents per pound, gives an average rate of return on capital employed in slave-labor cotton production of only 1.5 percent for the South as a whole. An upper-bound estimate of 8.2 percent is given for an exceptionally favorable case on alluvial soil and, at the other extreme, a rate of practically zero for poor upland pine land. In general, Saraydar concludes, slave-labor operations in cotton were unprofitable. The rate of return was generally less than the capital employed could have earned in other uses.

Was Saraydar right? If he was, maybe Phillips had been right too. And maybe those had been right who had insisted all along, despite the buildup of evidence to the contrary, that slavery would have disappeared without the Civil War. A hard look at Saraydar's calculations, and a renewed scrutiny of what Conrad and Meyer had in fact done, were certainly in order. The task was undertaken by Richard Sutch, in a reply to Saraydar published a year later in the same journal. His counterattack is two-pronged. First, he charges Saraydar with omitting from his calculations of profitability the income earned from slave breeding, despite the fact that he had included the cost of maintaining wives and children in his estimates of the cost of maintaining a male field hand. And second, he undertakes to show that Saraydar had substantially underestimated the average yield of a field hand. The records on which Conrad and Meyer had based their yield estimates had referred to plantations that grew their own provisions; no case for alleging an upward bias in their productivity figures could be built on that basis. Sutch's own estimates give an average yield of 2.6 bales per year per *slave,* which clearly suggests that Saraydar's estimate of 2 to 3.6 bales per year per *field hand* is an underestimate (an estimate of yield per hand is not required in Sutch's own formulation of the problem). By revising the yield estimates upward and including the effects of appreciation in the stock of slaves, Sutch arrives at estimates of the rate of return in 1849 and 1859 which (for the latter year) range from a low of 3.6 percent per year in the older areas to a high of 15.1 percent per year on the best soil. His estimate for the South as a whole is very close to that of Conrad and Meyer.

Saraydar's rebuttal to these criticisms, included below as the last of the three selections in this section, turns in part upon the particular price and crop data used by Sutch, but it becomes clear that the major issue at stake is the differing estimates of slave productivity. And this is, of course, precisely what one would expect. Whether Saraydar adequately defends his position is a matter you should judge for yourself. You will undoubtedly note, however, that both in the Conrad and Meyer analysis and in that by Sutch the income yielded by slave breeding plays an important role in the calculation of the rate of return on capital. Conrad and Meyer used two production functions, one for production of slaves, the other for the production of cotton; Sutch prefers to use a single function which includes as one of its variables the appreciation rate of the stock of slaves. The difference is one of technique only; both analyses interpret productivity to mean more than the output of cotton per field hand. Saraydar explicitly excludes this; he is interested only in the rate of return to be realized from an investment in field hands, and the appreciation rate of the stock of slaves is, to him, simply irrelevant. It is hardly surprising, therefore, that their productivity figures and their estimates of the rate of return on capital differ significantly.

As frequently happens, the interest in this exchange of views lies only partly in the issues that the two participants regarded as of prime importance. Particularly worth noting is the way in which both authors try to distinguish clearly between profitability and viability. Sutch is explicit on the point. Even if Conrad and Meyer were wrong, he argues, (that is, even if Saraydar were right), this would not prove that slavery was about to disappear. Profitability is a short-run phenomenon. Even if slave-labor cotton production were, in the short run, unprofitable, this would prove only that slaves or land were over-priced, or that resources were misallocated, not that the institution of slavery was economically unsound. As long as slave prices were higher than zero, alternative uses for slaves could be found and the institution would remain viable: " . . . slavery will always be able to compete with free labor through adjustments in the price of slaves."

Was it true, then, as Sutch asserted, that these difficult and perplexing calculations of profitability were irrelevant to the question of the viability of the slave system? Did their importance lie only in the fact that they helped us to judge how important "nonpecuniary returns," such as status and prestige, were in slaveholding? And was this latter question really important enough to justify all the labor and argument that had gone into the debate over profitability? Could the viability of slavery in the South be analyzed without raising questions about the long-run effects of the slave system on Southern economic development? And could these questions be tackled within the conventional limits of economic theory?

EDWARD SARAYDAR

A Note on the Profitability of Ante Bellum Slavery

ALFRED H. CONRAD and John R. Meyer, in a stimulating article published some years ago,[1] attempted to answer such questions about ante bellum slavery as these: (i) Was investment in slave capital at least as remunerative as were alternative investment opportunities, or was slavery—as many have contended—on the verge of 'toppling of its own weight' because of insufficient returns? (ii) Was slavery viable; that is, did the system include an efficient market for generating and allocating slave labor? (iii) Was the institution of slavery inimical to southern economic growth because of such factors as slave inefficiency in industry, excessive use of credit, and the rigidifying of capital in slave holdings?

[1]"The Economics of Slavery in the Ante Bellum South," *Journal of Political Economy,* April 1958, pp. 95-130.

This paper will only be concerned with Conrad and Meyer's treatment of the first question—the profitability of ante bellum slavery—and will further restrict itself to a consideration of the returns to be realized from only one production process: the production of cotton after 1830 by male prime field hands. Utilizing the same methodology as that employed by Conrad and Meyer (calculation of the internal rate of return via the capital-value formula), it is possible to demonstrate that Conrad and Meyer's conclusion—that investment in prime field hands was indeed as remunerative as a typical investment in an alternative capital asset (which would return, say, 6%)—is quite possibly erroneous.

Conrad and Meyer use the capital-value formula[2] to determine the profitability for the slaveholder of purchasing a 20-year-old prime cotton hand and employing him in cotton production for the remainder of his life. In order to compute the internal rate of return (so as to compare it with the interest rate in order to establish profitability), it is necessary to estimate slave longevity, the cost of the slave together with additional capital used in the production process, and the annual net return.

Conrad and Meyer, then, take the life of the investment to be equivalent to the life-expectancy for a 20-year-old slave working as a prime cotton hand in the period 1830-50. After pointing out that "there is a scarcity of good longevity data for the period," they estimate this life-expectancy at 30-35 years, and use 30 years in their calculations. Although there is some reason to believe that this estimate may be on the high side,[3] it will nevertheless be used here as a basis for calculating the internal rate of return.

[2]This well-known formula as given by Conrad and Meyer is: $y = x_t/(1+r)^t$, where "y is the cost of the investment, x_t is realized return t years hence, and r is the internal rate of return . . . " (*ibid.*, p. 98).

[3]Conrad and Meyer discount Charles Sydnor's estimate of 22-year life-expectancy for 20-year-old Mississippi slaves in 1850 (Charles S. Sydnor, "Life Span of Mississippi Slaves," *American Historical Review*, April 1930, pp. 566-74) for two reasons: (i) Sydnor's estimate involves "the dubious assumption that there was no advance in medical and dietary knowledge around the middle of the century," and his procedure is really more relevant to life expectancy in the years preceding 1850 than after (Conrad and Meyer, *op. cit.*, p. 99); and (ii) " . . . estimates from deaths reported at the end of ten-year intervals and averaged back over the decade would tend to underestimate life-spans at the younger ages" *(ibid.)*

Conditions prevailing during the 19th Century may have been such that Sydnor's 'assumption' as to medical and dietary knowledge did not in itself introduce a sizeable estimating error. According to vital statistician Paul Jacobson:

. . . most persons born around 1850 encountered during their lifetime much

In calculating the cost of the capital investment, the price of field hands is a prime consideration. U. B. Phillips' estimates of prices for prime field hands are based—among other sources—on thousands of bills of sale recording actual market transactions; his remains the most exhaustive such study available, and, as such, it is the prime source of information on slave prices. Conrad and Meyer quite properly use Phillips' data in arriving at an estimate of prime field hand prices over the period 1830-50. Their information is taken from a summary table included in an article written by Phillips in 1905,[4] which estimates average slave prices in Georgia in selected years. Conrad and Meyer calculate the mean price for prime field hands to range from $900 to $950 in the period 1830-50.

This is confirmed to some extent when prices for intermediate years are filled in and data from another Lower South market included. Visually estimating, then summing, yearly average New

---

the same health and mortality conditions that prevailed at the time of their birth. In consequence, the actual average lifetime for a cohort of persons born a century ago did not differ to any considerable extent from their expectation of life at birth. In fact, the indications are that they lived only about one year longer, on an average, than that expected when they were born. (Paul Jacobson, "An Estimate of the Expectation of Life in the United States in 1850," *Milbank Memorial Fund Quarterly*, April 1957, p. 201.)

As for Sydnor's underestimating life-spans at younger ages, some notion of the possible size of error involved may be had if one makes the extreme assumption that all those who died between ages 20 and 60 died at the very end of each age interval instead of at the midpoint. This would yield a life-expectation of 26 years instead of 22 years.

Even if one were to accept Conrad and Meyer's estimate and also assume that slaves were fully productive until they were fifty or fifty-five years old (*cf.* U. B. Phillips, *Life and Labor in the Old South,* p. 174), productivity must surely have declined as slaves moved into old age and dotage. In their sixties they produced very little (*cf.* Kenneth Stampp, *The Peculiar Institution,* p. 319), and when over seventy they were usually superannuated (Phillips, *op. cit.,* p. 175), or at best only paid for their maintenance (Stampp, *loc. cit.*). Phillips cites a case where a broker paid the seller of a plantation gang of 85 slaves being sold as a unit $2000 more than the asking price if the seller would only keep 10 old slaves in the lot (Phillips, *loc. cit.*).

Therefore, if, for example, a group of 20-year-old prime hands were purchased with a life-expectancy of 30 years, use of the capital-value formula and 30-year longevity to calculate rate of return would imply that the loss in returns realized through the early death, say, of a slave at 30, would be made up by a slave who lived to 70. But decreasing productivity into old age implies that the loss would not be made up by the older slave. One way to offset the effects of this would be to revise longevity downward.

[4] U. B. Phillips, "The Economic Cost of Slaveholding in the Cotton Belt," *Political Science Quarterly,* Vol. XX, No. 2 (1905), p. 267.

Orleans and middle Georgia slave prices[5] yields an over-all average slave price for prime field hands in the Lower South of approximately $925 for the period 1830-50. This is the figure which we shall utilize in further calculations.

Land investment per hand is, of course, also an important part of Conrad and Meyer's profitability calculation. They first of all state that a range of $6 per acre for poor upland pine land in Alabama and $35-$40 per acre for Mississippi alluvium pretty well covers prices in the period 1830-50.[6] Since they do not cite the source of this information, it is assumed that they refer to estimates made by Lewis Gray, who—on the basis of capital account statements from a number of cotton plantations—gives figures for what he believes to be a typical large plantation devoted to growing upland cotton.[7] Gray puts the average price of cleared Mississippi alluvium at $35 an acre; uncleared land at $10 an acre. His 'typical' large plantation requires 16 acres of cleared and 10 acres of uncleared land per hand—and these are the figures used by Conrad and Meyer. As for poor upland pine land, the only pertinent data in Gray is a reference to the capital account of a small Alabama poor pine land plantation in 1846 which indicates a requirement of 36 acres of land—at $6 an acre—per hand.

Conrad and Meyer, assuming 10-year exhaustion of upland pine land, 30-year slave longevity, an 8% interest rate, and a 30-35 acre per hand land requirement, estimate the present value of investment in upland pine land per hand at $302-$350.[8] Making the same depreciation, slave longevity, and interest rate assumptions, but adopting the 36 acre per hand requirement as cited in Gray, the figure which emerges—and will be used in our calculations— is $362.

Land investment in the alluvial area totals to $660 per hand, if one assumes—as do Conrad and Meyer—that usefulness of land and slave lasted the same number of years. Conrad and Meyer, in fact, maintain that such land "typically" outlasted the slave in usefulness, although Gray refers only to "a number of rich river bottoms" which "were exceptions to the rule of exhaustion and migration."[9] Else-

---

[5] From Phillips' chart "Prices of Slaves in Four Markets . . . ," *Life and Labor,* p. 177.

[6] Conrad and Meyer, *op. cit.,* p. 50.

[7] Lewis Gray, *History of Agriculture in the Southern United States to 1860,* pp. 541-42.

[8] Conrad and Meyer, *op. cit.,* p. 101.

[9] Gray, *op. cit.,* p. 447.

where, he estimates the usefulness of cotton lands to range from 10 to 20 years.[10] We shall assume here that the alluvium lasted 20 years. A 30-year slave life-expectancy, 8% interest rate, and requirement of 16 acres of cleared and 10 acres of uncleared land per hand would then yield a land investment of $769.

Again, Conrad and Meyer apparently use figures from Gray's "typical" alluvium operation for their estimate of the investment in farm implements—$25.[11] Assuming that they were renewed every 15 years,[12] their present value would be about $33 on the assumption of 30-year slave longevity and 8% interest—the estimate we shall use.

Over wide areas of the South, farms and plantations were largely self-sufficient. According to Conrad and Meyer—since livestock was probably self-replenishing—the costs involved should be limited to interest on the investment. Gray's "average" alluvium plantation implies an investment in livestock of $73 a hand. A 30-year slave life-expectancy would require an interest cost of about $66, again on the assumption of an interest rate of 8%.

Capital costs per hand in terms of present value, then, are $1386 for the upland-pine operations, $1793 for the alluvium operation. This compares with Conrad and Meyer's estimate of $1250-$1300 for the upland-pine operation, and $1700 for the alluvium operation.[13]

Annual net return to the cotton operation is the difference between gross sales and expenses. In estimating annual out-of-pocket expenses, Conrad and Meyer use three principal sources: J. L. Watkins' *The Cost of Cotton Production* [U. S. Dept. of Agriculture, Division of Statistics, Miscellaneous Series, Bull. 16 (Washington, D. C.: U. S. Govt. Printing Office, 1899)], Lewis C. Gray's

---

[10]*Ibid.,* p. 543.

[11]This estimate does not include an allowance for buildings (although it does include investment in a cotton gin). It was characteristic of large plantations especially to have numerous buildings constructed for, e.g., plantation office, carpenter shop, blacksmith's shop, loom house, smoke house, grist mill, wash house, stable and sheds, gear and implement sheds, storehouses, etc. Although an estimate should be included, information is scanty. Gray speaks of outbuildings as being of an "inexpensive character," with Negro houses generally representing an "inconsiderable expenditure." (*Ibid.,* p. 540.)

[12]Conrad and Meyer do not indicate what this assumption is based upon. There seems to be no obvious reason to expect "plows, gins, wagons, cabins, and miscellaneous implements" (Conrad and Meyer, *loc. cit.*) to have an average life of 15 years, but in the absence of any compelling reason to change it, the assumption will be retained in this paper. Gray does cite a cotton planter as calculating that *buildings* required replacement every 15 or 20 years. (Gray, *op. cit.*, p. 543.)

[13]Conrad and Meyer, *op. cit.,* Table 9, p. 107.

History of Agriculture in the Southern U. S. to 1860, and Kenneth Stampp's *The Peculiar Institution.* These sources in turn have drawn on a large amount of material—agricultural and business journals, diaries and plantation records—in making their estimates of expenses, and these estimates seem to represent the best information available.

However, Conrad and Meyer have apparently confused out-of-pocket expenses per *slave* with out-of-pocket expenses per slave *hand* when recording maintenance costs. Thus, in Table 5,[14] they indicate a range of $7 to $10 for "out-of-pocket costs where some ready-made clothing and meat, fish, and other food 'delicacies' were purchased." Gray states that "plantations purchasing a portion of the clothing ready-made, together with fish or other meat and a few delicacies, averaged about $7 to $10 a slave, or $14 to $20 per *hand"* (italics mine).[15] Similarly, medical care ($1.50-$2) and taxes ($.39-$1.20) are computed on a per slave basis, and should be doubled.

The cost of supervision is not so clear-cut. Stampp refers to a range of salaries for overseers of $100 to $1200 per year.[16] According to Gray, "typical" salaries were from $400 to $600.[17] One plantation manager informed Olmsted during his travels that 50 hands to each overseer was optimum;[18] if we were to make the assumption that this ratio was "typical," this would imply supervisory costs of $8 to $12 a hand. Phillips mentions an instance of a $120 salary being paid on a plantation with less than a dozen working slaves ($10 a hand).[19] Olmsted refers to four Mississippi plantations, each with over 100 hands, directed by overseers paid $500 to $1000 each ($5 to $10 a hand).[20] On balance, an estimate for supervisory costs of $10 a hand does not seem unreasonable, and this is the figure which shall be used.

[14]*Ibid.,* p. 104.

[15]Gray, *op. cit.,* p. 544. There is an assumption here that plantations typically carried one hand to every two slaves. This seems to be borne out by contemporary records and observations. *Cf.* Stampp, *op. cit.,* p. 57, Frederick Olmsted, *The Cotton Kingdom,* I, pp. 59-60, II, p. 177.

[16]Stampp, *op. cit.,* p. 38.

[17]Gray, *op. cit.,* p. 545. In addition to his salary, the overseer generally received food, a house, and the services of a slave servant (Stampp, *loc., cit.*)—but the cost of these perquisites per hand would seem to be negligible.

[18]Olmsted, *op. cit.,* Vol. II, p. 201.

[19]Phillips, *Life and Labor, op. cit.,* p. 313.

[20]Olmsted, *op. cit.,* Vol. II, pp. 195, 201.

In toto, means of the above estimates for maintenance, together with the approximation of supervisory costs, sum to an annual out-of-pocket cost per field hand of $32, as compared with Conrad and Meyer's estimate of $20-$21. This cost should be deducted from annual gross sales of cotton per hand.

Product per hand is an important part of the profitability calculus. Conrad and Meyer refer to "frequent statements in contemporary journals that in the typical case a prime field hand could be expected to raise from 3.5 to 4 bales (of cotton) a year. The maximum seems to have been 7-8 bales on the best lands, and 2-3 bales was the minimum on the poorest land." [21] Further, they cite several reported yields found in Watkins and in Gray for the period around 1850 which indicate a range of from 3 bales in South Carolina (around 1850) and 4 bales in one Mississippi county (1849), to 8 bales in the Vicksburg area of Mississippi (1855). [22]

Unfortunately, it is not indicated whether the estimates above are inclusive of the slave hand's non-cotton (subsistence) product. That is, are these estimates of output for a hand working in cotton alone, or output based on the assumption that the slave also made provisions? The latter estimate should be the one used, because the profitability calculation is being made on the assumption of self-sufficiency.

If the cotton output per hand figures used by Conrad and Meyer do *not* refer to self-sufficient cotton production, these figures should be revised downward; this in turn could have a significant impact on their internal rate of return estimates. One way to determine whether "reported yields" refer to self-sufficient production would be to assume that they do, and then see whether the per-acre yield implied is compatible with historical data relating to cotton production.

Regrettably, relevant historical data for different grades of land are not available. However, we can test the validity of the self-sufficiency assumption as it applies to the 7-8 bale per hand figure accepted by Conrad and Meyer as an average for the alluvium operation. (The figure which they use to calculate the rate of return on alluvium is 7 bales per hand.) If output per hand as hypothesized for the alluvium operation should turn out to be more consistent with slave hands working on cotton alone, rather than on cotton and

[21]Conrad and Meyer, *op. cit.,* p. 104.
[22]*Ibid.,* Table 6, p. 105.

rations, this would lend weight to a like interpretation of the output figures cited for other grades of land as well.

Assuming, then, a 'self-sufficient' 7-8 bales per hand on alluvium, a "typical" alluvium operation of 10 acres of cotton and 6 of corn per hand[23] would yield a product of .7-.8 bales or 280-320 pounds of cotton per acre of cotton planted. Now, cotton production after the Civil War surpassed the 1860 prewar peak (of nearly 5 million bales) in 1878 (a year after Federal troops left the South), and reached triple that figure by 1915.[24] The nearly unprecedented increase in cotton production after the Civil Was was augmented to a large degree by an increase in yield per acre partly brought about by a new and greatly expanded use of fertilizers.[25] Further, yield per acre in recent years has exhibited a striking upward trend with the introduction into cotton culture of significant innovations in seedbed preparation, fertilization, methods of planting, thinning and weed control, insect control (such as DDT), and breeding (such as the development of strains incorporating high yields, and storm and disease resistance).[26]

It is interesting to note that the period of greatest increase in yield per acre—from about 1930 to 1951—is also the period during which harvested acreage of cotton decreased by about one-half.[27] That is, the harvested acreage of cotton in 1951 was about the same as acreage in cotton in 1900; yet increases in yield per acre were sufficient to push cotton production to a point one-third greater than that in 1900—in fact, to about what it was in 1930 when twice as much acreage was harvested. Since 1910, there has been a vigorous expansion in cotton acreage into the Western irrigated areas—with unusually rapid increases in production recorded in New Mexico, Arizona, and California.[28] These areas are characterized by much greater yields than the older cotton areas.[29] It would seem

[23]Gray, *op. cit.,* pp. 707-08.

[24]James Street, *New Revolution in the Cotton Economy,* p. 26.

[25]*Ibid.,* p. 24.

[26]*Ibid* chap. 7.

[27]*Ibid.,* Fig. 1, "Cotton in the U.S.," (1873-1951), p. 25, where the source is given as the U. S. Dept. of Agriculture, Neg. 48046-VX, Bureau of Agricultural Economics.

[28]*Ibid.,* p. 37.

[29]Over the period 1919-27, Mississippi had an average yield per acre of 174 pounds, California 285 pounds, Arizona 280 pounds, and New Mexico (for the period 1923-27) 268 pounds. The average yield per acre for all cotton-producing states was only 156 pounds. (John Todd, *The Cotton World,* Table III. p. 10.)

reasonable to assume that the acreage taken out of cotton over the period 1930-51 was the poorest, least productive land.

Again, a 'self-sufficient' output of 7-8 bales per hand on Mississippi alluvium in 1850 implies a product per acre of 280-320 pounds. Yet, despite the increases in product per acre which have occurred (especially since the period just before World War II), yield per acre (calculated as a five-year average beginning in 1866) did not reach 280 pounds until the period 1946-50 (when it was 284 pounds), and did not reach 320 pounds until the period 1951-55 (when it was 340 pounds)—a full century after 1850.[30]

Thus, if the 7-8 bale per hand figure does indeed accurately reflect average 'self-sufficient' yield per acre on alluvium in 1850, this would have the dubious implication that the significant innovations in cotton culture which have served to boost yield per acre since the 30's have been only just sufficient to increase per acre yield to a level commensurate to that achieved on alluvium in 1850— even though these innovations have been applied to land the average quality of which was increasing. Therefore, although instances of 7-8 bales per hand may well have occurred and been reported, as an average for *self sufficient* cotton hands working on alluvial land 7-8 bales is very probably high.

In an attempt to arrive at an independent estimate of cotton per 'self-sufficient' slave hand, we utilized data from the 1850 Census. The Census lists information for each county which includes the number of slaves resident therein, together with production data for the various agricultural products including cotton.[31] In order to use these data for the estimate desired, it was assumed first of all that all of the slaves listed were employed in agriculture. This may not have been too strong an assumption, since probably not more than 10 percent did in fact live in cities and towns.[32] It was further assumed, on the basis of footnote 15 above, that only one-half of all the slaves were working field hands—the rest being children, infirm, aged, or other slaves who for one reason or another did not go into the fields. Finally, it was assumed that the output of all non-cotton products went into providing for the maintenance of slaves in cotton produc-

[30]Computed from the table "Hay, Cotton, Cottonseed Acreage, Production, and Price: 1790-1957," in U. S. Bureau of the Census, *Historical Statistics of the United States,* p. 301-02.

[31]J.D.B. De Bow, *Statistical View of the U.S.,* (Compendium of the Seventh Census), pp. 194-337.

[32]Stampp, *op. cit.,* p. 31.

tion. In order to make this last assumption more palatable, counties were deliberately chosen which produced zero or relatively negligible quantities of non-cotton staples: tobacco, rice, sugar, and hemp. The estimate of cotton yield per field hand in each county was reached through a simple divison of total bales of cotton by (estimated) number of field hands.

In order to make an estimate for cotton per field hand working on alluvium, those cotton counties were chosen which Gray lists as comprising the alluvial regions of the South.[33] The majority of these counties were in Mississippi, with some in Louisiana, Alabama, and Arkansas. The estimate was made on the basis of 21 counties in all. Both the mean and median turned out to be 3.6 bales per field hand, with a high of 6.1 bales, and a low of 1.6 bales.

Moving east, into the older areas of cotton production, an estimate for Alabama was made which excluded the alluvial and relatively fertile (calcareous) black prairie areas. Information from seven counties yielded a mean of 3.3 bales and a median of 3.5 bales—with a high of 3.9 bales and a low of 2.4 bales.

Further, two upland cotton counties were chosen in Northwestern Alabama which were characterized by remoteness from market and poor soils;[34] they were assumed to be representative of this class of cotton operation. Cotton output per hand in one was 2.4 bales, in the other 1.7 bales.

Moving east even further into the older upland cotton regions, an estimate was made for Georgia on the basis of information from 25 counties. Both the mean and median for Georgia were 3.0 bales. There was a high of 4.3 and a low of 1.2 bales.

Finally, an estimate for South Carolina was màde utilizing information from seven counties. The mean for South Carolina was 2.8 bales per hand, the median 2.7 bales, with a high of 3.6 bales and a low of 2.5 bales.[35]

The average, then, for alluvial lands seems to have been some 3.6 bales per hand, for the older areas of the South 3.0 bales per hand, and for very poor land some 2.0 bales per hand. A weighted average of the alluvial with older areas of the South yields what could be

---

[33]Gray, *op. cit.*, Table 12, p. 531.

[34]*Ibid.*, p. 534, Table 13, p. 536.

[35]Interestingly enough, around 1850 Governor Hammond of South Carolina asserted that he believed the average for South Carolina would not exceed 3 bales, and that a great many planters did not grow over 2.5 bales per hand. (*Ibid.*, p. 709.)

Table I Returns on Prime Field Hands

Type of Operation	Capital Cost Per Hand	Bales Per Hand	Internal Rate of Return at:	
			7¢ lb.	8¢ lb.
Poor Upland Pine	$1386	2.0	#	#
	$1250–1300*	3.0*	2.2%*	3.9%*
Older Areas	$1640	3.0	#	1.1%
	$1690	3.2	#	1.5%
Average for South	$1350–$1400*	3.75*	4.5%*	5.2%*
	$1600*	4.5*	5.0%*	7.0%*
"Somewhat Better Land"	$1793	3.6 (avg.)	.9%	2.3%
Alluvial Land	$1793	6.1 (high)	6.5%	8.2%
	$1700*	7.0*	10.0%*	12.0%*

*Conrad and Meyer estimates, from their Table 9, p. 107.
#Less than .025%.

considered to be a rough estimate for the Lower South as a whole: 3.2 bales per hand.

Conrad and Meyer's 7-8 cents per pound average realized farm price for cotton[36] seemed reasonable enough and was used in further calculations.

Putting all of this information together made it possible to compute rates of return for prime field hands in cotton culture as indicated in Table I. The cost per hand of the capital investment in older cotton areas of the South—$1640—as well as in what might be called average land—$1690—was calculated on the assumption that such cost was proportional to cotton output per hand. (Conrad and Meyer estimate investment in average areas at $1350-$1400,[37] on the assumption that investment per hand in average land was halfway between that in pine land and that in alluvium;[38] they make no separate estimate of investment in the older cotton areas as such.) Further, a calculation was made for alluvial land on the basis of 6.1 bales per hand (which was the high for alluvial land achieved in one county in 1850), to see what the return might have been in an *exceptionally favorable* case.

We see, then, that contrary to Conrad and Meyer's conclusions, ante bellum cotton production under the slave system generally failed to earn returns which were in any sense comparable to a 'normal' return of, say, 6%—even if the assumption of 30-year longevity is retained. However, even though cotton culture dominated southern agriculture in the ante bellum period, slaves might well have been profitably employed in other pursuits. What can be said, and what this paper has shown (by demonstrating the general unprofitability of slave operations in cotton), is that Conrad and Meyer may well have been premature in stating that the "argument that slavery must have destroyed itself can no longer rest upon allegations of unprofitability."[39]

[36]Based on Gray, *op. cit.,* Table 41, pp. 1027-29.
[37]Conrad and Meyer, *op. cit.,* Table 9, p. 107.
[38]*Ibid.,* p. 101.
[39]*Ibid.,* p. 122.

RICHARD SUTCH
The Profitability of Ante Bellum Slavery—Revisited *

A RECENT NOTE in this *Journal* by Edward Saraydar[1] undertakes a criticism of Alfred Conrad and John Meyer's well known
article, "The Economics of Slavery in the Ante Bellum South."[2] By
reconstructing a typical cotton plantation's production function,
Conrad and Meyer had attempted to prove that southern slavery in
the latter part of the 1850's was at least as profitable as alternative
investment opportunities.

Mr. Saraydar charges that Conrad and Meyer in the course of
their calculations confused data from plantations that purchased all
food and clothing from outside sources with data from self-
sufficient plantations. By using the average yield per slave from the
specialized plantations and estimates of yearly slave maintenance
from *self-sufficient* plantations, one would arrive at too high a profit
rate. Saraydar recalculates what he feels to be consistent data and
uses them to demonstrate "the general unprofitability of slave
operations in cotton."[3]

The relevancy of the rate of profit earned on ante bellum cotton
plantations to a number of historical questions has been pointed out
by Conrad and Meyer. Primarily, however, interest has been
focused on the proposition that the institution of slavery would have
destroyed itself without political intervention through its own
unprofitability had not the Civil War intervened.[4]

It was primarily to test this hypothesis, and to test it on the
historians' ground, that Conrad and Meyer undertook to calculate
the rate of return on slave holdings in the last decades before the
Civil War. They concluded that:

> In sum, it seems doubtful that the South was forced by bad states-
> manship into an unnecessary war to protect a system which must

*I would like to thank Dr. Douglass C. North and Dr. Donald F. Gordon of the
University of Washington for their helpful comments on earlier drafts of this paper.

[1]Edward Saraydar, "A Note on the Profitability of Ante Bellum Slavery," *The
Southern Economic Journal,* April 1964, pp. 325-32.

[2]Alfred H. Conrad and John R. Meyer, "The Economics of Slavery in the Ante
Bellum South," *The Journal of Political Economy,* April 1958, pp. 95-130.

[3]Saraydar, p. 331.

[4]Conrad and Meyer, p. 95.

soon have disappeared because it was economically unsound. This is a romantic hypothesis which will not stand against the facts.[5]

It is true, if Conrad and Meyer's figures are valid, that the historians' arguments "can no longer rest upon allegations of unprofitability."[6] On the other hand, it is important to note that if Conrad and Meyer's calculations are wrong (as Saraydar suggests), this alone would not be sufficient to prove that slavery was about to "topple of its own weight." For what is really of importance to this test is not the profitability of cotton production, which is a short-run phenomenon, but the viability of slavery. If cotton production was unprofitable, it would not mean that slavery was doomed, for presumably alternative uses for slaves existed. If at the existing prices no alternative uses for slave labor were profitable, then the price of slaves, the price of land, or both, would have fallen (had emancipation not taken place) until it was once again profitable to own slaves and to grow cotton. In other words, temporary unprofitability of cotton operations would only mean that land and slaves were overvalued or that resources were misallocated, not that the institution of slavery was economically unsound.

Since slavery is only a peculiar method of providing a labor force, we would expect slavery to be viable as long as it could provide labor at a cost equal to or below that of free labor. Since the cost of owning a slave is the cost of his maintenance plus the amortization of his initial price, slavery will always be able to compete with free labor through adjustments in the price of slaves. If free labor posed a threat to slave labor, slave prices would fall and slavery's viability would be maintained. Only if slave prices fell to zero would the institution become economically unviable, and this could happen only if the wages of free labor were at the subsistence level.[7] But this would imply that the free labor force was multiplying at Malthusian rates—a highly unlikely assumption for any period of American history. Thus, it is fairly certain that given reasonably flexible slave prices economic forces could not have brought about an end to slavery directly.

[5]*Ibid.*, p. 121.

[6]*Ibid.*, p. 122.

[7]The wages of free labor would not have to fall quite to the subsistence level if a slave were a less productive worker than the free laborer. For even if the free laborer's wage were above subsistence, we would prefer him to a slave for whom we had to provide subsistence, if the free laborer's product were higher.

While the profitability figures of both Conrad and Meyer and Saraydar are irrelevant to the question of slavery's viability, they do have a relevance to other questions often connected with ante bellum slavery. For example, a number of historians have argued that low monetary returns to slave owning were counterbalanced by nonpecuniary returns.[8] In other words, the owning of slaves conferred upon the master a higher status in his community, or gave him a feeling of power, or gave him political prestige, or some other nonmonetary return which compensated for low rates of profit.

By calculating the monetary returns, we can test whether such nonpecuniary returns are necessary to explain the patterns of slaveholding. Saraydar's calculations imply that they are necessary, and that Conrad and Meyer were wrong. Despite the fact that there are some problems with Conrad and Meyer's data, it is our contention that Saraydar has made even more critical mistakes in his calculations, and that they vitiate his conclusion.

There are two sources of error in Saraydar's estimates: (1) he employs an unrealistic assumption about the cotton plantation's production function, and (2) he underestimates the yearly yield of cotton per slave hand. The balance of this note attempts to demonstrate how serious these two factors are to the estimates of profit rate in cotton production.

I

The incorrect specification in Saraydar's production function arises from his implicit assumption that no reproduction of the slave stock takes place. Conrad and Meyer, in their article, employed a concept of a dual production function. One function was used to measure the return from the labor of male field hands, the other the return from the sale of children produced by the female slaves. The two production functions were completely independent of each other.

Saraydar tested only the first of these two production functions; however, he did not retain their independence. Instead, he increased the estimate of the yearly maintenance cost of a male hand used by Conrad and Meyer to include an amount necessary to maintain the

---

[8]Ulrich Bonnell Phillips, *American Negro Slavery,* 2d ed. (Gloucester, Mass.: Peter Smith, 1959), p. 394.

females and children.[9] Yet he did not include the returns the females generated by producing salable offspring.

In other words, Saraydar calculates the return to slaveholders by assuming that only the labor in the cotton fields was productive of revenue and that no increase in the stock of slaves took place. In his model, the stream of income provided by an investment in slaves remains constant for thirty years and then stops. In reality, of course, the slave population actually grew throughout the whole period. Thus, an investor in this form of capital would find that as time passed his stock of capital was growing—since under southern law, the children of a female slave belonged to the woman's owner. This growth in the stock of capital would produce a rising stream of income that would continue growing indefinitely.

Thus, if we wish to switch from Conrad and Meyer's dual production function to a single production function (including both male and female slaves as inputs), we must include the appreciation in the slave stock as part of our formulation. Alternatively, if we wished to retain Conrad and Meyer's dual concept, we would not properly include the females and children as inputs to the males' production function, for they are inputs to their own distinct production function. If this is the case, Conrad and Meyer's maintenance costs *are* the appropriate estimates and we cannot charge that they confused "out-of-pocket expenses per *slave* with out-of-pocket expenses per slave *hand* when recording maintenance costs."[10]

To obtain an idea of how critical this error in specification of the production function is, we have recalculated the rate of profit using a single production function concept. This approach has an advantage over the dual production function of Conrad and Meyer in that the rate of appreciation of slave capital can be calculated directly from Census data rather than requiring a large number of assumptions concerning fertility and mortality rates of the slave population.

The single production function model is embodied in the following formula:[11]

$$r = \frac{1 + a}{1 - \left[\dfrac{pY - c}{K}\right]} - 1,$$

[9]Saraydar, pp. 327-28.
[10]Saraydar, p. 327.
[11]The formula is derived in the following way:

where

> r is the internal rate of return,
> a is the appreciation rate of the stock of slaves,
> p is the price of cotton to the farmer,
> Y is the yield per hand in pounds,
> c is the yearly out-of-pocket expense per hand, and
> K is the initial investment per hand.

Consulting the Census figures, we find that between 1850 and 1860 the slave population increased 23.4 per cent which represents an annual increase of 2.15 per cent.[12] Between 1850 and 1860, slave prices rose 72 per cent or, after adjustment for the increase in the general price level, 68 per cent.[13] Thus the capital value of the slave stock increased 107.6 per cent in ten years—an annual increase of 7.56 per cent.

When we recognize this general appreciation of an investment in slaves, it puts a totally new light on the profitability question. For

$$V_t = R_t (1/1 + r)^t$$

is the capital value formula where R_t is the return in the year t and V_t is the present value of this return. But the return per hand is $pY - c$, and the number of hands in year t is $(1 + a)^t$ times the original number of hands purchased; since we are looking for the present value of a single slave we have:

$$V_t = (pY - c)(1 + a)^t (1/1 + r)^t,$$

since a purchase of slaves will yield an infinite stream of income, the present value of this stream is obtained by summing:

$$K = (pY - c) \sum_{t=0}^{\infty} \left[\frac{1 + a}{1 + r} \right]^t$$

which simplifies to:

$$K = \frac{(pY - c)}{1 - \left[\dfrac{1 + a}{1 + r} \right]}$$

and solving for r gives us our formula.

[12] Census Office, *Population of the United States in 1860*, Eighth Census (Washington, D. C.: U. S. Government Printing Office, 1864), p. ix. The age distribution of the population also shifted between "fifty and 'sixty, but a calculation of "prime field hand equivalents" showed that they increased only one tenth of 1 per cent more over the ten years than the population as a whole.

[13] Robert Evans, Jr., "The Economics of American Negro Slavery, 1830-1860," *Aspects of Labor Economics,* National Bureau of Economic Research (Princeton, N.J.: Princeton University Press, 1962), p. 224. Evans used a New Orleans price index.

this 7.6 per cent increase in and of itself is greater than the 6 per cent alternative rate of return. However, if these capital gains are to be solidly based on rising profitability of slave-operated cotton plantations rather than on short-term speculation effects, we must demonstrate a return to cotton production above 6 per cent *exclusive* of the effects of rising slave prices. For this reason an appreciation rate of 2.15 per cent is used in the following calculations.

To measure how significant the growth of the slave population is to the estimates of profit rate, we recalculated the internal rate of return using Saraydar's own estimates of the yields per hand for each of the regions he examined, and the seven- to eight-cent range in the price of cotton used by Saraydar. However, increases are necessary in both the yearly maintenance cost and the initial investment required to be consistent with the altered assumptions.

For the cost of slave maintenance, Saraydar uses $32 per hand. Since the number of slaves increased at the rate of 2.15 per cent, the stock of land and associated capital must be increased at the same rate to prevent diminishing returns. Using Saraydar's figures of $640 and $793 for the cost of these inputs per hand for the Old South and for the highly fertile alluvial soils respectively means that new investment of $13.76 to $17.05 per hand per year must be added to the $32 maintenance cost.

The nursery costs associated with the birth of slave children must also be included in the yearly maintenance allowance if we are to bring all the costs into the picture. In 1860 there were 113,650 slaves under one year old[14] which would imply 2.87 successful births per year for every one hundred slaves. Conrad and Meyer assumed that the nursery costs were $50 per successful pregnancy[15] which in turn implies a cost of $2.87 per slave hand per year for nursery costs.[16] Thus the total yearly outlay per hand ranges from $48.70 to $52.00, the numbers we use for *c* in the formula.

For our calculations, we need to have an estimate of the initial capital investment per hand; this variable should include the cost of the slaves, land, and equipment, and the value of a sinking fund to replace the land as it wears out. Saraydar calculates the value of the land, the equipment, and the sinking fund at $640 for plantations in

---

[14]*Eighth Census of Population,* p. 594.
[15]Conrad and Meyer, p. 108.
[16]Assuming, with Saraydar, that 50 per cent of the slaves are hands.

the Old South and $793 for alluvial soil. The sinking fund was calculated to last only thirty years; however, the necessary increase required to extend this to a perpetual fund is negligible. These data, then, seem reasonable enough as they stand. However, in calculating the necessary investment in slaves we must now include, not just the investment in male field hands, but in women and children as well.

In 1850, 45.4 per cent of the slaves in the United States were under fifteen years of age and 50.87 per cent were between 15 and 60.[17] Conrad and Meyer have reported the average price of a male field hand in prime condition in 1848 as $900 and an adult female as $750 to $800.[18] Assuming that children and slaves over 60 are worth only one half of their adult prices, we can calculate that the average value of a slave was roughly $630 in 1849, the year for which Saraydar measured his yields. Thus, if 50 per cent of the slaves are field hands, the average investment in slaves per hand was $1,260; adding the cost of the other capital as estimated by Saraydar, we come to the final estimate of capital expenditures: $1,900 for the Old South, and $2,053 for alluvium.

Table I compares the returns computed by Saraydar with those from the single production function model. As can be seen, his neglect of the growth of the negro population produced a significant downward bias in his estimates.

Saraydar originally calculated a yield for "poor upland pine land"; however, this figure is not reported in Table I since Saraydar's calculations for this region are incorrect by his own method. He chose two counties in northwestern Alabama which he felt had poor soils,[19] and he reported a cotton output per hand of 2.4 bales in one and of 1.7 bales in the other.[20] Yet the correct figures, *using his method,* should be exactly twice this. Apparently he did not divide the slave population in half before calculating his returns.

---

[17]J. D. B. DeBow, *Statistical View of the United States, Compendium of the Seventh Census* (Washington, D. C.: Beverley Tucker, 1854), p. 103.

[18]Conrad and Meyer, p. 100.

[19]Fayette and Marion Counties, Alabama. There is no evidence that I could find that would indicate that these counties had poor soils. Indeed, E. A. Smith reports the soils are above average in fertility and "quite productive." Eugene A. Smith, "Report on the Cotton Production of the State of Alabama," in Eugene W. Hilgard, Census Office, *Report on Cotton Production in the United States, Part I* (Washington, D. C.: U. S. Government Printing Office, 1884), pp. 120-21.

[20]Saraydar, p. 330.

Table I Effect on Estimated Returns of Alternative Models of the Production Function

Region and model	Yield (bales per hand)	Capital cost	Maintenance cost	Return with cotton selling for 7¢/lb.	8¢/lb. (percentage)
Older Areas:					
Saraydar's Model	3	$1,640	$32.00	—	1.1
Single Production Function Model	3	1,900	48.70	4.1	4.8
Average for the South:					
Saraydar's Model	3.2	1,690	32.00	—	1.5
Single Production Function Model	3.2	1,950	49.70	4.3	5.0
Average for Alluvium:					
Saraydar's Model	3.6	1,793	32.00	0.9	2.3
Single Production Function Model	3.6	2,053	52.00	4.6	5.4
High for Alluvium:					
Saraydar's Model	6.1	1,793	32.00	6.5	8.2
Single Production Function Model	6.1	2,053	52.00	8.4	9.8

—, less than .025%.
Source for Saraydar's Model: Saraydar, Table I, p. 331.

II

As Table I has shown, the effects of appreciating stocks are fairly significant to the profitability estimates, but they are not generally sufficient to raise the return above the 6 per cent interest available on alternative investments. This brings us to the second source of error in Saraydar's estimate: his underestimation of the average yield per hand.

Conrad and Meyer's data on the average yield were drawn from three authoritative secondary sources: J. L. Watkins, *The Cost of Cotton Production;* Lewis C. Gray, *History of Agriculture in the Southern United States to 1860;* and Kenneth Stampp, *The Peculiar Institution.*[21] The yields used in Conrad and Meyer's calculations ranged from three bales per hand per year on the worst land to seven bales per hand on the best.[22]

Saraydar charges that these figures are unrealistic in light of present day yields from cotton plantations of the South. He calculates that Conrad and Meyer's average yield of seven to eight bales per hand on alluvial soil (regarded as the best for cotton) implies a yield per acre of 280-320 pounds; yet it was not until 1946-1950 that 280 pounds per acre was achieved as an average for the South, and not until 1951-1955 that it reached 340 pounds. Saraydar concludes:

> . . . this would have the dubious implication that the significant innovations in cotton culture which have served to boost yield per acre since the 30's have been only just sufficient to increase per acre yield to a level commensurate to that achieved on alluvium in 1850. . . . [23]

However, this finding is not as unreasonable as it might first appear. For one thing, Saraydar is comparing the yield from the best lands of the South before the Civil War with the average for all the United States in recent years. It is not immediately obvious that

[21]James L. Watkins, *The Cost of Cotton Production,* U. S. Department of Agriculture, Division of Statistics, Miscellaneous Series, Bulletin No. 16 (Washington, D. C.: U. S. Government Printing Office, 1899); Lewis Cecil Gray, *History of Agriculture in the Southern United States to 1860,* 2d ed. (Gloucester, Mass.: Peter Smith, 1958); Kenneth Stampp, *The Peculiar Institution* (New York: Alfred Knopf, 1956).

[22]Conrad and Meyer, p. 107.

[23]Saraydar, p. 329-30.

agricultural technology should have improved *average* yields to the extent that they equalled the yields obtainable from the *best* soils before the Civil War.

In fact, if we look at the growth in productivity on alluvial soil we find that it has grown at a reasonable rate. The Census of 1880 provides us with the earliest data on cotton yields per acre by county. We can use these data to compare the 280-320 pounds per acre yield implied by Conrad and Meyer's data, with yields from alluvium in 1879. Table II presents the average yield per acre for the 13 counties in Arkansas, Mississippi, and Louisiana that border the Mississippi River and are characterized by the Census Office as having primarily alluvial soils.

Table II *Yields per Acre on Mississippi Alluvium in 1879*

County	Pounds of lint per acre	Page reference
Mississippi County, Arkansas	390	p. 587
Tunica County, Mississippi	285	p. 318
Crittenden County, Arkansas	330	p. 587
Coahoma County, Mississippi	380	p. 318
Desha County, Arkansas	430	p. 586
Bolivar County, Mississippi	399	p. 320
Washington County, Mississippi	413	p. 321
Chicot County, Arkansas	470	p. 548
East Carroll Parish, Louisiana	451	p. 145
Issaquena County, Mississippi	418	p. 323
Madison Parish, Louisiana	394	p. 149
Tensas Parish, Louisiana	394	p. 149
Concordia Parish, Louisiana	375	p. 149
Weighted Average	396	

Source: Computed from data in Eugene W. Ililgard, Census Office, *Report on Cotton Production in the United States, Part I*, (Washington, D.C.; U.S. Government Printing Office, 1884). The data were reported in bales and converted to pounds according to the average weight of bales reported on p. 18.

Since these 13 counties produced one half of all the cotton grown on alluvium in that year,[24] the average yield of 396 pounds can probably be taken as an average for a typical Mississippi alluvium

[24]Hilgard, Part I, p. 16.

operation in 1879. This figure is 24 to 41 per cent higher than the yield implied by Conrad and Meyer's seven to eight bales per hand for Mississippi alluvium.

Saraydar has suggested that the yields reported by Conrad and Meyer were too large, because they came from plantations that bought all their food from the outside rather than growing most of their own.[25] Since the production costs used by Conrad and Meyer are based on the assumption of self-sufficiency, such an error would bias their calculated returns upward.

However, a check of the three sources used by Conrad and Meyer reveals in two of them that the figures given were explicitly stated to be from plantations that *did* produce their own foodstuffs. Conrad and Meyer's figure for the Vicksburg area of Mississippi, for example, is obtained from Watkins:

> A Vicksburg, Miss., cotton planter [who owned in 1855] . . . a plantation of 1,600 acres, 1,000 of which was cleared land, and worked with 75 effective hands worth $600 each and 50 mules worth $130 each, *the corn and meat being produced on the plantation,* states that the yield for an average of ten years would be about 600 bales of 400 pounds each.[26] [Italics mine.]

Simple calculation gives an average yield of eight bales per "effective" hand.

Similarly, the figure from Watkins cited by Conrad and Meyer for DeSoto County, Mississippi (1849), was from a self-sufficient plantation. Here "4 bales of 500 pounds each per hand [was] a fair average."[27] Since Conrad and Meyer based their price on a four-hundred-pound bale, they should have reported five bales a hand from this county—as it is, they *underestimate* the average yield.[28]

Conrad and Meyer cite from Gray a yield of five bales on new land in the Southwest. Gray reports a hand could work eight to ten acres

[25]Saraydar, p. 328.

[26]Watkins, p. 46.

[27]*Ibid.*, p. 45.

[28]Similarly, Conrad and Meyer's 1844 figure of seven bales to a hand was underestimated; as the reference was to 450-pound bales (Watkins, p. 43), the correct figure should be 7.875 bales. And the Cherokee County, Alabama (1855), yield of four bales was for 500-pound bales; the correct figure is therefore five bales. It should also be noted that the yield of $4\frac{1}{3}$ bales per hand for South Carolina coastal plantations cited by Conrad and Meyer actually refers to a plantation in Marengo County, Alabama (Watkins, pp. 44-45).

of cotton "besides making provisions."[29] Eight to ten acres with a product of 250 pounds each, yields five to six-and-a-quarter bales, of four hundred pounds each, to the hand.

Thus, it would seem that Saraydar was incorrect in arguing that "as an average for self-sufficient cotton hands working on alluvial land 7-8 bales is very probably high."[30] It can be easily shown that Saraydar's range of 2 to 3.6 bales is an underestimate. In 1859, seven southern states[31] produced 4,824,308 bales (400 pounds each) of cotton (90 per cent of the U.S. crop). The 1860 slave population of these same states was 2,361,722, but only 1,594,888 were between 10 and 70 years old.[32] If we subtract 10 per cent from this figure for the slaves in the cities,[33] we get an average yield of 3.36 bales per slave, and this completely ignores the fact that a sizable proportion of these slaves were not cotton hands, but worked in tobacco, rice, sugar, or other cash crops, or were domestic servants, or were unable to work for one reason or another.

Because he felt Conrad and Meyer had overvalued the average product of a field hand, Saraydar recalculated yields for several regions of the South. His estimates were arrived at by dividing one half of the slave population of several southern counties into the counties' cotton production, the raw data being taken from the Seventh Census (1850).[34]

The major bias in such a procedure is introduced by using the Seventh Census, which reported the 1849 cotton crop—for this year saw particularly low yields.[35] The total crop of the preceding year (considered a particularly good one) was 25 per cent higher; and not until the outbreak of the War, over a decade later, did the cotton crop fall below the trough reached in 1849.[36] The average annual crop of the 50's was 3,091,843 five-hundred-pound bales, a full 50 per cent above the 2,064,028 bales of the 1849 season.

The short crop sent the price of cotton up to 10.8 cents a pound.[37]

[29]Gray, p. 912.
[30]Saraydar, p. 330.
[31]Alabama, Arkansas, Georgia, Louisiana, Mississippi, South Carolina, and Texas.
[32]*Eighth Census of Population*, pp. 594-95.
[33]This figure is given by Kenneth Stampp and is cited with approval by Saraydar.
[34]DeBow, pp. 194-337.
[35]Watkins, p. 34.
[36]Gray, Table 40, p. 1026.
[37]*Ibid.*, Table 41, p. 1027. It should be noted that when Conrad and Meyer reproduced these data of Gray in their Table 17, p. 117, they matched average cotton

If Saraydar had used a price based on this rate in his calculations, then the error in using the 1849 crop would not be so great; instead, he used a 7- to 8-cent range that was valid for more normal years. Thus, even if Saraydar's yields accurately measured 1849 productivity, his profit rates could not be considered correct.

Between September 1849 and August 1850, the period in which the 1849 crop was sold, cotton prices at New Orleans rose from 9.3 cents a pound in September to 12.2 cents in July 1850. The weighted average price for the year was 10.8 cents.[38] Conrad and Meyer have calculated the cost of marketing the cotton (the cost of freight, insurance, storage, drayage, and commissions) at 0.7 to 0.8 of a cent per pound.[39] Thus, if we use 9-10 cents a pound as the price of cotton, we should not be overstating the farm-gate price relevant to Saraydar's yields.

Table III *Estimated Return for 1849*

Region	Yield	Internal rate of return	
		9c/lb.	*10c/lb.*
Older areas	3.0	5.5	6.1
Average for South	3.2	5.7	6.4
Average for alluvium	3.6	6.2	6.9
High for alluvium	6.1	11.2	12.8

Table III presents the results of calculating the rate of return using 9- to 10-cent cotton. The model used was the single production function model, with the same capital and maintenance allowances used in Table I.

These calculations show that slavery was profitable for a good many planters in 1849. But still we can hardly expect to find "normal" profits in a year of particularly poor crops. What we would like to do is to recalculate yields for different years than 1849.

If we wish to avoid the cotton crop data from 1849, we are forced to use the data reported in the Census of 1860 for the 1859 crop.

---

prices with the wrong years' cotton production. If the years are meant to be crop years, then Conrad and Meyer have reported the crop a year late (i.e., the crop of 1849 is reported as that of 1850). If the years are meant to be commercial years, the prices are reported a year early.

[38]*Ibid.*

[39]Conrad and Meyer, p. 105.

But, then we have the opposite problem, for 1859 was one of the best years for cotton production and the yields calculated from these data will overrepresent an average for the decade of the fifties.

However, there are several reasons why it would be interesting to examine the yields of 1859. First, a test for 1859 is more relevant than one for 1849 to the hypothesis of the major proponent of the unprofitability thesis, U. B. Phillips. It was his contention that:

> . . . by *the close of the 'fifties* it is fairly certain that no slaveholders but those few whose plantations lay in the most advantageous parts of the cotton and sugar districts and whose managerial ability was exceptionally great were earning anything beyond what would cover their maintenance and carrying charges. [Italics mine.][40]

Secondly, there were a number of important changes in the cotton economy between 1849 and 1859. Cotton output more than doubled—largely through expansions into new lands in Louisiana, Arkansas, and Texas (these states' cotton output rose 335 per cent, 462 per cent, and 643 per cent respectively). And, as we have noted, the price of slaves rose 68 per cent during the decade. The price of cotton seemed to be increasing slowly.

Finally, the more detailed data available from the 1860 Census will enable us to devise a more precise method of estimating the yields. Saraydar's method of simply dividing one half the number of slaves into the cotton production of each county introduces several biases into the estimates. We should like to correct for as many of these as possible.

As Saraydar realized, his method assumes all the slaves in the country lived on cotton plantations. Yet an examination of the fourteen alluvial-soil counties of Mississippi, used in part by Saraydar in his calculations, turned up Adams County with 688 slaveowners in 1860 but only 214 farms, and Warren County with 821 slaveholders and only 396 farms.[41] Of the fourteen alluvial

---

[40]Phillips, pp. 391-92.

[41]United States Census Office, *Agriculture of the United States in 1860,* Eighth Census (Washington, D. C.: U. S. Government Printing Office, 1864), pp. 206 and 232. According to the Census Office, "It would probably be a safe rule to consider the number of slaveholders to represent the number of families directly interested in the slave population in 1860," p. clxxii. Since there is no reason (such as tax advantage) to believe that there would be more than one slaveholding family per farm, it can be safely assumed that the excess of slaveholders over farmers represents the minimal number of persons who held slaves for non-agricultural purposes.

counties examined, all but one had a greater number of slaveowners than of farms in 1860. By including slaves who were obviously not on farms in his calculations, Saraydar's method will bias the yields downward.

A bias in the opposite direction will be present, in so far as free men worked in the fields producing cotton. Data in the *1860 Census of Population* enable us to make at least a partial correction for both of these effects. So that we do not count slaves who lived in cities as farm hands, we have deducted from each county's population the number of slaves reported in each of the towns enumerated by the Census. Since the listing by towns is partial, this will be only an incomplete adjustment. Furthermore, for South Carolina, a number of towns had only the free population reported; for these it was assumed that the same proportion of slaves resided in the city as was found in those towns of South Carolina (excluding Charleston) for which the slave population was reported.

The Census reported in 1860 the occupations of the free population by state. We calculated for each state the percentage of the free population who were reported as farm laborers (see Table IV), and assumed that this ratio held in every county. From this was calculated the estimated number of free field hands, which was added to the slave population. In general, this adjustment had negligible effects on the productivity.[42]

Table IV Percentage of the Free Population Who were Farm Laborers, 1860

State	Per- centage	State	Per- centage
Alabama	2.7	Mississippi	2.2
Arkansas	2.6	South Carolina	2.1
Georgia	3.3	Texas	1.6
Louisiana	1.5		

Source: *Eighth Census of Population*, pp. 662–63, 607.

[42]It might be argued that the white slaveowners should be included in the number of cotton hands along with the slaves and free farm laborers. However, the best evidence is that it was not common for the slaveowner to work alongside his chattel particularly in the planting regions that we are considering. See Gray, p. 486. Furthermore, a check of the census figures reveals that such inclusion would have little effect on the results.

A minor downward bias is introduced into the calculations because the 1850 Census reports the crops of 1849 but the population of 1850. Since the population grew between 1849 and 1850, too many slaves will be included in the calculations. On the average, this amounts to only about 2 per cent; although in counties that experienced a large in-migration of slaves, this factor might be significant. No adjustment was attempted to correct this bias.

Saraydar's method assumes a labor force participation rate of 50 per cent; although this figure is supported by a number of contemporary sources, it would seem open to doubt. For this rate implies that *all* slaves, male and female, fifteen to sixty years old, would be engaged as full-time hands.[43] Yet, it must be that a number of slaves in this age group were domestic servants or craftsmen, and that many of the women were unable to work in the fields because of advanced pregancy or child-caring activities. Moreover, very few of the children below fifteen could be expected to be as helpful as a prime field hand (32 per cent of the slave population were under ten).

The problem of measuring the labor force participation rate is particularly tricky. One of the important advantages of the single production function is that it allows us to bypass the problem entirely. As can be seen by referring to the formula, the calculation of the internal rate of interest is independent of the proportion of slaves assumed to be field hands. For we can calculate the yield as well as the yearly outlay and capital costs on a per-*slave,* rather than a per-hand, basis. In other words, the proportion of slaves assumed to be hands cancels out of the interest formula. This makes the calculated return for each region dependent on the total cotton output, the total number of slaves on cotton plantations, the price of cotton, and the yearly outlay and capital costs per slave.

Since Saraydar assumes a 50 per cent labor force participation rate, we need only halve the initial capital cost and the yearly maintenance allowance already calculated to return the data to the original per-slave basis.

Table V presents the estimated average yield per slave for several cotton producing regions of the South. The counties included in each region are cited by Gray as the major cotton producing counties of 1859. They follow the groupings which he prepared according to soil and climatic conditions.[44] This method of selecting

[43]DeBow, p. 91.
[44]Gray, pp. 531-37.

Table V Yields of Cotton—Alluvial Regions—1859

Region	Bales per slave (400 lbs.)
Mississippi River Counties, Louisiana	6.27
Alluvial Counties, Southeast Arkansas	4.35
Yazoo Delta, Mississippi	3.88
Upper Red River Counties, Louisiana	3.40
River Counties, Southwest Mississippi	2.69
Tennessee River Valley, Alabama	1.72
28 Alluvial Counties, Miss., La., Ark., and Ala.	3.69

Yields of Cotton—Other Cotton Regions of the New South—1859

East Texas Cotton Counties	3.83
Northwest Alabama	2.74
Black Prairie, Alabama	2.69
Clay Hills Region, Alabama	2.33
Eastern Piedmont, Alabama	2.24

Yield of Cotton—Cotton Regions of the Old South—1859

Upper Coastal Plain, Georgia	2.39
Southern Piedmont, Georgia	1.74
Middle and Upper Coastal Plain, South Carolina	1.13
Southern Piedmont, South Carolina	1.17
17 Counties, Georgia	2.03
13 Districts, South Carolina	1.25

---

[a] Carrol, Concordia, Madison, and Tensas Parishes, Louisiana.

[b] Arkansas, Chicot, Deshia, and Jefferson Counties, Arkansas.

[c] Bolivar, Coahoma, Issaquena, Tallahatchie, and Tunica Counties, Mississippi. Part brown-loam uplands.

[d] Bossier and DeSoto Parishes, Louisiana.

[e] Adams, Claiborne, Jefferson, and Wilkinson Counties, Mississippi. Part brown-loam uplands.

[f] Limestone and Madison Counties, Alabama. Rich alluvial river bottoms offset by poorer uplands.

[g] All counties listed in notes a through f, as well as Carrol, Hinds, Madison, Warren, and Yazoo Counties, Mississippi; Rapides Parish, Louisiana; and Crittenden County, Arkansas.

[h] Austin, Fort Bent, Grimes, Walker, and Washington Counties, Texas.

[i] Fayette and Marion Counties, Alabama.

[j] Dallas, Greene, Lowndes, Marengo, and Montgomery Counties, Alabama.

[k] Butler and Pike Counties, Alabama.

[l] Chambers and Coosa Counties, Alabama.

[m] Burke, Clay, Dougherty, Houston, Stewart, Sumter, Thomas, and Washington Counties, Georgia.

[n] Coweta, Hancock, Harris, Meriwether, Monroe, Morgan, Newton, Putnam, and Troup Counties, Georgia.

[o] Barnwell, Clarendon, Richland, and Sumter Districts, South Carolina.

[p] Abbeville, Edgefield, Laurens, and Newberry Districts, South Carolina.

[q] All districts listed in notes o and p as well as: Cheste, Darlington, Marion, Marlborough and Union Districts, South Carolina.

counties has the advantage of including only those economies known to be primarily based on cotton production, thus preventing the downard bias that would result in counties that produced other staple crops with slave labor. A total of 74 counties was examined; together, they accounted for 38 per cent of the 1859 crop. The average yield from the entire sample was 2.6 bales per slave.

Before we can calculate the returns implied by these yields, we must adjust the data to take account of changes in the price of cotton and of slaves.

The bumper crop of 1859 caused the price of cotton to fall from the previous year's price of 11.5 cents a pound to 10.8 cents. At no time during the selling year did the price fall below 10.5 cents. Thus, a 9- to 10-cent farmgate price is the appropriate one for these yields.

By 1859, the price of slaves had risen substantially. Using the same technique we applied to the 1849 slave prices, we find that the average slave was worth $1,221. This increases the capital costs to $1,861 per *slave* for the Old South and to $2,015 per slave for the alluvial lands.

Table VI presents the returns calculated from the 1859 data, and Table VII digests them into averages, which are compared with Conrad and Meyer's and with Saraydar's estimates.

As the tables show, cotton production was clearly profitable for the alluvial or prairie lands of the New South, when compared with the 6 per cent alternative interest rate.[45] Particularly striking is the close parallel between the returns for the South as a whole calculated in 1849 and 1859, and Conrad and Meyer's estimates for a typical cotton plantation, with the 6 per cent return on other forms of capital. This would indicate that we need not rely on the assumption of nonpecuniary returns to slaveholding so often used to explain the willingness of southerners to own slaves.

Another interesting result emerges from the data; it seems that while the return to slave operated plantations remained fairly constant over the decade, returns in the New South were rising while the profits of the older states were declining. This would lead us to expect a more rapid expansion of cotton production in the new areas than in the older states, as capital reallocates itself to correct

---

[45]It should be noted that Conrad and Meyer estimated this 6 per cent return by looking at the interest rates on prime commercial paper in New York and Boston. Though this is not the ideal technique the paucity of data makes it about as good as we can do. The 6 per cent rate seems reasonable enough, agrees with contemporary sources, and is accepted by Saraydar.

Table VI The Rate of Return on Cotton Operations in the Ante Bellum South, 1859

	Yield (bales per slave)	Rate of return with:	
		9c cotton	10c cotton
		(percentage)	
Rich Cotton Lands (K = $2,015,			
c = $26.00)			
Mississippi River Counties, La.	6.3	11.9	15.1
Alluvial Counties, S. E. Ark.	4.4	8.3	10.4
Yazoo Delta, Mississippi	3.9	7.4	9.2
East Texas Cotton Counties	3.8	7.2	9.0
28 Alluvial Counties, Miss., La.,			
Ark., and Ala.	3.7	7.1	8.7
Upper Red River Counties, La.	3.4	6.5	8.0
Northwest Alabama	2.7	5.3	6.5
River Counties, S. W. Miss.	2.7	5.3	6.5
Black Prairie, Ala.	2.7	5.3	6.5
Tennessee River Valley, Ala.	1.7	3.6	4.3
Older Areas (K = $1,861,			
c = $24.25)			
Upper Coastal Plain, Georgia	2.4	5.6	6.2
Clay Hills Region, Ala.	2.3	5.5	6.0
Eastern Piedmont, Ala.	2.2	5.3	5.8
17 Counties, Georgia	2.0	4.8	5.3
Southern Piedmont, Ga.	1.7	4.2	4.6
13 Districts, South Carolina	1.3	3.4	3.7
Southern Piedmont, So.			
Carolina	1.2	3.2	3.5
Middle and Upper Coastal			
Plain, So. Carolina	1.1	3.0	3.2

the disparities in income. This should be accompanied by transfers
of slaves from the Old to the New South.

And this is exactly what was happening. Table VIII demonstrates
this by comparing the expansion in cotton production, slaves, slave
owners, and the average size of slave holdings for several states of
the Old and the New South.

The rather high rates of return calculated for several areas of the
New South indicate that the price of land was not high enough to
capture its full rent. In long-run equilibrium, we would expect the
land rents to adjust so that returns in all parts of the South are equal,
save for the differences caused by unequal risk premiums. In the late

Table VII The Profitability of Ante Bellum Slavery

| Region | Rate of Return on Slave-Operated Cotton Plantations | | | |
	1849[a]	1859	Conrad and Meyer[b]	Saraydar—1849[c]
Older areas	5.5–6.1	3.6–4.0	2.2–5.4	0–1.1[d]
Average for the South	5.7–6.4	5.8–6.3[e]	4.5–6.5	0–1.5[d]
Average for alluvium	6.2–6.9	7.1–8.7	10.0–13.0	0.9–2.3
High for alluvium	11.2–12.8	11.9–15.1	—[f]	6.5–8.2

[a] From Table III.
[b] Conrad and Meyer, Table 9, p. 107.
[c] Saraydar, Table I, p. 331.
[d] The lower value in the range reported by Saraydar was less than 0.025 per cent.
[e] Calculated from a yield of 2.5 bales per slave, which is the simple average of the 3.7 bales on alluvium and the 1.4 bales of the Older areas.
[f] Conrad and Meyer did not report a high for alluvium.

fifties, it was undoubtedly the case that the free or very cheap (yet highly fertile) lands to the west prevented rents from rising, thus causing disequilibrium.

Several regions of the Old South show normal returns, and if we take into account the capital gains earned in these states when they sold their slaves to buyers in the New South, it is fairly certain that even the poorest areas could show a profit. If this process had been allowed to continue for some time, it might have been the case that the Old South would have run out of slaves before returns were equalized. In this regional sense, therefore, and only in this sense, could slavery have destroyed itself through its own unprofitability.

It is not our intention, however, to exhaust the subject of slave profitability but only to show that Mr. Saraydar was incorrect in challenging Conrad and Meyer's conclusion.

Table VIII Expansion of Cotton Production in the New and the Old South—1850 to 1860

State	Year	Cotton production (400 lb. bales)	Number of slaves	Number of slave holders	Average number of slaves per owner
The Old South:					
Georgia	1850	499,091	381,682	38,456	9.9
	1860	701,840	462,198	41,084	11.2
(Percentage change)		(40.6)	(21.1)	(6.8)	(13.1)
So. Carolina	1850	300,901	384,984	25,596	15.0
	1860	353,412	402,406	26,701	15.0
(Percentage change)		(17.5)	(4.5)	(4.3	(0)
The New South:					
Arkansas	1850	65,344	47,100	5,999	7.8
	1860	367,393	111,115	11,481	9.7
(Percentage change)		(462.2)	(135.9)	(91.4)	(24.4)
Louisiana	1850	178,737	244,809	20,670	11.8
	1860	777,738	331,726	22,033	15.0
(Percentage change)		(335.1)	(35.5)	(6.6)	(27.1)
Texas	1850	58,072	58,161	7,747	7.5
	1860	431,463	182,566	21,878	8.3
(Percentage change)		(643.0)	(213.9)	(182.4)	(10.7)
Total for the *Old South:*	1850	799,992	766,666	64,052	12.0
	1860	1,055,252	864,604	67,785	12.8
(Percentage change)		(31.9)	(12.8)	(5.8)	(6.7)
Total for the *New South:*	1850	302,153	350,070	34,416	10.2
	1860	1,576,594	625,407	55,392	11.3
(Percentage change)		(421.8)	(78.7)	(60.9)	(10.8)
Total for all *Slave States:*	1850	2,445,779	3,204,051	347,516	9.2
	1860	5,385,354	3,953,696	395,196	10.0
(Percentage change)		(120.2)	(23.4)	(13.7)	(8.7)

Sources: Cotton production 1850: DeBow, p. 173; 1860: *Eighth Census of Agriculture*, p. 189. Slave population: *Ibid.*, pp. 247–48, 224. Slaveholders: *ibid.*

EDWARD SARAYDAR

The Profitability of Ante Bellum Slavery—A Reply

RICHARD SUTCH states that the intent of his paper is "only to show that Mr. Saraydar was incorrect in challenging Conrad and Meyer's conclusion." At the outset, I should like to restate the "conclusion" which I attempted to test, since Sutch himself seems to be somewhat confused as to my purpose.

Conrad and Meyer concluded that, in the period 1830 to 1860, investment in male prime field hands to be utilized in cotton production yielded a rate of return of at least 6% (the relevant interest rate). Although they did not delimit their analysis to the particular thesis that ante bellum investment in field hands was unprofitable (or profitable)—e.g., their article was also concerned with slavery's viability, as well as its implications for Southern economic growth—my paper was clearly concerned with their treatment of this problem alone. Therefore, it is quite appropriate to utilize the capital-value formula which incorporates returns over the life of this particular investment (indeed, Sutch does not disapprove of this identical production function as employed by Conrad and Meyer; he cites their results with approval, and compares his own rates of return with theirs).

Consequently, I am at a loss to understand the relevance of Sutch's charge that there is an "incorrect specification" in my production function which arises from my "implicit assumption that no reproduction of the slave stock takes place." I do not make this assumption, because it is not required. Reproduction of the slave stock is relevant to Conrad and Meyer's *second* function, the production of the intermediate good, slave labor—i.e., slave breeding.

Sutch argues that I erred in increasing out-of-pocket expenses to include those necessary to maintain females and children as well as male field hands. I am inclined to agree with him; these expenses should properly be charged to the production function for the intermediate good. However, I object to Sutch's use of this rather slim reed to support his allegation that I assumed "that only the

From *The Southern Economic Journal*, XXXI (April 1965), 377-383. Copyright © 1964 by *The Southern Economic Journal*. Reprinted by permission of the Editor and the Author.

labor in the cotton fields was productive of revenue and that no increase in the stock of slaves took place." In fact, the significance of using $21 rather than $32 out-of-pocket costs for the profitability calculation is reflected by, and should be adjudged solely in terms of, the 1.9% rather than .9% rate of return on alluvium which emerges at 7¢ a pound for cotton, and the 3.0% rather than 2.3% rate of return at 8¢ a pound.

The pertinence of Sutch's single production function analysis to the determination of the rate of return to be earned from an investment in slave hands over the period 1830 to 1860 is surely questionable. Conrad and Meyer's (as well as my own) analysis involved an estimate of an *average* price for field hands over the period 1830-50 (since slave prices in the 50's would have introduced an upward bias), *typical* prices for cotton lands over the period 1830-50, an *average* interest rate for the period 1830-60, *typical* out-of-pocket costs in the period 1840-60, and an *average* price for cotton over the period 1830-60. Our major point of dispute centers on the question of whether their estimates or my own (based on 1850 Census data) more accurately reflect slave productivity for the entire period. Neither Conrad and Meyer nor I tried to calculate the rate of return in 1849, 1859, or any other single year.

Why, then, does Sutch insist that a 9¢ to 10¢ range for cotton is more appropriate to my output-per-hand estimates—which are intended to represent an average for the period 1830-60—than the average price for cotton over that same period? Sutch maintains that the higher price is more relevant because my productivity figures are necessarily low, since 1849 was "a year of particularly poor crops." But was 1849 really a year of "particularly low yields"? On the contrary, it could be argued that 1849 was particularly representative.

The 1849 crop was actually well above (some 10% above) the average for the 40's.[1] Prior to 1849, there were only three cotton crops which were larger: 1844, 1847, and 1848. The 1844 and 1847 crops were not significantly so (1% and 3% respectively), but the 1848 crop stands out; it was almost 39% greater than the average for the 40's. It makes no sense to compare 1849 with the bumper-crop year of 1848, as does Sutch. In an effort to establish that 1849 was

[1]Lewis Gray, *History of Agriculture in the Southern United States to 1860* (Washington, D. C.: The Carnegie Institution of Washington, 1933), Table 40, p. 1026.

not a normal year, Sutch notes that the average crop of the 50's was "a full 50 per cent" above that of 1849. But this proves only that the 50's were especially good years for cotton, not that 1849 was a particularly poor year. The average annual crop of the 50's was also almost 20% larger than the bumper crop of 1848, and "a full" 45% greater than the one-year-earlier 1847 crop (which sold for 7¢ a pound)—and both of these were record years to that time.

Even if we accepted the 9¢ to 10¢ price range, this alone would not be enough to ensure a rate of return greater that 6%. These prices imply rates of return of 4.4%-5.4%, 3.7%-4.8%, and 3.3%-4.3% respectively, on alluvium, as an average for the South, and for older areas.

But these rates of return are calculated without the benefit of Sutch's single production function concept. As noted above, the rate of appreciation is simply not relevant to the production function with which I was concerned. Nevertheless, Sutch recalculates rates of return with his function, to see how "critical" was my "error in specification" in ignoring the growth rate of the negro population.

Sutch devotes a major portion of his paper to a critique of the estimates which I used for slave productivity in my model. First, I should like to acknowledge that he has indeed correctly spotted an arithmetic error in my calculation of output per hand for the two Northwestern Alabama counties of Fayette and Marion. I wanted to choose representative counties characterized by remoteness from market and poor soils; Gray implies that these two counties quite possibly fitted the description.[2] Although cotton producers in both counties faced major transportation problems—even in 1879[3]— which lowered average realized farm price (and thus the rate of return) sufficiently to keep cotton production quite low, cotton acreage was relatively fertile in both counties, and therefore output per hand was relatively high. In fact, of the 52 Alabama counties which produced cotton in 1849, Fayette ranked number four in output per hand at 4.8 bales, and Marion ranked number seventeen at 3.4 bales per hand. More representative counties, for example, were Greene, at 2.3 bales and Sumter, at 1.9 bales per hand.

In an attempt to confirm Conrad and Meyer's 7 to 8 bale per hand estimate as an average for ante bellum slave productivity on alluvium, Sutch cites a yield per acre figure of 396 pounds as an

[2]*Ibid.*, Table 13, p. 534, p. 536.
[3]Census Office, *Report on Cotton Production in the United States, Part II* (Washington, D. C.: U. S. Government Printing Office, 1884), pp. 120-21.

average for the 13 counties which produced one half of all the cotton grown on alluvium in 1879. He notes that this figure is 24% to 41% higher than the yield implied by Conrad and Meyer's estimate. A weighted average for those alluvial areas which produced 99.8% of all the cotton grown on alluvium generates a figure of 361 pounds per acre on alluvium in 1879.[4] This is some 13% to 29% higher than Conrad and Meyer's implied yield. We may thus conclude that yield per acre on alluvium in 1879 does not in itself invalidate Conrad and Meyer's estimate for ante bellum slave productivity.

But, surely, neither does it support that estimate. Cotton production in 1879, twenty years after the ante bellum period, exceeded that of any previous year.[5] The 1879-80 season was "propitious" for cotton in all states other than Georgia and Alabama.[6] In fact, contemporary reports by the Department of Agriculture indicate that 1879 was an especially good year for cotton—i.e.:

> In the States bordering on the Mississippi River there is considerable increase (in pounds of lint per acre). Louisiana and Mississippi each show the effects of the favorable fall, and make decided gains over last year. Arkansas and Tennessee equal their magnificent yield of 1878.[7]

In reference to this 1879 crop, quoted extracts from correspondence from counties in Louisiana, Mississippi, and Arkansas are replete with statements such as: "unprecedented good weather for gathering," "yields more clear lint to the 100 pounds than previous years," "season very favorable," "as good a yield per acre as ever made in this county," "so far the most favorable fall ever known," "weather finest for years," "better than ever before."[8] I should think, then, that yield per acre figures for alluvium in 1879 are useful only in the sense that they provide some kind of an extreme upper limit for ante bellum yield per acre estimates.

As to the 7 to 8 bale per hand estimates of Conrad and Meyer, I am perfectly willing to concede that *all* of the nine reported yields per field hand listed in Conrad and Meyer's Table 6 might have

---

[4] *Ibid.*, Part I, p. 16, and summary reports for Louisiana, Mississippi, and Arkansas.

[5] U. S. Bureau of the Census, *Historical Statistics of the United States* (Washington, D. C.: U. S. Government Printing Office, 1960), p. 302.

[6] U. S. Department of Agriculture, *Condition of Crops*, Special Report No. 19 (Washington, D. C.: U. S. Government Printing Office, 1879), p. 15.

[7] *Ibid.*

[8] *Ibid.*, pp. 17, 18.

involved self-sufficient cotton production,[9] whether explicitly reported as such or not. But Conrad and Meyer did not make their estimates for slave productivity on the basis of these reports. They merely used them to "illustrate the possible variation in productivity per hand."[10] They do note that this relatively small sample of reported yields agrees (I would say, rather, that it does not disagree) with the "frequent statements in contemporary journals" upon which they base their *own* estimates. I merely suggest that the "frequent statements in contemporary journals" might not have referred to output inclusive of the slave hand's non-cotton (subsistence) product, and this would introduce an upward bias into their estimates.

Sutch avers that "it can easily be shown that Saraydar's range of 2 to 3.6 bales is an underestimate (of ante bellum slave productivity)." He proceeds to do so by dividing total cotton output in 1859 of the seven major cotton states by the total number of slaves (discounted by 10% to account for city-dwellers) between 10 and 70 years old. He gets an average yield of 3.36 bales per slave. The joker in this particular deck is his use of the 1859 cotton crop. The 1859 crop was by no means an "average"; it was 47% greater than the average for the 50's—a pre-Civil War high. In fact, Sutch himself notes that "1859 was one of the best years for cotton production and the yields calculated from these data will over-represent an average for the decade of the fifties." Slave productivity based on this crop would have a strong upward bias. If we utilize the 1850 Census, we find that the seven states cited by Sutch produced 2,150,866 bales in 1849; 1,192,718 slaves in these seven states were between 10 and 70 years old; subtracting 10% to account for those living in cities ("not more" than 10% probably lived in cities and towns), we get an average of 2.0 bales per slave. But, like Sutch's average of 3.36 bales, this neither proves nor disproves that my range of 2 to 3.6 bales is an underestimate.

Recognizing that 1859 was a bumper crop year, and therefore that productivity estimates based on this crop would not be representative of the ante bellum period, Sutch nevertheless feels that "a test for 1859 is more relevant than one for 1849" in spite of U. B. Phillips' contention that by the close of the 50's only a few

[9]Alfred Conrad and John Meyer, "The Economics of Slavery in the Ante Bellum South," *The Journal of Political Economy*, April 1958, p. 105.

[10]*Ibid.*, p. 104.

slaveholders "were earning anything beyond what would cover their maintenance and carrying charges." I would have thought that a test for *neither* year would be, in itself, sufficient to determine the profitability of slave operations in cotton over the period 1830-60. Surely, this is the proper target toward which Sutch should direct his inquiry if, as he says, he wishes to test whether "non-pecuniary returns are necessary to explain the patterns of slaveholding."

Sutch's contention that an analysis of 1859 is superior to one relating to 1849 cotton yields because "the more detailed data available from the 1860 Census will enable us to devise a more precise method of estimating the yields" is frankly puzzling. As far as I can see, the only information he utilizes which is not available in the 1850 Census has little or no effect on productivity estimates arrived at through a simple division of cotton output by slave population.

Sutch dislikes my method of estimating yield per hand, which involves dividing cotton production in particular counties (chosen on the basis of type of soil and zero or relative-negligible production of the non-cotton staples) by one-half of the slave population in each county (on the assumption that plantations typically carried one hand to every two slaves). I claim no great precision for this method; nevertheless, I do maintain that the productivity estimates which emerge *are* more precise than Conrad and Meyer's estimates based on "frequent statements in contemporary journals."

Sutch apparently does not think so. He feels that there must be a significant downward bias, for example, connected with the assumption that "not more" than 10% of the slaves in each county lived in towns or cities. To support his assertion, he points out that "an examination of the fourteen alluvial-soil counties of Mississippi . . . turned up Adams County with 688 slaveowners in 1860 but only 214 farms, and Warren County with 821 slaveholders and only 396 farms," and that "all but one (of these counties) had a greater number of slaveowners than of farms in 1860." Apart from the obvious fact that my calculations involved slave residency in 1850 while his figures relate to 1860, it is not clear at all that his results imply that there is a significant downward bias in my method. In fact, for what it's worth, an examination of the 21 alluvial counties which I used for estimating slave productivity on alluvium reveals not one, but *six* counties that had a greater number of farms than slaveowners in 1860.

More importantly, if we subtract the number of farms from the number of slaveholders in the remaining counties, the number of slaves which each of these presumably non-farm slaveholders could have owned, and still not have left more than 10% of the slave population living off farms, ranges from 3 in Adams County, Mississippi, to 66 in Issaquena County, Mississippi; the mean for all 15 counties is 30.

Further, one may judge to some extent the relative importance of farming to slave employment by noting that the median slave holding in each of these counties[11] times the number of farms in each county yields—in every case—a number of slaves which is more than sufficient to account for the total slave population of each county.

Finding that the 1850 Census reports 50.87% of all slaves in the United States as being between the ages of 15 and 60, Sutch is disturbed by my assumption of a 50% labor force participation rate. He feels that this must imply that all slaves in the 15 to 60 age bracket were employed as hands. According to Sutch, this rate is suspect because "a number" of slaves in this age bracket must have been utilized as craftsmen or servants, and "many" slave women in this group were incapacitated by advanced pregnancy, or cared for children instead of working in the fields. Furthermore, "very few of the children below fifteen could be expected to be as helpful as a prime field hand."

Since the quantities implied by "a number," "many," and "very few" are necessarily vague, I wonder what the proportion of slaves in the 15 to 60 age group would have had to have been in order to satisfy Sutch as permitting a 50% participation rate—52%, 55%, 60%, 100%? It could just as credibly be argued that the proportion of slaves in this age group who were craftsmen or servants, or who were in advanced pregnancy, was insignificant. Moreover, child-caring activities might well have been within the province of older slaves. And, although it is true that not many of those below the age of 15 could be expected to have been as productive as a prime field hand, this is not really the relevant consideration.

Field work age encompassed the years 10 to 54,[12] and, in fact, children were assigned fractional work in the fields at an age as early as six.[13] For the six states that provided the data for my productivity estimates, 52% (in the alluvial counties, 57%) of the slave

[11]As estimated by Gray, *op. cit.,* Table 12, p. 531.
[12]Conrad and Meyer, *op. cit.,* p. 116.
[13]Gray, *op. cit.,* p. 549.

population was between the ages of 15 and 60 in 1850. But if we (properly) include the 10 to 15 year old group, roughly 65% of the slave population was of field work age. The relevant question, then, is not how many below the age of 15 were as productive as a prime field hand, but rather how many field hands would it have taken to do the field work performed by those less than 15 years old? My point is that Sutch's observation that 50.87% of all slaves in the United States were between the ages of 15 and 60 does not, in itself, provide sufficient information to cast serious doubt on the 50% labor force participation rate assumption.

The participation rate assumption can in fact be tested. Suppose we make the perfectly reasonable assumption that the highest yield per acre on the best soil in 1879 (470 pounds, Chicot County, Arkansas; see Sutch, Table II) was no less than yield per acre in those areas which Sutch identifies as producing a high for alluvium twenty years earlier in 1859 (the Louisiana Parishes of Carroll, Concordia, Madison, and Tensas). Sutch estimates average yield per *slave* in these areas as 6.27 bales. This in turn would imply a labor force participation rate of *at least* 53% on alluvium in 1859, and (since there is no obvious reason to expect the rate to differ significantly) in 1849 as well. [The participation rate t is derived from the formula $(400b)/(10t) = q$, where: b = bales per slave, q = pounds per acre, at 400 pounds per bale, and 10 acres of cotton land per hand. In 1859, $b = 6.27$, $q \leq 470$. Therefore, $t \geq (40)(6.27)/470 = 53\%$.]

Sutch feels that he can bypass the problem of estimating the labor force participation rate altogether by using his single production function concept. He estimates yield per slave for a number of counties using 1859 data, and revises upward the price of cotton and of slaves to more accurately reflect the 1859 situation.[14] He then calculates rates of return for the several types of cotton operations, and compares them with those of Conrad and Meyer and myself.

I would like to reiterate two points applicable to Sutch's results.

[14]However, he ignores the possibility of rising land prices in the 50's. One might reasonably expect the magnitude of this price increase to be reflected in the movement of the ratio of "cash value of (acres of land in) farms" to "acres of land in farms." Over the census period 1850-60, this ratio increased by 1.7 times for those counties (in Table 5) which Sutch includes in "Cotton Regions of the Old South," by 2.5 times for those counties comprising "Other Cotton Regions of the New South," by 2.6 times for counties which make up his "Alluvial Regions," and by 3.1 times for those Mississippi River counties which he identifies as yielding a high output per slave on alluvium.

First, whatever the single production function does measure, it does *not* measure the rate of return to be realized from an investment in field hands. Although the participation rate does indeed cancel out of Sutch's formula, the appreciation rate does not—and that rate is just not applicable to a consideration of the returns to be realized from male field hand investment.

His function has implications for profitability which are immediately obvious. For example, Sutch's construction has the property of guaranteeing at least a 2.15% rate of return on an investment in slave hands—*regardless* of the price of slaves, land, or cotton, of slave productivity, or out-of-pocket costs—as long as return per hand is not negative. In other words, if slaves were multiplying at the rate of 6% or more a year, there would be no question of profitability, as long as each slave yielded a net return of, say, as little as 1¢ a year.

Further, his single production function model implies a positive rate of return even if yearly out-of-pocket expense per hand *exceeds* the value of his product. Suppose $c>pY$. As long as $(c-pY)/K< a$, $r>0$.

According to Sutch then, it might still be profitable for a planter to purchase a male field hand, even though his yearly net return is negative, if the price of the hand is high enough. In any event, if the hand working in cotton yields a positive net return—no matter how small—it is always profitable to purchase him as long as the negro population is growing at a rate which is no less than the rate of interest. Needless to say, the validity of both of these propositions is at least open to doubt.

The final point is that Sutch's estimates in any case are not comparable to those of Conrad and Meyer and myself. Sutch attempts to estimate presumably expected rates of return for the specific years of 1849 and 1859, while we attempted estimates of average rates of return over the period 1830-60. Sutch apparently does not realize this, for he incorrectly labels my estimates in his Table VII as "Saraydar—1849."

EUGENE D. GENOVESE

The Significance of the Slave Plantation for Southern Economic Development

The work of Yasuba, Evans, Saraydar, and Sutch represented one line of development from the Conrad and Meyer analysis: the checking of the results by alternative methods, and the reexamination of the quality of the data. Saraydar's criticisms excepted, these revisions and recalculations in general left intact the major conclusion of the Conrad and Meyer article: slave-labor agriculture in the South before the Civil War was profitable.

In the meantime, analysis of the economic significance of slavery shifted to a different though related issue—one that had already been hinted at when viability rather than profitability had become the focus of discussion. This line of analysis was adopted by writers who accepted, or at least did not choose to question, the fact that the slave system had been profitable, but who asked, in effect: "So what?" And having asked this always disconcerting question, they reverted to the class of issues that Douglas Dowd had raised in his initial response to Conrad and Meyer and that earlier had attracted the attention of Robert Russel. Was it or was it not correct that the slave system, even though profitable, had adversely affected Southern development?

To phrase the question in these terms implied posing a problem for economic analysis intrinsically more complex than the estimation of a rate of return on capital. The techniques for estimating the present value of an anticipated flow of future incomes were essentially straightforward, however difficult it might be to identify and locate the statistical information required to make the estimate. But analysis of the dynamics of economic development was a task to which economic theory had only recently returned, after a prolonged period of neglect, and there was no general consensus, except in the most abstract terms, regarding what "counted" and what did not. Furthermore, the type of problem that presented itself in the analysis of economic development was such as to make it very difficult for economists to remain comfortably behind the shelter of their disciplinary barricades. When measuring the profitability of an investment in slaves, it made sense to

From *The Journal of Southern History*, XXVIII, Number 4 (November, 1962), 422-437. Copyright © 1962 by the Southern Historical Association. Reprinted by permission of the Managing Editor.

stipulate that you proposed to analyse the matter "from a strict economic point of view." It made much less sense when you turned to discussing the effects of slavery on Southern development.

One rather ironic result of this shift of emphasis was that a number of traditional themes in the analysis of slavery, discussed many years before by Cairnes and Phillips but pushed into the background by the intervening concentration on the profitability issue, now raised their heads again. Once again, for example, we find questions being raised about the absorption of capital by investment in slaves, about the rigidity and inherent inefficiency of a slave labor force, about the inhibiting effect of slavery on the development of manufacturing. And again we find appearing the traditional assumption that, in the antebellum years, the economic development of the South had been in some meaningful sense unsatisfactory.

One of the best examples of this return to broader issues is the article on "The Significance of the Slave Plantation for Southern Economic Development" by Eugene Genovese which is reprinted here. In its very first paragraph Genovese explicitly rejects the assumption that slavery can sensibly be discussed as a purely economic institution—an assumption which, in his view, underlay the Conrad and Meyer analysis. Surely it is undeniable, he argues, that a slave system gives rise to a distinctive politics, ideology, and pattern of social behavior? And who would question that these had immense economic consequences? Whether or not slavery was profitable in an economic sense, what the historian has to explain is how and why it retarded Southern economic development, and in particular the industrialization of the South.

Setting to one side the other ways in which slavery probably exercised an influence hostile to economic development, Genovese concentrates on one channel of influence which economic history and the contemporary experience of the underdeveloped countries suggest was probably vital and which in itself "provides an adequate explanation of the slave South's inability to industrialize": the restricted size of the home market for industry and agriculture. This limited home market in the South resulted, he believes, from the absence of "an agrarian revolution which shatters the old regime of the countryside." Lacking such a revolution, the South remained burdened by an agrarian regime which provided little effective demand for the products of Southern agriculture and little prospect of an adequate market for Southern industries, should any such be established. Limitation of the home market, he argues, was not primarily the result of plantation self-sufficiency but rather of the low income levels prevalent among slaves, subsistence farmers, and poor whites. This in its turn reflected the income distribution that resulted from the dominant position in the economy of slave-labor plantation agriculture. It was reinforced by an ideology, among the planter class, which regarded industrialization and urbanization as a threat to the power structure which they controlled, by the low population density characteristic of the South, and by a transportation system designed to tie staple-producing plantations to seaports but not to open up the back country for independent farmers.

Thus the South was trapped in a quasi-colonial situation not unfamiliar in the contemporary world: it provided a market large enough to be attractive to established outside industry, but not large enough to sustain domestic industry on a scale adequate to compete with imports from the outside. What industry did exist in the South catered to the luxury demands of the planter class, to the crude textile and hardware requirements of slaves and the rural poor, and to Northern demands for semi-agricultural exports like hemp and tobacco. Fundamental to the economic problems of the South was the low level of demand characteristic of a plantation-based slave system, and until this restraint was removed by thorough-going agrarian reform, combined with changes in ideology and in the structure of power, little prospects for successful urbanization and industrialization existed.

The argument is without doubt a powerful one, gaining strength not only from its own inherently good fit to much that we know to have been true about the South, but also from a wide range of other supporting generalizations which we know or believe to be true about staple production, economies of scale, income distribution, the relationships that tend to grow up between economic power, ideology, and political control, and like matters. It is, in fact, a brilliant synthesis, deserving to be ranked with Kenneth Stampp's "Peculiar Institution." But once again we must ask: Is it a proof? Does Genovese demonstrate his assertions, or does he induce you to believe them?

Too quick and ready an answer to this question must confront the criticisms of Robert Fogel, one of the leading figures of the new economic history, who in an article published in the *Journal of Economic History* in September 1967 ("The Specification Problem in Economic History," Volume XXVII, Number 3) painstakingly listed no less than six implicit counterfactual statements and theoretical assumptions on which Genovese's case critically depended. It is an excellent exercise for the student, after reading Genovese's article, to try to identify these assumptions, but for our present purposes the point to be noted is that none of these counterfactual statements is proved by

Genovese, nor are the theoretical assumptions justified, within the context of his article. This is not to say that the assumptions are incorrect or the counterfactuals invalid; nor is it to assert that good history can be written as if it were a series of theorems in Euclidian geometry. But it is to emphasize once again the contrast between the "convincingness" at which a first-class historian aims, and the logical proof and operational verification which are the goals of the new school of economic history.

HISTORIANS are no longer sure that plantation slavery was responsible for the economic woes of the Old South. The revisionist doubts rest on two propositions of dubious relevance. The first is that slave labor could have been applied successfully to pursuits other than the raising of plantation staples; the second is that slave agriculture was possibly as profitable as were alternative industries and can not be held responsible for the unwillingness of Southerners to use their profits more wisely.[1] The first confuses slave labor and its direct effects with the slave system and its total effects; it is the latter that is at issue, and the versatility of slave labor is a secondary consideration. The second rests on the assumption that the master-slave relationship was purely economic and not essentially different from an employer-worker relationship. Yet, when confronted with the issue direct, who could deny that slavery gave rise to a distinct politics, ideology, and pattern of social behavior and that these had immense economic consequences?

We need not examine at the moment the precise relationship between slavery and the plantation. Certainly, plantation economies presuppose considerable compulsion, if only of the *de facto* type now prevalent in Latin America. The historical fact of an ante bellum plantation-based slave economy is our immediate concern, although, undoubtedly, post bellum developments preserved some of the retardative effects of ante bellum slavery.

Those retardative effects were too many even to be summarized here. A low level of capital accumulation, the planters' high propensity to consume luxuries, the shortage of liquid capital aggravated by the steady drain of funds out of the region, the low

[1]See, for example, the well known writings of R. R. Russel, including his "The General Effects of Slavery upon Southern Economic Progress," *Journal of Southern History*, IV (February 1938), 34-54, or the more recent statement of Alfred H. Conrad and John R. Meyer, "The Economics of Slavery in the Ante-Bellum South," *Journal of Political Economy*, LXVI (April 1958), 95-130.

productivity of slave labor, the need to concentrate on a few staples, the anti-industrial, anti-urban ideology of the dominant planters, the reduction of Southern banking, industry, and commerce to the position of auxiliaries of the plantation economy—all these are familiar and yet need restudy in the light of the important work being done on the economics of underdeveloped countries. For the present let us focus on another factor, which in itself provides an adequate explanation of the slave South's inability to industrialize: the retardation of the home market for both industrial and agricultural commodities.

Thirty years ago Elizabeth W. Gilboy complained that economic historians studying the process of industrialization were too much concerned with supply and insufficiently concerned with demand.[2] Her complaint was justified despite brilliant work on the problem of markets by a few outstanding men from Karl Marx to R. H. Tawney and Paul Mantoux. Since then, demand has received much more attention, although possibly not so much as it deserves. Important essays by Maurice Dobb, Simon Kuznets, H. J. Habakkuk, and Gunnar Myrdal, among others, have helped to correct the imbalance,[3] as has new research on European industrialization and the economics of underdeveloped countries. If there is one lesson to be learned from the experience of both developed and under-developed countries it is that industrialization is unthinkable without an agrarian revolution which shatters the old regime of the countryside. While the peasantry is tied to the land, burdened with debt, and limited to minimal purchasing power, the labor recruitment and market pre-conditions for extensive manufacturing are missing. "Land reform"—*i.e.* an agrarian revolution—is the essential first step in the creation of an urban working class, the reorganization of agriculture to feed growing cities, and the development of a home market.

---

[2]Elizabeth W. Gilboy, "Demand As a Factor in the Industrial Revolution" in *Facts and Factors in Economic History; Articles by the Former Students of Edwin F. Gay* (Cambridge, Mass., 1932), 620-39.

[3]Maurice Dobb, *Studies in the Development of Capitalism* (New York, 1947), 6 ff., 87 ff., 98 ff., 290-96; Simon Kuznets, "Toward a Theory of Economic Growth," in Robert Lekachman (ed.), *National Policy for Economic Welfare at Home and Abroad* (New York, 1955), 12-77; H. J. Habakkuk, "The Historical Experience on the Basic Conditions of Economic Progress," in L. H. Dupriez (ed.), *Economic Progress* (Louvain, Belgium, 1955), 149-69; Gunnar Myrdal, *Rich Lands and Poor* (New York, 1957), *passim,* 23-38 especially.

There are several ways in which agricultural reorganization can provide markets for manufactures; for our immediate purposes we may consider two. First, when the laborers are separated from the land, as they were during the English enclosures, they necessarily increase the demand for clothing and other essentials formerly produced at home. Paradoxically, this expansion of the market is compatible with a marked reduction in the laborers' standard of living. Second, the farmers left on the countryside to produce for growing urban markets provide an increased demand for textiles, agricultural equipment, and so forth.

The rapid extension of the rural market was the way of the North, but the slave plantations dominated the South until such time as reorganization was imposed from without by a predatory foe interested primarily in a new system of rural exploitation. An adequate home market could not arise in the ante bellum South and has only evolved slowly and painfully during the last century.

In 1860 about seventy-five per cent of the Southern cotton crop was exported; during no ante bellum year did the grain exports of the United States exceed five per cent of the grain crop. No doubt, cotton profits were an important element in the financing of America's economic growth. The question is, were the profits syphoned off to build up the Northern economy? We know that the credit mechanisms alone, to a considerable extent, did just that. The South's dependence on the export trade, in contradistinction to the North's primary reliance on its home market, indicates not merely a social division of labor but the economic exploitation of the exporting South.

Robert G. Albion, in his excellent examination of the colonial bondage of the South to the North, concludes that the South's lack of direct trade with Europe constituted an irrational arrangement secured by the impudence of New York's aggressive entrepreneurs. We can agree that, had the South imported from abroad as much as the North and West, there could have been no sensible reason to route through New York either the South's cotton or its share of European goods; but Albion's assumption of a rough equality of imports, an assumption shared by contemporaries like George McDuffie and T. P. Kettell, can not be substantiated. The slave South's total market for manufactured goods was small relative to that of the free states; and even though the South depended upon Europe as well as the North for manufactured goods, its imports from Europe were smaller in value than imports into the North and

West and smaller in bulk than the staples it exported. If the ships carrying cotton had sailed from Southern ports direct to Europe and back, they would have had to return in ballast.[4] New York's domination of the South's export trade was, therefore, not accidental. Furthermore, if the South's share in American imports had been as Albion suggests, and if the coastal trade had been as large as he implies, the greater part of the goods sent from New Orleans to the plantation areas would have originated in Europe and been re-shipped through New York rather than being—as is known—of Western origin.[5]

Albion's acceptance of the assumption of nearly equal imports is the more surprising in view of the evidence of restricted Southern demand. The Southern cotton, iron, paper, wool, and railroad industries—to mention a few—struggled with indifferent results against a low level of Southern patronage. Antislavery leaders like Henry Ruffner and Cassius M. Clay made slavery's effects on the home market a cardinal point in their indictment. Thoughtful proslavery Southerners also commented frequently on the market problem. The opinion of the editor of the *Southern Agriculturist* in 1828 that the South lacked sufficient customers to sustain a high level of manufacturing was echoed throughout the ante bellum

[4]See Robert Greenhalgh Albion, *The Rise of New York Port, 1815-1860* (New York, 1939) and Albion, *Square-Riggers on Schedule: the New York Sailing Packets to England, France, and the Cotton Ports* (Princeton, 1938). For similar arguments presented by contemporaries, see James D. B. De Bow (ed.), *The Industrial Resources, etc., of the Southern and Western States . . .* (3 vols., New Orleans, 1852-1853), 125, 365; and *De Bow's Review*, IV (1847), 208-25, 339, 351. For a perceptive Northern reply, see the anonymous pamphlet, *The Effects of Secession upon the Commercial Relations Between the North and South and upon Each Section* (New York, 1861), 15. For the weakness of the Southern import trade, see George Rogers Taylor, *The Transportation Revolution, 1815-1860* (New York, 1951), 198; Philip S. Foner, *Business & Slavery; the New York Merchants & the Irrepressible Conflict* (Chapel Hill, 1941), 6-7; and Samuel Eliot Morison, *The Maritime History of Massachusetts, 1783-1860* (Boston, 1921), 298-99. Many of the lines carrying cotton from Northern ports were deeply involved in bringing immigrants to the United States, which was one of the reasons why their ships did not have to return from Europe in ballast. John G. B. Hutchins, *The American Maritime Industries and Public Policy, 1789-1914; an Economic History* (Cambridge, Mass.; 1941), 262-63.

[5]Emory R. Johnson and others, *History of the Domestic and Foreign Commerce of the United States*, (2 vols., Washington, 1915), I, 242; R.B. Way, "The Commerce of the Lower Mississippi in the Period 1830-1860," Mississippi Valley Historical Association, *Proceedings*, X (1918-1919), 62; Louis Bernard Schmidt, "The Internal Grain Trade of the United States, 1850-1860," *Iowa Journal of History and Politics*, XVIII (January 1920), 110-11.

period. The speech of Col. Andrew P. Calhoun to the Pendleton, South Carolina, Farmers' Society in 1855, for example, was strikingly similar in tone and content. On the other side, someone like Beverley Tucker would occasionally argue that Northerners would never risk a war "which, while it lasted, would shut them out from the best market in the world."[6] It is difficult to imagine that many, even those who adopted such arguments for political purposes, took seriously a proposition so palpably false.

Alfred Glaze Smith, Jr., and Douglass C. North have traced the low level of Southern demand, in part, to plantation self-sufficiency. This view is not borne out by the data in the manuscript census returns from the cotton belt, which reveal only trivial amounts of home manufactures on even the largest plantations and which bear out the judgments of Rolla M. Tryon and Mary Elizabeth Massey on the weakness of Southern household industry.[7] In De Soto and Marshall counties, Mississippi, the big planters (those with thirty-one or more slaves) averaged only seventy-six dollars worth of home manufactures in 1860, and farmers and small planters averaged much less. In Dougherty and Thomas counties, Georgia, the small planters (those with from twenty-one to thirty slaves) led other groups of slaveholders with one hundred and twenty-seven dollars, and the big planters produced only about half as much. Most of the planters in both clusters of counties recorded no home manufactures at all.[8] Sample studies from Virginia's tobacco area, wheat

[6]*Southern Agriculturist* (Charleston), I (September 1828), 404; *Farmer and Planter,* VI (December 1855), 270-71; *Southern Quarterly Review,* XVIII (September 1850), 218.

[7]Alfred G. Smith, *Economic Readjustment of an Old Cotton State: South Carolina, 1820-1860* (Columbia, S. C., 1958), 134; Douglass C. North, *The Economic Growth of the United States, 1790-1860* (Englewood Cliffs, N. J., 1961), 132-33; Rolla M. Tryon, *Household Manufacturers in the United States, 1640-1860; a Study in Industrial History* (Chicago, 1917); Mary Elizabeth Massey, *Ersatz in the Confederacy* (Columbia, 1952), 80, 98.

[8]From the five Mississippi and the five Georgia cotton belt counties regarded as typical by Lewis C. Gray in his *History of Agriculture in the Southern United States to 1860* (2 vols., Washington, 1933), I, 334-35, II, 918-21, I have analyzed for each state the two that come closest to the mode in the only variable for which there is clear evidence, the size of slaveholdings. A review of the economic and natural conditions of the South reveals nothing to suggest that the four counties so chosen are not roughly typical of the cotton belt. I have used the four counties primarily for an investigation of purchasing power—to gain clues to the general structure of the market—and the insignificant expenditures recorded indicate that even with due allowance for the possibility of a wide, say 50%, deviation in other counties and for

area, and tidewater reveal the same situation. Plantation manuscripts show surprisingly frequent, and often quite large, expenditures for artisans' services and suggest that plantations were much less self-sufficient and exhibited much less division of labor than is generally appreciated.[9] The root of the insufficient demand must be sought in the poverty of the rural majority composed of slaves, subsistence farmers, and poor whites.

In nineteenth-century America as a whole both capital and labor were in short supply. Industrial development was spurred by farmers who provided a large market for goods and tools, and manufacturing arose on the foundation of this immense rural demand. Eastern manufacturers gradually awoke to their dependence on this rural market and by 1854 were supporting homestead legislation not only to gain support for higher tariffs and for purposes of speculation but to expand the market for their goods. Farmers in New England saw their futures linked with industrial development, and their hostility toward commercial middlemen was not usually transferred to the manufacturers.[10] The same was true in

---

incorrect reporting in the census returns, the results could not conceivably be substantially different.

As a random sample, I selected the first ten names on each page of U. S. Census, 1860, Georgia, Schedule 4, Productions of Agriculture, Dougherty and Thomas counties (Library, Duke University, Durham, North Carolina) and U. S. Census, 1860 Mississippi, Schedule 4, De Soto and Marshall counties (Mississippi State Archives, Jackson). From the U. S. Census, 1860, Georgia, Schedule 2, Slave Inhabitants, Dougherty and Thomas counties, and U. S. Census, 1860, Mississippi, Schedule 2, De Soto and Marshall counties (National Archives, Washington), I determined the number of slaves held by each agriculturist in my sample. Where Schedule 4 gave the amount of produce but not its monetary value, I used a specially prepared price schedule in order to translate the amounts into dollar values. See Eugene D. Genovese, The Limits of Agrarian Reform in the Slave South (unpublished Ph.D. thesis, Columbia University, 1959), appendixes.

[9]These expenditures were for blacksmiths' services, road building, cabin building, and even for such trivial tasks as the erection of door frames. The accounts often run into hundreds of dollars. See, for example, Moses St. John R. Liddell and Family Papers (Library, Louisiana State University, Baton Rouge), Haller Nutt Papers (Library, Duke University, Durham, N. C.), Everard Green Baker Papers (Southern Historical Collection, University of North Carolina, Chapel Hill), I, 139; Killona Plantation Journals (Mississippi State Department of Archives and History, Jackson), I, 60 ff.

[10]Roy M. Robbins, *Our Landed Heritage; the Public Domain, 1776-1936* (New York, 1950), 177; Joseph Brennan, *Social Conditions in Industrial Rhode Island, 1820-1860* (Washington, 1940), 18; Samuel Rezneck, "The Rise and Early Development of Industrial Consciousness in the United States, 1760-1830," *Journal of*

the West. As the shrewd Achille Murat noted in the 1830's, the manufacturing interest of the West "is not constituted by the manufactories which exist, but those which they look forward to in prospective."[11] An agrarianism uncompromisingly hostile to industry and urbanization—to what was called "manufacturing as a system"—existed only in the South and can not be separated from the ideological leadership of the slaveholding planters. Even there, those seriously interested in economic progress saw the link between agricultural reform and industrialization and tried to work out proposals for increased manufactures that would be palatable to their fellow slaveholders.[12]

The West was able to import capital because Eastern manufacturers and European creditors were confident of her growth and prosperity. Outside credits at that time had to be accumulated by the importation of commodities and the maintenance of an unfavorable trade balance. The immense internal market guaranteed the West an import surplus until 1850. Its insatiable demand for manufactured articles contributed to the unfavorable trade balance of the United States, but on the whole this was not a serious problem for the country because American importers were strong enough to obtain long-term credits on relatively easy terms; and, during the 1850's, profits from shipping and other invisible gains largely restored the balance.[13] Thus, on the one hand, the national economy was sufficiently strong to overcome the worst effects of a trade deficit, and, on the other hand, the agrarian West was able to obtain the credits required for industrial development. The South did not benefit from this arrangement. It provided an exportable surplus, which, although of great help to the national economy in offsetting

---

Economic and Business History, IV (1932), 784-811; Isaac Lippincott, *A History of Manufactures in the Ohio Valley to the Year 1860 . . .* (New York, 1914), 63-65; Grace Pierpont Fuller, *An Introduction to the History of Connecticut As a Manufacturing State* (Northhampton, Mass., 1915), 45; James Neal Primm, *Economic Policy in a Development of a Western State, Missouri* (Cambridge, Mass., 1954), 56-59; Frank W. Taussig, *The Tariff History of the United States* (7th ed., New York, 1923), 68-108; and Bray Hammond, *Banks and Politics in American, from the Revolution to the Civil War* (Princeton, 1957).

[11]Achille Murat, *America and the Americans* (New York, 1849), 19.

[12]For examples, see the remarks of M. W. Phillips and John J. Williams, *Mississippi Planter and Mechanic,* II (May 1858), 157-58; of Thomas J. Lemay, *Arator,* I (November 1855), 237; and of Andrew Johnson, *Congressional Globe,* XXIII, 312.

[13]See Simon S. Kuznets, *Economic Change; Selected Essays in Business Cycles, National Income, and Economic Growth* (New York, 1953), 307 ff; and Charles F. Dunbar, *Economic Essays* (New York, 1904), 268.

the large quantity of imports, was exploited by Northern capital. The invisible gains that were so important to national growth were made partly at the expense of the South.

The population statistics for 1860 offer a clue to the structure of the market. If we exclude Maryland, in which slavery was declining, and Delaware, which was a slave state in name only, the median population per square mile in the slave states was 18, and Kentucky was high with 31. In comparison, Massachusetts had a population of 158 per square mile; Rhode Island, 138; Connecticut, 98; New York, 84; New Jersey, 81; and so forth. In the West, Ohio had 59; Indiana, 40; and Illinois, 31.

These figures do not tell the important part of the story. A country that is sparsely settled, in absolute terms, may have a high population density, in economic terms, if its system of transportation and commodity production are well developed and integrated. For example, the Northern states in 1860 had a much higher population density—from an economic point of view—than the thickly populated countries of Asia. When we consider the superiority of Northern transportation and economic integration, relative to those of the South, we must conclude that the difference in the magnitude of the market greatly exceeded that suggested by the population figures.

Historians have long appreciated—at least since the pioneer researches of U. B. Phillips—that the Southern transportation system tied the staple-producing areas to the ports and that this was the best possible arrangement for the planters. The planters controlled the state legislatures in an era in which state participation was decisive in railroad construction and generally refused to assume the tax burden necessary to open the back country and thereby encourage and strengthen politically suspect farmers. Without a fully developed railroad network tying the South into an economic unit, the absorption of nonstaple producers into the market economy, except in a peripheral way, was impossible. Poor transportation was, for example, one important factor in the retardation of the Southern cotton textile industry.[14]

With good reason alert Southerners spoke of the connection

---

[14]See Milton S. Heath, *Constructive Liberalism; the Role of the State in Economic Development in Georgia to 1860* (Cambridge, Mass., 1954), 290-91, and Seth Hammond, "Location Theory and the Cotton Industry," *Journal of Economic History,* II (1942), Supp., 101-17. The opposition of entrenched landowning classes to the extension of transportation has been general in colonial, underdeveloped countries. See George Wythe, *Industry in Latin America* (New York, 1945), 4.

among railroads, markets, diversified agriculture, and manufacturing. James Robb pointedly described improved transportation and greater industry as necessary ingredients in the process of unifying the South. Oscar M. Lieber noted that without an adequate transportation system South Carolina farmers were prevented from entering the market as corn producers. John Bell warmly supported federal land grants to railroads to strengthen the bonds of commodity production.[15] Within the South these men could, at best, expect to be received with an impatient silence. Where their message was sometimes listened to attentively was in the upper South, as for example in what came to be West Virginia; the subsequent construction of road and railroad links to existing markets generally bound parts of the upper South to the free states and helped remove them from the slaveholders' domain.

In the slave South the home market consisted primarily of the plantations, which bought foodstuffs from the West and manufactured goods from the East. The planters needed increased Southern manufacturing but only for certain purposes. They needed cheap slave clothing, cotton gins and a few crude agricultural implements, rope for cotton bagging, and so forth. This narrow market could not compare with the tremendous Western demand for industrial commodities of all kinds, especially for agricultural implements and machinery on the more capital-intensive Western farms. The Northeast had the capital and skilled labor for fairly large-scale production and had established its control over existing markets in the North and West. Southern manufacturers could not hope to compete with Northern outside the South, and the same conditions that brought about Northern control of the Northern market made possible Northern penetration of the Southern market despite the costs of transportation.

The South was caught in a contradiction similar to that facing many underdeveloped countries today. On the one hand, it provided a market for outside industry. On the other hand, that very market was too small to sustain industry on a scale large enough to compete with outsiders who could draw upon wider markets. Only one fifth of the manufacturing establishments of the United States were in the South, and their average capitalization was well below that of

[15]De Bow (ed.), *Industrial Resources,* II, 154; Oscar M. Lieber, *Report on the Survey of South Carolina . . . 1857* (Columbia, 1858), 106; *Congressional Globe,* XXI, pt. 1, 867-68.

the manufacturing establishments of the free states. Consider the situation in two industries of special importance to the South—cotton textiles and agricultural implements. New England had almost three times as many cotton factories as the entire South in 1860, and yet the average capitalization was almost twice as great. The concentration in this industry had proceeded so far by 1850 that of the more than 1,000 cotton factories in the United States only forty-one had one half the total capital investment. As for the agricultural implement and machinery industry, New York, Pennsylvania, Ohio, and Illinois each had a greater total capital investment than did the entire South, and in three of these the average capitalization was between two and two and a half times as great as the average in the South.[16] This Northern advantage led Edmund Ruffin and T. L. Clingman, among others, to look forward to a Southern confederacy protected by high tariffs against Northern goods.[17]

In view of the nature of the plantation market it is not surprising that data on the cotton textile industry almost invariably reveal that Southern producers concentrated upon the production of the cheapest and coarsest kind of cloth to be used in the making of slave clothing.[18] Even so, local industrialists had to compete for this market with Northerners who sometimes shipped direct and some-

---

[16]U. S. Census Office, *Manufactures of the United States in 1860* . . . (Washington, 1865), xxi, ccxvii, lxxiii, 729-30; Evelyn H. Knowlton, *Pepperell's Progress; History of a Cotton Textile Company, 1844-1945* Cambridge, Mass., 1948), 32. The average capitalization of manufacturing establishments was in 1850 more than 25% higher in the free states and territories than in the slave states, and the gap widened in the 1850's when the increase in average capital investment was 68% in the free states and territories and only 51% in the slave states. The lower South (North Carolina, South Carolina, Georgia, Florida, Alabama, Mississippi, Louisiana, and Texas) fell even further behind. The average capitalization here, 38% less than in the free states in 1850, was 47% less by 1860. Furthermore, the rate of increase in the number of establishments during this decade was appreciably greater in the North than in the South.

[17]Edmund Ruffin, Incidents of My Life, 19-20, in Edmund Papers (Southern Historical Collection, University of North Carolina); T. L. Clingman's speech to the House of Representatives, January 22, 1850, in *Selections from the Speeches and Writings of Hon. Thomas L. Clingman of North Carolina* . . . (Raleigh, N. C., 1877), 233-54, especially 250.

[18]See Patent Office, *Annual Report, 1857, Agriculture, Senate Exec. Docs.*, 35 Cong., 1 Sess., No. 30, pt. 4 (Serial 928), 308-309, 318; and Richard H. Shryock, "The Early Industrial Revolution in the Empire State," *Georgia Historical Quarterly*, XI (June 1927), 128.

times established Southern branches and who had facilities for the collection and processing of second-hand clothing.[19] Just as New England supplied much of the South's "Negro cloth," so it supplied much of the boots and shoes. Firms like Batchellor Brothers of Brookfield produced cheap shoes especially for the Southern market and as early as 1837 opened a branch at Mobile to consolidate its Southern market.[20]

Producers of better cotton goods had little hope of making a living in the South. Occasionally, a William Gregg could penetrate Northern markets successfully, but Southern demand for such goods was too small to have much effect on the industry generally. Northern firms like the Pepperell Manufacturing Company or A.A. Lawrence Company did little business in the South. On the other hand a rising demand for textiles in the agrarian West had greatly influenced the New England cotton industry since 1814.[21]

The Southern iron industry, hampered as it was by the restricted railroad development in the slave states, also had a poor time of it. American iron producers generally were handicapped because much of the country's railroad iron was being imported. The small scale of operations and resultant cost schedule, which hurt the industry nationally, hit the Southern manufacturers especially hard. Dependent upon a weak local market, Southern iron manufacturers had great difficulty holding their own even during the prosperous 1850's.

No wonder the Augusta, Georgia, Commercial Convention added to its demand that Southerners buy Southern goods the qualification, unless you can get Northern cheaper. And no wonder the proposal was ridiculed as amounting to "Never kiss the maid if you can kiss the mistress, unless you like the maid better."[22]

We can not measure precisely the extent of the Southern market nor even make a reliable, general, quantitative comparison between the Southern and Western rural markets, but we can glean from various sources some notion of the immense difference. For exam-

[19]Jesse Eliphalet Pope, *The Clothing Industry in New York* (Columbia, Mo., 1905), 6-7.

[20]Blanche Evans Hazard, *The Organization of the Boot and Shoe Industry in Massachusetts Before 1875* (Cambridge, Mass., 1921), 57-58.

[21]Knowlton, *Pepperell's Progress,* 83-84; Caroline F. Ware, *The Early New England Cotton Manufacture; a Study in Industrial Beginnings* (Boston, 1931), 48, 55.

[22]Herbert Wender, *Southern Commercial Conventions, 1837-1859* (Baltimore, 1930), 25.

ple, Phelps, Dodge & Co., a prominent cotton shipping firm that also distributed metals, tools, machinery, clothing, and an assortment of other items, reported at the beginning of the Civil War that only five per cent of its sales were to the South and that those were primarily to the noncotton states. We do not know the extent of the firm's participation in the cotton export trade, but it was considerable. Phelps, Dodge & Co. was in an excellent position to exchange industrial goods for cotton, but the Southern demand for imported goods could not compare in bulk or value with the supply of cotton. In the West, on the other hand, farmers and townsmen provided a growing and lucrative market, and the firm had more customers in Ohio than in any state except New York.[23]

An examination of the 1860 manuscript census returns and other primary sources pertaining to two representative cotton counties in Mississippi and to two in Georgia permits us to judge roughly the extent of the market in the cotton belt by estimating the expenditures made by planters and farmers in these counties. (See above, note 8.) The estimates are the most generous possible and exaggerate the extent of the Southern rural market in relation to the Western in two ways: There were far more rural poor with little or no purchasing power in the cotton belt than in the West, and the concentration of landholdings in the South resulted in fewer landowners than could be found in a Western area of comparable size. Thus, even if the estimate of the expenditures made by these Southern planters and farmers had been larger than the expenditures of a similar group of individual proprietors in the West—which was by no means true—the total purchased in each county would still have been far less than in a comparable Western area. Furthermore, as food was a major item in the expenditures of the Southerners, the market for industrial commodities was much smaller than might appear.

The concentration of landholding and slaveholding in the Mississippi counties meant that six per cent of the landowners commanded one third of the gross income and probably a much higher percentage of the net. That is, the majority of landowners were faced with a disproportionately small portion of the total income accruing to the cotton economy as a whole.

Only the largest planters—ten per cent of the landowners—spent

[23]Richard Lowitt, *A Merchant Prince of the Nineteenth Century, William E. Dodge* (New York, 1954), 31 ff., 37.

more than $1,000 a year for food and supplies, and they rarely spent more. These expenditures include the total purchases for the slaves. The slaveholding farms and plantations in Mississippi annually spent about thirty or thirty-five dollars per person for food and supplies; nonslaveholders spent about twenty-five dollars per person. In Georgia slaveholding farms and plantations spent about twenty-five dollars per person, and nonslaveholders were just about self-sufficient.[24] In contrast, Philip Foner reports that contemporary newspapers and other sources indicate that the small farmers who made up the great majority of the rural population of the West accumulated store bills of from one hundred to six hundred dollars.[25] Even if we allow for considerable exaggeration and assume that the accounts were generally closer to the lower estimate, these figures, which are exclusive of cash purchases, mail orders, payments to drummers, and so forth, are at least a clue to the impressive purchasing power of the Western countryside.

However imprecise the estimates for the South may be, they indicate the lack of purchasing power among the rural population of the cotton belt and demonstrate how greatly the situation there differed from that in the West. With such a home market the slave economy could not sustain more than the lowest level of commodity production apart from that of a few staples. The success of William Gregg as a textile manufacturer in South Carolina and the data produced by Professor John Hebron Moore showing that a cotton textile industry could and did exist in ante bellum Mississippi would seem to contradict this conclusion; but Gregg, who was aware of the modest proportions of the home market, warned Southerners against trying to produce for local needs and suggested that they focus on the wholesale market. His own company at Graniteville, South Carolina, produced fine cotton goods that sold much better in New York than in the South. Gregg's success in the Northern market could not easily be duplicated by others, and when he discussed the Southern market, he felt compelled, as did Benjamin L. C. Wailes and other astute observers, to advocate production of cheap cotton goods for the plantations.[26] Moore's conclusion that his data prove

[24]In Mississippi a sample of 584 units with 7,289 slaves and an estimated 2,480 whites spent about $316,500; in Georgia a sample of 100 units with 2,354 slaves and an estimated 710 whites spent about $73,300.

[25]Foner, *Business & Slavery,* 143.

[26]William Gregg, *Essays on Domestic Industry; or An Inquiry into the Expediency*

the adaptability of manufacturing to the lower South requires for substantiation more than evidence of particular successes, no matter how impressive;[27] it requires evidence that Southern producers were strong enough to drive out Northern competition and, more important, that the market was large enough to sustain more than a few firms.

The plantation system did have its small compensations for industry. The planters' taste for luxuries, for example, proved a boon to the Petersburg iron industry, which supplied plantations with cast-iron fences, lawn ornaments, balconies, fancy gates, and other decorative articles.[28] A silk industry emerged briefly but was destroyed by climatic conditions as well as by a shortage of capital.[29] The hemp industry, which supplied rope for cotton baling, depended heavily on the plantation market.

Some Southern industrialists, especially those in the border states, did good business in the North. Louisville tobacco and hemp manufacturers sold much of their output in Ohio. Botts and Burfoot of Richmond, Virginia, reported the sale of $1,000-worth of straw cutters in the North during a six-month period. The more successful Southern iron producers were those of the upper South, who were able to sell outside the slave states. Smith and Perkins of Alexandria, Virginia, began production of locomotives and railroad cars in the 1850's and obtained a good many orders from the North; but the company failed because shipping costs made consolidation of its Northern market difficult and because only a few orders were forthcoming from the South. Similarly, the paper industry in South

---

of Establishing Cotton Manufactures in South-Carolina (Graniteville, S. C., 1941), 4; Benjamin L. C. Wailes, *Address Delivered in the College Chapel Before the Agricultural, Horticultural and Botanical Society, of Jefferson College* (Natchez, Miss., 1841), 22-23; *De Bow's Review,* XXIX (October 1860), 496-97; Broadus Mitchell, *William Gregg, Factory Master of the Old South* (Chapel Hill, N. C., 1928), 106.

[27]John Hebron Moore, "Mississippi's Ante-Bellum Textile Industry," *Journal of Mississippi History,* XVI (April 1954), 81.

[28]Edward A. Wyatt, IV, "Rise of Industry in Ante-Bellum Petersburg," *William and Mary College Quarterly,* s. 3, XVII (January 1937), 32.

[29]Southerners were very much interested in silk cultivation and manufacture and saw fine market possibilities. See Charles G. Parsons, *Inside View of Slavery; or a Tour Among the Planters* (Boston, 1855), 71 ff; C. O. Cathey, "Sidney Weller: Ante-Bellum Promoter of Agricultural Reform," *North Carolina Historical Review,* XXI (January 1954), 6; Spaulding Trafton, "Silk Culture in Henderson County, Kentucky," *Filson Club History Quarterly,* IV (October 1930), 184-89.

Carolina did well until the 1850's, when Northern orders dropped and no Southern orders appeared.[30] The political dangers of these links with the free states were widely appreciated. The Virginia Commercial Convention, for example, reported that West Virginia was being cut off from the South in this way.[31] During the Civil War, William Henry Holcombe, a thoughtful doctor from Natchez, listed in his diary various reasons for the adherence of the border states to the Union and placed close commercial ties high on the list.[32] One suspects that there was more than hindsight here, for politically sophisticated Southerners were alert to the danger well before 1861. But what could they have done about it?

The inability of the slave South to generate an adequate rural market inhibited industrialization and urbanization, which in turn limited the market for agricultural produce and undermined attempts at diversification. With the exception of New Orleans and Baltimore, the slave states had no large cities, and few reached the size of 15,000. The urban population of the South could not compare with that of the Northeast, as is generally appreciated; but, more to the point, it could not compare with that of the agrarian West either. The urban population of the lower South in 1860 was only seven per cent of the total population, and in the western part of the lower South, embracing most of the cotton belt, there was a relative decline during the preceding twenty years. In New England, the percentage was thirty-seven; in the Middle Atlantic states, including Ohio, thirty-five; and perhaps most significantly, in Indiana, Illinois, Michigan, and Wisconsin, fourteen.[33]

The urban market in the South was even less developed than these figures suggest. If we except New Orleans, which was a special case,

---

[30]Lippincott, *Manufactures in the Ohio Valley,* 64; *Southern Planter,* III (April 1843), advertisement on back cover; Lester J. Cappon, "Trend of the Southern Iron Industry Under the Plantation System," *Journal of Economic and Business History,* II (February 1930), 361, 371, 376; Carrol H. Quenzel, "The Manufacture of Locomotives and Cars in Alexandria in the 1850's," *Virginia Magazine of History and Biography,* LXII (April 1954), 182 ff; Ernest M. Lander, Jr., "Paper Manufacturing in South Carolina Before the Civil War," *North Carolina Historical Review,* XXIX (April 1952), 225 ff.

[31]De Bow (ed.), *Industrial Resources,* III, 465.

[32]William Henry Holcombe Diary (Southern Manuscript Collection, University of North Carolina), entry for September 6, 1855, but obviously written in 1861.

[33]Urban area defined as incorporated places of 2,500 or more. See U. S. Bureau of the Census, *Urban Population in the U. S. from the First Census (1790) to the Fifteenth Census (1930)* . . . (Washington, 1939).

three cities of the lower South had a population of 15,000 or more: Mobile, Charleston, and Savannah, with a combined population of 92,000. Of this number, thirty-seven per cent were slaves and free Negroes, who may be assumed to have represented only minimal purchasing power. In the 1850's American families certainly did not spend less than forty per cent of their incomes on food, and the importance of a large urban market for foodstuffs may be judged accordingly.[34]

Eugene W. Hilgard, state geologist of Mississippi, explained his state's failure to develop a cattle industry largely by the absence of a local market. Similarly, Oscar M. Lieber, state geologist of South Carolina, warned farmers in a state that was never comfortably self-sufficient in corn not to produce more corn than they could consume, for there was no place to market the surplus. Charles Yancey of Buckingham County, Virginia, wrote that planters and farmers would not grow oats because the only possibility of disposing of them lay in person to person barter.[35]

The weakness of the market for agricultural produce had many detrimental consequences for the South, of which we may mention only two. First, those sections of the border states which found markets in the Northern cities were increasingly drawn into the political-economic orbit of the free states at the very moment when the slave states required maximum solidarity to preserve their system. Second, the weakness of the market doomed the hopes of agricultural reformers and transformed their cry for diversification into a cry for a backward step toward natural economy.

When that great antislavery Kentuckian, Cassius M. Clay, finally receives from historians the honor and attention that he deserves, he will surely be recognized as one of the most penetrating commentators on the economics of slavery. Consider his remarks on the problem of markets, with which we are presently concerned:

[34]This estimate is from Edgar W. Martin, *The Standard of Living in 1860* (Chicago, 1942), 11-12, and may greatly underestimate the situation in urban households. According to Richard O. Cummings, laborers in Massachusetts probably spent about three fourths of their weekly wages on food in 1860. R. O. Cummings, *The American and His Food; a History of Food Habits in the United States* (Chicago, 1941), 266.

[35]Eugene W. Hilgard, *Report on the Geology and Agriculture of the State of Mississippi* (Jackson, 1860), 250-51; Lieber, *Report*, 106. See also Patent Office, *Annual Report, 1849, Agriculture, Senate Exec. Docs.*, 31 Cong., 1 Sess., No. 15, pt. 2 (Serial 556), 137.

Lawyers, merchants, mechanics, laborers, who are your consumers; Robert Wickliffe's two hundred slaves? How many clients do you find, how many goods do you sell, how many hats, coats, saddles, and trunks do you make for these two hundred slaves? Does Mr. Wickliffe lay out as much for himself and his two hundred slaves as two hundred freemen do? . . . All our towns dwindle, and our farmers lose, in consequence, all home markets. Every farmer bought out by the slave system send off the consumers of the manufacturers of the town: when the consumers are gone, the mechanic must go also. . . . A home market cannot exist in a slave state.[36]

Plantation slavery, then, so limited the purchasing power of the South that it could not sustain much industry. That industry which could be raised usually lacked a home market of sufficient scope to permit large-scale operation; the resultant cost of production was often too high for success in competition with Northern firms drawing on much wider markets. Without sufficient industry to support urbanization, a general and extensive diversification of agriculture was unthinkable. Whatever other factors need to be considered in a complete analysis, the low level of demand in this plantation-based slave society was sufficient to retard the economic development of the South.

ALFRED H. CONRAD and JOHN R. MEYER

Slavery as an Obstacle to Economic Growth in the United States

It has long been the custom, and generally it has been a useful one, to organize the program for the annual meetings of the Economic History Association around a single theme. The advantages of the practice, and

[36]Horace Greeley (ed.), *The Writings of Cassius Marcellus Clay* . . . (New York, 1848), 179, 227. For a recent biography, see David L. Smiley, *Lion of White Hall: The Life of Cassius M. Clay* (Madison, Wis., 1962).

From *The Journal of Economic History,* Volume XXVII, Number 4 (December, 1967) pages 518-531. Copyright 1967 by the Economic History Association. Reprinted by permission of the authors and the Business Manager.

in particular the way in which it provides an integrating focus for discussion, have generally been substantial enough to offset the headaches involved in identifying topics likely to attract and hold the interest of a diverse and individualistic membership. One of the more successful ventures along this line took place in 1967, when the theme selected was *Obstacles to Economic Growth*. On the one hand this topic concentrated attention on what had become a dominating interest for many economists and economic historians; on the other, by emphasizing "obstacles", it departed from conventional approaches to the subject which had, with questionable success, attempted to identify factors likely to promote or accelerate growth, rather than those likely to impede or retard the process.

The topic also provided a convenient opportunity to review some long-standing differences of opinion. With this in mind, one of the sessions was devoted to a discussion of the question whether or not, and in what ways, slavery had been an obstacle to economic development in the United States. A distinguished panel of discussants was brought together, including not only Alfred Conrad, John Meyer, and Douglas Dowd, who had debated closely related issues at the Association's meeting ten years before, but also other scholars who had contributed to the debate in the intervening period.

The session produced an informative and sometimes eloquent restatement by the major protagonists of the positions they had held for some time, but showed no noticeable narrowing of the gap between them on the original issues. From the transcript subsequently printed in the *Journal of Economic History* there is reproduced here, first, the statement presented by Alfred Conrad and John Meyer. This includes three principal components: first, a review of the major criticisms made of their original paper; second, a vigorous defense of their method and conclusions, including a restatement of what they had and had not tried to do; and third, a series of observations on the issue that had *not* been central to their original article, namely the effects of slavery on the economic development of the South.

Some comment on the relation between slavery and economic development was of course required by the topic assigned. But the attention paid by Conrad and Meyer to this issue in 1967, as compared with 1957, also reflected the way in which the focus of discussion had shifted away from the profitability of investment in slaves and toward the economic viability of a society based on slavery and its potential for development.

Of the greatest significance was the fact that discussion of this issue in 1967 took place against a background of statistical information on Southern economic development which had not been available ten years earlier. Most of this new information stemmed from the work of two investigators who had played no direct role in the slavery controversy: Richard Easterlin of the University of Pennsylvania, who had published in 1961 a set of estimates of regional income shares, the implications of which were profoundly disturbing to conventional notions; and Robert Gallman of the University of North Carolina, who had in 1966 published a path-breaking set of estimates of the gross national product of the United States between 1834 and 1909. The relevance of these statistical estimates to the slavery issue became evident when they were combined to yield estimates of relative rates of economic growth in the major regions of the country. Stanley Engerman of the University of Rochester played the major role in combining the Easterlin and Gallman estimates, making some significant revisions in the figures in the process (see below page 317).

The net result was that, while the controversy had in a sense reverted to the great issues of social structure and economic change which had engrossed Cairnes and Phillips and which writers like Dowd and Genovese had consistently stressed, it had done so in a drastically changed context. For the research of Gallman and Easterlin, and the reworking of their figures by Engerman, pointed to the conclusion that the rate of economic development in the South before the Civil War had been eminently satisfactory. Between 1840 and 1860, according to Engerman's figures, per capita income in the South had grown at an average rate of 1.6 percent per year; the national average for the same period was only 1.3 percent per year. These figures, moreover, included slaves as part of the population. If, reflecting the dominant values of Southern society at the time, slaves were regarded as intermediate goods and not as consumers (and thus were excluded from the denominator of the fraction), the rate of Southern economic development between 1840 and 1860 was 1.8 percent per year, compared to the national average of 1.3 percent.

U. B. Phillips, believing that slave ownership had become economically unprofitable by the 1850s, had found it no hard matter to argue that it had also become a burden on the regional economy, retarding its growth and inhibiting its industrialization. Conrad and Meyer in 1957, having no reason at that time to question the conventional view of the South as an economically retarded region, had had to content themselves with the assertion that, whatever the reasons for this state of affairs might have been, absence of profits in slave-labor agriculture was not one of them. But now the wheel had come full circle. Not only had slavery not been unprofitable, it had also not retarded Southern economic development. Quite the contrary, in fact; for out of the statistical findings of Gallman and Easterlin, supplemented by the work of economic historians like Douglass North, there was beginning to emerge a picture of the economic significance of the ante-bellum South quite at variance with the accepted truths of earlier days. Slave-labor staple agriculture, and particularly cotton, had generated in the antebellum South a rate of economic development higher than the national average. Further, if North's interpretation was to be accepted, the direct and indirect effects of Southern staple production had sustained and reinforced the rate of development of the entire national economy in the pre-Civil War period. And it was precisely in these pre-Civil War decades that the foundations had been laid for massive postwar industrialization and for the explosive geographical expansion that was to carry American empire to the Pacific and beyond. All this, it would appear, stemmed originally from the slave-labor economy of the antebellum South, an economy that had not only been profitable at the time to the owners of slave capital but had also initially set in motion the great groundswell of economic expansion that sustained American economic growth through the nineteenth century.

But if this were the case, where had there arisen the conventional view of the South as a retarded region? And what explanation was to be given for the fact that, in the second half of the nineteenth century, the South had unquestionably been poorer than the rest of the nation? The first question was perhaps easily answered: contemporary observers and later commentators had been misled by the absence of substantial industrialization in the South, and had illogically concluded from this that its rate of growth of income per head must have been low. Or perhaps they had generalized too readily from the obvious poverty that resulted from a skewed income distribution. Perhaps no further explanation was necessary: the South had specialized in that line of production in which it had the greatest comparative advantage, and consequently manufactures had languished while agriculture thrived. As for the second question, there was of course the destruction caused by the Civil War, and the fact that new sources of cotton production, particularly in the East Indies, had been developed during the War to take over the markets lost by the South. The relatively low *level* of Southern development in the second half of the nineteenth century, in short, resulted basically from the fact that for two crucial decades—the 1860s and the 1870s—its *rate* of development had been seriously retarded, primarily because of the loss of foreign markets for its staple export. And for this, directly and indirectly, the Civil War was responsible. Morally repugnant Southern slavery might well have been; but it had not been economically detrimental.

The context of argument had indeed changed. And although at first glance it might appear that none of the leading participants in the 1967 discussion had significantly altered his position, in fact the basis of debate and the issues on which judgments seriously differed were far different from what they had been ten years earlier. The new information, the new statistical estimates, and the new interpretations of national economic growth that grew out of them clearly tended to favor the Conrad and Meyer position, in the sense that it absolved them from any need to reconcile a profitable slave agriculture with an apparently lagging economy. But, on the other hand, there was room for lingering doubts. Could it be true that a society dominated by slavery, and specifically by the kind of slavery that existed in the antebellum South, was capable of sustained economic development? Did the new statistics show any more than that, until the end of the 1850s, a profitable staple agriculture, geared to expanding foreign markets and enjoying easy access to rich natural resources, had directly and indirectly generated a relatively high rate of growth of per capita income? Did they give any warrant for belief that the process could have continued? If so, on what assumptions? Could the South have continued in its path of development without precipitating civil war? If not, should the costs of the Civil War, including its long-run impact on the South, be included in the costs of slavery? Was the development path of the South before the Civil War perhaps too easy, too immediately rewarding, too closely adjusted to resources and markets that were too easily available? Would a more difficult and more demanding path, based less exclusively on slave-labor agriculture and export staples, have brought greater benefits in the long run? And might these greater benefits in the long run have been achieved without civil war?

EVERY ECONOMIST must be pleased to start some hares; it can become embarrassing, however, when they begin to breed like rabbits. In the ten years since we first tried our slavery model in public, in Professor Gerschenkron's history seminar, more than thirty published arguments addressed to that model have come to our attention. We don't pretend to know whether that represents an increased output over preceding decades. Besides, in our youthful enthusiasm we gave the impression that we were disposing, once and for all, of a piece of intellectual game that was already rather high. In any event, the apparent egocentricity that turned up all those papers and articles may be explained, if not justified, by Ralph Barton Perry's dictum that every reader looks up two references in an index: sex, and his own name.

The recent discussion on the profitability of slavery in the ante-bellum South can be surveyed along three lines. First, a number of questions of fact, or evidence, have been raised. Second, the capital model that we used has been criticized as irrelevant. And third, the model, as a piece of economic analysis, has been attacked as insufficient to answer the historical questions we put to it.

As for factual or data questions, Fritz Redlich is not a man to mince words. He has characterized Part II of our paper, which is where the model works, as simply "fictitious." He means more by this remark than what is implied by saying that *I Promessi Sposi* is a work of fiction and not an historical account of the Counter-Reformation in the Duchy of Milan, or that John Motley could not really know the drunken indiscretions of Egmont or the midnight fears of William of Orange (though Motley may come closer to Mr. Redlich's definition of history than does Fishlow or Fogel, for example). What he *means* is that our Table 9 presents estimated returns on investments in prime field hands under a number of assumptions as to yield per hand, capital outlay, farm-gate cotton price, and slave longevity. Modal values and other measures of central tendency were used where we had distributions of estimated values, but the range over various land fertilities and capital outlays was given in full, so that the sensitivity of our results to different price and interest rates might be tested. The individual values are old-style historical facts; the modal values are statistical estimates, which is a class neither necessarily nor epistemologically equivalent to fiction. We were aware that the census data on longevity were questionable, and we considered whether the estimates were consistent with population trends. Such a comparison is presumably a form of "source criticism." But how does one estimate the rate of return on a piece of capital *without* estimating its life expectancy?

What new information, then, has emerged from the recent literature? Eugene Genovese urges that the medical costs should be at least 50 per cent higher and perhaps double our estimate. He raises the cost of overseers from a range of $5 to $15 per hand, to $22.50. He points to our unfortunate assumption that a stock consisting largely of mules and oxen could be self-reproducing, but he doesn't really reveal how large a proportion of horses and donkeys would be sufficient to maintain the stock—in Mississippi cotton counties, for instance, horses accounted for one-quarter to almost half of the total work animals in 1860, depending upon the size of the farm. He would raise our food and clothing expenses, and he would have us add as costs "several dollars worth of Christmas presents per slave," the "regular and expensive vacations in watering places," and the large sums planters spent on tutors, academies, and finishing schools for their children. However secure or insecure may be the inference that the regular vacations were widespread in the South, the gross analytic error of counting trips to Saratoga as costs should make it unecessary to pursue the question further.

A more serious factual objection was raised by Edward Saraydar. He argues in a note in the *Southern Economic Journal* that we used data from plantations that *purchased* all provisions as though they represented the costs on self-sufficient plantations. Combining such underestimates of costs with *upward*-biased average yields from specialized plantations, we would obviously have overestimated the rate of profit. Saraydar redid the average yields by returning to the 1850 Census, but at the cost of several downward biases and one arithmetic oversight. Richard Sutch, after raising a disturbing question about the relevance of our model, which we will discuss below, observed, first, that our yields did come from self-supporting plantations, and second, that yields estimated from the 1860 Census data are much closer to the ones we used than to Saraydar's estimates. Mr. Sutch then went on to calculate the rate of appreciation on slaves—an annual increase of 7.56 per cent—from population and slave price increases. To remove speculative effects, he turned more directly to cotton plantations and estimated the internal rate of return exclusive of the rising slave prices, by limiting the appreciation rate only to the 2.15 per cent slave population increase. He found that cotton farming was clearly profitable in the new South and concluded that land prices in the new areas could not rise fast enough to capture the full rent, from which one should predict the press of cotton production (as it actually occurred) into the new western lands.

Robert Evans has contributed to the evidence on slave-hiring practices—and, incidentally, on training and skills—and on the internal slave trade. Most of the interest in his two papers arises from the alternative model that he proposed for estimating rates of return, but his evidence on slave-hire-to-purchase ratios and trading differentials both lend strong support to the conclusion that the slave economy was viable. When he compares the specific slave *trade* returns to skilled wage rates, he finds some compensation in the traders' labor income, presumably to pay for the social disrepute in which the trade was held. But even admitting the difficulties of comparing occupational requirements, the evidence does not indicate that the traders were treated as pariahs.

In criticizing Evans, and later in a review of our book, Thomas Govan raised again (cf. his 1942 work) several factual questions, the most troubling of which relate to the depletion of the fertility of cotton lands. Our discussion of soil exhaustion is a "perverse belief" and a "disregard of reality." From the other side, however, Genovese claimed that we did not take sufficient account of the soil depletion pressed upon the South by the slave-and-cotton economy, and he cites further evidence on fertilizer requirements as well as contemporary discussion. At worst, we may have been clumsy in identifying the central tendency.

We would argue with Fogel and others that the social savings Genovese computed and the rates of return we calculated could both well be *facts*. But that is not the point. There has been much use of the word "guessing" in the discussion, but very little unearthing of new, direct evidence to refute the estimates we used. Only Sutch and Evans have contributed new evidence and in both cases it buttresses the case for the profitability of slavery.

There has been novelty in the model-building department, however. Let us start by reviewing what we actually did. In order to estimate the profitability of Southern slavery we computed the rate of return on an investment in slaves by the familiar procedure of capitalizing an income stream. In order to include all the relevant income we considered two production functions, one, for the production of cotton, in which the labor of prime field hands was the major input, and a second, in which the natural increase of the marketable slave population was looked upon as the production of capital goods. It should not be necessary to repeat that we did not need to assume, and that we never did assume, the existence of specialized breeding farms, in order to make the computation meaningful. However, to answer some of the denials that have appeared in the literature, let us repeat that we found enough references to "breeding wenches" and "proven breeders" in the secondary and primary source material to suggest, at least, that some ante-bellum Southerners got the idea.

We also did not estimate the returns *as-if* there were breeding farms. Slaves, like other people, reproduced themselves, and their children were sold as capital instruments. We estimated the returns from that appreciation of the capital stock of the slave South. We made the estimates because it has been argued, repeatedly, that southern slavery had been about to disappear because it was not profitable. We asserted that the values which we derived from the market data led directly to the inference that enough individual men in the South were making a commercial profit that large-scale slavery was not likely to disappear automatically.

A number of alternative models have appeared in the last few years. We have already mentioned Robert Evans' procedure. He computed the net yearly income from the yearly hire received by owners of slaves when they were rented out to work. The advantage of this procedure is the relatively direct, as opposed to residual, nature of the income data. A major danger, of course, is that evidence from slave hires might be biased in the direction of a special class of slave stock. Evans did try to restrict his observations to unskilled labor, but we have been unable to judge his success in this regard. The rates of return on slave capital from his computation are safely above contemporary railroad bond yields and short-term money rates.

Yasukichi Yasuba introduced the problem of *economic* rent—the difference between the price of capital instruments and the net reproduction cost—in an alternative evaluation of the viability of the slave system as a whole. For a given region or crop, he argues, the market price is relevant, but for the viability of the system as a whole, only the costs of reproduction of the capital—that is, the costs of rearing slaves—are relevant. He rewrote our basis postulate, therefore, as follows:

> . . . If the portion of the price of slaves which represents capitalized rent was increasing, it is a sign of the increased profitability of slavery . . . To say that capitalized rent was positive is the same thing as to say that the rate of return based on the reproduction costs of slaves was above the market rate of interest, provided that non-economic factors did not affect the determination of the price and there was no lag or anticipation in capitalization . . .

Because the supply of slaves, especially after the prohibition of further imports from Africa, was largely independent of profits, a discrepancy between prices and costs could last longer than would be the case for ordinary capital. This, he argued, is precisely what happened: the demand curve shifted to the right more rapidly than the supply curve could shift, with the result that the economic rent persisted, and indeed increased, over the ante-bellum period. Capitalized rent rose continuously from 1821 to 1855, with a decline between the prosperous late 1830's and the depressed early 1840's. On this basis, as distinguished from our findings on the marginal efficiency of slave capital, valued at market prices, Yasuba concluded that the slave system was viable.

This argument was pressed further by Richard Sutch and Douglass North. Much further, since North concluded that we failed to accomplish our objective and simply perpetuated the miserable controversy around profitability and viability. In fact, he says, "there is no possibility that slavery was economically not viable." Given the existence of rent on land and on slaves, short-run unprofitability would result in a readjustment of land rents or slave prices, sufficient to restore equilibrium. Only if the wages of free labor fell to subsistence, they argue, so that slave prices fell to zero, or at least below their cost of reproduction (in which case the rents would fall to zero), could the system become economically nonviable. If this argument simply refers to the fact that with upward sloping supply curves there will apparently always be a margin of private rent, then it must come up against Mrs. Robinson's demonstration that the rising supply curve is a necessary, but not sufficient, condition for the existence of rent in a particular industry. To be more specific, refutation of the arguments of those who said slavery was uneconomic, required proof that slave markets were viable and operative. Those who insist that there was "no possibility of slavery being unprofitable" come very close to assuming away the central question by simply assuming that viable slave markets existed. Furthermore, North is arguing as if slavery were a self-contained system. Actually, the cotton-slave-plantation system was *not* a closed system; it had to bid slave labor away from other uses. One of the results of our study was the demonstration that slave labor was highly mobile. Quasi-rents probably existed in the alternative uses and would have to be part of the plantation bid. Therefore, the presence of some rent or quasi-rent in the price of slaves and of cotton lands is not enough to make viability a foregone conclusion. Something more remains to be proved.

Sutch and North both recognize that if the slaves were less efficient than free labor, slave prices need not have fallen to zero to render the system nonviable. The lower limit would be the subsistence or reproduction cost of slaves; in the face of all the literature on the inefficiency of slave labor this hardly seems an empty question. Slave rents or quasi-rents should have been continuously threatened by the supply of presumably more efficient free labor. Now, in order to argue that market prices will respond successfully to such erosion, one must visualize that the declining stream of rents is instantaneously reflected in falling slave prices, and that those prices will not hover above the subsistence margin set by the difference in productivity. The stream of rents yielded by slaves from the time they could cover their variable—that is, subsistence or reproduction—costs, to the time when they retired or expired, is the key variable. It is not self-evident that the capitalized sum of that stream must always equal the prices of slaves in a period of declining prices and yields. With any lag in price adjustments, the system might well become nonviable. North's closing point, that if slave prices were pegged by the requirements of conspicuous consumption, land prices must have fallen to an equilibrium solution, seems to ignore the possibility that the land would be in demand for the production of cotton or many other commodities with more efficient free labor. We may have underestimated the returns by using market price rather than the cost of reproduction, but we were certainly not tilting at windmills.

In general, an exclusive reliance upon calculation of quasi-rents to establish the economic viability of slavery *as a system* greatly oversimplifies. And it was definitely not the context in which the historical arguments were conducted. Rather, those who contended that slavery was uneconomic argued that slave markets were pathological and disequilibrated. Stress was placed upon investor irrationality and a divergent pattern in the development of cotton and slave prices. The specific contention was that in the immediate ante-bellum period a rational investor would not find it profitable to "buy into" the slave system. We demonstrated that this was certainly not obvious and almost certainly was fallacious.

Importance also attaches to differences in the pattern of economic viability of slavery by regions and particular applications, particularly since much political controversy in the pre-Civil War period centered about the issue of whether new lands should be admitted to slave culture. We demonstrated that this emphasis upon growth of slave lands was hardly quixotic. An expanding slave system was much more profitable than a stagnant system, not only for those who occupied the new lands, but for those who remained back on the older lands of the South, engaged in a combination of agriculture and slave breeding. Indeed, looking at the political controversies of the period immediately prior to the war, it is perhaps not too extravagant to claim that the war might have been avoided if southerners had been satisfied to restrict their slave system to lands on which it was already established.

In another set of papers the irrelevance of our model has been argued on very different grounds. From a variety of starting points, Douglas Dowd, Eugene Genovese, Harold Woodman, Thomas Govan, and Fritz Redlich all arrived at the conclusion that we could not settle any significant issues with a business model, or a capital model, because slavery was not *simply* a business or a capitalist enterprise. There may be a meaningful distinction to be drawn between the question of the *relevance* of a model of the slave system as a business enterprise, and the *sufficiency* of such a model for the problems of growth and development. Let us look first at the question of relevance.

Why is our economic model argued to be irrelevant by these historians? In Douglas Dowd's words:

> . . . For the southerner to convert himself to beliefs and behavior which would support and comport with slavery required a concentration so intense that all else became secondary—including the process of capital accumulation . . . Who would be inclined to use the term "capitalist" to describe the owners of Southern wealth? Apart from a William Gregg here and there, southern capital was *planter* capital. Planters were of course interested in profits; so were medieval "businessmen" (as jarring a term as "southern capitalists"). But neither group approached the question of capitalist accumulation in the sense in which the northern manufacturers did . . .

In Genovese's terms, the argument runs as follows:

> . . . however brisk the slave trade, considerable sentimental pressure existed to inhibit a purely rational approach to buying and selling slaves. Any notion that slaveholders as a class could or would have abandoned their estates to invest in more remunerative pursuits . . . —in other words, to transform themselves into ordinary capitalists— rests on a vulgar economic determinist outlook, contradicts the actual historical experience, and ignores the essential qualities of slave-based Southern life.

The question of whether or not the slaveholders earned a return equal to that accruing to Northern capitalists is not an especially significant political or social question.

. . .

Economists have assumed that an affirmative answer would prove slaveholding to have been just another business; as Schumpeter warns us, statistics can never disprove what we have reason to know from simpler and more direct methods.

Now, to be accused of vulgar economic determinism, which must be related to vulgar Marxism, is a serious business, and we would like to say something on that point. First of all, we were not attempting to prove that slaveholding was "just another business"—that explication has nothing to do with our thesis, and is itself untrue. We were looking for evidence on profits, because their alleged absence has been offered as a reason why the American Civil War was unnecessary. We believe that we did find evidence of competitive profit rates in slavery and concluded, first, that they were an additional and significant reason, along with any possible Southern quixoticism and Gothic imagination, to explain the South's willingness to fight; and second that those profits could have provided the capital for further growth.

Having read our Schumpeter, too, we are prepared to wear the Marxist shoe, if it fits. But we reserve the right to reject the vulgar model, on grounds of taste. Let us see if we can outline a Marxist interpretation of history that will admit the relevance of our capital model. We shall borrow liberally, but not slavishly, from Maurice Merleau-Ponty.[1] Discussions of Marxism and historical determinism have often been conducted as if causality implied that each event had to have a linear relationship with another event, about which it could then be determined whether it was "economic" or "ideological," or even *simply* economic or ideological. Marxism, or economic explanation, is then thought to be vanquished when one can point to "ideological" causes. But neither materialistic history nor econometric history is more abstract than idealistic history or spiritualistic history. At the heart of the Marxist interpretation is the idea that nothing can be isolated in the total context of history, but also that because of their greater generality economic phenomena

[1]Maurice Merleau-Ponty. *Sense and Non-Sense.* Translated by H. L. and P. A. Dreyfus. (Evanston, Ill.: Northwestern University Press, 1964), chs. viii, ix.

make a greater contribution to historical discourse. Now, to recognize that the economic phenomena do not explain everything is not the same as to relegate the production of material conditions to the outbuildings of history. We don't believe that slaves were simply or merely capital, or that the southern gentleman was simply or merely *homo faber,* but that does not make a capital model irrelevant or a precise limitation of the opportunity costs of the enterprise a waste of time, nor does it render the capitalization of an income stream from slaves a figment or a fiction. History passes through *homo faber,* and the production of material conditions, the production and transformation of laws, customs, beliefs, styles of civilization, even the content of consciousness—all these are mutually penetrating and fully reciprocal.

Let us quote from the last paragraph of our conclusion, before going on to consider the *sufficiency* of our model:

> Although profitability cannot be offered as a sufficient guarantee of the continuity of southern slavery, the converse argument that slavery must have destroyed itself can no longer rest upon allegations of unprofitability or upon assumptions about the impossibility of maintaining and allocating a slave labor force. To the extent, moreover, that profitability is a necessary condition for the continuation of a private business institution in a free-enterprise society, slavery was not untenable in the ante-bellum American South.

In this last part, now, we well be less polemical. The arguments of Genovese, Dowd, and many before them, have linked Southern slavery directly to Southern stagnation. In Genovese's words:

> Even if it could be established that plantation profit levels did stay high and that long-range prospects looked good, it would not follow that capital was being accumulated in a manner guaranteeing a politically viable economic development.

Frankly, we never had a model sufficient to deal with this question. About the best we can do on this matter is to define the problem in terms of some recent work on agrarian reform and Southern development.

There are two essential points that are frequently overlooked when the discussion settles down to Southern backwardness. To begin, the ante-bellum Southern economy was not stagnant. North,

Easterlin, Williamson, and Nicholls have all demonstrated that the prosperity of the plantation economy was real, that income grew as rapidly in the prewar South as in the rest of the nation, and that cotton was the most important influence in the ante-bellum growth of the economy. Apparently, though, retardation did occur in the rate of Southern economic growth in the period between 1860 and approximately 1880. As Engerman has pointed out, it was 1890 before the South again achieved the per capita income levels enjoyed in 1860. In very large measure both the absolute and relative failure of the South to achieve standards of economic welfare comparable to the rest of the country can be attributed to the losses or the growth not achieved in the two decades of the 1860's and the 1870's. Stanley Engerman and Louis Rose have examined the devastation and capital losses due to the war and the emancipation, and William Nicholls has discussed with deep insight how in the postwar period agrarian values persisted, then rigidified, and finally corrupted the southern social structure to the point where tradition hardened into a dense barrier against further progress.

Perhaps the most important single illustration of the war's disruptive impact is to be found in the pattern of British cotton imports during the second half of the nineteenth century. Statistics on these are shown in Table 1. Quite noticeably, a sharp rise in world prices for cotton in the early 1860's elicited a rather rapid increase in the supply of cotton from areas outside the American South. In particular, an almost fourfold increase occurred in the average level of East Indian cotton exports to Britain between 1860 and 1865. By contrast, almost fifteen years were required to displace this new cotton from the British market after the war terminated; it was not until the 1880's that the South had regained its absolute and relative prewar position in the British markets once more. Displacement from conventional market outlets would, of course, have retarded southern development during the 1860's and 1870's even without any war-induced physical destruction.

The timing of southern economic retardation also seems important. If most southern underdevelopment is attributable to only two decades of stagnation, difficulty resides with any insistence that it was slavery or some southern slave-induced mentality that lies at the root of southern economic problems. Such an argument is confronted with the difficulty of explaining why these problems should have been particularly pronounced or observable only during two decades. Why was Southern growth not retarded during the

Table 1 Prices and Quantities of British Cotton Imports, 1850 to 1889

| Year or Decade | Imports by Origin (in thousands of bales per year) | | | | | | Average Prices by Types | | |
	Ameri-can	Brazil-ian	Egyp-tian	Peru-vian	East Indian	Total	Ameri-can	Brazil-ian	East Indian
1850's	1,638	132	103	9	406	2,288	$5^{11}/_{16}$	$7^7/_{16}$	$4^5/_8$
1860	2,581	103	109	10	563	3,366	$6^1/_4$	$8^3/_{16}$	5
1861	1,841	100	98	10	987	3,036	$8^9/_{16}$	$9^3/_4$	$6^5/_{16}$
1862	72	134	147	20	1,072	1,445	$17^1/_4$	$18^1/_8$	$12^7/_8$
1863	132	138	248	23	1,391	1,932	$23^1/_4$	$24^1/_4$	$19^1/_4$
1864	198	212	319	60	1,798	1,587	$27^1/_2$	$28^3/_4$	$21^1/_2$
1865	462	340	414	131	1,408	2,755	19	$19^1/_4$	$14^1/_2$
1866	1,163	407	200	112	1,867	3,749	$15^1/_2$	$17^1/_8$	12
1867	1,226	437	198	129	1,511	3,501	$10^7/_8$	$11^5/_8$	$8^3/_4$
1868	1,269	637	201	101	1,452	3,660	$10^1/_2$	$11^5/_8$	$8^1/_2$
1969	1,040	514	226	106	1,496	3,382	$12^1/_8$	$12^1/_2$	$9^3/_4$
1870's	1,977	388	277	102	899	3,643	$7^7/_8$	$8^3/_8$	$5^3/_4$
1880's	2,755	246	260	57	631	3,949	$5^{15}/_{16}$	$6^1/_8$	$4^1/_8$

Note: Taken from the *Cotton Trade of the United States* as in turn derived from the Senate Report on Cotton Production and Consumption, Fifty-third Congress, third session, Report 986.

height of the slaveholding period or just before the Civil War? Or why did slavery-induced mental attitudes not prove such a hindrance after 1880? By contrast, hypotheses that emphasize war dislocations and destruction are completely consistent with retardation's being restricted to the war period and its immediate aftermath.

Economic considerations or (if you wish) profit-seeking are also quite sufficient to explain the South's concentration upon agricultural development. The South seemed fully capable of developing manufacturing capacity when technological or economic circumstances made such a course attractive, as in the pre-Civil War period and subsequently around the turn of the century. When steam-powered textile mills became possible or more economical than water-powered mills, the locus of the textile industry slowly but surely shifted from New England to the South, eventually resulting in the substantial post-World War II trauma of New England textile mill towns.

In short, the South was not an isolated, self-contained economy. It is a gross exaggeration to talk about the ante-bellum Southern states as a colonial or tributary economy, locked into dependence upon the North. The terms of trade with England, as well as with New England, were excellent, and the South was well represented in the national government.

Of course, agricultural development, whether a "prerequisite" for industrialization or not, might hold back the initial growth of the industrial sector, especially if agriculture is stuck in a traditional and static position. In that case, agrarian reform is apparently the prerequisite. Alexander Gerschenkron identifies two aspects of this reform:

> . . . it is supposed to increase the productivity of agriculture so that its growing produce will allow shifts of population out of agricultural areas and will support the increasing numbers of men engaged in non-agricultural pursuits. . . . it is supposed to eliminate the traditional restraints on the mobility of the agrarian population and its freedom to exercise a free choice of occupation.

Now, some increase in productivity in the ante-bellum cotton culture can be easily demonstrated, but there is a distinguished chorus to remind us that having once revived the almost moribund institution of slavery as an answer to labor shortage, the South stopped where it was, eagerly abetted in this tendency by its machines—the slaves. Abolition, then, was apparently necessary as the first item on the reform agenda, though the postwar experience must make us question whether it could lead to an essentially different system of cultivation. In the American South it is not obvious that the problem was ever one of moving from a communal to an individualistic system of production.

With regard to eliminating traditional restraints on mobility, obviously the slave population was without free choice of occupation. But, given the market conditions for cotton, and the ease with which market incentives drew production to the fertile western lands, it is not clear exactly what increased mobility might have accomplished for Southern agricultural development in the prewar period.

Indeed, let us speculate that the crucial moment for agrarian reorganization and the formation of prerequisites came not in 1860, in the United States, but in the last decade of the eighteenth century. At that point southern agriculture had recovered effectively and rapidly from the Revolutionary War. Then, in 1794, there came the gin and forty-cent cotton. Some kind of structural response was called for, especially in the face of an impending labor shortage. Two alternatives seem plausible: (1) a thoroughgoing agrarian reform to freehold, individualist cultivation, as in the northern cereal lands; or (2) the extension of slavery and the evolution of the slave market to facilitate the movement of productive resources to the West. The actual choice that was made does not seem to have been necessarily eccentric or irrational. Certainly that was not the moment at which agrarianism became stagnant, rigid, and inimical to development in the South. Instead of searching, fruitlessly, for the signs of morbidity which were supposed to lead inexorably to a "genuine" agrarian reform, we can observe that slavery was profitable, indeed viable, and that the moral conflict, instead of appearing to be an avoidable blunder, takes on real meaning. What remains is the devastation of the War years, and the failure of the thoroughgoing reform to take hold. There is still much to be explained, and it may be at this point, where the institutions are less boldly outlined, that the social history is most sorely needed.

DOUGLAS F. DOWD
Slavery as an Obstacle to Economic Growth in the United States: a Comment

Revised interpretations of the course of economic development in the South called for revised interpretations of the economic significance of slavery. But did they require abandonment of the view that a society based on slavery was incapable of sustained economic development? By no means, claimed Douglas Dowd. Economic development means more than maintaining a certain rate of growth of income per head; it implies qualitative as well as quantitative change—change, that is to

From *The Journal of Economic History,* Volume XXVII, Number 4 (December, 1967), pages 531-538. Copyright © 1967 by The Economic History Association. Reprinted by permission of the author and the Business Manager.

say, in the structure of the economy and, at one remove, in the values and structure of the society. A society whose whole efforts were compulsively devoted to maintaining, justifying, and defending domination of the black man by the white was not capable of this kind of development. To prove the contrary surely required more than a demonstration that prewar growth rates had attained a certain height, reinforced by references to war destruction and East Indian cotton. Readjustment after the Civil War to a legally emancipated labor force and to foreign competition in cotton called for structural changes in Southern society, and these were not forthcoming. The economic effects of slavery were evident not in the high growth rates of the prewar years—easily explained in terms of the economic circumstances of the period—but in the inability of the South to restructure its economy and society after the war. And why this inability? Because in essence, despite emancipation, Civil War, and Reconstruction, social, political, and economic power in the South was still held by the group that had created slavery and fought to maintain it. If such a society is to develop, says Dowd, the distribution of power has to be changed; that is to say, the possessors of power have to be changed.

Along lines like these, in the 1967 debate, Douglas Dowd argued in vigorous defense of the same philosophy of history as had inspired his remarks ten years earlier. It is clear that he intended his remarks to be as applicable to the problems of our world today as to the interpretation of Southern history. Must a philosophy of history such as his necessarily find itself set in opposition to the work of the statisticians and the new economic historians? Or was this an accidental result, and perhaps a regrettable one, of the way in which this particular controversy had developed?

WHETHER in the slavery or the new economic history controversies of the past decade, one moves to a feeling that the participants are often talking past one another, talking to themselves and to what may loosely be thought of as their respective adherents. The new economic historians, it may be said, put one in mind of rather light-hearted evangelists; while those who dissent from their innovations seem, by comparison, stuffy, old-fashioned, fearful of the new truths, perhaps of truth itself.

As is well-known, when controversies take on such characteristics, it is because procedures and conclusions, rather than assumptions and aims form the stuff of the controversy. Only apparently are the discussions concerned, then, with the same subject matter, for the parameters are different, and they are different because—quite appropriately for both parties—the purposes are different. The slavery controversy provides a useful basis for an exploration of this question, not least because it came as the opening gun of the new economic history, a decade ago, when Messrs. Conrad and Meyer presented their twin papers on methodology and on slavery to the joint EHA-NBER meetings and I served as a critic.

Then, as still today, I puzzled over what Conrad and Meyer were trying to show. If they were attempting to demonstrate that Ulrich B. Phillips (in his *American Negro Slavery, inter alia*) was wrong, there was much more than profitability of slavery on which to focus, for by the time they wrote Phillips had been quite thoroughly discredited on both narrow and broad questions, perhaps most completely by Kenneth Stampp (in his *Peculiar Institution*). I had thought, by then, that contemporary historians had come to view Phillips and his works more as sociological than as historical materials; documents, almost, revealing how a partisan of the Lost Cause viewed the evolution of that society. And was it not generally accepted by students of the South that writers like Phillips took the position that slavery was unprofitable because to do otherwise would muddy the more fundamental justifications for the system?

There is often something to be said for precise refutations of mistaken notions, to be sure. But what can be said that is positive diminishes to the degree that a general analysis would do. It is of course reasonably obvious that in any functioning social system, slave or otherwise, there will be incomes that are high at the top and decrease as one moves to the bottom of the social scale; and that power will be roughly proportionate to income and wealth. What is less obvious are the costs of a given system—costs in terms of alternatives foregone, as well as the social and human costs of the existent reality.

For the American South, it surely was good business sense that led planters to emphasize cotton cultivation, slaveholding, and slavebreeding; and good business sense was also good economic sense, if the short run and the interests of those in power are taken as guiding criteria. But when we speak of economic development it is not business sense or economic sense for the short run as viewed by those in power that are, or should be, taken as the appropriate referents for judgment; for then we are speaking not only of structural realities and changes in the economy, but also of far-reaching social and political structures and changes.

As I said a decade ago, one cannot evaluate the meaning of

slavery as though it were merely one kind of a labor force rather than another, *ceteris paribus.* Slavery normally implies and requires, and especially in the United States implied and required, a slavery-dominated society as much as a society dominating slaves. In turn, this meant that whatever business considerations might support the continuation of the slave-cum-cotton system, these were immeasurably reinforced by the social and political imperatives—ever more on the defensive in the ante-bellum South—of maintaining a slave society. Is this not made more evident when we examine the post-Civil War development of the South?

I should have thought it would be unnecessary to raise these questions once more, except that here we are meeting again on the subject; and, more vividly, we are aware of new work tending to move in the same directions as the earlier work of Conrad and Meyer. I have been away from the United States for a year, having just returned a week ago. Consequently, I have been unable to read Stanley Engerman's latest contributions on the South, slavery, and the Civil War. But may I not assume that Robert Fogel represented Mr. Engerman accurately in his article[1] on the new economic history? There it is said:

> The retarded development of the South during the last third of the nineteenth century and the first half of the twentieth was due not to stagnation during the slave era, but to the devastation caused by the Civil War. As Stanley Engerman points out, if *ante-bellum* growth-rates had continued through the war decade, southern *per capita* income would have been twice the level that actually prevailed in 1870. So disruptive was the war that it took the South some thirty years to regain the *per capita* income of 1860 and another sixty years to reach the same relative position in national *per capita* income that it enjoyed at the close of the *ante-bellum* era. The case for the abolition of slavery thus appears to turn on issues of morality and equity rather than on the inability of a slave system to yield a high rate of economic growth (p. 647).

In a paper delivered to this Association in 1956, in which I attempted to explain the late nineteenth- and early twentieth-century retardation of the southern economy, I did not say, nor do I

[1]Robert W. Fogel, "The New Economic History: Its Findings and Methods," *Economic History Review, XIX* (Dec. 1966), 642-56.

recall anyone else having said, that southern stagnation was due to "stagnation during the slave era." But I do recall arguing that it was the consequence of slave society, in all its ramifications, that explains that stagnation. To reopen that argument here and now would be impossible, as well as unrewarding, just as it would be impossible to come to grips even partially with all the questions that arise from the works of Messrs. Conrad, Meyer, Fogel, Engerman, and others now cultivating the new vineyards. But perhaps our brief excursion can provide a basis for fruitful discussions in the meeting today.

Perhaps I am mistaken, but I believe I am correct in seeing the new economic history as an attempt to incorporate the methodology of neoclassical economics and the procedures of econometrics with the materials and the questions of economic history—with the added notion that economic history will thereby be strengthened, made more scientific. In its essence this entails the central use of partial equilibrium analysis. Such an approach may or may not be appropriate for the analysis of questions of narrow focus and very short time periods, where the pound of *ceteris paribus* can serve as a temporary safe haven for "other things." Can it do so when we concern ourselves with changes taking a long period, and that neither begin nor end with economic, let alone quantitative, matters?

It was of utmost significance that slavery in the United States could not be maintained without vitally affecting "all other things," whether that slavery was profitable or not. As Stanley M. Elkins has so capably shown in his *Slavery,*[2] American Negro slavery was the very "worst" the world had known, in its nature and in its consequences, whether it be compared with ancient or contemporaneous slavery (in, for example, Brazil or the Caribbean). What does "worst" signify in this context, and why should it have been so? Slaves have always and everywhere been cruelly treated (and always with exceptions), and black slaves especially. Even so, their treatment, their rights (or total lack of rights), their "family" lives, the depths to which racism sank, the manner in which the present and long-distant future of black slaves (even, as we know, their past) was distorted and doomed—in social, psychological, political, and of course economic terms—in the United States reached the lowest of depths. Why should this be so, in the land of the free and the home of the brave? Was not economic individualism adhered to in the

[2]Stanley M. Elkins, *Slavery* (New York: Grosset and Dunlap, 1963).

South? It surely was, extending even to trafficking in human beings as commodities. Did not the Enlightenment, did not Christianity, extend into the American South? Most assuredly, but as with economic individualism, certain exotic notions had to be grafted onto otherwise healthy plants. To achieve such exoticism took a mighty effort, an effort that became obsessive, compulsive, and sickening not just to those who lived under the system, but also to those who lived from it and with it and for it.

Which brings me to the postwar period, if a bit abruptly, with Mr. Engerman's contributions in mind. Without asking how *ante-bellum* growth rates could have continued indefinitely; without asking, that is, how the South could have maintained its power in the nation while it also maintained slavery (with or without westward expansion); without asking whether or not there was some determining relationship between the Civil War and the socioeconomic system of the South and its power struggle with the North; without asking any of these questions, let us point to some questions that relate growth to development, and war destruction to growth and development.

Keeping in mind the well-recognized distinctions between growth and development, between quantitative and qualitative change (and keeping in mind, too, their connections), let us examine the notion of *"ante-bellum* growth rates continuing through the war decade" and even more, beyond that time. By 1860, the South showed few significant signs of moving away from its dependence on slaves and cotton. The signs that such a concentration might be something less than promising had begun to appear already during the Civil War; but what were then mere whispers turned into a roar in the years after 1870. Were the falling cotton prices (among other prices) in the last quarter of the century a function largely, if at all, of the Civil War? Is there any reasonable basis to assume either (1) that slave-breeding would have maintained the supply of slaves within economically viable magnitudes, or (2) that political realities would have allowed the reopening of the external trade? Has anyone specified how the maintenance of slavery (and the power of those who would so maintain it) in the United States in the late nineteenth century might be made compatible with economic development? Or how its forceful abolition (apart from the Civil War) would have been accomplished? Or its peaceful abolition, by those squarely dependent upon it? Is there any ground for believing that the kinds of structural (economic, political, social) changes that are implied by economic development would have ensued in a South whose economy could no longer "thrive" on the basis of agriculture (for the majority of either its white or its black population)? And, given that the slaves were in fact (legally) emancipated, how does one explain the persistence of all the essential qualities of *ante-bellum* southern society in *post-bellum* southern society, down to the very recent past? Civil war damage? But is it not difficult to believe that for eighty years the southern economy was retarded by war destruction, in the light of what we have seen of so many other war-damaged economies in our own lives? Can the answers to any of these questions be turned to the advantage of the relevant conclusions of the new economic history? Or to its procedures? Can we learn nothing about our own economic development from our studies of the complex interrelationships of development (or its lack) in the contemporary underdeveloped world?

Furthermore, and in a different vein: What is the point of the analyses that have occupied these studies? "The case for the abolition of slavery" *of course* "turns on issues of morality and equity rather than on the inability of a slave system to yield a high rate of economic growth." To state otherwise would be to say, one presumes, that an economically viable slave system is to be recommended to . . . whom? The underdeveloped countries? Of course not, and the sneers of the new economic historians to such a query are appropriate. But then what is the point? If students of the South had earlier believed the system was profitable, what then, besides elegance, was the point of going on? Or did we have to be told, once more, that the Civil War was terribly destructive? Are we going back to Ranke, "simply" recording the facts, with technical trimmings? Or are there more vital tasks facing social scientists today; more vital, more demanding, more promising?

Of course slavery was profitable. And of course imperialism has been profitable. And of course the status quo in today's underdeveloped countries is profitable. Profitable, in all cases, to investors, whose definitions of profit do not go beyond the balance sheet and the income statement, and whose definitions of propriety are quite identical with their definitions of property. And of course slavery damaged both whites and blacks in the long run (and most, also, in the short run). And imperialism damages most citizens of both metropolis and colony, in the long run; and similarly with underdevelopment. Nor is it difficult to show that the damage that accrues from such systems is not solely, or mostly, economic; it is social, psychological, political, cultural. As it is also true that economic development both requires and brings about social, political, psychological, and cultural changes.

We are concerned in these meetings with obstacles to economic development, a focus that requires us to look at reality. That is a considerable improvement over the earlier inclinations of economists to develop and to use abstract models that, if they had any application at all, were relevant only to highly industrialized, political stable societies, operating within basically capitalist institutions. But improvements do not constitute sufficiencies; and especially they do not if their effect is to fragmentize an area of inquiry that requires broadening, deepening, and an enhanced sense of relevance.

Because in practice the meaning of economic development extends out and down so broadly and deeply, the analysis of development, not to say its implementation, must be as broad and as deep. This is to say that "experts" in economic development must take on the staggering task of attempting to understand the functioning of *societies,* and the manner in which *social* change takes place. One of my criticisms of the new economic history, and not only in its manifestations as regards the South, is that its methods, its thrust, are in exactly the opposite direction from that so desperately needed in the field today. Market relationships (for capital, commodities, labor) are indeed central to the functioning of an economy, as the heart is to the body. But the heart functions in relationship with a nervous system, and a circulatory system, and, among other things, in an environment. If the problem is a heart murmur, perhaps—no more than perhaps—total concentration on the heart itself will do. But those who will understand a cardiac condition, and prescribe for it, require themselves to understand the body in all its essential functions and charactertistics. The lack of economic development is a problem in today's world that does not fall within the purview of the man who thinks in terms of heart murmurs. And the South had a cardiac condition in the nineteenth century.

To say that slavery was profitable and yet it inhibited economic development is not to say that slavery but that slave society in the United States in the nineteenth century, during and after its existence, inhibited economic development. But this is to say something else: Both before and after emancipation, social, economic, and political power in the South was held by those who had helped to create, and fought to maintain, slavery; nor was there a lack of interested parties in the North either before or after the War. For the

South to develop economically, it was essential—and it is essential—either for a social upheaval within the South to take place, and/or for steady pressures, positive and negative, to be introduced from "outside." Power—its sources and its uses—has to be changed; that is, its possessors have to be changed.

What is true for the South is true for other societies that would develop. To detail such changes, let alone to understand, advocate, and support them, on a country-by-country basis is not only to move out from partial equilibrium analysis, but to move into the swirl and turbulence that characterize the world. And that suggests the stance of the committed and concerned social scientist—distasteful though such an idea is to our profession—more than that of the cheerful and comfortable economist.

STANLEY L. ENGERMAN
The Effects of Slavery upon the Southern Economy: A Review of the Recent Debate

The name of Stanley Engerman, of the University of Rochester, has already appeared in this volume in connection with the reinterpretations of Southern economic development called for by the Gallman-Easterlin findings on national income and its regional distribution. The selection which follows contains Engerman's calculations of Southern growth rates before the Civil War, as well as an extensive and thorough review of the controversy over the economics of slavery, paralleling and contrasting with the review by Harold Woodman with which these readings began. Published late in 1967, the article had been circulated earlier among interested scholars in provisional form.

The interest and utility of Engerman's article for those who lack the time or patience to read the contributions to the debate in the original, or the sophistication in economics necessary for them to find their way

From *Explorations in Entrepreneurial History* (second series), Volume 4, Number 2 (winter, 1967), pages 71-97. Copyright 1967 by the Graduate Program in Economic History, The University of Wisconsin. Reprinted by permission of the author and the editor.

through the tangled underbrush of controversy, are so obvious as to require little comment. But it is not for these reasons that it is included here. What Engerman offers is not merely a summary of past arguments but also an analysis of what have emerged as the central issues, an appraisal of what has been tentatively settled and what has not, and a program of research for the future. Its principal value lies in its perspective—the perspective of an economic historian of the new school, concerned to evaluate where our work has taken us and where we go next.

With this in mind, you should be alert, in reading the article, to the points at which Engerman's dissatisfaction with the present state of knowledge clearly emerges. Sometimes this dissatisfaction focuses on the use that has been made of statistical averages—estimates justifiable as first approximations or as indications of a central tendency, but likely to obscure significant variations among different regions or sub-periods. Measures of profitability are sensitive to the particular years chosen for averaging. Prices of cotton fluctuated widely from year to year; so did crop yields. In the same way, prices for slaves were not uniform throughout the South, and the use of an average price for the whole region can lead to significant distortion. Our knowledge of slave productivity is imperfect; the possibility of a significant trend over time, and of significant variation among regions, cannot be overlooked. What Engerman is calling for here is more of the dirty work of economic history—the patient scanning of census returns and plantation records, work which quickly burns up enthusiasm and energy but without which, after a certain stage has been reached, no further progress is possible.

But Engerman's prescription for further progress involves more than a retreat to the archives. He calls also for clearer thinking and better analysis. As an example, note his succinct statement of what the various estimates of the rate of return on slave ownership proved *beyond* the fact that this investment paid as well as any available alternatives. The fact that ownership of slaves brought prestige and status does not have to be introduced to explain why slaves brought the prices they did. Field productivity alone in the case of male slaves, and field productivity plus the value of children in the case of females, provides sufficient explanation. This is true, furthermore, regardless of how inefficient slave labor was relative to free labor: planters who used slaves profited from their use. Investments in slaves were not sub-marginal, undertaken for purposes of prestige or social obligation: most planters made profits. And note too how the point of the profitability controversy looks subtly different when Engerman trans-lates its findings into a generalization about the efficiency of slave markets: supply and demand in Southern markets set the price of slaves at a figure which yielded the market rate of return to the purchaser.

Engerman adds an interesting corollary: the rate of return on slaves to the Southern economy exceeded the rate of return to the individual planter, since the latter was based on the market price of slaves, the former on rearing costs. As Yasuba emphasized, these were not the same. In addition, slaves satisfied a demand for prestige and conspic-uous consumption on the part of their owners; these consumer services were obtained essentially free, since the general level of slave prices was determined by their field productivity.

Where Engerman breaks new ground in this article is in his cal-culation of per capita income and rates of economic growth in the South. The estimates of relative *rates* of growth are cited frequently. Less attention is usually paid to the income *levels* estimated for 1840 and 1860 on which the growth calculations are based. Worth noting, for example, is the degree to which the high level of average per capita income in the South in 1860 (whether or not slaves are counted as consumers) depended on the very high level in the West South Central region. It is this high level in 1860, of course, that tilts the trend line to produce the high rate of growth. The significance of the westward movement of the slave-cotton frontier into Texas (and of Engerman's inclusion in the regional averages of an 1840 estimate for Texas, which had not been included in Easterlin's original calculations) needs no additional emphasis. If we were to exclude the West South Central region and count slaves as consumers, the level of per capita income in the South in 1860 would be less than half that in the Northeast (which includes, in these estimates, Delaware and Maryland), and slightly below the North Central region. Furthermore, as Engerman points out, the rate of growth in each component region of the South between 1840 and 1860 is below the national average; it is the increasing weight of the West South Central region in the aggregate, as population moved westward, that raises the rate for the South as a whole above the national rate. These considerations make it clear why continued territorial expansion was so important for the South. They also help clarify the economic importance of such earlier steps in the creation of the American continental empire as the Louisiana Purchase and the Mexican War, normally highlighted in history books for their constitutional and military interest.

What remains to be done? The refinement of existing statistical estimates, of course; but also, Engerman argues, the measurement of quantities and statistical distributions of which we at present know little. It is ironic to consider what a key role beliefs about these statistics have played and must play in any discussion of the economic effects of slavery, despite the fact that the underlying calculations have never been made. Lack of evidence has clearly been no bar to speculation. How, for example, can we say anything sensible about the effects of slavery and cotton on capital accumulation until we know something about Southern income distribution? Engerman's admittedly crude estimate suggests that it was no more skewed in the antebellum South than it was in the United States as a whole in 1929. And even if Southern income distribution was badly skewed, that does not by any means imply a low savings rate, any more than does the lavish scale of living conventionally associated with planter status. Most of the explanations for slow Southern industrialization, in fact, either rest upon highly dubious chains of reasoning or require, to be acceptable, statistical confirmation that is at present not possible.

The basic generalization from which all theorizing on the subject must start is that slave-based cotton production in the antebellum South paid well. To say that, nevertheless, the South *should* have tried deliberate industrialization is to place more confidence in twentieth-century strategies for economic development than they should properly be asked to bear. Given the world demand for cotton, the nature of the human and natural resources of the South, and the rate of growth of incomes actually achieved, confident assertions that the South was following the wrong strategy of growth sound like the worst kind of Monday-morning quarterbacking. If indeed the South was following the "wrong" strategy, the reasons are to be found in the fact that this strategy led to civil war and to the crystallization of a type of social system in the South that made structural change after the Civil War very difficult. Black slavery was of course fundamental to both of these reasons.

The tone of Engerman's article is not that of a man who regards the controversy as essentially settled. There is a strong suggestion, indeed, that in his view the really difficult questions have hardly yet been asked, far less tackled as problems for research. If so, the new economic history is hardly likely to leave them in that virgin state for long. Predictions are hazardous, but it begins to look as if we are on the eve of a major reinterpretation of the economic history of the antebellum South—and, for that matter, of the nation as a whole before 1860.

Revised calculations of the rate of return on capital in the cotton economy will probably yield figures higher than the original Conrad and Meyer estimates, reinforcing belief that incomes generated in this sector had a catalytic effect elsewhere in the economy. Research on interregional trade flows and on Southern food output has already led to substantial revisions in the older view of the South as a food-deficit region. Despite criticisms, North's view of cotton exports as the major dynamic factor in pre-1860 *national* economic development still carries conviction. What is in the offing is a vastly changed interpretation of the ways in which the South, the North, and the West were economically integrated before the Civil War, and specifically of the ways in which the economic fortunes of the rest of the nation depended, despite political repugnance and moralistic opprobrium, upon the institution of slavery and the incomes generated by slave-labor cotton production.

THE ECONOMIC EFFECTS of slavery have long been a subject of great interest.[1] Hotly debated in the antebellum period, the question has been discussed extensively by historians ever since. Over the years there emerged among historians a general consensus which held that slavery not only prevented the economic development of the South, but that by 1860 it had become unprofitable to the slaveholders. Consequently the slave system was economically decadent before the onset of the Civil War. The chief architects of this interpretation were Ulrich B. Phillips and Charles W. Ramsdell. Although challenged by several writers in the 1930's and 1940's, the Phillips-Ramsdell position continued to be dominant until the late 1950's. However, during the past decade a series of attacks on the views of Phillips, Ramsdell, and their main supporters has substantially modified the old consensus.

In this critical review of the long debate on the economics of slavery I shall discuss both the basic arguments of the Phillips-Ramsdell view and the recent attacks on it. It will be important to

The author is indebted to Robert Fogel, Robert Gallman, Sherwin Rosen, and Edward Zabel for comments and suggestions. Several parts of this article have been extended in "The Economics of Slavery", co-authored with Robert W. Fogel, which appear in Robert W. Fogel and Stanley L. Engerman (editors), THE REINTER-PRETATION OF AMERICAN ECONOMIC HISTORY, to be published by Harper and Row.

[1]For another critical review of the debate, from a different perspective, see Harold D. Woodman, "The Profitability of Slavery: A Historical Perennial," *Journal of Southern History,* 29:303-325 (August, 1963).

distinguish three related but different issues often confused in the debate. These are:

1. The profitability of slavery to the individual slave-owner.
2. The viability of slavery as an economic system.[2]
3. The effects of the slave system on the economic development of the South.

The answers to these questions do not necessarily fall into a simple pattern; a positive answer to any one does not imply the answer to the others. Much disagreement in the literature can be traced to the failure to recognize the differences among these questions.

I. THE PHILLIPS-RAMSDELL POSITION

Historical work on the slavery question has been dominated by the writings of Ulrich B. Phillips.[3] Phillips discussed almost all the economic aspects of slavery and much of the subsequent debate has been within the framework which he set forth. Phillips' study led him to conclude that slavery was economically unprofitable to the planter, was undoubtedly moribund on the eve of the Civil War, and that it was the crucial factor in the presumed retarded development of the southern economy. Phillips granted that his conclusions were not always true, since slavery had been established and initially expanded "because the white people were seeking their own welfare and comfort." However, he argued, "in the long run [private gain and public safety] were attained at the expense of private and public wealth and of progress."[4]

Central to this position was his view that the Negro slave was an

---

[2]Viability is defined as the ability of an industry to continue existing. In economic terms an industry would be considered viable if a market rate of return could be made on the replacement cost of capital used. In the case of slavery the test for viability is the equating of the present value of the future stream of income from slaves with the costs of rearing them. If the present value, computed on the basis of the market rate of interest, was less than the present value of rearing costs, slavery would have been economically unviable—there would have been no incentive for anyone to raise slaves.

[3]The most pertinent of these are: "The Economic Cost of Slave-holding in the Cotton Belt," *Political Science Quarterly*, 20:257-275 (June, 1905); and *American Negro Slavery* (New York, 1918).

[4]Phillips, "Economic Cost," p. 259.

innately ignorant savage and an inefficient worker who could handle only simple tasks and who required constant control. To use such crude labor the plantation system, which provided the necessary supervision, was essential. Therefore, the slave system and the plantation system became identical in the South.

In an early article, Phillips presented his basic arguments for the conclusion that slavery had become unprofitable and moribund by the time of the Civil War.[5] His major piece of evidence was a comparison of the ratio between the price per pound of cotton and the price of male field hands. Observing a ten- to twelve-fold increase in the ratio of slave prices to cotton prices between 1800 and 1860, he stated (without supporting evidence) that such an increase was much too great to be explained by increased slave productivity. He went on to point out that the cost of using slave labor included: "expense of food, clothing and shelter"; interest on the capital invested in the slave; economic insurance against death, illness or escape; the "wear and tear" of years; and taxation on the capitalized value of the slave. While no conclusions were drawn concerning the sum of these costs, in context they seem clearly designed to buttress the argument of unprofitability. Phillips noted that account should have been taken of the market value of offspring, but he claimed this was offset by the cost of supporting the aged. The existence of high and rising slave prices he attributed to overspeculation—"an irresistible tendency to overvalue and overcapitalize slave labor."

Phillips stated that another important factor in bidding up the price of slaves was economies of scale in cotton production. This, he contended, would explain in part the high and rising slave prices since a price in excess of the value of each particular slave would be paid. It also explained why larger plantations expanded relative to smaller holdings, and how these larger plantations could have shown profits while losses were widespread. For this reason, according to Phillips, all funds that the planter could earn or borrow went to purchase slaves, "not into modern implements or land improvements."[6]

[5] *Ibid., passim.*

[6] *Ibid.,* p. 272. The question of economies of scale in cotton production is one of the key questions concerning the plantation which remain to be answered. The primary evidence for increasing returns to scale is the increased plantation size and concentration of holdings in larger plantations before 1860. See Lewis Cecil Gray, *History of Agriculture in the Southern United States to 1860* (2 vols., Washington,

The existence of a demand for slaves for purposes of prestige and conspicuous consumption was also mentioned as a cause of high slave prices. Implicit is the statement that only part of the slave's price was based upon the value of production, the remainder representing a form of consumption expenditure by the owners of slaves.[7] If this were true, slavery could be viable even if it were an unprofitable investment as measured by the return from business operations alone. The large extent of the prestige demand, however, was considered an important element in explaining the low rate of capital formation and economic growth in the southern economy.

Phillips argued that the slave system further retarded southern economic development because "the capitalization of labor and the export of earnings in exchange for more workmen, always of a low degree of efficiency," deprived the southern economy of capital which presumably could have been used for other (industrial) purposes, and made the South a chronic debtor to northern merchants and bankers.[8] Phillips' argument about labor capitalization and export of earnings is rather confusing. He realized that after the closing of the external slave trade in 1808 the export drain went to the Upper South rather than outside the southern states. However, he claimed, "there it did little but demoralize industry and postpone to a later generation the agricultural revival"—but the mechanism explaining this outcome was never clearly stated.[9] The capitalization of the labor force presumably reduced labor elasticity and versatility: "it tended to fix labor rigidly in one line of employment."[10] This

1933), 478-480, 530. William Parker apparently doubts the existence of economies in production attributable to the costs of management and equipment, or at least he doubts that they alone can explain the observed size distribution of plantations. William N. Parker, "The Slave Plantation in American Agriculture," First International Conference of Economic History, *Contributions and Communications* (Paris, 1960), 321-331.

[7]Rising slave prices in this period could be attributed to either increased consumption of prestige by slaveowners or to increased value of slave production in business operations (with the consumption expenditure remaining constant), or to some combination of the two. The observation that the price of slaves fluctuated with the price of cotton does not itself suggest that southerners were behaving to maximize profits from business operations alone. Such variations are consistent with the hypothesis that the expenditure for prestige remained constant.

[8]Phillips, "Economic Cost," p. 275.

[9]*Ibid.*, p.273.

[10]*Idem.* Phillips later argued that the slave system had the advantage of providing for mobility of the labor force (*Slavery*, P. 395). The distinction intended was apparently that between occupational mobility and geographic mobility.

was significant in the South's one-crop economy, particularly since the profitability of cotton production exhibited considerable cyclical variation. However, Phillips was not clearly on the side of those blaming the South's ills on agricultural specialization. At one point he argued that slavery "deprived the South of the natural advantage which the cotton monopoly should have given it."[11]

Given all the adverse effects, why maintain the system? Because it was essential to keep the "savage instincts from breaking forth"—in other words, for race control and protection.[12] Maintaining slavery and letting slaves produce agricultural commodities was, in Phillips' opinion, less expensive than sending slaves back to Africa or supporting the police and army which would have been required if the slaves were freed.

The Phillips position was modified and extended in an influential article by Charles W. Ramsdell, which claimed that while profitable before 1860, slavery had become unprofitable and moribund by that year.[13] Ramsdell held that economic factors would have made slavery unprofitable to the planting class and that slavery would have ended in the late nineteenth century without the Civil War. In his view, the decline of slavery was likely because the planters had reached the end of the land upon which cotton could be grown profitably. Ramsdell suggested that by 1860 the western limits of slavery had been reached in Texas, and no room existed for expansion northward. Geographic containment would have caused a rise in the labor/land ratio and, as a consequence, the slave prices would have fallen until it became too expensive for the owners to maintain their slaves. The end result would have been manumission.

The Ramsdell position—frequently called the natural limits hypothesis—is theoretically plausible, but Ramsdell argued as if there were little room for downward adjustment of slave prices before freedom of the slaves would become an attractive alternative to owners. He also exaggerated the potential pressure on slave prices by ruling out the possibilities that soil in the older areas might be refurbished or that slaves might be profitably employed in other agricultural or non-agricultural pursuits. Nevertheless the natural limits hypothesis has attracted a large number of adherents.

The Phillips position received new support during the 1930's

[11]*Ibid.*, p. 275.

[12]*Ibid.*, p. 259.

[13]Chas. W. Ramsdell, "The Natural Limits of Slavery Expansion," *Mississippi Valley Historical Review,* 16:151-171 (September, 1929).

when several southern historians turned to the records and diaries of individual plantations.[14] Focusing on the profitability of slavery to the planter, they uncovered evidence which appeared to indicate a low rate of return in most of the cases reviewed. Although the accounting techniques used were open to question, and it was never established whether those plantations whose records were used were representative, these studies were used to buttress the Phillips position.

The most recent support for the Phillips conclusion has come from writers who have revived antebellum arguments concerning the effects of slavery upon the course of southern economic development. While generally accepting the profitability of slavery to the planter, they argue that the socio-economic system associated with slavery nevertheless retarded the growth of the overall southern economy. Perhaps the most prominent exponent of this position is Eugene Genovese, who stressed the effects of the slave system upon the size of the internal market in the South.[15] Genovese posited that the skewed income distribution which slavery created made for low demand for domestically manufactured goods within the South; wealthy planters preferred to import goods, slaves had no purchasing power, and low income whites had little market income. This situation contrasted with that of the North and Midwest where a large "middle-class" market was held to have led to the internal development of industry and a more diversified economy. Genovese argued that this restriction of the internal market deprived the South of economies of scale upon which to create an efficient industrial base. The result was a rural, agricultural southern economy dependent upon outsiders for modern industrial goods. An additional effect of the skewed income distribution was that it caused, or at least permitted, conspicuous consumption and lavish living on the part of the rich planters. Consequently savings and capital formation were reduced.

Douglass North has recently put forward the suggestion that the most important effect of slavery upon capital formation was to be

[14]See, in particular:

Ralph Betts Flanders, *Plantation Slavery in Georgia* (Chapel Hill, 1933).

Charles Sacket Sydnor, *Slavery in Mississippi* (New York, 1933).

Charles S. Davis, *The Cotton Kingdom in Alabama* (Montgomery, 1939).

[15]Eugene D. Genovese, "The Significance of the Slave Plantation for Southern Economic Development," *Journal of Southern History,* 28:422-437 (November, 1962). Reprinted in his *The Political Economy of Slavery: Studies in the Economy and Society of the Slave South* (New York, 1965), 157-179.

found in the small amount of investment in human capital in the South.[16] Unlike Phillips, who had earlier make a similar point, North considered the South wasteful of the potential of both white and Negro workers. Phillips had argued that slavery prevented the development of a skilled labor force by discouraging the non-planter whites, but he dismissed the possibility of improving the skills or intelligence of the Negro.

II. THE REVISIONS

The attack on the arguments of Phillips, Ramsdell, and their followers began in the thirties when Lewis Gray and Robert Russel presented strong arguments for the profitability and viability of slavery, although both did consider the South stagnant relative to the rest of the nation.[17] Gray's work was particularly important since it clearly set forth most of the general considerations to be found in the recent discussions of the profitability and viability. However, Gray did conclude that slavery indeed retarded the growth of the southern economy. In the early forties Thomas P. Govan pointed to serious mistakes in several of the studies based on plantation records. He contended that correction of these mistakes led to the conclusion that slavery was profitable.[18] Kenneth Stampp, in his thorough study of slavery (published in 1956), reached the same conclusion as did Govan, and he went on to dismiss most of the arguments which had been used to connect slavery and the backwardness of the southern economy.[19] However, it apparently was not until after the appearance of the widely discussed essay on "The Economics of Slavery in the Antebellum South," by Alfred H. Conrad and John R. Meyer that the old interpretation lost its clearly dominant position.[20]

[16]Douglass C. North, *The Economic Growth of the United States, 1790-1860* (Englewood Cliffs, 1961), 133-134. See also his *Growth and Welfare in the American Past: A New Economic History* (Englewood Cliffs, 1966), 90-97.

[17]Robert R. Russel, "The General Effects of Slavery upon Southern Economic Progress," *Journal of Southern History*, 4:34-54 (February, 1938), and Gray, *op.cit.*, 462-480, 940-942.

[18]Thomas P. Govan, "Was Plantation Slavery Profitable?" *Journal of Southern History*, 8:513-535 (November, 1942).

[19]Kenneth M. Stampp, *The Peculiar Institution: Slavery in the Ante-Bellum South* (New York, 1956), 383-418.

[20]Alfred H. Conrad and John R. Meyer, "The Economics of Slavery in the Ante Bellum South," *Journal of Political Economy*, 66:95-130 (April, 1958). Reprinted in

Profitability to the Planter. As noted above, Phillips' contention that slavery was unprofitable to the planters found support in several studies of plantation records. Recent attacks on these studies have come from two directions. First, the records were found to be incomplete and to contain a crucial conceptual error. Second, economists have applied the traditional tools of economic analysis to test for the profitability of slavery in a manner which removed the reliance upon the fortunes of those particular plantations whose complete records survived. The results of this analysis contradicted the Phillips hypothesis.

It was never clear how much reliance should be placed upon conclusions drawn from the analysis of those few plantations whose records survived. Not all plantations kept records and even fewer were preserved. Special factors could have affected each plantation, but no adjustment can be made without prior knowledge of the biases. It is therefore not certain that the existing sample of plantations is representative. There were long and short cycles in prices and output, regional variation was pronounced, and there were apparently differences based upon size of plantation. Conrad and Meyer did use these records, but they used only certain of the data they contained as sample observations in determining estimates of particular variables. They did not generalize from the profit position of a small number of plantations.

Moreover, the use of plantation records by Phillips and his followers contained several errors, the importance of which were first stressed by Govan, and later reiterated by Stampp. A conceptual error in accounting technique led to an erroneous conclusion. Phillips included interest on the capital invested in slaves and land as costs in his discussion of the expenses of plantation owners. The later accounting studies similarly included the imputed interest on invested capital as a cost to be deducted from revenues in calculating net profits. This net profit figure was then divided by the capital value of the plantation to measure the average rate of return on capital. Since the rate of return computed in this manner was below the rate of return on alternative investments, slavery was considered unprofitable.

Govan and Stampp both pointed out that this was an illegitimate calculation, since it resulted in double-counting the cost of capital.

---

their *The Economics of Slavery and Other Studies in Econometric History* (Chicago, 1964), 43-92.

Net profits are computed by deducting all expenses (including depreciation) from gross revenues. A positive residual includes the imputed return on the capital of the owner, as well as the wages of management and "pure profits." When imputations for capital cost and the wages of management are deducted any positive sum remaining would be "pure profits." The existence of such "pure profits" would indicate that the investment was profitable. There is no need to then compare this with the alternative rate of return, since deducting the imputed capital cost allows for this. The same test could be made by deducting from net profits the imputed wages of management, computing the rate of return upon this investment, and then comparing it with the rate of return upon alternative assets. If the rate of return on the investment exceeds that upon alternative assets, the investment is considered to be profitable. Both methods described provide the same answer; what is shown to be profitable by one computation is profitable under the other. (Accounting and economic approaches differ in the way costs are measured—the accounting calculations using historical costs and the economic current opportunity costs.)[21]

An important omission from plantation income was the capital gain derived from the reproduction of the slave labor force. As long as slave children could be sold or used on the plantation, this was an additional source of income. A capital gain was also to be derived from the increased value of existing slaves. The slaves held in the 1850's were usually purchased in earlier years at below their current market value. Other errors were the exclusion of slave household services and slave land clearing and maintenance services, and the treatment of the personal expenditures of planters as costs rather than as a use of profits. Govan and Stampp argued that correcting the omissions and errors of earlier historians showed that their samples clearly demonstrated high rates of return to slave ownership in the antebellum period.

The path-breaking essay by Conrad and Meyer was more general in scope, based on an economist's as opposed to an accountant's approach to the problem. Rather than confining their attention to measuring the rates of return of particular plantations, they asked whether, on the average, a planter who purchased slaves and land at

---

[21]For a criticism of the accounting calculations, based as they are upon historical

an "average" price for the period (1830-1860) could have expected to make as high a rate of return as if he had invested in some alternative asset. While not arguing that every plantation made money, their important conclusion was that, on the average, profits were to be made from slave ownership.

In their analysis, Conrad and Meyer separated the slave economy into two sectors, and estimated the profitability of slave ownership in each. Male slaves were regarded as capital goods used in the production of marketable output of agricultural staples. Female slaves, however, not only were used to produce staples but also were the source of additional slaves. Thus the female slave could be considered a capital good who produced the capital goods used to produce final output.

By regarding both male and female slaves as capital goods, Conrad and Meyer were able to test for the profitability of slavery by computing the rate of return on the total investment in slaves, including the land and other assets which the slave used. The basic computation involved solving to find that rate of return which equated the cost of obtaining slaves with the net stream of earnings derived from using the slaves. Separate rates of return were computed for male and female slaves.

These calculations involved the estimation of four variables. First, the period over which the stream of earnings was obtained was estimated by using an average life expectancy drawn from mortality tables. Second, the total cost of the investment in the slave and the complementary assets was derived from information on slave prices collected by Phillips, with various sources providing the basic information for other assets. Third, the rates of return from bonds and commercial paper were used to compare with the rate of return on slaves. The fourth variable, the annual value of earnings from the slave's productive activities was computed differently for males and females. For the male, gross earnings were measured by multiplying the estimated quantity of cotton produced per slave by the farm price per pound of cotton. Net earnings were obtained by subtracting the costs of maintaining and supervising the slave from gross earnings. For the female, net earnings depended not only on the value of the cotton she produced but also on the market value of offspring. The computation involved estimates of the expected number of offspring, a deduction for nursery and other costs of effect, all the costs of raising slave children to productive age were charged against the female slaves, and all proceeds from sales were attributed to her.

Conrad and Meyer estimated the rate of return from slave ownership for different types of land using various selling prices of cotton. For the majority of plantations they estimated the return on male slaves to range between 4¹/₂ per cent and 8 per cent. On poor soils, such as upland pine or the worked-out lands of the east, the rate of return varied from 2.2 per cent to 5.4 per cent. On the best lands of the South the returns varied from 10 per cent to 13 per cent. These rates of return meant that males yielded a rate of return equal to or in excess of the return on alternative assets on all but the poorest lands.

For female slaves a rate of return was computed for land of average quality only. If the females had only five marketable offspring, the estimated lower limit, the rate of return was 7.1 per cent. If there were ten offspring, the estimated upper limit, the rate of return was 8.1 per cent. Conrad and Meyer then argued that slaveholders in the older regions of the South, where males were yielding a low rate in cotton production, were able to achieve a profitable rate of return by selling the offspring of their female slaves to the newer areas where profitable cotton production was possible. They demonstrated the existence of this type of slave reallocation by pointing out differences in the age structure of slaves in the newer and older states, as well as by citing testimony of contemporaries.[22]

The computations of Conrad and Meyer have been attacked as showing too high a rate of return from investment in slaves. While their estimates of each of the four variables—slave life expectancy, capital costs, the rate of return on alternative assets, and the income

---

[22]They also directly answered Phillips' charge that slaves were overpriced by pointing to a sharp rise in productivity in this period, justifying the rise in slave prices in terms of cotton prices. (See *op. cit.*, pp. 116 and 117, particularly Table 17). However, the increase in productivity they show may be too large. First, their estimates ignore the secular and cyclical variations in the proportion of slave labor used in cotton production. Second, a published estimate of man-hours per bale of cotton shows a fall from 601 in 1800 to 439 in 1840 and 304 in 1880. Department of Agriculture, *Progress of Farm Mechanization* (Miscellaneous Publication No. 630, Washington, 1947), p. 3. This study, however, shows no change in yield per acre

obtained from slaves—have been criticized, the revision which most sharply challenges their conclusion is Edward Saraydar's downward adjustment of the productivity of prime male field hands in cotton production.[23]

Saraydar was interested in testing a more restricted hypothesis about slave profitability than were Conrad and Meyer. He was concerned only with the profitability of owning male prime field hands; thus ignoring the gains from slave offspring which Conrad and Meyer accounted for in computing the rate of return upon females. This means that Saraydar understated the profitability of slave ownership to the individual plantation owner (as well as to the southern economy) as long as female slaves were a profitable investment. The specific formulation of the test for the profitability of male slaves used by Saraydar was the same as that of Conrad and Meyer. He computed the rate of return from the use of males in cotton production using averages of the period 1830-1860. His one major change was to provide an alternative measure of physical productivity in cotton operations. Rather than an average of estimates presented in various "contemporary journals," Saraydar used a sample of counties taken from the 1849 census to estimate slave yields in various parts of the South. The particular year chosen, 1849, was justified as being one of average crop size for the 1830–1860 period. Saraydar selected counties in which little was produced besides cotton, and then adjusted the total slave population to obtain an estimate of the average number of field hands. Dividing total cotton output in these counties by the estimated number of field hands gave cotton productivity per field hand. This resulted in a lowering of the all-south average yield per field hand from Conrad and Meyer's 3.75 bales to 3.2, and the yield on alluvial soil from 7.0 bales to 3.6.[24] Using these lowered yields, Saraydar computed sharply lower rates of return on male slaves. On average land the computed rate of return was below that upon alternative assets, and only on the best alluvial land were field hands a profitable investment to the planter. Even there the rates of return

[23]Edward Saraydar, "A Note on the Profitability of Ante Bellum Slavery," *Southern Economic Journal*, 30:325-332 (April, 1964).

[24]Saraydar also claimed that Conrad and Meyer must have overstated alluvial yields since the average yield per acre for the nation didn't reach their implied level until after World War II. Richard Sutch pointed out that alluvial yields in 1879 exceeded those implied by Conrad and Meyer. Richard Sutch, "The Profitability of

were distinctly lower than the rates computed by Conrad and Meyer.

Both Saraydar's form of the test for the profitability of slavery and his specific productivity estimates were challenged in turn by Richard Sutch. Sutch incorporated into one production function the computations which Conrad and Meyer did separately for males and females, thus providing for a single overall test of slave profitability. In effect, Sutch's formulation considered the plantation owner to purchase a slave whose price was determined by applying to Phillips' data the age-sex composition of the slave population and allowed the owner to benefit from the growth of the slave labor force. Unlike Conrad and Meyer, however, the benefits of the increased labor were not attributed to the female alone. This formulation meant that the purchase of a slave provided a per-manent stream of income to the owners as long as average slave productivity exceeded average costs of rearing and maintenance. By applying this production function to Saraydar's figures, Sutch estimated rates of return on slave ownership roughly similar to those of Conrad and Meyer.

Sutch, however, also attacked Saraydar's estimates of income from slaves by preparing specific tests of profitability for the years 1849 and 1859. His main correction of Saraydar's 1849 figures was the use of the higher cotton price of that year, while for 1859 both the higher cotton price and increased physical productivity were used. However, these corrections provide too favorable an estimate of slave profitability for the thirty-year period studied. Although the 1849 crop was below that of the preceding two years, it was rather high for the decade of the 1840's, and Sutch's argument that the marked price rise that year is indicative of a small crop is weak. The 1849 price was unusually high—only one year of the seventeen from 1839 to 1855 had a higher cotton price. The 1859 crop, on the other hand, was abnormally large. It was almost half-again as large as that of the average of the 1850's, and was not exceeded until 1879. Thus, while they indicate that Saraydar's adjustments may not be relevant for those specific years, Sutch's corrections of price and yield seem excessive when applied to the years between 1830 and the outbreak of the Civil War.

There are several questions concerning the profitability of slaves in cotton production which require further analysis. First, the argument that profits should be measured using data from a large gives an element of arbitrariness to the calculations. Since prices and output of cotton varied considerably during the thirty years presumably averaged, and slave prices did move sharply, the measurement of profitability is sensitive to the particular numbers chosen. The use of averages also ignores the possibility of an upward trend in slave productivity above that attributable to the movement to newer soils. Computations for specific years may provide a better indication of profitability than does the thirty-year average, though sensitive to the particular years studied. Saraydar and Sutch, of course, may both be correct. Slavery may have been unprofitable in the earlier part of the interval studied, but profitable in the 1850's.

Second, the use of an average price of slaves for the entire South overlooks the fact that the market adjustment between the Upper South and the Lower South did not lead to price uniformity. Evans' data suggest an average price spread of about 25 per cent in the years from 1830 to 1860, with no marked trend in the size of the differential over time.[25] The use of Lower South slave costs in all regions results in an understatement of the rate of return in the older regions, though the computations for the better soils are not affected.

Third, better estimates of slave productivity are necessary. To obtain these more detailed work on census manuscripts and plantation records is necessary. Questions as to the degree of self-sufficiency on plantations, the possible production of other marketed crops on what are primarily cotton producing plantations, the other functions of an income-yielding nature performed by slaves, and the quantity of cotton produced by whites both on and off plantations require further study, some of which is currently being undertaken.[26]

What Saraydar has done is to throw into some doubt the profitability of owning male slaves. This does not mean that slavery would be unprofitable to planters, as long as females were owned and

[25]Robert Evans, Jr., "The Economics of American Negro Slavery," in National Bureau of Economic Research, *Aspects of Labor Economics* (Princeton, 1962), 185-243. The Phillips estimates do show an increased differential in favor of the Lower South after 1856.

[26]Robert Gallman and William Parker have been studying the manuscript census for southern states in 1860. In a related study, James T. Foust and Dale Swan have

produced marketable offspring. Saraydar's result, in fact, suggests that female slaves were underpriced, given the market value of slaves. If he were correct we would expect the price of male field hands to fall below that of females, since it is the offspring who are the source of profits. It is the maintenance of the higher price on male slaves which raises questions about the meaning of Saraydar's (and Conrad and Meyer's) separate production functions for male and female slaves, as well as the accuracy of Saraydar's yield estimates.

Moreover, a study by Robert Evans using a different set of data and testing the same hypothesis as did Saraydar, reached the same conclusion as Conrad and Meyer. Evans estimated the rate of return on male slaves only, excluding the value of offspring. He used data on the prices paid to hire slaves as estimates of the income to be derived from using slaves. If the slaves hired were equal in productivity to the slaves used elsewhere, the hiring rate should provide an estimate of the income produced per slave. Evans' treatment of the problem of slave mortality also differed from Conrad and Meyer's. Evans adjusted slave incomes for the proportion of deaths each year rather than using an average expected life span. Rates of return were computed for five-year periods between 1830 and 1860. They ranged from 9.5 per cent to 14.3 per cent in the Upper South, and between 10.3 per cent and 18.5 per cent in the Lower South. Evans further tested the sensitivity of his results to possible errors in the data, and concluded that it was improbable that his conclusion was in error. The maximum cumulation of probable errors would not be sufficient to reduce the rate of return from ownership of male slaves below the return from alternative assets.

We should be clear as to exactly what has been measured in these studies. If Conrad and Meyer and Evans are correct, a planter who purchased either a male or female slave at the market price could have made a rate of return equal to or better than that upon alternative investments. This would mean that prestige demand does not have to be used in explaining the price of slaves. It means further than regardless of how inefficient slave labor was relative to white labor, the planters who employed slaves were profiting from their use. The market price could be justified on the basis of the productivity of the male slave in market activities, and labor made a presumption of viability. The finding of profitability also means that any retardation the South experienced could not be attributed to sub-marginal investments made by slaveowners.

Viability to the Economy. Yasuba, Evans, and Sutch have each pointed out that the conclusion that slavery was profitable to the planter did not prove the viability of the slave system. It is possible that a profitable rate of return be made on the market price of existing slaves although the system was moribund. If the value of slaves (as reflected in the market price) was below the rearing cost, there would be an adjustment over time, resulting in a decline in the number of slaves until the institution disappeared. If the demand for slaves fell, but the market price for a reduced number of slaves was equal to the rearing cost, the slave industry would decline without disappearing. However, not only was the market price of slaves in excess of rearing costs in the years before the Civil War, but as Yasuba has demonstrated, this surplus—or capitalized rent—was growing in the late 1840's and 1850's.[27]

Capitalized rent would exist in the price of slaves as long as the market price exceeded the cost of producing slaves—the cost of raising them to the age at which they became productive or were sold. This surplus was not eliminated because once the importation of slaves from Africa was forbidden, the increase in supply set by either biological or institutional constraints was not sufficient to reduce the market price of slaves to their rearing cost. The surplus of market price over cost of production is the measure of the potential fall in slave values which could have occurred without making slavery unprofitable to the southern economy.[28] A falling price of slaves due to a decline in demand would mean that it was possible for the same rates of return to be made on the market price of slaves before and after the decline in demand.[29] However, this

---

[27]Yasuba's calculations are based on the estimates of Conrad and Meyer. Even if, as discussed above, the latter overstate cotton yields per slave the existence of rent and the trend remain.

[28]As Sutch pointed out, flexibility also existed in the price of land.

[29]This point is overlooked by Govan in his discussion of the Evans paper. He rejected as implausible Evans' finding that the profits of slave purchasers not only did not fall, but actually rose in the early 1840's. Thomas P. Govan, "Comments" in National Bureau of Economic Research, *Aspects of Labor Economics* (Princeton, 1962), 243-246. Yasuba found the capitalized rent in this period lower than in

price decline, resulting in a capital loss to those who owned the slaves, need not imply that slavery as an institution was not viable, as long as the lowered price still exceeded the costs of producing slaves.

Thus studies which indicate slave purchasers made a rate of return roughly equal to that upon alternative assets would not be surprising. Rather, since supply was inelastic at any moment of time, the price of slaves was set by the demand for them. It therefore would mean that the price of slaves was set at a figure which yielded the market rate of return to the purchaser.

The level of the price of slaves could be based upon elements of both prestige demand and demand for use in production. As long as the total price southerners were willing to pay for slaves exceeded rearing costs, the institution was viable. However, Conrad and Meyer and Evans argued that the market price could be justified on the basis of slave productivity alone. This means that slavery's viability was not attributable to an element (prestige demand) which caused apparent business losses and lowered southern capital formation. (If prestige demand were high it would not necessarily mean that, properly defined, business losses occurred, or that capital formation was reduced. Rather, the profitability test should be based upon the business value of slaves—deducting the imputed consumption element—and the capital formation comparison would need to bring in the expenditures upon goods for conspicuous consumption in the North, which also reduced the investible surplus.)

Yasuba separately estimated the rent element in the price of male slaves and of female slaves. Since the form of the calculation attributes the value of the offspring to the female slave, the rent on the female is based not only upon her productivity in growing cotton, but also upon the future value of her marketable offspring. Thus, the demand for female slaves would be based upon expectations covering not only her life-span but also that of her offspring. If there was an anticipation of an early end to slavery, for economic or other reasons, the demand for female slaves would decline. That Yasuba finds the rent rising before 1860 implies that the southern planters did not expect slavery to decline, let alone be abolished, until at least several decades elapsed. Whatever merit there is in the

---

this period to have made high rates of return, since they obtained slaves at a lower price. Apparently investors as a group were overly pessimistic.

natural limits hypothesis, its presumed effects were not anticipated in the South before the Civil War. Indeed the magnitude of the rent calculated by Yasuba makes it clear that a substantial decline in slave values would have had to occur for the institution to be threatened.[30]

Richard Sutch independently arrived at the same result concerning slavery's viability as did Yasuba, although he stated his argument differently. Sutch's analysis was based upon a comparison of the costs of using free labor with the costs of using slave labor to the economy (the annual "maintenance cost" plus the amortization of rearing costs). The value of the marginal productivity of the slave to the southern economy exceeded the costs of using the slave, thus creating an economic surplus. The free laborer was paid the value of the marginal product, so that no such surplus existed. If we assume that slave and free labor are equally productive, and that the cost of using slaves was at a subsistence level, then slavery would be viable as long as the free wage rate exceeded subsistence. (If the productivity of the two types of labor differed, the condition for viability is that the ratio of the cost of using slave labor to the wages paid free labor be less than the ratio of their marginal value products.) This would be equivalent to Yasuba's result if slavery were profitable to the planter, since the present value of the surpluses from the use of slave labor would then be equal to the capitalized rent in the price of the slave.[31]

The discussion of the viability of the slave economy points out that the rate of return to the southern economy from its investment in slave labor exceeded the rates of return earned by planters. This was because the latter studies measured the rate of return based upon the market price of the slave, while, as Yasuba notes, for the economy it would be based upon rearing costs. The difference between rearing costs and the market price resulted in capital gains for slaveholders—the question of who received the capital gains

[30]John Moes has suggested another possible economic end to slavery. If the productivity of the freed Negro was sufficiently in excess of his productivity while enslaved he would have been able to compensate his owner for granting freedom. John E. Moes, "Comments," in National Bureau of Economic Research, *Aspects of Labor Economics* (Princeton, 1962), 247-256.

[31]If slavery were unprofitable this would mean that rent as measured by Yasuba, based upon the excess of market price at age 18 above rearing costs, would exceed that implied by Sutch, which is based upon the excess of productivity above rearing and maintenance costs.

depending upon the foresight with which slave values were predicted once the importation of slaves was prohibited.

A Stagnant Economy? The strongest argument against slavery on economic grounds has been the image of a poor and stagnant southern economy in the antebellum period. Some historians have argued that slavery was both profitable and viable, but have introduced other factors to contend that the long-run effect of the slave system was to retard southern economic development. As described in Section I, major emphasis has been upon the presumed effects of the slave system upon income distribution (and thus the size of the internal market) and the rate of capital formation. Stagnation has also been attributed to southern specialization in the production of agricultural staples, particularly cotton, for export. A long debate has taken place as to whether slavery caused specialization, or whether specialization in cotton promoted slavery. In either case, analogy has been made with the supposed weak position of agricultural export producers in the world today. The argument is that a shift away from agricultural specialization would have led to a more rapid rate of economic growth in the South.

Many discussions of the antebellum southern economy start with the presumption of a low income, slow growing region. Thomas Govan had used the wealth estimates of the 1850 and 1860 censuses to question the concept of a stagnant southern economy, but it is only with the recent estimates of regional income by Richard Easterlin that this point can be examined in more detail. By applying Easterlin's estimates of the income shares by region to Robert Gallman's estimates of national income for 1840 and 1860 we can calculate the level of income by region for the two decades preceding the Civil War, and compute regional growth rates. The regional income estimates can be placed on a per capita basis by dividing by regional population.[32]

[32]Richard A. Easterlin, "Regional Income Trends, 1840-1950," in Seymour Harris, ed., *American Economic History* (New York, 1961), 525-547; Robert E. Gallman, "Gross National Product in the United States, 1834-1909," in Conference on Research in Income and Wealth, Volume Thirty, *Output, Employment, and Productivity in the United States After 1800* (New York, 1966), 3-76; Department of Commerce, *Historical Statistics of the United States: Colonial Times to 1957* (Washington, 1961), Series A123-180, p. 13. There were a number of revisions applied to Easterlin's data in obtaining the estimates of Table 1. The major revision was the estimation of income for Texas in 1840, so that Texas could be brought into the southern region in both years. To downward bias the growth rate Texas per capita

Easterlin's estimates of regional income include slaves as part of the population and their "incomes" (maintenance costs) in the income total for each region. On this basis the level of southern per capita income in 1860 was 80 per cent of the national average (Table 1). While less than 60 per cent of the per capita income in the Northeastern states, it was higher than the per capita income in the North Central states. Comparing rates of growth of per capita income between 1840 and 1860, the southern economy does not appear stagnant. The southern rate of growth, 1.6 per cent, exceeded that of the rest of the nation, 1.3 per cent.[33]

The pattern of income change within the southern economy is of interest. The per capita income within each component section grew at a rate below the national average. Nevertheless, it is clear that growth did occur within the period in each of the sections. The shift of southern population into the richer West South Central states, particularly Texas, explained the high southern growth rate. However, since it says nothing about the imminence of any possible decline in that area nor anything about declines in the older parts of the South, this population redistribution cannot be used to support the natural limits thesis. As Sutch has argued, the greater profita-

---

income in 1840 was assumed equal to the 1860 level. The 1840 population was interpolated between the 1836 and 1846 estimates presented in Lewis W. Newton and Herbert P. Gambrell, *A Social and Political History of Texas* (Dallas, 1932), p. 280. Thus the regional breakdown in Table 1 differs from Easterlin's in including Texas in the South, but accords with his placement of Delaware and Maryland in the Northeast. The Mountain and Pacific states were excluded from the national and regional totals in both years.

Easterlin's estimates are the most detailed available for this period, but, of course, may not be perfectly accurate for the conclusions made. Genovese, for example, has stressed the inferior quality of livestock in the South. (See "Livestock in the Slave Economy of the Old South—A Revised View," *Agricultural History*, 36:143-149 (July, 1962). Reprinted in his *The Political Economy of Slavery*, 106-123.) The importance of such biases awaits further study. However, two points should be made. First, it is improbable that such corrections could reverse the finding that growth did occur in the slave economy. Second, while it is possible that such corrections would reduce the level of southern income in 1860, it need not affect the relative growth rate if the same relative quality existed in 1840 and 1860.

[33]As I have indicated elsewhere, southern backwardness appears to be mainly attributable to the effects of the Civil War and its aftermath. If per capita income in the South had grown as rapidly between 1860 and 1870 as it had between 1840 and 1860, the 1870 level would have been about twice the observed level. Stanley L. Engerman, "The Economic Impact of the Civil War," *Explorations in Entrepreneurial History*, Second Series, 3:176-199 (Spring, 1966).

Table 1 Per Capita Income by Region, 1840 and 1860
(In 1860 Prices)

| | Slaves as Consumers | | Slaves as Intermediate Goods[1] | |
	1840	1860	1840	1860
National Average	$ 96	$128	$109	$144
North:	109	141	110	142
Northeast	129	181	130	183
North Central	65	89	66	90
South:	74	103	105	150
South Atlantic	66	84	96	124
East South Central	69	89	92	124
West South Central	151	184	238	274

[1] "Maintenance cost" equal to $20.

Source: See text and footnotes 32 and 35.

bility of slavery in the New South immediately prior to the Civil War meant that land (and slave) prices had not reached equilibium. The low level of land rent is indicative of a relative abundance of cheap lands.[34] Similarly the higher levels of land values in the Old South do not suggest that this area had lost economic potential.

The comparisons in the previous paragraphs included slaves in the population and their "income" in the income totals. For those imbued with twentieth-century mores this seems the obvious thing to do, but we should remember that to southern planters slaves were intermediate goods, used in the production process, not individuals for whom society was producing final output. From the viewpoint of these planters, the comparisons of per capita income should be based upon the income of the free population only, deducting the "maintenance cost" as the expense of using slave labor.[35] This

[34]Sutch, *op. cit.,* p. 377.

[35]The "maintenance cost" per slave used in these calculations was $20 (see Gray, *op. cit.,* p. 544). It should be noted that while a higher maintenance cost would reduce the relative per capita income of free southerners in 1860, it would raise the rate of growth of their income between 1840 and 1860. E.g., if a $30 figure were used the southern per capita income would have been $144, compared to the North's $142, but the growth rate would have risen to 1.9 per cent, with that of the North remaining the same as in the previous calculation. For similar comparisons see Easterlin, *op.cit.,* p. 527, and Robert William Fogel, "The Reunification of Economic History with Economic Theory," *American Economic Review,* 55:92–98 (May, 1965).

redefinition of "Southern society" raises both the level and rate of growth of southern per capita income relative to that of the rest of the nation. With the exclusion of slaves from "society" the level of southern per capita income in 1860 exceeds the national average. Southern per capita income was two-thirds again as large as the per capita income of the North Central states, and the gap between the South and the Northeast is reduced by over 50 per cent. Treating slaves as intermediate goods also has an effect upon rates of growth. The southern growth rate becomes 1.8 per cent, in contrast with the rest of the nation's 1.3 per cent.

Given these findings, how do we account for the widespread impression of southern backwardness? Three factors seem most important. First, the fact that the South had only 33 per cent of the nation's population in 1860 (24 per cent of the free population) means that comparisons based upon total output (perhaps useful in discussing war potential) provide a less favorable comparison for the South than do the per capita measures.[36] Second, the commercial dependence upon the North for financial and transport services, as well as for manufactured goods, upset the southerners, who seemed unwilling to acknowledge fully their comparative advantage in the production of cotton and other staples. Third, if growth is equated with urbanization and industrialization, the South does compare unfavorably with the rest of the nation. Comparisons with the agricultural states of the North Central region, however, are less unfavorable to the South. The percentage of population in urban areas in 1860 was 36 per cent in the Northeast, 14 per cent in the North Central states, and 7 per cent in the South. Of the total national employment in manufacturing in that year, 72 per cent was in the Northeast, 14 per cent in the North Central states, and 10 per cent in the South. (The population shares were 36 per cent, 29 per cent, and 33 per cent, respectively).[37]

[36]Hinton Helper's classic attack was restricted to measures of total output, overlooking population differences. Hinton Rowan Helper, *The Impending Crisis of the South: How to Meet It* (New York, 1963). His comparison was based upon a more complicated model, since it is also intended to explain the net outflow of population from the South. Southern total income grew at 4.1 per cent. from 1840 to 1860 as contrasted with the rest of the nation's rate of 4.7 per cent. The northeastern growth rate, however, was only 4.0 per cent (With slaves treated as intermediate goods, the southern growth rate becomes 4.2 per cent, still below the rest of the nation's rate of 4.7 per cent.)

[37]Bureau of the Census, Sixteenth, *Population* (Washington, 1942), Vol. I, p.20. Census, Eighth, *Manufactures of the United States in 1860* (Washington, 1865), p. 729

The last two of the indicators have been widely used as proxy measures for southern economic development, in the absence of a more complete set of income estimates. Thus their usefulness as proxies has been superseded by Easterlin's measures, which directly give us the information we want. While it is true the South lacked industry and was not urbanized relative to the rest of the nation, this clearly did not mean that the South was a poor or a stagnant area.

Other of the arguments which have been used to suggest southern backwardness can also be misleading. The particular nature of cotton as a crop may explain the low level of farm mechanization in the South, since cotton was profitably farmed without mechanical equipment. It is of interest that no important cotton harvesting equipment was adopted until the middle of the twentieth century. Profitability of new lands can explain the frequent mention of presumably exhausted soil in the older areas of the South. Given a choice between investing in older soils (fertilizing) and in new soils (clearing), at the relative prices existing before the Civil War, movement to new soil was apparently economically rational. It is not clear, moreover, that this behavior would not have changed had the relative prices for these types of investment in land shifted.

Emphasis by Phillips on the effects of slavery upon capital formation has made this a standard argument for southern retardation. The slave system has been considered to be the cause of low southern investment in physical capital, since investment in slaves presumably absorbed capital which would have had other uses in the economy.[38] However, once the external slave trade was forbidden, there was no capital drainage out of the South—funds were merely being transferred from one region to another within the southern economy. Therefore, it is necessary to determine what the seller of the slave did with his funds.[39] It is, in fact, possible that slave

[38]Moes has pointed out a theoretically plausible way in which such a decline in investment could have occurred. If in a non-slave society expenditures on rearing children are considered consumption to the parents while in a slave society such expenditures are considered part of capital formation, slave societies which have the same savings-income ratio as non-slave societies would devote less to non-human capital. However, if the ratio of savings to income was higher the more unequally income was distributed, the slave society might devote more to all types of capital formation than the non-slave. John E. Moes, "The Absorption of Capital in Slave Labor in the Ante Bellum South and Economic Growth," *American Journal of Economics and Sociology,* 20:535-541 (October, 1961).

[39]It is not clear in which direction within the South net capital flowed. If a slave was sold from an older region to a new region, there would be a net flow of funds to the

ownership increased the ability of southerners to borrow from the North (as well as the planter's ability to borrow within the South) by providing a marketable asset which could be used for collateral on loans, and thus permitted increased capital formation.

Other explanations of low southern capital formation can also be questioned. That a skewed income distribution and the social climate attributable to slavery resulted in conspicuous consumption and waste of money on the part of the plantation owners has often been argued.[40] At present, however, no reliable income distribution statistics exist for the antebellum South which can be compared with other regions and years. For a rough indication of the inequality of the income of the free population in 1860, I have estimated the share of income going to the top approximately 1 per cent of free southern families in 1860. The basic assumption is that all the top income earners were plantation owners. By using data on the size distribution of plantations by number of slaves owned, it was estimated that the share of free southern income going to the top 1 per cent of the free population was about the same as the income share of the top 1 per cent of the population in 1929.[41] While crude,

---

older area in exchange for human capital. If the planter moved with his slaves there would be a net inflow of human and other capital into the new region, with no corresponding outflow. See William L. Miller, "A Note on the Importance of the Interstate Slave Trade of the Ante Bellum South," *Journal of Political Economy,* 73:181–187 ((April, 1965).

[40]The distribution of income in the South is still debated. For an argument that inequality was not as great as often implied, see Frank Lawrence Owsley, *Plain Folk of the Old South* (Baton Rouge, 1949). For a rebuttal to this position see Fabian Linden, "Economic Democracy in the Slave South: An Appraisal of Some Recent Views," *Journal of Negro History,* 31:140–189 (April, 1946).

[41]The key assumptions were that only plantation owners fell in the top 1 per cent of income earners, and that dividing estimated plantation income by five (the average family size) does not change the rankings. Thus what is actually measured is the share of income going to families owning large plantations. The size distribution of plantations is in Census, Eighth, *Agriculture of the United States in 1860* (Washington, 1864), p. 247 and errata sheet. Each slave was considered to represent capital (including land, etc.) of $2500. Capital was then decapitalized at 6 per cent, roughly the market rate of interest. If slavery were unprofitable, the capital estimate would be decapitalized at a lower rate, and the income amount and share would be correspondingly lower. Total free southern income was taken from the detail underlying Table 1. The top 0.8 per cent of free population, representing plantations with over 50 slaves, received 15 per cent of income, while the top 1.2 per cent (plantations with over 40 slaves) received 18.5 per cent. In 1929 the top 1 per cent of the population received 17.2 per cent of income (economic variant). See Simon Kuznets, *Shares of Upper Income Groups in Income and Saving* (National Bureau of

it does suggest the need for more detailed examination of southern income distribution.

The essential point of the conspicuous consumption argument is not that planters purchased more land and slaves—this could represent a productive use of capital—but that they lived too lavishly. This is usually supported by fragmentary mentions of wasteful expenditures by planters. Unfortunately, we again lack sufficient data to determine if the spending propensities were higher in the South than in the North, as well as if the South had more and/or richer upper income families. We do know, however, that the large consumption expenditures do not imply low savings. In the somewhat atypical year of 1928, the per capita consumption of the top 1 per cent of income earners in the United States population was about $5200, while that of the remaining 99 per cent was under $600. Certainly this is a pronounced difference, and given normal human reactions this could (and did) lead to discussions of wasteful expenditures by the rich. Yet in this year the top 1 per cent had a savings-income ratio of 43.3 per cent, and accounted for over 100 per cent of estimated personal savings.[42] This suggests the possibility that the effects of large consumption expenditures on southern capital formation may be overstated. That conspicuous consumption which did exist was probably carried on mainly by planters who were wealthy by the standards of the times. Their conspicuous consumption possibly absorbed only part of their incomes, and their savings rates could have exceeded the national average. Indeed, given what we now know about the relationship between income and savings, it is quite possible that savings in the South were higher than they would have been with a less skewed income distribution.

Another way in which slavery was presumed to have retarded southern capital formation was by necessitating debt payments to be

---

Economic Research Occasional Paper 35, New York, 1950), p. 67. For a study of the wealth distribution in 1860, based on census manuscripts, see Robert E. Gallman, "The Social Distribution of Wealth in the United States," unpublished paper presented to the International Economic History Conference, August, 1965.

[42]See Robert J. Lampman, *The Share of Top Wealth-Holders in National Wealth, 1922-56* (Princeton, 1962), p. 236. This is the boldest comparison, but more typical years of the 1920's can be used to demonstrate the same point. In 1925, e.g., the ratio of consumption per capita of the upper 1 per cent to that of the rest of the population was 9:1; yet the upper income groups had a savings-income ratio of 42.9 per cent, and accounted for 51 per cent of personal savings.

made to the North. Payments on loans led to a drain of funds from the South, as did southern purchases of services from the North. However, the existence of such flows are part of the costs to be paid for profitable borrowing and specialization. Certainly the existence of capital imports for the South need not result in any reduction in income or capital formation. If the capital imports permitted a higher level of investment in the South it could have raised, rather than lowered, the rate of growth of the economy.

It has been argued that the income estimates do not provide the relevant comparisons—that the South should have industrialized for long-term growth irrespective of its prewar condition. This implies that a deliberate effort should have been made to shift resources from agriculture to manufacturing. This policy has been advocated on two grounds. The first is that the southern entrepreneurs were backward, and therefore were unwilling or unable to take advantage of modern developments. It appears, however, that the South did not ignore all modern developments. The South had 31 per cent of the nation's railroad mileage, with per capita mileage only slightly below the national average.[43] This network was financed predominantly by indigenous capital, a fact which is of interest for the capital formation hypothesis discussed above. While the track to area ratio was lower in the South than elsewhere, the southern economy was favored by a transportation network based upon navigable streams and rivers. Thus the absence of an entrepreneurial spirit within the confines of the slave system is not clearly established.

The second reason for advocating a shift to manufactures is the proposition that growth based upon an agricultural export commodity was doomed to ultimate failure. The more rapid the shift away from cotton, the better the longer-term prospects for the southern economy. Implicit in this is the statement that southern whites would not have responded to changing profit opportunities. This statement is usually justified by the argument that industrialization was prevented because it would have meant the end of slavery.

---

[43]See George Rogers Taylor, *The Transportation Revolution, 1815-1860* (New York, 1951), p. 79. Similarly, Allen Fenichel shows that in 1838 (the only ante bellum year for which data exist) the South had 38.2 per cent of the nation's total capacity of steam power in manufacturing. Allen H. Fenichel, "Growth and Diffusion of Power in Manufacturing, 1838-1919," in Conference on Research in Income and Wealth, Volume Thirty, *Output, Employment, and Productivity in the United States After 1800* (New York, 1966), 443-478.

While the hypothesis that with the existence of shifts in profitability the South would not have shifted into industry is widely debated, it should be repeated that cotton production was apparently profitable in most of the antebellum period, that geographic mobility in response to income differentials existed, and that, at least within agriculture, there were responses to changing profitability.

In concluding this section, we can raise further questions about two of the arguments previously given for slavery's deleterious effect upon southern economic development. The first, arguing for retarded development of the internal market, needs more justification. The question is not slave purchasing power but the amount of demand which existed for products the slaves consumed. Southern discussions of the clothing and shoes for slaves which were imported from the North suggest the existence of a substantial market for consumer goods on plantations. That the planters paid for these goods rather than the slaves does not diminish the effect on demand. It can be argued that the products ordered by planters were more standardized and amenable to mass production techniques than would have been the situation if the slaves were themselves the source of demand.

Given the small optimal size of manufacturing plants in 1860, it seems probable that the southern market could have been large enough to support internal industry, if the South's comparative advantage had been manufacturing. Estimates presented by Genovese of cash expenditures per person in the South suggest that the region could have supported over 50 cotton textile plants and more than 200 boot and shoe establishments of Massachusetts size. While an admittedly crude calculation, it is more probable that the estimates are too low rather than too high.[44] For a more complete answer the important questions are those of plantation self-sufficiency and the nature of the products purchased by southerners.

[44]Genovese estimates 1860 cash expenditure in Mississippi at about $25 per person (Genovese, *Political Economy,* p. 169). If we assume this amount to hold throughout the southern states, this amounts to about one-fourth of southern per capita income in that year. Making the extreme assumption that outside of the South all income went into cash expenditures, while the southern share was only one-fourth, and that expenditures on boots and shoes and cotton textiles were proportional to all cash expenditures, we can use the value of output of those sectors to estimate total southern cash expenditures on the specific goods. Total value of output and average output per Massachusetts plant are from Census, Eighth, *Manufactures,* pp. xxi and lxxiii. In 1860 there were 217 cotton textile plants and 1,354 boot and shoe establishments in Massachusetts.

To settle this, detailed records of the magnitude and composition of southern purchases from other regions and from abroad are needed.[45]

The second argument, the relative deficiency of education in the South, is clearly supported by the relevant data. The education of slaves was forbidden by law, while that of the whites was certainly below that in the rest of the nation.[46] However, given the world demand for cotton and the rate of growth of income in the antebellum South, it may be that whatever costs it did impose were negligible relative to the effects in the late nineteenth and twentieth centuries. Here again, more research is needed in order to establish the size of the penalty paid by the South for its educational backwardness before the Civil War.

III. CONCLUSION

The recent works of historians and economists have resulted in revisions of the conclusions about the economics of slavery which derive from the pioneer works of U. B. Phillips. Indications are that on the eve of the Civil War slavery was profitable to the planters, viable, and consistent with a growing economy.

There are many aspects of the overall impact of slavery which have not been discussed. The effects on political decision-making, the psychology of the white population, and the propensity to innovate, for example, must be answered before a full determination of the social and economic effects of the slave system can be made.[47]

Perhaps the basic economic question would be the comparison of southern developments under free and slave labor. It is possible that growth might have been more rapid and the returns to investment higher had the slave system never been introduced. Yet we do know

[45]For an attempt to measure this trade see Albert Fishlow, *American Railroads and the Transformation of the Antebellum Economy* (Cambridge, 1965), 269-288, as well as the articles by Fishlow and Fogel in Ralph L. Andreano, ed., *New Views on American Economic Development* (Cambridge, 1965), 187-224.

[46]See Albert Fishlow, "The Common School Revival: Fact or Fancy?," in Henry Rosovsky, ed., *Industrialization In Two Systems: Essays in Honor of Alexander Gerschenkron* (New York, 1966), 40-67.

[47]For a study of some of these effects see Stanley M. Elkins, *Slavery: A Problem in American Institutional and Intellectual Life* (Chicago, 1959).

that up to the Civil War the South had a relatively high level of per capita income, that because of the surplus above subsistence costs the planters as a class made a return on their investments in slaves greater than that on alternative investments possible at that time, and that even if slave labor had been less efficient than free, its use probably did not cause losses to the owners. While the broader and more difficult questions are still unanswered, the recent revisions have improved the analytical and factual framework in which they can be pursued.

MARVIN FISCHBAUM *and* JULIUS RUBIN

Slavery and the Economic Development of the American South

In the two decades before the Civil War the South achieved a rate of economic growth higher than the national average. Could this rate of growth have been maintained, if the Civil War had not occurred? Was the retarded economic development of the South after the Civil War the result, directly and indirectly, of the War itself? Or did it reflect the exhaustion of the potential for development of the South's great staple, cotton, aggravated by the South's inability to escape the social, political, and economic consequences of slavery?

Here once again we are in the realm of hypothetical history: ". . . . if the Civil War had not happened." But, hypothetical or not, we confront questions that must be answered, one way or the other, if we want to form a judgment about the economic effects of American slavery. Did slavery pay—in the long run? Did the South pay, after the Civil War, by poverty, stagnation, and political humiliation, for the economic gains it had achieved in the antebellum years?

The article which follows, by Marvin Fischbaum and Julius Rubin, ends our collection of readings on the economics of slavery. And it is a particularly appropriate selection for the purpose, because it offers, not

From *Explorations in Entrepreneurial History* (second series), Volume 6, Number 1 (Fall, 1968) 116–127. Copyright 1968 by The Graduate Program in Economic History, The University of Wisconsin. Reprinted by permission of the authors and the editor.

answers, but questions, doubts, and uncertainties. Its point of departure is the article by Engerman which you have just read—an article which tried to summarize, appraise, and plot out future work. Fischbaum and Rubin also summarize, appraise, and lay out future tasks, but their frame of reference is very different from Engerman's, and so are the questions they ask.

Engerman's view is that Southern backwardness in the last four decades of the nineteenth century was mainly due to the Civil War and its aftermath: the destruction of the War itself, the political and social instability of the reconstruction period, and the loss of foreign markets to other suppliers. He asks us to extrapolate the 1840-1860 rate of growth of per capita income in the South to 1870; and he leaves at least the impression, though he nowhere explicitly asserts, that this would probably have been the level of per capita income in the South in 1870, if there had been no Civil War.

What is acceptable as a statistical exercise, or as an imaginative device designated to highlight the significance of a trend, is less acceptable if it is intended as a serious statement of what would in fact have happened, if a catastrophe had not intervened. This is particularly so where what is involved is the extrapolation of a geometric progression. It is on this vulnerable point in Engerman's defenses that Fischbaum and Rubin concentrate their fire. Part I of their article, which raises a series of questions about the interpretation in welfare terms of per capita income statistics, is ingenious and interesting, but falls into the category of preliminary skirmishes. The main force attack is in Part II, which offers a demonstration that by 1860 the South was receiving "all the income it possibly could get from cotton," or in other words that no further potential existed for regional development along those lines. Such a finding clearly implies that further development required diversification—the creation of new "leading sectors" in the Southern regional economy. Part III of the article undertakes to show why this was impossible: the reasons are essentially the long run social, political, and economic consequences of slavery.

The article is, on the surface, a critique of Engerman's position—one which Engerman had anticipated and to some extent guarded himself against by the caveats with which he surrounded his conclusions. But its implications transcend the immediate occasion for the exchange. Fischbaum and Rubin are not offering negative criticisms of an adversary so much as arguing positively for a viewpoint of their own. What distinguishes their viewpoint from Engerman's? Not a hostility to statistics, although they are rather more vehement than Engerman that measurement is only a prelude to interpretation. Not a dislike of extrapolation and the hypothetical, for they write about "What would have happened if . . . " with a self-confidence no less than his. And not a reluctance to theorize, for underlying their analysis is a quite explicit model of the demand and supply conditions that governed the course of Southern incomes. Where they differ is, first, in their insistence that sustained economic growth in any society requires of that society the ability to transform itself; and secondly, in their conviction that the American South was incapable of these transformations.

The first of these propositions is one most economists would probably agree with in principle; the heart of the matter is in this particular case the assertion that such a transformation was due, or overdue, by 1860 and that, without it, the prewar rate of development could not have been sustained. The second assertion rests upon the analysis of the persistent influence slavery and the plantation system exercised on Southern values, politics, and social structure, as well as on the pattern and rate of urbanization, the education of the labor force, and the layout of the transportation system. The two propositions are closely related: if sustained economic development after 1860 was not contingent upon a transformation of Southern social structure, it is irrelevant whether or not slavery made such a transformation impossible.

In his article on the economics of slavery in the Winter 1967 issue of this journal, Professor Stanley L. Engerman distinguishes three issues which, as he remarks, are often confused: the profitability of slavery to the individual slaveowner; the viability of slavery as an economic system, with viability defined as "the ability of an industry to continue existing"; and "the effects of the slave system on the economic development of the South." The first two issues are admirably elucidated, the third requires some comment.

The principal piece of evidence on the economic development issue is the relatively rapid rate of growth of per capita income in the South between 1840 and 1860—1.6 per cent a year as against 1.3 per cent for the rest of the country—while the level of southern per capita income in 1860 was 80 per cent of the national average. But these figures underestimate the success of the slave economy, Engerman believes, because they include the slaves in the population and slave incomes in the income totals. "For those imbued with twentieth-century mores this seems the obvious thing to do, but we should remember that to southern planters slaves were intermediate goods . . . not individuals for whom society was producing final output." With slaves as intermediate goods, the southern growth rate becomes 1.8 per cent and southern per capita income in 1860 is actually above the national average.

Engerman's use of these estimates raises a number of issues. In Part I we deal with the meaning to be assigned to these relative growth rates: Do they actually measure changes in the relative economic well-being of the two regions? But then in the remainder of this paper we question the relevance of any income statistics for that period to the long-period economic development of the South. In Part II we try to demonstrate that southern economic advance before the Civil War was based upon a world demand for cotton textiles that could not support continued regional growth after the war; and in Part III we suggest that slavery, by its various direct and indirect long-term effects, helped to prevent successful regional diversification out of cotton both before and after the war. We conclude that Engerman's ante-bellum income figures, even if accepted as they stand, have little to do with the effect of slavery on the economic development of the South and that a study of the deterrents to diversification, particularly as they relate to the political, social, and economic effects of the slave plantation, would be far more relevant.

I

Though this is not our principal criticism of the income figures, the difficulties of estimation for that period should be noted. Easterlin has warned that the 1840 estimate required a great deal of extrapolation, while the 1860 estimate was derived in part by extrapolating the 1840 figures. Thus these estimates, though an important contribution to our knowledge of the period, are subject to errors of uncertain magnitude. More important, however, are the peculiar difficulties involved in applying these figures to the economy of the ante-bellum South.

There is first of all the peculiar institution itself: Is the slave to be considered a consumer or an intermediate good? Engerman's suggestion that we accept the viewpoint of the planter has some interesting implications for future work in historical income accounts. Southern spokesmen never tired of describing the brutal exploitation of workingmen in the North. Is it possible that northern capitalists considered their workmen as "intermediate goods" and that modern economic historians should adjust their income figures accordingly? Or take any exploitation colony. Is it right to consider the mass of natives as part of the population? Presumably we should first discover the attitudes of the governing elite on the question. And what about a personal dictatorship?—but here the mind boggles. Since a most important purpose of the investigation of nineteenth-century growth rates is to throw light upon twentieth-century growth problems and the theory of economic development, it may be best simply to accept our twentieth-century mores and to consider slaves as consumers, adding however that a part of the explanation for the existence of a long-term difference in regional incomes per capita in a country with an otherwise freely mobile population lies in the existence of a large non-competing group in the South. This point applies as well to the regional gap of the post-bellum period when Negroes, despite their freedom, stayed in the South because their income opportunities in all regions were minimal.

The well-known difference in the amount of migration to the two regions poses a much more serious problem in the interpretation of Engerman's income statistics. In an open economy regional differences in the rate of growth of real per capita income do not necessarily reflect differences in the rate of improvement of economic welfare. Assume an increase in the opportunities for unskilled workers in one of the regions, the North, and the consequent immigration of such workers from the South and from abroad. Average per capita income would fall in the North and rise in the South, but this would reflect only the changes in each region's mix of skills. There was no fall in either the income or the welfare of individuals in the North. Since there was in those decades a massive migration to the United States of which very little went to the South, as well as a modest northward migration from the poorer sections of the South, we must conclude that the per capita income figures are biased against the North.

Finally there are the cyclical factors. Phillips characterized 1840 as a time of cotton crisis, when average crops combined with low prices created acute distress.[1] In contrast, the 1859 crop exceeded

[1]Ulrich B. Phillips, "The Economic Cost of Slaveholding in the Cotton Belt," *Political Science Quarterly,* 20 (June, 1905), p. 267.

the previous record harvest by 10 per cent, the 1860 crop grew an additional 20 per cent, and yet the price held up. This was possible because several factors led Great Britain to import cotton at an unsustainable rate. The threat of war led to an unusual accumulation of raw cotton, a cobweb type of response to an unusually large demand for coarse cotton goods in the Indian and Chinese markets led to their overproduction, and liberalization of trade with France led to speculative production for what turned out to be a rather disappointing market.[2] Cotton was in for rough times with or without a war, and the growth rate between 1840 and 1860 has far less meaning that Engerman attributes to it.

II

Even more doubtful than the growth figures themselves is their use to predict the developmental capacities of the region. Assume rapid southern growth between 1840 and 1860. Does this by itself justify a presumption of continued growth? Obviously not. If the gain resulted from a windfall created by some fortuitous circumstance such as a war overseas, then we would write off the gain as merely temporary. On the other hand, the gain might have been related to some more permanent exogenous factor or involved a transformation of the economy such that the growth would be expected to feed upon itself. Engerman apparently believes that the gain was of the latter type. As he puts it in his footnote 33, referring to his earlier article in the Spring 1966 issue of this journal:

> Southern backwardness appears to be mainly attributable to the effects of the Civil War and its aftermath. If per capita income in the South had grown as rapidly between 1860 and 1870 as it had between 1840 and 1860, the 1870 level would have been about twice the observed level.

But southern growth was not of this nature. In an undiversified—and, as we shall argue, an undiversifiable—economy producing for export, foreign demand is a crucial factor and an essentially fortuitous one. This will be illustrated first of all by an examination

---

[2]Eugene Brady, "A Reconstruction of the Lancashire Cotton Famine," *Agricultural History* 37 (July, 1963), 156-62.

Commodity Output in the South, 1860-1880
(1879 prices; millions of dollars)

Year	Total Product	Agriculture	Manufactures and Mining
1860	$710	$639	$ 71
1870	534	477	57
1880	838	738	100

of the product estimates Engerman used to arrive at the above conclusion. They appear in his Spring 1966 article on page 180.

Following the normal procedure for estimating national income through the product approach, the physical output of each commodity was weighted by its base year (1879) price. The estimate obtained indicates a sharp decline in physical output. But we cannot infer from this a corresponding fall in incomes, because in an export economy, falling output can be associated with improving terms of trade. In the case of the South's single most important commodity, such an association did exist.

Table 1 Value Of Cotton Crop, 1859-1880

	Census Data			Agriculture Department Data		
	(millions of dollars)					
Year	Crop Value Current $	Output 1879 $	Income 1879 $	Year	Crop Value Current $	Income 1879 $
1859	$200	$222	$208	1860	$217	$226
1869	248	124	168	1870	343	232
1879	269	269	269	1880	354	354

Source: For Census Data, Robert E. Gallman, "Commodity Output, 1839–1899," in Conference on Research in Income and Wealth, Volume 24, *Trends in The American Economy in the Nineteenth Century* (Princeton, 1960), pp. 46–47; for Agriculture Department data, Marvin W. Towne and Wayne D. Rasmussen, "Farm Gross Product and Gross Investment in the Nineteenth Century," in same volume, pp. 292–293, 308. For both sets of data, income from crop in 1879 dollars is value of crop deflated by Gallman's all-commodity implicit price index, p. 43.

Physical output, weighted by 1879 prices, fell $176,000,000 between 1860 and 1870; and the statistics underlying Engerman's estimate indicate that cotton accounted for $98,000,000 of this drop. From the same data one finds that the purchasing power of the cotton crop fell only forty million dollars, while data from the Department of Agriculture suggests no drop at all. Part of the difference between the Census and Agriculture estimates can be attributed to the difference in year and part to under-reporting in the 1870 census. It is likely that the real income from the first postwar-crop—which sold for forty-three cents per pound— equalled that of the last, and most lucrative, prewar crop.[3] The cost of the disruption in cotton production was borne largely by people outside the South.

Furthermore, the drop in physical output, though real, was temporary. The small size of the postwar cotton crops has been attributed to the problem of adaptation to the new status of the Negro. Initially, freedmen failed to recognize how little, and land-holders failed to recognize how much, conditions had changed. Planters offered wages that corresponded to slave rations; Negroes expected a standard more in line with that enjoyed by white men. As a result, fertile lands remained uncultivated or were abandoned in mid-season. As sharecropping replaced gang labor, production rose to prewar levels and beyond.[4] But in turn this increase in southern product was not reflected in southern income. Indeed, neither the size of the cotton crop nor the productivity of cotton laborers had much to do with the level of southern income or the potentialities of southern development.

Southerners have long suspected that the nature of the demand for their crop is what today would be called inelastic. In 1852, C. F. McCay derided this notion:

> It is a common opinion among the planters and factors of the South, that a short crop not only brings a higher price, but actually produces a larger amount of money than a large or an average crop. It would be strange if this were true. Fine seasons, instead of being the kind gifts of a bountiful Providence would then be an injury and a curse. The destructive drought and early frosts would be a positive advantage to the agriculturist. The planter would be acting wisely for his own interest if he should destroy a large portion of what he had produced. These seem like strange propositions. . . .

[3]James L. Watkins, *Production and Price of Cotton for 100 Years* (United States Department of Agriculture, Division of Statistics, Miscellaneous Series Bulletin No. 9, Washington, 1895), pp. 13-17. General price index: Warren and Pearson's all-commodity wholesale price index in U.S. Bureau of the Census, *Historical Statistics of the United States, Colonial Times to 1957* (Washington, 1960), p. 115.

[4]Theodore Saloutos, "Southern Agriculture and the Problems of Readjustment, 1865-77," *Agricultural History* 30 (April, 1956), 66-72.

McCay compared five-year moving averages of the size of and revenue from the cotton crop with the actual crops and receipts in each year. He found that prior to 1840 large crops were associated with large receipts and small crops with small receipts; after that date, large and small crops tended to yield average receipts. McCay's evidence for the latter period is not at all inconsistent with the hypothesis of unitary elasticity of demand for southern cotton.[5]

Henry Ludwell Moore was the first to derive statistically a demand curve for cotton. Each of his three estimates, covering 1889-1913, placed the elasticity of demand close to one.[6] In 1938 Henry Schultz, in a careful statistical study, attempted, as far as the data allowed, to derive rigorously-defined demand curves for commodities, including cotton. He assumed that the price of American cotton depended upon domestic supply, composed of production and crop carry-over; foreign supply; world business conditions; and a time factor in order to eliminate trend. But for the period 1875-95 only data on the size of the American crop, the size of the foreign crop, and an index of industrial production and trade for the United States were available. Elasticity was estimated at 1.5 for 1875-95, 1.7 for 1896-1913, and 1.2 for 1914-29. For the first period fit was rather poor, with R equal to .55. In the latter two periods the slope of the coefficient of foreign production was positive—a suspicious result indicating that the greater the amount of foreign cotton, the higher the price of American cotton. After 1905 Schultz had data for domestic crop carry-over in Britain. Since cotton from large crops is saved for lean years, this data should, and did, lower estimated elasticity. In the period 1905-1929 elasticity was placed at .73; from 1918 to 1929 it was .78. Fit improved, but the coefficient of foreign production remained positive. After 1920, Schultz could use data on foreign crop carry-over and on world as opposed to United States business conditions. Results were more satisfactory: the artificial

---

[5]C. F. McCay, "Cotton Trade of the South," in J. D. B. DeBow, ed., *The Industrial Resources of the Southern and Western States* (New Orleans: J. D. B. DeBow, 1852), I, 139-41; reprinted in Stuart Bruchey, ed., *Cotton and the Growth of the American Economy, 1790-1860* (New York: Harcourt Brace and World, 1967), pp.200-204. A study by Peter Temin, published after this article was written, suggests that the elasticity of demand for American cotton from 1820 to 1859 was about 1.4. "The Causes of Cotton Price Fluctuations in the 1830's," *The Review of Economics and Statistics,* 49 (November, 1967), p. 46.

[6]*Forecasting the Yield and Price of Cotton* (New York: Macmillan Company, 1917), pp. 140-62.

trend variable, no longer significant, dropped out; R equalled .95; the coefficient for foreign supply turned negative; and the elasticity of demand, at .72, was two standard errors below the point of unitary elasticity. Schultz concluded that the demand for cotton was inelastic.[7]

It is clear that the income the South could derive from cotton was limited and that demand rather than supply constraints determined the effective limits. In the ante-bellum period two demand factors permitted a growth of southern income comparable to that of the North with little loss in the region's share of national population. Up to 1840, when it achieved a virtual monopoly in cotton production, the South increased its cotton receipts at the expense of other producing areas.[8] And up to 1860, world consumption of cotton goods was stimulated by cost-reducing innovations in cotton manufacturing which included the self-acting mule, the ring spindle, the self-acting loom temple, and the warp slasher. After 1860 technological progress in cotton manufacturing slowed and the ability of cotton to prop up the southern economy diminished. By the last two decades of the century the demand for American cotton was apparently approaching the region of unitary elasticity. A substantial increase in production would lead to inelastic demand and falling receipts; a substantial decrease in production would lead to increased foreign competition, elastic demand, and falling receipts. The South was receiving all the income it could possibly get from cotton.

At the same time the relative income obtainable from cotton diminished and the relative per capita income of the South reached its nadir. The share of national income accounted for by raw cotton production rose from 4.6 per cent in 1839 to 5.7 per cent in 1849

---

[7]Henry Schultz, *The Theory and Measurement of Demand* (Chicago: The University of Chicago Press, 1938), pp. 310-320, *et passim.* Schultz performed linear regressions on the logs of the variables. The inverse of the coefficient of domestic supply provides what Schultz considers to be an upward-biased estimate of the elasticity of demand.

[8]Bruchey, *op. cit.,* p. 7 places the American share of world cotton production at 9.0 per cent in 1801, 16.3 per cent in 1811, 28.6 per cent in 1821, 49.6 per cent in 1831, 62.6 per cent in 1840, 67.8 per cent in 1850, and 66.0 per cent in 1860. As early as 1850, and as late as 1890, the South supplied over 80 per cent of the cotton consumed by mills in the United States and Europe. United States Congress, Senate, Committee on Agriculture and Forestry, *Report on the Condition of Cotton Growers in the United States,* 83rd Congress, 3rd Session, Report 986, 1 (Washington, 1895), p.499.

and 6.0 per cent in 1859; but thereafter it fell, reaching 5.3 per cent in 1869, 4.5 per cent in 1879, 4.1 per cent in 1889, and 3.4 per cent in 1899.[9] This had nothing to do with the destruction of the Civil War. So long as the South was tied to cotton-growing, no conceivable effort—neither new technology, nor increased skill, nor greater marketing efficiency—could reverse the trend of incomes with respect to the North. Here is the point at which slavery had its greatest impact upon the economic development of the South. For the political, social, and economic conditions produced by slavery and its major agricultural institution ruled out a successful diversification out of cotton.

III

That the slave-labor system had long-term effects upon the ability to diversify has been denied on a number of grounds: in the ante-bellum period, the high relative profitability of agriculture and the existence of a small amount of diversification; in the post-bellum period, the much-vaunted but limited industrialization. Let us begin with the evidence regarding diversification in the ante-bellum period.

Engerman's Table I reveals that the rate of growth of income per capita in every component section of the South was well below the rate for the South as a whole. The reason, of course, is the shift of population into the more fertile West South Central states, particularly Texas. This by itself, Engerman notes, indicates nothing about the imminence of a decline in either the newer or the older southern states. But there is nevertheless a telling difference between North and South in this respect. Whether in 1840 or in 1860, as one moved westward in the North (from Northeast to North Central), per capita incomes declined considerably. But as one moved west in the South, incomes per capita increased. In the North, the older the region, the higher the income. In the South, the reverse. This reflects, of course, successful industrialization and agricultural adaptation in the Northeast. It also reflects the difficulty of such diversification in the

[9]Income data from Robert E. Gallman, "Gross National Product in the United States, 1834-1909," in Conference on Research in Income and Wealth, Vol. 30, *Output, Employment, and Productivity in the United States After 1800* (New York, 1966), p. 27; value of crop from Towne and Rasmussen, *loc. cit.*

Southeast. Engerman denies that there were any such difficulties; when "modern developments" were profitable, southern entrepreneurs had no difficulty in providing them—31 per cent of the nation's railroad mileage (presumably in 1860), with per capita mileage only slightly below the national average (p. 90), and 38.2 per cent of the nation's total steam power capacity in "manufacturing" in 1838 (fn. 43). But neither the possession of railroads to carry the crops to the ports nor steam power to process staple crops furnishes evidence of an ability to diversify. We are informed of the use made of steam engines in one state, Louisiana, which accounted for 7,800 of the 13,800 horsepower reported from the entire South. All of Louisiana's engines were in saw mills, cotton gins, or, most often, sugar mills.[10]

It is true, however, that the South did have a number of small factories, mines, and mills and that slaves were used in some of these. Some writers have inferred from this that slaves could be efficient in such activities and that consequently slavery was no obstacle to diversification. But one could as easily infer instead the existence of values opposed to the entry of white labor into southern industry. It is true that the importance of such values is often denied, because of evidence that the southern farmer worked hard (how could it be otherwise?), often side by side with his slaves. But the relevant attitude is to the idea of work under supervision, to the humiliation of wage-slavery. Finally, the efficient use of slaves in non-agricultural pursuits required the granting of greater freedom and more powerful incentives, particularly the promise of manumission. Richard C. Wade has ably documented the anxieties these tendencies produced in the cities of the ante-bellum South. In view of the intense fear of the Negro in the prewar decades, any significant urban-industrial trend, with its concomitant development of a skilled, mobile, free and semi-free Negro sector, might well have provoked an overwhelming political reaction.[11] But this is ahistorical. If from the beginning slavery had not produced conditions that strongly inhibited diversification, slavery in the South as

[10]Allen H. Fenichel, "Growth and Diffusion of Power in Manufacturing, 1838-1919," in Conference on Research in Income and Wealth, Vol. 30, *Output, Productivity and Employment in the United States After 1800,* (New York, 1966), pp. 456, 463-64.

[11]See John E. Moes, "The Economics of Slavery in the Ante-Bellum South: Another Comment," *Journal of Political Economy* 68 (April, 1960), 183-7; and Richard C. Wade, *Slavery in the Cities* (New York, 1964).

well as attitudes toward the Negro might have been entirely different than what they actually were by the mid-nineteenth century.

What were those slavery-induced conditions that inhibited diversification? Unfortunately only an outline of the relevant relationships can be suggested at this point. We begin with the fact that slavery made plantations possible, that these tended to concentrate in river valleys and to trade long-distance—usually directly with the port cities—and that consequently interior town development was inhibited. Towns are growth points; they provide the indispensable conditions for a sustained diversification process. But even more important, they transform the agricultural environment. In the North the enterprising towns of the great river valleys drove with all their might to conquer the back country with their local transportation lines and their commercial networks. But in the cotton South, towns were sparse, and where they existed they were more passive. The mutual economic interrelationships between town and country, which were essential to northern economic and social development, were not possible in an agricultural environment dominated by the plantation. Consequently the back country remained largely in its pristine state and a dualism developed: on the one hand, a commercialized and progressive plantation sector; on the other hand, an isolated, largely subsistent farming sector.

At this point the political factor is crucial. Slavery made it possible for a relatively small group to wield enormous political power. At the same time, slavery, in its indirect effects, weakened the formerly dominant political power of the farmer by isolating him. The economic consequences of these political relationships are evident in at least two fields: in education, where the southern farmer, in sharp contrast to his northern counterpart, could not get, and often did not want, an adequate public educational system; and in transportation, where planter interests produced a railroad system principally designed to carry plantation crops to the ports.[12]

Finally the various direct and indirect effects of the slave system determined the characteristics of the potential labor force for southern industry. On the one hand, the ex-slaves—illiterate, unskilled, and irresponsible; on the other hand, the back-country

[12]For a theoretical discussion of the economic effects of political power in the development of a planter-farmer economy, see William H. Nicholls, "An 'Agricultural Surplus' as a Factor in Economic Development," *Journal of Political Economy*, 71 (February, 1963), 1-29.

farmer—isolated from the influences of towns and a modern transportation network, far less literate than his northern counterpart,
subject in varying degrees to the narrow outlook and the intense
conservatism so often produced by generations of subsistence
farming. This was the heritage of the post-bellum South, a heritage
far more harmful and long-lasting in its economic effects than the
destruction of a war and the humiliation of an occupation.

It is against this background that the income growth of the
ante-bellum period should be considered. That growth was based
upon the remarkable world demand for cotton produced by the
industrial revolution and the availability of virgin soils. But the
institution which could take advantage of these windfalls—the slave
plantation—produced conditions of a far more permanent character.
In later decades when large transfers of population from old to
virgin soils were no longer possible and when the level of raw cotton
prices no longer justified specialization in cotton-growing in large
parts of the South, those conditions still inhibited adaptation. And
even after the capture of the cotton-textile industry, successful
diversification eluded the South. As Douglas Dowd has remarked, a
virtually one-product industrial sector was added to a virtually
one-product agricultural economy.

Our conclusion that a respectable rate of growth of twenty years
duration should create no presumption whatsoever regarding the
continuation of that growth may seem extreme, but it is in line with
historical evidence which goes far beyond the experience of the
American South. It is not at all difficult to provide evidence that
there is a kind of rapid growth that produces the conditions for
successful growth in a later period, while there is another kind of
rapid growth that produces precisely the conditions for later stagnation. The history of the Americas provides some dramatic examples.
Consider the growth rate of the Spanish mining colonies in the
seventeenth century and compare it to that of the British colonies.
Or compare the West Indies with the North American mainland in
the same period. Economies based upon an exportable resource
produced by unskilled and uneducated forced labor can advance
extremely rapidly—until conditions change and a more complex,
more diversified response is required. Then the conditions produced
by the initial period of growth—the lack of investment in human
skill and intelligence, the polarized political and social structure, the
inhibition of urban growth points—can prevent a successful response for a very long time.

To sum up, the investigation of the effects of slavery on the economic development of the South requires the kind of analysis appropriate to a development rather than to a short-run income problem, and this requires an adaptation, not a mechanical application, of the economic concepts and statistical tools developed for income analysis. Income accounts work best when applied to closed economies over short periods, and anyone attempting to apply them more broadly must bear in mind the inevitable distortions. Simple extrapolation of income growth, justified though it may be for very short time periods, cannot be applied over longer periods without a careful analysis of the factors that determined the growth of income. Finally, the simplication of a problem by considering economic factors alone—a method which produces interesting results when applied to periods in which everything else does remain pretty much the same—is inappropriate when applied to development problems. Economic historians, when wearing their historian's hat, have of course always known this, but in their economist's cap they often prefer to forget it.

A Final Word

A good teacher, like a good friend, should not talk too much. If he does, it suggests vanity and a self-regarding belief that what he has to say is probably more important than anything else you might happen to hear, or to think about, at that moment. A good editor should follow the same rule. He should choose selections that are good; he should introduce them briefly; and then he should stand aside. But, in this case, a final word seems necessary, in order to say something that none of these readings says, although most of the authors might well agree.

What appears to be involved, through this whole controversy, is a series of differences of opinion about slavery, the South, and cotton. But when you probe a little deeper, these particular differences of opinion seem to stem from different views about how change happens in human societies. And when you probe deeper still, there seem to emerge differing philosophies about what counts in making humans behave the way they do and about how we, who want to understand their behavior, should best go about analyzing it.

Without the subtle and sophisticated analysis of men like Conrad and Meyer, Yasuba, Evans, and Engerman, there is no doubt that our understanding of slavery and of American history in general would be infinitely poorer than it now is. The long-drawn-out controversy has, particularly in its later stages, generated some of the best work in economic history that American scholarship has yet produced. And yet, in the reactions of scholars like Dowd and Genovese, one senses a feeling that, in the search for precise definition and rigorous verification, much that is important and much that is essentially human has been lost to view. Many students react in the same way: it is the apparent inhumanity of the analysis that bothers them. The reaction is, perhaps, a little like what many people feel when they hear nuclear war discussed in terms of the theory of games.

Is there an inevitable conflict here? Can the points of view be reconciled? The fact that a social scientist tries to be ideologically neutral, to define his terms clearly, and to test his hypotheses rigorously, surely does not mean that it has somehow escaped his attention that, at bottom, he is dealing with people who live and breathe and can be hurt. What he is after is clear thinking; and the more complex the problem, the more he believes clear thinking to be necessary. What else would you have him do? What alternative intellectual attitude would you recommend? A comfortable admission that everything depends on everything else, and that "values" are important? That is where understanding begins, not where it ends. It is easy to insist that reality is complex—more complex than any of our ways of describing it. But who denies it? It is difficult to find fault with the search for accuracy and verifiability. After all, do we not want to know, and to know *when* we know?

And yet, there are limits to what social science can do. In particular, there are limits to what economics can do. When we talk about the many ways men have devised to live with each other, and to live off each other, it is prudent to remember that some valuable things cannot be traded, because what you give to another, you still have yourself, and sometimes in greater measure than before. And among these things that no market can price are hatred, love, and the respect one man has for another. These things, or their absence, and not the rate of return on capital, gave American slavery its unique character in human terms. Because they could not be bought or sold nor carry a price, they cannot figure in any economic calculus. No economist or economic historian can, in his professional capacity, tell you much about them, and you should not expect him to. But what he *can* tell you about is fundamental. It is important that we have a correct understanding of the economics of American slavery, because men and women were bought and sold in organized markets in this country and we should not be in ignorance of how and why this was done. If we fail to get the economics of the matter straight, we are not likely to understand much else about it.

ABCDEFGHIJ— M —76543210